HINDUS AND THEIR CHRISTIAN BIBLE

HINDUS AND THEIR CHRISTIAN BIBLE

R. S. Sugirtharajah

LONDON • NEW YORK • OXFORD • NEW DELHI • SYDNEY

T&T CLARK

Bloomsbury Publishing Plc, 50 Bedford Square, London, WC1B 3DP, UK
Bloomsbury Publishing Inc, 1359 Broadway, New York, NY 10018, USA
Bloomsbury Publishing Ireland, 29 Earlsfort Terrace, Dublin 2, D02 AY28, Ireland

BLOOMSBURY, T&T CLARK and the T&T Clark logo are trademarks
of Bloomsbury Publishing Plc

First published in Great Britain 2024
Paperback edition published in 2025

Copyright © R. S. Sugirtharajah, 2024

R. S. Sugirtharajah has asserted their right under the Copyright, Designs and Patents
Act, 1988, to be identified as Author of this work.

For legal purposes the Acknowledgements on p. vi constitute an extension
of this copyright page.

Cover artwork © Rohini Mani

All rights reserved. No part of this publication may be: i) reproduced or transmitted
in any form, electronic or mechanical, including photocopying, recording or by means
of any information storage or retrieval system without prior permission in writing from the
publishers; or ii) used or reproduced in any way for the training, development or operation
of artificial intelligence (AI) technologies, including generative AI technologies. The rights
holders expressly reserve this publication from the text and data mining exception as
per Article 4(3) of the Digital Single Market Directive (EU) 2019/790.

Bloomsbury Publishing Plc does not have any control over, or responsibility for,
any third-party websites referred to or in this book. All internet addresses given in
this book were correct at the time of going to press. The author and publisher
regret any inconvenience caused if addresses have changed or sites have ceased
to exist, but can accept no responsibility for any such changes.

A catalogue record for this book is available from the British Library.

Library of Congress Cataloging-in-Publication Data
Names: Sugirtharajah, R. S. (Rasiah S.), author.
Title: Hindus and their Christian Bible / R.S. Sugirtharajah.
Description: London ; New York : T&T Clark, 2023. | Includes index. |
Summary: "Shows how Hindu reformers scrutinized, adapted and interacted
with the sacred text of their colonizers, interpreting the bible in their own
contexts and for their own means"– Provided by publisher.
Identifiers: LCCN 2023027509 | ISBN 9780567711533 (hb) | ISBN 9780567711533 (pb) |
ISBN 9780567711540 (epdf) | ISBN 9780567711564 (ebook)
Subjects: LCSH: Bible. | India–Colonies. | Hinduism.
Classification: LCC BS475.3 .S875 2023 | DDC 220.6/1—dc23/eng/20230919
LC record available at https://lccn.loc.gov/2023027509

ISBN:	HB:	978-0-5677-1153-3
	PB:	978-0-5677-1157-1
	ePDF:	978-0-5677-1154-0
	eBook:	978-0-5677-1156-4

Typeset by RefineCatch Limited, Bungay, Suffolk

For product safety related questions contact productsafety@bloomsbury.com.

To find out more about our authors and books visit www.bloomsbury.com
and sign up for our newsletters.

CONTENTS

Acknowledgements	vi
INTRODUCTION	1
Chapter 1 A MORAL TESTAMENT	5
Chapter 2 TEXTUAL ORDINANCES FOR TEMPLE WORSHIPPERS	25
Chapter 3 UNIVERSAL AND INTUITIVE TRUTHS	51
Chapter 4 A SAIVA CĀSTIRAM	79
Chapter 5 A WORLD-RENOUNCING GOSPEL	103
Chapter 6 BAPU'S BIBLE	125
Chapter 7 A VARIANT OF THE VEDAS	155
Chapter 8 FANATICAL AND FRAUDULENT	181
AFTERWORD: CHALLENGES AND CONFRONTATIONS	205
General Index	211
Scriptural References	215

ACKNOWLEDGEMENTS

This book evolved at a time when Covid-19 posed unexpected challenges. Given the perilous nature of the times, I would like to thank those who showed tremendous understanding and sympathy. I am grateful to Dominic Mattos, the inspirational Senior Publisher at T&T Clark for his continuing encouragement and support. I also extend my gratitude to Katherine Jenkins for her skilful guidance throughout the various stages of production. Additionally, I appreciate Ronnie Hanna for his expertise and efficient copy editing. And also thanks to Ralph Broadbent for his astute observations and helpful comments which strengthened the text. Rohini Mani deserves my thanks for creating an imaginative cover image for the book. Finally, thanks to Sharada, my wife who has been by my side providing inspiration and intellectual support for all my endeavours. Without her unstinting support, I wouldn't have been able to write a single line.

INTRODUCTION

The idea for the book on the Hindus' use of the Bible came to me when I was doing the research for *Jesus in Asia*. I came across an enormous number of references to the Bible and biblical allusions in the works of the nineteenth- and twentieth-century Hindu reformers, both of the Brahmo Samaj and the Arya Samaj, and that of the Indian nationalists. Although there are books on the Hindus and their portrayals of Jesus, there is no work which brings together their views on the Bible in a single volume. The book you are holding in your hands tries to rectify this lamentable lacuna.

Indian Hindus have been pioneers in developing Indian Christianity, making especially significant contributions to biblical studies which have gone unnoticed by mainstream Western biblical scholarship. In the Indian context, the first search for the historical Jesus, the first modern line-by-line biblical commentary, the first comparative exegesis, the first modern harmonization of the Gospels, the first identification of biblical religion as Asiatic and the first use of what was known at that time as higher criticism to interrogate the biblical texts were all initiated by Hindus, some of whom you will meet in this volume. Their articulations exemplify extraordinary attempts to explain biblical teachings through the prism of the Indian sacred textual tradition.

None of the Hindu reformers and Indian nationalists studied here wrote a full-scale volume on the Bible but their ideas are scattered around in their various writings. For instance, almost all the writings of Keshub Chunder Sen, Swami Vivekananda, Gandhi and Radhakrishnan have some biblical quotes, or an allusion to biblical texts. What is evident in their works is not only an intense knowledge of the Bible but also a total confidence in handling biblical passages. Some of them show familiarity with the then prevalent biblical scholarship and were not afraid to question some Western scholars' cherished ideas and findings. Some of them knew biblical languages and put this into effective use to query the missionary translations which were at odds with their own theological presuppositions. Most of their interpretative engagements were done during the colonial era and some in post-colonial India. It was the aggressive missionary activity and the Christian Church's alleged alliance with the British government which galvanized and provided the impetus for these Hindus reformers.

Their response to the Bible varies from accepting it as one of the revelations of God to dismissing it as not being worthy of being God's word. Some were genuine in their search to understand the Bible in relation to Hindu sacred texts which they saw as their proud possession, and others were keen to refute the Bible's uniqueness and prove the superiority of the Vedic revelation. All of them had a curiously ambivalent attitude towards the Bible and Christianity. In other words, their appropriation of the Bible varied from being generous to ambiguous to a totally adverse posture.

This volume is structured by a series of chapters, seven of them devoted to the writings of individuals such as Rammohun Roy, Arumuga Navalar, Keshub Chunder Sen, M. K. Gandhi, Ponnambalam Ramanathan, Swami Vivekananda and Sarvepalli Radhakrishnan. The eighth chapter looks at the works of a group of Hindu nationalists from both the colonial and post-colonial eras who took a hard-line position which ranged from revisionist to blasphemous to downright rude.

The chapters provide a brief biographical sketch and their interpretative context; the hermeneutical principles they employ; the authority they accord to the Bible; their exegetical methods; their textual selections; their view of the Bible and its relation to the Bhagavad Gita, the Upanishads and the Saiva texts; the role of the Vedanta and the Saiva Siddhanta in interpreting the Bible; their challenges to the prevalent translations; and their lexical and grammatical skills in extracting particular meanings which suited their vested interpretative stance, or to refute the interpretation of the missionaries. The essays here also inquire into their interpretative motives – establishing common grounds for inter-religious living, or asserting the superiority of Hinduism. The volume narrates how these interpreters detached the Bible from the Christian milieu and gave it a new Hindu flavour, and at the same time demonstrate how they drew on biblical themes, ideas and metaphors to undergird, redefine and forge a Hindu religious identity.

The personalities studied here are by no means a thorough representation of the Hindu world. The obvious omissions are the female voices. My attempts to find Hindu women who used the Bible in their discourse proved futile.

Therefore, the stories of the men told here represent pivotal hermeneutical moments in the history of biblical interpretation in India. They reflected and crystalized a certain stance rather than shaping the discipline. The figures assembled are linguistically and geographically distinct. They did not even belong to the same Hindu tradition. But they are connected by the desire to refute the routine missionary claim that salvation was a gift of the Bible and the denial of any liberatory potential in the Indian religious texts. The essays presented in this book are a challenge to this view.

One hopes that their voices will be recognized and, more importantly, be included in the current scholarly exchanges regarding the methods and meaning of the Scriptures. The personalities discussed here are fairly well known in Hindu Studies, inter-faith dialogue and missiology, but they hardly feature in Biblical Studies. Some genuinely wanted to understand and interpret this new imported book and others were uncompromising in their anti-Christian posturing. Whatever their hermeneutical presuppositions and aims, they struggled on undaunted by the insults levelled against them by Western and missionary interpreters and questioned the central tenets of biblical faith. This is not simply a matter of letting them into the academic fraternity. They should be studied as a sterling example of challenging the myth of the historical-critical method as the only way to mine meanings in the Bible. The historical value of their articulations may be tenuous, but they help to draw attention to aspects of the narrative that might otherwise have gone unnoticed or be overlooked by mainstream biblical scholarship. And there is an additional reason for paying them attention – this is the voice of those once written about by the West now coming back and writing about the Christian West. If only for this reason, these voices deserve a hearing despite being unpalatable and at times sounding rude. Perhaps it is beneficial that Christian biblical scholarship learns a thing or two from non-Christian outsiders over whom it has time and again claimed superiority.

Chapter 1

A MORAL TESTAMENT

The year was 1820. Sake Dean Mohomed, an early Indian immigrant to England and grandiosely named 'surgeon', introduced a new method of shampooing and cleansing the bodies of the British upper crust in London. In the same year another Indian in Calcutta (now Kolkata) was cleansing the text of the British establishment. The text he purified was the Christian Bible, more specifically the Gospels. His name was Raja Rammohun Roy (1772-1833)[1] and the resultant text was *The Precepts of the Jesus: The Guide to Peace and Happiness*.[2]

Roy's story is often condensed into the appellation 'Father of the Nation'. This patriarchal trope suggests a secure, confident privilege. Beside this laudable label, the ascription 'first' is also often attached to his name, which varied from publishing newspapers in India to championing the cause of women's rights to the abolition of child marriage. Among his 'firsts', one that is often overlooked is his realization that Christianity was going to play an important role in India. The power of the Mughal samrājya was waning, and the English were in the wings, waiting to take over. Roy, who lived under the Mughals and experienced the complex and unwelcome consequences of their imperial rule in India, was well aware of what colonialism could do. It was a time fraught with uncertainty and Roy thought that it was his role to prepare his country to face the impending British rule, so he sought out a morality that would meet the challenges of the time. He was also alert to the fact that the Vaishnavism that was practised in Bengal at that time was not 'well calculated to promote their political interest', and he deeply felt that for the 'sake of their political advantage and social comfort'[3] a new moral purpose was needed. He found one in the teachings of Jesus. The result was *The Precepts of Jesus*, which Roy thought was 'so admirably calculated' to elevate 'high and liberal notions of one God' and to 'regulate the conduct of the human race in the discharge of their various duties to God, to themselves, and to society'.[4] He declared that there was nothing that was as 'sublime' or 'equal to the simple doctrines' inculcated by Jesus.[5] Roy genuinely felt that the *Precepts* would be a suitable scripture for India's uncertain future.

The Reduced Version

The introduction that Roy wrote for the *Precepts* was both expressive and perturbing, especially to the Serampore Baptist missionaries with whom, up until the publication of this slim and seditious volume, he had had a cordial relationship. Ironically, it was published by the press run by the Baptist missionaries. In gleaning extracts from the Gospels, he made it clear that some Gospel materials were far more important than others. What stood out for him was the 'simple code of religion and morality', which he summarized as 'man should do unto others as he would wish to be done by'. Roy conceded that this moral maxim was partially taught by other religions, but he assiduously maintained that it was 'principally inculcated by Christianity'.

Taken as it is, the *Precepts* was a harmless text, even a commendable one coming from a Hindu. His hermeneutical misdemeanour according to his missionary opponents in Calcutta was to compress the entire Gospel message into a simple ethical code. What really annoyed them was his disregard for some of the staple and sensitive elements of Christianity. He discarded the historical details, the miraculous, supernatural events, and what he called the 'mysterious doctrines' found in the Gospels as having no desirable effect on the Indians. He was of the view that the historical events were liable to 'doubts and disputes'; that the miracle and supernatural accounts were much less wonderful than the Asian tales, and would not carry any 'weight'; and that the doctrines did not have 'sufficient novelty and force' to attract his readers. There was no possibility that Roy, who rejected the miracles and doctrines in his own tradition, would embrace these 'heathenish' notions advocated by this alien faith.

Just as Western Orientalists were seeking pure Hinduism in the ancient Indian texts, Roy reversed the gaze and was searching for the authentic teachings of Jesus in the canonical Gospels. The *Precepts* was staid, sober and occasionally repetitive. Roy defended his selection of the Gospel material on the grounds that the moral precepts of Jesus had become entangled with doctrinal matters and mangled by later theological interpretations, hence it had to be rescued. He further stated that the missionaries themselves were not in a position to establish the truth of the Gospels because they were already prejudiced and their partiality had prevented them from paying attention to doctrines which were 'consistent with the laws of nature' and 'acceptable to common sense'. What Roy implied was that as an outlier with his independent mind, he was in an ideal position to ascertain and inquire what the Gospel was and, more crucially, to rectify 'extremely incorrect' versions propagated by missionaries.

The principal purpose of bringing out the edited version of the Gospels was to introduce the foreign faith to his fellow Bengalis and not to denigrate Christianity or disgrace Jesus. He believed that the pure-principled moral teachings of Jesus had to be detached from the abuse of the denominational churches, and that this redeemed Jesus and his message should be presented to his people. Roy strongly believed that the Christian faith that was introduced to India by missionaries was riven by denominational divisions that would be beyond the reach of the learned and the unlearned people of India.

The resultant volume appeared without major ingredients of the Gospels. The *Precepts* left out supernatural episodes such as Jesus' walking on water, calming the storm, feeding the 5,000, raising Lazarus to life, and Jesus rising from the grave on the third day. Next, he edited out the historical events associated with Jesus. So out went the genealogy of Jesus, the birth narratives, his baptism, his temptation, the choosing of his disciples, the transfiguration, his entrance into Jerusalem, the cleansing of the temple, the betrayal, the trial and his crucifixion. Roy feared that the historical events could be doubted and, even worse, be ridiculed by freethinkers and anti-Christians among Indians. All references or allusions to doctrines such as the Trinity, the atonement and the Holy Spirit disappeared. The Trinity, Roy maintained, was a 'human invention'. The doctrine of atonement, where Jesus offered his blood to propitiate God, in his view appeared to 'every civilised being' as 'monstrous'. He argued that the missionaries who rejected the allegorical representation of the triune God in Hinduism as a fanciful idea could not realistically expect the Hindus to 'adopt' the Trinity. Similarly, Roy found the language applied to the Holy Spirit, such as 'she was found with child of the Holy Ghost', was offensive to the feelings of those who ascribe 'purity and perfection' to God. He redefined the Holy Spirit as the 'miraculous power of the Deity'.

So, what then did Roy include in the *Precepts*? It starts innocently with the Matthew's version of the Sermon the Mount – a sermon with which Jesus allegedly launched his first public engagement. This sermon contained the famous Beatitudes which were primarily about God's favour in response to certain human predicaments, achievements and behaviours. The other material included Jesus' teaching on anger, human relationships, adultery and male lust, divorce and mistreatment of women by men, the ineluctable link between word and action. It also contained acts of piety – almsgiving, prayer and fasting. Roy did not reproduce the entire sermon – he omitted nearly ten verses from Chapter 5, which were about vows and resistance to evil (5.33-44). Later, in his dispute with Joshua Marshman, the Baptist missionary who spoke for orthodox Christianity, Roy stated in his characteristic fashion that these three chapters of Matthew contained 'every duty of man, and all that is necessary to salvation'. In his view, the Sermon on the Mount had no historical or doctrinal materials that were 'calculated to do injury'. It was probably this reason which prompted him to include Luke's shorter version of the same sermon.

The rest of his selections from the Synoptic Gospels included Jesus' strong views on material wealth and how it is a hinderance to entering the Kingdom of God, with complete renunciation seen as a suitable stance towards it. Strangely, Roy left out Jesus' sterner instructions to his disciples that could exemplify such ascetical living. He deleted all Jesus' recommendations for austere living for those on missionary journeys – taking no money, bread or putting on two coats, and wearing sandals. His other selections included anxiety about covetousness and lack of generosity towards those who were in need. While Roy incorporated the incident when Jesus advised a rich man to give up his wealth in order to enter Kingdom of God, he inexplicably left out the story of Zacchaeus, the tax collector who precisely embodied this ideal by giving up half of his wealth. Roy missed here a great opportunity to press his point home.

The other passages which found their way into Roy's text, sometimes twice, were Jesus' redefinition of family, which transcended traditional blood ties to include those who did the will of God. He also chose passages which emphasized the inner moral aspect rather than external rituals – the very issue with which Roy was involved with his fellow brahmin priests. His selection also included instances in Jesus' life where he questioned the religious authorities of the day. Just like Roy, Jesus challenged their strictures as unjust and oppressive.

The other materials that Roy endorsed were the parables of Jesus and the pedagogical reason for teaching in them, the cost of discipleship and instructions on how to pray. Some of Luke's special material found its way into the *Precepts*, including parables such as the Prodigal Son, the Good Samaritan, the Friend at Midnight, the Shrewd Manager, the Widow and the Judge, the Rich Fool, the Pharisee and the Tax Collector, Severe and Light Beatings and the Rich Man and Lazarus. All of them expanded the view of God, and God's dealing with humans and their conduct. Roy's approval of these materials could have been influenced by his cardinal moral precept – the love of God and showing love to fellow human beings.

Curiously, besides the moral teaching, Roy retained passages which revealed the missiological purpose of Jesus, such as the verses 'He that receiveth you receiveth me, and he that receiveth me receiveth him that sent me' (Mt.10.40) and 'All things are delivered unto me of my Father: and no man knoweth the Son, but the Father; neither knoweth any man the Father, save the Son, and he to whomsoever the Son will reveal him' (Mt.11.27). These sayings fitted in well with Roy's view of Jesus as an envoy sent by God to 'preach and impart divine instruction'. Jesus was basically a 'distributor of eternal life'.

Roy's selection of John's materials was modest and meagre, confined to fifty-six verses. He blamed the fourth Gospel for being the principal source and origin of the most difficult-to-comprehend dogmas of the Church. Nonetheless, this did not prevent him from using the fourth Gospel's anti-idolatry cause – a cause Roy himself advocated: 'God is a Spirit: and they that worship him must worship him in spirit and in truth' (4.23–4). Sadly, however, Roy missed out on some of the choicest sayings on love recorded in John's Gospel, which could have strengthened his case, for example: 'Greater love hath no man than this, that a man lay down his life for his friends' (15.13).

Roy, who championed the rights of women and fought against the immolation of wives on the funeral pyre, included only a few biblical women in the *Precepts*. His approach to women is a mixture of avoidance or overuse for his hermeneutical purposes. The women, as in the Gospel narratives, do not accompany Jesus. The Widow who made the offering at the temple appears twice, whereas the Samaritan Woman and her intriguing liturgical questions are omitted, yet the that part of Jesus' answer which anticipated ritual-free worship which Roy encouraged was retained.

There are puzzling passages included in the *Precepts* which were contrary to the tolerant and forgiving nature of Jesus and the high moral standard he expected of others. A specific example of this is Jesus' instruction to the disciples as to how they should respond to the cities which refused to welcome or accept them. Instead of working among those who resisted them, Jesus' advice to the disciples was that they should leave the city and issue them with a stern warning 'that it shall be more tolerable in that day for Sodom, than for that city'. Such threats and admonitions did not sit well with Roy's much-commended teaching of Jesus: 'Love your enemies.'

Roy's *Precepts* was not always faithful or consistent, and did not live up to the noble goals set out in his Introduction. He claimed that he would remove all the Gospel accounts of miracles, but he retained a few that formed part of Jesus' challenge to the religious authorities of the day. The healing of the man with the withered hand is illustrative of this. Unaccountably, Roy included the harsh words Jesus aimed at Herod, which contained references to his ability to drive out devils and heal the sick, which would not have passed the reason-test he himself set: 'Go ye, and tell that fox, Behold, I cast out devils, and I do cures today and tomorrow, and the third day I shall be perfected' (Lk. 13.32). A supernatural event which did make an appearance in the *Precepts* were allusions to the resurrection of Jesus – the principal focus of Christianity. At Caesarea Philippi, after charging Peter to maintain strict silence, Jesus went on to reveal his intention to go to Jerusalem, face death and the subsequent resurrection. This is further alluded to in his harsh words to Herod, already noted, that on the 'third day I shall be perfected' (Lk. 13.32).

Roy also stated that he would delete historical accounts – but he did not define what he meant by historical. It could mean historical and prophetical predictions about Jesus' lineage and the role he was assigned to play. He retained a number of historical events in Jesus' life which varied from the sublime to the mundane. These included the Caesarea Philippi incident, where Jesus sought validation from his disciples about his identity, and everyday events such as Jesus simply walking in the corn fields with his disciples. Strangely, Roy, who edited out the question about Jesus' identity raised by the disciples of John the Baptist, retained Jesus' question about himself.

One of the concerns that prompted Roy to produce the *Precepts* was the adverse effect of the Gospels as they were propagated by the missionaries. He believed that the *Precepts* he edited was 'well fitted to regulate the conduct of the human race in the discharge of their various duties to themselves, and to society, that I cannot but hope the best effects from its promulgation in the present form'.[6] Roy found the morality he was looking for was better represented in the Gospels than in the Vedic texts because in the Hindu texts moral precepts were randomly scattered and marked by deplorable errors that had accumulated over the years, distracting from their ethical content.

The intention of Roy's truncated text was not to scorn or minimize the Bible as the rationalists, English Deists and Enlightenment radicals did at that time, but to maximize its message and renegotiate it for India which was going through a period of uncertainty. He believed that it could be profitably related to the lives of Indians. For Roy, the *Precepts* was a genuine religious expression which the Serampore Baptists did not appreciate. He accepted the Gospel accounts without questioning their veracity or considering their own internal theological and ecclesiastical proclivities. Unlike the lives of Jesus that appeared in the eighteenth and early nineteenth centuries, which showed a 'lack respect for the language of Jesus' and were 'reproduced in the most respectable modern style',[7] Roy hardly changed a word, or updated its language, or added anything to his Gospel selections.

He simply redacted the canonical Gospels without any regard for their individuality or the intention with which they were initially composed. What the *Precepts* did was to diminish the diversity enshrined in the four Gospels and conflate them into one single story. The text virtually expunged the individual character of the of the Gospels and moulded them into one solitary narrative. In Roy's hands, the Gospels became indistinguishable, merely containing moral codes.

The *Precepts* surprisingly left out three notable sayings of Jesus which later Indians, both Hindus and Christians, treated as *mahāvākyas* (Great Sayings) and used them profitably with a view to indigenizing the message of Jesus. One is the Matthean saying of Jesus – 'that ye resist not evil' – a saying which provided textual ammunition for Gandhi, whom we will meet later, to launch his resistance against the British government. The other two missing sayings – Luke's 'behold, the kingdom of God is within you' and John's 'I and my Father are one' – were mobilized to support the advaitin notion of the metaphysical union of Father, Son and the believer by Hindu thinkers like Radhakrishnan. Though this Johannine saying was missing in the *Precepts*, Roy used this verse to challenge the missionaries' understanding of the metaphysical union of Father and Son, and interpreted it as a 'union of will and design that subsisted' between Jesus and God. This idea of moral union has been repurposed by Indian reformers like Keshub Chunder Sen and a number of Indian Christian theologians, including Appasamy, who argued for a moral union based on love and obedience without crediting Roy.

Devising a single story out of the four Gospels has been going on ever since various accounts of Jesus came into existence. The earliest attempt was the second century *Diatessaron* by the Assyrian Christian Tatian. The aim here was to get rid of contradictory and duplicate materials in the Gospels. Roy did not engage in such an exercise. His *Precepts* contains a number of duplicates, such as: the disciples' question about who was greatest among them; their concern about the future rewards; the request that the sons of Zebedee sit at the right hand and left hand of Jesus; the Rich Man and Jesus' teaching on wealth; the Lord's Prayer; the Parable of the Sower; and the widow who made an offering at the temple; and blasphemy against the Holy Spirit.

A compilation of the moral teachings of Jesus teaching is nothing new. The Apocryphal Gospel of Thomas provides a collection of sayings and parables of Jesus and some scholars give it an earlier date than the canonical Gospels. The Bible itself contains aphoristic texts such as the Wisdom literature. Where the *Precepts* differed from other harmonizations of the Gospels was that it was aimed at Roy's fellow Hindus, whereas the Western compositions targeted Christians.

Roy did not clearly define what cardinal virtues Jesus revealed to the world and how these were beneficial to India. In his exchanges with Marshman, he was more interested in simply providing biblical verses as if he had gone through a concordance and gathered texts which had some semblance of what he had in mind rather than expounding what the morality Jesus proclaimed looked like. The principal marks of ethical conduct that Jesus identified were prudence, courage, justice, compassion and humility. His selection of parables shows how people act when motivated by compassion. In the parable of the Unforgiving Servant, the servant was moved with 'compassion, loosed him, forgave him the debt'. In the parable of the Prodigal Son, the father had 'compassion' and ran and hugged his son when he returned. The Good Samaritan showed 'compassion' for the man who was left for dead by the thieves.

Besides Roy's *Precepts* there were other modern abbreviated Gospels. The most prominent and at the same time much pilloried was composed by Thomas Jefferson, the third president of the United States. *The Life and Morals of Jesus of Nazareth* was completed in 1820, the same year that Roy published his *Precepts*. Widely known as the Jefferson Bible, it excluded miracles and the resurrection,[8] but was far from being a secularized Gospel, retaining angels and devils, the healings of Jesus and many references to God and exhortations to fear him.[9] The other main abbreviation of the Gospels was Leo Tolstoy's *Gospels in Brief*, a synthesis of the four Gospels, eliminating miracles and the resurrection, but with Jesus still remaining a Son of God and the Messiah.[10] The most recent abbreviations include Julian Baggini's *The Godless Gospel: Was Jesus a Great Moral Teacher*? His Jesus embodies in secular form Christian exceptionalism as a countercultural hero who makes you a 'better person' in the vein of American televangelists.[11]

Editing of the Gospels texts has a long history, and the proliferation of post-canonical Gospels is indicative that the relevance of the Bible depends on its continual retelling. Roy's *Precepts* played its part in the long process of removing the incongruities embedded in the texts. The Bible is essentially a work in progress.

Just like the Bible itself, the *Precepts* was not composed so much as gathered, redacted and reconstructed over time. Roy's motivating question was not 'What did the Gospels really look like?' but 'In what other ways we can imagine them?' The greatness of the *Precepts* lies not in the text itself but in what it signified – a depository of the moral teachings of Jesus. Roy rewrote the Scripture but far from secularizing the Word of God, he humanized it and created a moralistic narrative out of it. In Roy's *Precepts*, liberalism, Deism and rationalism converge in the egoistical belief that no one has understood the subject better than its author. The *Precepts* was simultaneously a pious and blasphemous document – both an endorsement and a critique of the Gospel message.

Jesus: Dispenser of Moral Maxims

Roy's depiction of Jesus was not conspicuously Indian. He was more interested in purifying his Vedas than fitting Jesus into an Indian framework. The Indian imaging of Jesus was undertaken later, at times brilliantly and at times blandly, by various Indian Christian thinkers like K. M Banerjea and A. J. Appasamy. What Roy achieved was to open up Jesus, who was the prime focus of devotion for Christians, to innumerable Hindus who did not view him in the conventional Christian sense.

Roy, like some of the eminent Enlightenment luminaries of the time, had an extremely high regard for Jesus, whose teaching he considered beneficial for India. As with these eighteenth-century thinkers, Roy, too, took the view that Jesus should not be confined to the past and portrayed as a person of his time, but should be a contemporary figure who had a message for the present day. Roy was not searching for a historical Jesus but rather a biblical Jesus whom Indians could comprehend. This Jesus, Roy believed, could serve as the basis of an undogmatic Christianity and morality.

One of Roy's astute hermeneutical achievements was to cast Jesus, the founder of the Christian faith, as an Asiatic. True, it was a vague and generalized geographical description, but it served an important theological purpose. At a time when the Orientalists and missionaries ridiculed Indians as people 'degraded by Asiatic effeminacy', Roy repositioned Jesus as an Asiatic. He sagaciously turned the accusation around: 'Almost all the ancient prophets and patriarchs venerated by Christians, were ASIATICS. So, if a Christian think[s] it degrading to be born or reside in *Asia*, he directly reflects upon them.'[12] The subtext was clear. You are not ridiculing us but *all* the biblical figures whom you worship and venerate.

In Roy's portrayal, Jesus was a 'messenger of God', a 'spiritual teacher', and a 'created being'. The most significant aspect of Jesus was that he revealed the divine will more fully than ever before. It was Moses who started to 'erect the everlasting edifice of true religion', which consisted of the unity of God and obedience to his will, but it was Jesus of Nazareth who 'completed the structure, and rendered his law perfect'.[13] It was Jesus who 're-established' what the Commandments had ordained according to the law and prophets.

All those grand divine privileges and titles that missionaries accorded to Jesus and drawn from the biblical sources, such as the 'Son of God', 'only begotten', 'first born', 'Holy one', 'the Most Holy', 'Saviour', 'shepherd', 'Messiah', were dismissed by Roy as commonplace designations. He drew from the same Bible to demonstrate that these assertions had been applied to other biblical personalities and even to inanimate objects: David had been called the 'first born' and there were several persons who were known as Messiahs, including Hezekiah, while the term the 'most holy one' was also applied to non-living matter, such as 'an altar most holy' (Exod. 29.37).

In the accusatory words of his missionary opponent, Marshman, Roy made Jesus 'the Teacher and Founder of a Sect, instead of adoring Him as the Lord of all'. Roy found deifying Jesus 'both an affront to God and an *unchristian* doctrine', persistently asking the missionaries how they could justify the idea that one who was in 'human shape', was possessed of 'human feelings' and was subjected to 'the calls of nature' was truly God and above 'all mortal causes and effects'.

Readers learn little of Jesus' infancy and nothing of his divine election or mission in the *Precepts*. Roy did not pay much attention to Jesus before he delivered the Sermon on the Mount. What the Serampore missionaries objected to was that the teachings of Jesus on which Roy lavished praise did not include many doctrinal and religious elements, without which Jesus' message was meaningless. The Jesus that emerges from the *Precepts* is neither the Sunday School image of a meek and mild babe born in the manger who was seen as the Prince of Peace nor the Jesus with a whip threatening the authorities. Roy's Jesus did not believe in using political means to achieve social goals and uplift his people. The priority for this Jesus was not social change but social happiness. This was achieved through changing oneself from within.

Though Jesus preached peace and harmony, in Roy's construal he brings division and discord. Roy's Jesus authorizes Peter to establish a church with power to bind and loose, to admit and to exclude people. He stokes unnecessary conflict, as exemplified in the statement 'He that is not with me is against me.' This Jesus even expected his disciples to cause disruption. The Lukan verse that crept into the *Precepts* is a startling illustration of this point: 'he that dispiseth you dispiseth me'. It looks as if dissension was to be the main thrust of Jesus' mission and not a by-product. In Roy's envisioning, Jesus was not a man of flawless character and superlative conduct. He exhibits un-Christlike characteristics. He curses his enemies and demands complete obedience. He is insensitive and hard even on his own disciples, preventing them from going to their own father's funeral.

The Jesus depicted in the *Precepts* is not the Jesus of two natures – Jesus as both human and divine – a confessional orthodoxy sanctioned by ecclesiastical councils and advocated by the missionaries. Roy flatly dismissed such a claim as 'unscriptural and irrational'. He wrote that as a person who had been solemnly linked to incarnations of a twofold- or threefold-God, this idea of dual identity had lost its 'novelty' for him. His point was that 'the doctrine God-Man, Man-God' had been preached by the Brahmins and that this same doctrine preached by 'another body of priests better dressed, better provided for and eminently elevated by virtue of conquest' would not excite his 'curiosity'.

Jesus is portrayed as a man of wisdom in contrast to the people he encountered. Those who showed wisdom equal to that of Jesus were omitted from the *Precepts*. Victims of this elision were the Syrophoenician Woman who exposed his racial arrogance, and the Samaritan Woman who posed serious theological questions to Jesus. Jesus was represented as a cool figure, a quality illustrated in the incident of the storm: while the disciples despaired, Jesus displayed calmness and authority.

Jesus comes across as a man without any claim to supernatural power. This Jesus does not perform godlike activities such as striding on the sea, rebuking the storm or feeding the hungry. He was a mere moral teacher without a sacrificial death. Naturally, such a Jesus did not appeal to the missionaries. Roy's Jesus forgives sinners without getting on to the cross. There was no reparation made on behalf of fallen humanity. Roy found the atonement, in which blood was 'offered to God to reconcile to God', to be 'unreasonable' and 'conducive to immoral practices'. Roy persistently declared that the redemption was affected through two means. One, Jesus saved people through the inculcation of the word of God: 'Now ye are clean through the word which I have spoken unto you' (Jn 15.3). The beneficiaries of this new divine pardon were the two sinners: one was the woman caught in adultery and the other a sinful woman who anointed Jesus. The other means of salvation was sincere repentance on the part of sinners. In his deliberations with the missionaries, Roy cited the case of the Prodigal Son whose repentance was enough for his father to pardon his transgressions. Roy reminded them of the numerous passages in both testaments which spoke of forgiveness being obtained by 'sincere repentance'.

In the canonical Gospels, Jesus set himself as an example to follow. This is clearly exemplified in Jesus' own words after the washing of the feet of the disciples, which is unfortunately omitted from Roy's version: 'For I have given you an example, that ye should do as I have done to you.' Jesus was most exemplary at his trial. His passive resistance, his calmness and the dignified way he faced the ridicule and abuse were all missing from the *Precepts*.

Roy's Jesus is not the conventional moral teacher issuing injunctions as a confident expert with authority. He did not even claim any originality. When people approached him, he responded to them by pointing out that they already had the Commandments. When the Rich Young Man wanted to know how to inherit eternal life, Jesus told him that he already knew what the Commandments were and quoted most of them to him. Apparently, even in Jesus' time not all were willing to follow the moral teaching of Jesus, one such being the Rich Young Man.

In the Jewish Scriptures, the moral codes were delivered by divine command. It was God who called Moses and gave him the Ten Commandments and told him that he should tell the house of Jacob and the children of Israel. Roy's Jesus did not demonstrate or profess such authority. When the Chief Priest, the scribes and the elders asked him who he was and by whose authority he spoke and acted, he deflected the question and posed his own – what did they think about the baptism of John and was it of men or of heaven?

Roy's Jesus simply encouraged people to show love to their fellow human beings in the way that God lavished love upon them. This teaching was not particularly innovative, having a certain connection and continuity with that of the sages of wisdom literature. Biblical scholars have identified similar sayings and ideas prevalent in the ancient world.[14] Not all Indians were enthused by the world-renouncing ethics of Jesus. Radhakrishnan found it to be a 'negative one' and 'not a humanist ethic' and cited Bishop Gore to strengthen his case. Bishop Gore saw it as a 'proclamation of unworldliness in its extreme form'.[15]

Roy's Jesus refused to be forced into an eschatological mould as the later nineteenth-century lives of Jesus tended to portray him. The *Precepts* was more interested in Jesus' moral utterances than in his announcement of the Kingdom of God. He was more of a teacher of human relationships and behaviour. Without the miracles and the resurrection appearances of Jesus, there is not much to say about the immediate impact of Jesus' ministry on the people who followed him. Roy's text is full of the sayings of Jesus, but there is no compelling reason why anybody should follow or believe in him. Roy's Jesus would have definitely warmed the hearts of the Unitarians and liberal Christians. Whether the Palestinians of his time would have warmed to him is another matter. Though Roy's aim was admirable, there is not much to admire in the Jesus who has been deracinated from his environment, his God, his fellow Jews, his followers, his Scriptures and his doctrines and theology. Once you uproot Jesus – or for that matter, anyone – from their immediate associations or connections which define them, what is there to cherish or commend?

The Brahmin, the Baptists and their Bible

Roy's *Precepts* inevitably caused concern for the Baptist missionaries in Calcutta. The Christian rebuttal was spearheaded by the Baptists Joshua Marshman,[16] William Yates, who wrote anonymously, and an Anglican, T. Scot.[17] The debate, which went on for three years, was largely waged by stringing together biblical passages which supported each other's position. The whole exchange was dense, detailed and repetitive. For every defence of the orthodox position, Roy was able to cite counter-texts which challenged it. Examples included Christ's divinity, the father–son relationship and the role and function of the Holy Spirit. It was clear that Roy and his missionary opponents were talking on two different wavelengths. On reviewing the debate, it is apparent that they all agreed on certain basics and differed only on intention and implication.

Roy and the missionaries concurred on one thing – the authority of the Bible. Both quoted copiously from the Scriptures to confirm their pre-existing stance. While the missionaries claimed that Bible *alone* was sufficient for salvation, Roy found the moral precepts of Jesus were more than adequate to lead people to achieve peace and happiness and cultivate 'universal love and harmony'. Each attributed different utility value to the Bible. While the missionaries used it as a perfect tool to save souls, Roy employed it as a fundamental manual to remind his people of their 'civil duties'. They also differed over the nature of the Bible. The missionaries accused Roy of placing the Bible 'on a level with any good book', whereas for them it was the depository of the unerring and unchanging word of God. Marshman saw the Bible as an effective tool for evangelism. They spoke of the 'two thousand editions of the New Testament as two thousand missionaries'.[18] Roy, on the other hand, considered it to be a moral self-help guide. While both the missionaries and Roy regarded the Bible to be the faithfully revealed Word of God, there was a difference between them. Whilst Baptists considered the Bible to be the final and full revelation, Roy saw it was a work in progress and he was anxious that one should not foreclose future revelations. In support of this, he quoted the Johannine saying of Jesus that he had 'many more things to say unto' them.

Roy and the missionaries both subscribed to the pre-critical assumption that the Gospels were the depositories of the words and deeds of Jesus, but they differed in their appropriation. The missionaries believed that these words could simply be applied irrespective of time and place, but Roy held the view that they had to be seen in their context, otherwise they were liable to be misunderstood and could be 'adduced to support any doctrine whatever'.

The missionaries, besides insisting on the all-sufficiency and the inerrancy of the Bible, kept on asking Roy whether he had been 'endued with authority from above' to summarize the entire Bible in the two sayings of Jesus. For them, the Bible was a 'harmonious whole' and it could not be sliced up to suit one's own theological needs. They wanted to know whether he had directions from above that no other parts were requisite for the peace and happiness of humankind. The missionaries dismissed Roy's claims as inferences and not revelations from God. They even cited the case of the prophet Mohammad who when abrogating the parts of the

Bible which did not conform with the Koran, claimed that he had divine direction to do so. They also pointed out the earlier examples of the Arians and Socinians, who 'tortured' some passages but did not 'disown the whole of the Bible' as Roy did. For Roy, there was no need to receive such divine direction. He was simply following the practice of Jesus. He understood the 'grand design' of Christ better than his opponents and reminded the missionaries that Jesus himself had drawn from many biblical books just two commandments – love of God and love for fellow human beings – as encompassing the whole of the Bible. Such a move was 'entirely founded on and supported by the express authorities of Jesus of Nazareth'.[19] It is not the inspiration he sought but rather corroboration from within the narratives. Authority, for Roy, did not come from heaven but was derived from the confirmative textual evidence embedded in the Gospels. For Roy, though the Vedas were dignified and established, they had only 'fluid sacred authority'. He did not overly worry whether the Scriptures were God-inspired – their truth status was determined by their potential to change and enhance life. He was further convinced that there was no need for any divine sanction to disregard a text, if it promoted polytheistic beliefs, irrationality and idolatrous practices.

Roy and the missionaries agreed that the moral precepts of Jesus were 'essential to our peace and happiness', but the issue between them was not who 'pays the most deference to the moral precepts of Jesus' but more crucially 'whether these precepts were ever designed to nullify the doctrinal ones and the rest of the scriptures'.[20] The missionaries' position was that the fact the law and the prophets contained in those two commandments did not permit one to abridge the Bible and render the original 'useless'. It was Jesus who used them for the convenience of the people so that they could 'recollect' in two sentences rather than require the whole of the law and the prophets. Roy pointed out that the missionaries themselves were not innocent in this matter and had the habit of publishing a selection of 'different passages of the scriptures for certain purposes'. The missionaries agreed that they did publish extracts from the scriptures but they did so on the basis that this did not supersede the 'other parts of the scripture'. They nobly claimed that their purpose 'was to give a sample of the whole, and not the whole of what we judged to be necessary'.[21] Roy's argument was that his compiled precepts had divine origin and came from the originator of the Christian religion and that they were a 'true substitute of the Gospel, without intending to depreciate the rest of the word of God'.[22]

Roy was a serial interferer with other peoples' texts. Just as he tampered with the Gospels to remove doctrines that were injurious to the Christian faith, so he did the same with his own Hindu texts that were offensive to the purity and perfection of God. Roy recalibrated the Upanishads, the Vedanta Sutra and the Laws of Manu to fit sufficiently with the cause he was espousing and reconfigured them as models for Hindu worship untainted by idolatry. The missionaries, however, were adamant that the Scriptures were 'sufficient' and that there was no need to improve them.

Roy and the Baptists had similar views on the salvific role of Jesus, but differed as to how this was to be accomplished. Roy's conception of salvation was free from paying debt as a recompense for human sin. Human repentance itself was enough.

The Baptists held to the view that it was Jesus who paid the debt through his sacrificial death. Hence, for them it was the person of Jesus, rather than his moral teachings as Roy steadfastly claimed, that was crucial to the salvation of humanity. Roy was very specific about the 'indispensability of repentance' for the remission of sins.

Each blamed the other for an excessive attachment to their pre-existing theological positions, which prevented them from looking at the texts objectively. Roy claimed that the Baptists' denominational upbringing hindered them from reading the biblical texts with fresh eyes, whereas the Baptists criticized Roy's anti-Trinitarian stance as coloured by the 'tenets of Musselman'. Roy's charge that his missionary opponents read their Bible to 'suit their peculiar ideas' could equally be said of him. Or, as an Irish minister who observed the debate colourfully put it, both were 'twisting and screwing to adjust them to particular formulas'.[23]

The Serampore Baptist missionaries were not always true to or straight with their arguments. There are wonderfully weird double standards in their accusations. When Roy maintained that there was no biblical evidence for the personality of the Holy Spirit, the Baptists retaliated by saying that his objection was merely 'trifling'. Their case was that '*truths* not *words* constitute the matter of revelation; and *words* are only the vehicle of *truths* to our minds'.[24] It was the same Baptists who objected to infant baptism because it did not have a biblical warrant or any reference in the Bible.

The debate between Roy and the missionaries was for most of the time courteous, except when Marshman called Roy a 'heathen' – a bad choice of word, especially in the colonial context. The trouble was that each had a different understanding of the term. For Marshman, a heathen was one who did not believe in the staple doctrines of Christianity whereas Roy understood it as a person who believed in irrational ideas like the Trinity. In the context of the controversy, Marshman employed it not as an argument but as a sneer, an epithet of reproach. Roy, in his turn, lobbed a bombshell at the missionaries and posed a question which the missionaries would not have expected: who is a Christian? And how do you define one? This ambiguity, Roy pointed out, was further exacerbated by the Apostles themselves who had 'several instances of different opinions'. Roy contended that there was no fixed meaning of who a Christian was, and listed a few of his definitions – the one who believed in the divine Christ, the Holy Spirit, the Bible as the revealed will of God, or adhered to the teachings of Jesus. The implication was that since there was no stable meaning of who a Christian was, Roy had every right to interpret the tenets of the biblical faith.

Roy and the missionaries concurred that the Hinduism that was practised at the time was in decay and was ill-adapted to meet the social needs of the Indians. For the missionaries, Hinduism was rotten to the core and had to be redeemed by the injection of the Gospel message. For Roy, both Hinduism and Christianity were corrupted by the 'subsequent intermixture of polytheistical ideas', aided and abetted by priests who sought to 'promote their own interests'. Hence both Hinduism and Christianity had to be cleansed.

Roy and the missionaries' approach to the Bible was akin to the ancient Indian parable of a group of blind people encountering a huge animal and each person creating their own version of reality from their partial perspective and experience. Similarly, Roy and the missionaries chose biblical texts which confirmed their entrenched theological views rather than grasping, to quote a phrase that often cropped up in their debate, the 'grand design' of the Bible.

'The Heathen' and his Hermeneutics

When the Bible was introduced to colonial India, it did not come as a confident and unifying authority of European culture. It appeared as a confessional document of Anglicans, Baptists, Methodists and Roman Catholics, riven with denominational divisions and rivalries. Roy's aim was not to supplant the denominational exegesis prevalent at that time. Rather, he hoped to develop a mode of interpretation that took full account of reason and the multi-religious context of the subcontinent. The way Roy handled the texts prompted W. H. Drummond, a Presbyterian turned Unitarian minister, to call him 'eminently qualified to discharge the office of a Biblical Critic'.[25]

Roy did a number of things with this pliable and adaptable Bible. First, he divorced it from denominational readings and introduced a reading which was a mixture of rationalism, liberalism, Islamic monotheism and Unitarianism. Second, he untethered the Bible from its ancient past and made it a contemporary textual product capable of reinvigorating India. Third, Roy made his fellow Indians realize that the Bible's contents were as good or as bad their own Scriptures. He informed them that both Scriptures – Hindu and Christian – 'firmly maintained' the doctrine of divine unity. He treated both – Hindu and Christian – as equal and having more or less the same contents. They differed from each other only minimally. Roy's placement of the Bible along with the Indic texts inevitably took the shine off the Englishman's book.

His general hermeneutical strategies involved studious scrutiny of relevant scriptural passages in the Bible, applying his knowledge of Greek, Hebrew and Arabic to smooth out confusion and misrepresentation caused by distorted translations. For example, on one occasion, he quoted a full verse in Greek, provided a literal translation and rewrote it to fit in with English grammar. The verse in question was John 3.13.

Roy's impressed his missionary opponents by referring to works of those Western thinkers and Jewish commentators whom they easily recognized and whose authority they acknowledged. Whenever he cited a Western author, Roy made a point of reminding the missionaries that the Christianity professed by these 'illustrious persons ... did not contain the doctrine of the Trinity'.[26] These included Locke and Newton, who were paraded as defenders of Christianity. On another occasion, Roy brought into his discussion Johann Jakob Griesbach and Johann David Michaelis, who he referred to as 'Trinitarian editors and commentors' who omitted 1 John 5.7 in their New Testament exegesis – the very text used by missionaries to support the Trinity.

He also relied on Jewish sources to combat the argument of the Christian apologists. When Marshman discredited Roy's use of the Targum of Jonathan as a paraphrase, and indicated his preference for Bishop Lowth's rendition, Roy retaliated by posing a question to Marshman – whose interpretation should one take seriously: 'celebrated Jewish writers' or 'one thousand Christian Bishops, to whom, at any rate Hebrew is a foreign language?' He made use of his Jewish knowledge to correct some of the Christian claims. When Ambrose Serle (1742–1812) in his book *Horae Solitaire* misrepresented Isaiah's Trisagion or Thrice Holy (6.3) as implying the Father, the Son and the Holy Spirit, Roy quoted the original Targum of Jonathan to prove his point: 'Holy in the most high heavens, the place of his glory – Holy upon the earth, the work of his power – Holy for ever and ever and ever.'[27] Incidentally, Roy had a personal copy of the 1656 edition and provided the name of the publishers and told Marshman that it was procurable.

Roy's hermeneutical activities were undertaken before biblical studies became professionalized and formed part of an academic discipline. Once it became a specialist subject, it lost its effectiveness as a socially active enterprise. This is evidence of the old adage that 'when academia moves in, activism moves out'. What Roy's work demonstrated was that there was no need to resort to the excessive use of technical terminology or slavishly follow critical theories in order to unravel the texts. What was needed was an intimate knowledge of the texts and an acute awareness of one's context – and the ability to interrogate them both. More pertinently, he cast aside all dogmatic presuppositions, a rule which he himself did not always follow. Roy did not have the benefit of more recent efforts to separate the authentic words of Jesus from the subsequent accretions. The modern attempt to distinguish between 'tradition' and 'redaction' had yet to be devised.

Roy was hermeneutically assured enough to instruct the missionaries as to how to do proper exegesis. He told them that first they must read the books of the Old Testament as arranged in the canonical order, then get familiar with the biblical phrases without being influenced or biased by any denominational teachings, and then engage in a comparative study of the two the testaments. In this way, he informed them, Christianity would not 'any longer be liable to be encroached upon by human opinions'.[28]

It was Roy who realized the potential of the biblical narratives and worked out an early form of composition criticism without employing any of the fancy techniques associated with the current approach. It took more than 100 years for Western biblical discipline to appreciate the Bible's narrative profile. At a time when the Bible had become incoherent due to the deadly dryness of historical criticism, sectioned and segmented by various theories, it was the narrative criticism which emerged in the 1990s that showed the way to look for theological meaning in the contents of the Bible rather than getting bogged down in its historicity. Roy grasped this point long ago.

Roy was engaged in what in biblical circles became known as 'demythologizing' before it was made famous by Rudolf Bultmann nearly 100 years later. In both cases, it was not just a matter of discarding Gospel elements which were unpalatable but rather stating the case afresh with a view to making it meaningful to their respective communities. In Bultmann's case, this was a community which had come of age because of scientific advancement, and in the case of Roy, it referred to a community which had become weary of and lost interest in supernatural elements.[29]

Roy's interpretation of Christianity drew wider public attention and deliberation. His reading of the biblical narratives sought to resurrect and energize traditions which the missionaries of the time considered irrelevant to the Christian faith they professed and advocated. He alerted them to their own diverse textual traditions which they were woefully unaware of or did not want to acknowledge because of their narrow evangelical view. He made missionaries engage with the diverse strands that lie within the biblical narratives and his hermeneutical efforts made Christians of different denominations converse with each other. An illustrative example of this development was the effort by Anglicans and Baptists to produce a volume on the Bible that they could defending in terms of its sufficiency and inerrancy.[30] Roy did not perceive Christian missionaries as simply agents of imperialism or impostors convinced of the superiority of their faith. He took up their challenge to further his knowledge of both his own ancestral faith and the religion which came with the Europeans.

English Man's Book and Ethical Teachings

Roy set out to repair the version of Christianity which the missionaries were eager to propagate. He did not recast biblical faith into Hindu forms that could resonate with Indic ideals – a task which Indian Christians later espoused earnestly to regain their indigenous credentials. Roy's central concern was rehabilitating Hinduism by unearthing Vedic texts which championed the cause of monotheism and rejected polytheistic beliefs. His search for a purer form of Christianity was only a marginal interest.

The Baptist missionaries who worked in Calcutta at that time were schooled in the nineteenth-century theological convictions of evangelical and pietistic revival in England. These convictions included the all-sufficiency of the Bible, the infallibility of the Word of God, the divinity of Jesus and the atoning power of the blood of Jesus Christ. They could not accept the idea that the Word of God was unimportant in attaining salvation, and worse, that the whole Bible could be reduced to two just sayings of Jesus seen as containing the whole essence of the Law, the Prophets and the Gospels. Their worry was what would become of the Bible 'if subjected to such encroachments?'[31]

In Roy, the missionaries in West Bengal encountered a different and an astute opponent. As dissenters in a mono-cultural, mono-religious England, they faced the heavy hand of the Church of England. Whereas in India, they came across an interlocuter who, from a multi-religious, multicultural and multi-linguistic perspective threatened their staple doctrines and, more worryingly, made the Bible, their principal mediator, a relative text. The missionaries were completely unprepared for this theological confrontation.

Roy believed that the ethical message of Jesus, which contained the 'essence of all that is necessary to instruct mankind in their civil duties', would be truly beneficial to his country. What is frustrating about reading the *Precepts* and the debate that ensued was that nowhere did Roy explain what the teachings of Jesus were, or which divine laws were applicable to India. He also did not outline how this alien faith would be incorporated into India – a country which was already crowded with many faith traditions. Instead, he reiterated routinely the overriding significance of love of God and love of neighbour and the instruction that 'whatsoever ye would that men should do to you, do ye even so to them'. The fact that the Golden Rule ended with the words 'for this is the Law and the Prophets' was indicative of the extent to which it was linked to the Jewish Scriptures. Neither of these teachings was original to Jesus. Roy, as an astute student of the Bible, was well aware that love of God and love of neighbour was a repetition of Jewish teaching and was taught by other religions including Hinduism. Roy had ambitions to build an India based on these ethical principles, but as an intelligent person he should have known that it was not possible to organize a society on such vague and aspirational codes.

It is plainly evident that the moral teachings of Jesus recorded in the Gospels are not a systematic discourse. Except for the Sermon the Mount, the rest of Jesus' ethical pronouncements emerged from specific encounters he had with a variety of people, including women, the sick and the priestly authorities, and how he responded to their particular demands and needs. The Gospel writers frequently delved into the ethical teachings of Jesus in response to various challenges presented to him. The parables he taught as a way of explicating his ethical ideas were enigmatic and ambiguous and it was not easy to draw moral principles from them. Some parables encouraged feudalistic ideas and others spoke of the levelling of society. The trouble with using moral teachings of an earlier era is that they are a product of the cultural convictions of that time and so may not speak to our context. A conspicuous example is that of slavery – Jesus has nothing to say about the ethics and evils of slavery.

The one question which is intriguing and remains unresolved is what made Roy focus on the moral teachings of Jesus, which were not even religious in character and could be practised without being affiliated or devoted to any religion. The injunction to love your neighbour as yourself dates back to the Hebrew Scriptures. In choosing the supposedly Christian moral precepts, was Roy simply playing into the hands of Western perceptions of Indians as having no morality and so he needed to import the ethical teachings found in the Englishman's book? Was he witlessly endorsing the typical Orientalist cliché that Indians lacked morality? Such a notion was held by John Mills, who never visited India but wrote in 1817 that the Indians did not have any morals. William Ward, one of the Serampore Baptist missionaries with whom Roy had a cordial relationship, stated in his volumes on Hinduism, which went through several editions, that 'there is not a vestige of real morality in the whole of the Hindoo system'.[32] Roy had a strong liking for anything English, admiring their superior scientific, medical and political knowledge, their parliamentary system, their legislative checks and their educational methods. He urged 'a large majority of Europeans and their descendants professing Christianity' to stay in India. Along with these foreign imports, was he trying to embrace the morals that came with the British?

The missionary expectation that India would embrace Jesus and would become a Christian nation did not materialise. Roy was one of the first to highlight the dangers of conversion and the exploitation by the missionaries of the hapless Indians. Although Roy admired the moral teachings of Christianity, this did not prevent him from criticizing its predatory nature as the religion of the ruling power.

What Roy did was to make India a more inclusive nation, incorporating inspiration from a variety of sources including Christianity. His study of other Scriptures – Christian, Buddhist, Islamic and Persian – showed his fellow Hindus that they could still be true to their scriptural tradition without accepting the foreign faith. Roy encouraged his fellow Indians to seek beyond the subcontinent for other sacred scriptures, godly manifestations, communications of truths and moral values without losing their 'Indianness'. His message was that there was no need to shield oneself from other texts and retreat from making more universal connections – an idea that Gandhi later took up energetically. He believed that Indians could follow foreign precepts without becoming Christians.

Roy's hermeneutical achievement was to bypass the priests and gurus and appeal directly to the Scriptures first. The word 'scriptural' occurs nearly thirty-seven times in his controversial dialogue with Marshman, and 'unscriptural' twelve times when the Baptist claimed scriptural validity for his trinitarian Christianity. As part of the Protestant tradition, a cry for a return to the Scriptures remained a central concern for the missionaries too. But there was a difference. While the Baptists were preoccupied with a single text – the Bible – Roy was interested in exploring several sacred texts: Hindu, Christian, Islamic and Persian.

While some of Roy's anti-Mughal ('savage conquerors') and anti-Islam ('religious horror of Mohammadi's') remarks might enthuse the present-day ultra-nationalists and turbo-charged followers of Hindutva ideology, they would be disappointed with his views on Sanskrit learning. He found that such studies would keep India in 'darkness' and 'perpetuate ignorance' as they had 'little or no practical value'. Some of his pro-British views might not endear him to them. His desire for English rule to prosper for many years and his veneration of the British monarch 'as the guardian of our lives, property, and religion', treating him as 'a father and a protector', would now be regarded as unpatriotic and would receive the default opprobrium hurled at such persons – see Pakistan.

Roy did not hesitate to expose the myopic hermeneutics of the missionaries, arguing that these gentlemen, who found fault and ascribed 'unreasonableness to every other system of religion', chose to close 'entirely their eyes upon the total want of reason and rationality in the faith which they themselves profess[ed] and preach[ed]'.[33] The Baptists, who themselves were seen as dissenters at home, were now faced with another form of dissension. The irony was that the Bible translation project of the Serampore Baptists was set up to expose the errors of Hinduism. But now that the very Bible was unveiled as riddled with superstitions and irrational doctrines.

What the *Precepts* and the controversy that followed its publication did was to expose the fact that the Christianity presented by the missionaries was basically similar to popular Hinduism. A religion which was so 'sublime' and 'respected' was in Roy's hands now reduced almost to the level of polytheistic faith. The claim that the imported faith was more moral and rational now looked hollow. To the annoyance of the missionaries, Roy was quick to point out that what they contemptuously called the 'standard' of Brahmanical religion prescribed in the Vedas was also found in Christianity – idols, crucifixes, saints, miracles, relics, the trinity, transubstantiation, holy water. Similarly, his demonstration of the idolatrous nature of the doctrine of the Trinity muted the missionary critique of Hindu polytheism. What annoyed the missionaries was that he told them that he found 'Christian doctrines resembling those of the Hindus [sic] in substance, though they were different from each other in minute interpretations'.[34] Roy made Christian faith as superstitious and polytheistic as Hinduism. In doing so, he challenged the very reasons for which the British claimed to be in India – their rationalistic and superior civilization. He hoped that the 'sameness' of these religions would 'produce attachment' between the worshipers of these faiths.

Roy made Indians realize that the white man's religion was not going to offer anything better than their own traditional religion, although it was beset with its own difficulties. This encouraged Hindu reformers like Keshub Chunder Sen and Swami Vivekananda, whom we will encounter later, to make similar claims. For this alone, his hermeneutical engagements deserve to be remembered and studied. Roy demonstrated effectively that just as the '[t]eachers of Christianity' used 'reason and persuasion' to defend their religion, the Hindus, too, could secure theirs with the 'same weapons'. What irritated the missionaries was that such criticism came from a member of the Hindu community, who were viewed as having 'no higher intellect than a dog, and an elephant, or a monkey'.[35]

Roy's *Precepts* indicated to missionaries in a clear manner that the great impediment to the Christian faith was its unscriptural and irrational doctrines and that Christianity was not a compilation of crude ideas gathered around an ancient book. Roy made it clear that the Bible was not a book of historical narratives and dogmatical conundrums but a practical rule of life exemplified in the moral precepts of Jesus. What exasperated the missionaries was that the remedy came from a Hindu. To promote Christianity, instead of their 'vapoury rodomontade', Roy argued that they should resort to reason and common sense – the very ideas which the missionaries thought were cherished and exceptional Western values.

Notes

1 Books on the life and work of Roy are legion. For a compact and competent introduction, see Amiya P. Sen, *Rammohun Roy: A Critical Biography* (New Delhi: Viking, 2012).

2 Rammohun Roy, *The Precepts of Jesus: The Guide to Peace and Happiness; extracted from the books of the New Testament, ascribed to the four evangelists with translations into Sanskrit and Sanskrit Bengalee* (Calcutta: Baptist Mission Press, 1820). For a detailed study of the production of this text, its history and the hermeneutical issued it raised, see R. S. Sugirtharajah, *The Brahmin and his Bible: Rammohun Roy's Precepts of Jesus 200 Years on* (London: T &T Clark, 2019).

3 Sophia Dobson Collet, *The Life and Letters of Raja Rammohun Roy*, ed. Dilip Kumar Biswas and Prabhat Chandra Ganguli (Calcutta: Sadharan Brahmo Samaj, 1900), 213.

4. Rammohun Roy, *The English Works of Raja Rammohun*, ed. Jogendra Chunder Ghosh (New Delhi: Cosmo Print, 1906), 547.
5. Collet, *The Life and Letters of Raja Rammohun Roy*, 213.
6. Roy, *The English Works of Raja Rammohun*, 485.
7. Albert Schweitzer, *The Quest of the Historical Jesus: A Critical Study of its progress from Reimarus to Wrede* (London: A.C. Black, 1910), 28.
8. For an up-to-date history and hermeneutics of Jefferson's Bible, see Peter Manseau, *The Jefferson's Bible: A Biography* (Princeton, NJ: Princeton University Press, 2020).
9. For a detailed study of these two versions, see Sugirtharajah, *The Brahmin and his Bible*, 69–80.
10. Leo Tolstoy, *Gospels in Brief*, trans. Isabel Hapgood (London: University of Nebraska Press, 1997).
11. Julian Baggini, *The Godless Gospel: Was Jesus a Great Moral Teacher?* (London: Granta, 2020).
12. Roy, *The English Works of Raja Rammohun*, 906 (capitalization and italics in the original).
13. Roy, *The English Works of Raja Rammohun*, 606.
14. For a careful catalogue of such sayings, see Runar M. Thorsteinsson, *Jesus as Philosopher: The Moral Sage in the Synoptic Gospels* (Oxford: Oxford University Press, 2018).
15. S. Radhakrishnan, *Eastern Religions and Western Thought* (Oxford: Clarendon Press, 1939), 69.
16. Joshua Marshman, *A Defence of the Deity and Atonement of Jesus Christ, in Reply to Ram-Mohun Roy of Calcutta* (London: Kingsbury, Parbury and Allen, 1822).
17. *A Defence of Some Important Scripture Doctrines* (Calcutta: Baptist Mission Press, 1822). This is a collection of twelve essays: seven by Yates and five by Scot.
18. J. B. Middlebrook, *William Carey* (London: Carey Kingsgate Press Limited, 1961), 61.
19. Roy, *The English Works of Raja Rammohun*, 550.
20. Marshman, *A Defence of the Deity and Atonement of Jesus Christ*, 88.
21. Marshman, *A Defence of the Deity and Atonement of Jesus Christ*, 95.
22. Roy, *The English Works of Raja Rammohun*, 569.
23. William Hamilton Drummond, *A Learned Indian in Search of a Religion: A Discourse occasioned by the death of Rajah Rammohun* (London: Hunter, 1883), 8.
24. *A Defence of Some Important Scripture Doctrines*, 70 (emphasis in the original).
25. Drummond, *A Learned Indian in Search of a Religion*, 11.
26. Roy, *The English Works of Raja Rammohun*, 666.
27. Roy, *The English Works of Raja Rammohun*, 670.
28. Roy, *The English Works of Raja Rammohun*, 666.
29. For a longer discussion on Roy and Bultmann, see Sugirtharajah, *The Brahmin and his Bible*, 31–3.
30. See the essays in A *Defence of Some Important Scripture Doctrines*.
31. *A Defence of Some Important Scripture Doctrines*, 97.
32. William Ward, *A View of the History, Literature, and Mythology of the Hindoos including a minute description of their manners and customs, and translations from their principal works in three volumes*, vol. 1 (London: Kingsbury, Parbury and Allen, 1822), 296.
33. Roy, *The English Works of Raja Rammohun*, 197.
34. Rammohun Roy, *The Correspondence of Raja Rammohun Roy, Volume 1 1809–1831*, ed. Dilip Kumar Biswas (Calcutta: Sarawat Library, 1960), 350.
35. *The Private Journal of the Marquess of the Hastings. KG Governor-General and Commander in Chief in India in two volumes*, vol. 1, ed. his daughter the Marchioness of Bute (London: Saunders and Otley, 1858), 31.

Chapter 2

TEXTUAL ORDINANCES FOR TEMPLE WORSHIPPERS

In the first month of 1856 there was a testy exchange of letters between a meddlesome Methodist minister labouring in colonial Jaffna and an 'uppity native'. The occasion was an incendiary text anonymously produced by this Jaffna man which not only questioned the basic tenets of Christianity but also decisively hampered its spread in the peninsula. The missionary, true to the arrogance that came with being part of the ruling race, wrote letters which were a mixture of condescension, plea and threat. He urged his recipient to repudiate the authorship, or he would expose him. To this he added the standard colonial insult and the practice of divide and rule. He reminded the colonized of his ungratefulness after benefiting from lengthy connections with the Protestant missionaries. The mischievous native (there were many in the colonies) was Arumukampillai (1822–79),[1] widely known as Arumuka Navalar – Navalar being the title conferred on him for his eloquence. The text that caused much concern to the missionaries was *Caivatūṣaṇa parikāram* (Remedy for Invective on Saivism). The combative reverend was John Walton (1823–1904), who ministered in the Jaffna circuit of the Methodist Church.[2]

It is fairly safe to say that nobody in nineteenth-century colonial Jaffna had a personal story to match that of Navalar. An opinion-dividing thinker and activist, he inspired reverence and revulsion in equal measure. Sir Muthu Coomaraswamy, the father of the *Dance of Shiva* author Ananda Coomaraswamy, called him the 'Hindu of Hindus'.[3] His opponents branded him a 'liar' and a 'person with a slanderous tongue',[4] but everyone agrees – some with enthusiasm and others with enmity – that he was one of the primary reasons for the survival of Saivism in Jaffna. Francis Kingsbury, another Jaffna Tamil whose Saiva–Christian relationship was fraught with ambiguity and suspicion, put it rhetorically: 'What would have happened to Saivism had not Navalar been born in Jaffna?' He answered his own question with these words: 'Navalar's days were good times for Jaffna.'[5]

Navalar was a vehement defender of Saivism who proved to be an excruciating thorn in the side of rampant missionary proselytization at the time. Navalar, by all accounts, was a complex character: engaged in endless disputes with Christians, his own temple authorities and with fellow Saivites, the most famous being his petulant arguments with Ramalinga Adigalar (1823–74).[6]

Navalar's life revolved around three interrelated areas – the religious, the literary and the educational. He produced a large number of texts which included grammars, dictionaries and poems, which Kamil Zvelebil, a notable and respected scholar in Tamil linguistics and literature, found 'mostly faultless and accurate'. He also found Navalar's prose style 'spotlessly correct, very elegant, lucid, vigorous and expressive, free of Sanskrit loans but not purist, although somewhat pedantic'.[7] In opposition to Christian schools, he set up educational institutions in Jaffna and in the South Indian town of Chidambaram to spread Saiva education and knowledge. To these, one could add his social welfare initiatives.

This chapter specifically looks at a short but significant aspect of Navalar's life involving his engagement with the Christian Bible, which was a complex one. By all accounts he was a willing participant in rendering the Bible into readable Tamil, and later he made use of this same Bible as a weapon to dispute and discredit the missionaries' version of Christianity, saying the doctrines missionaries preached were pure fabrication and had nothing to do with the Bible, which sanctioned only temple rituals.

Tendentious Translations

Navalar had three serious forays into the Bible. The first one was when he assisted Peter Percival in translating the Bible into Tamil. This provided an opportunity for him to learn the contents of the Christian Scriptures. The second was when he wrote an anonymous letter to *Utayatārakai/Morning Star*, a bilingual periodical, perhaps Asia's oldest newspaper, published in 1843 under the name of 'Saiva Youth and a devotee of virtuous religion'. In the letter, Navalar pointed out the staggering parallels between Saiva and Jewish temple worship and their continued relevance. His third incursion into the Bible happened eleven years later, in 1854, when he published the booklet *Caivatūṣaṇa parikāram* (Remedy for Invective on Saivism),[8] expanding on the parallels he had already outlined in the *Utayatārakai/Morning Star* letter. This pithy booklet was primarily meant to be a spiritual and textual resource for his fellow Saivites, who faced relentless attacks from Western missionaries and Jaffna Tamil converts. This polemical pamphlet was also Navalar's answer to the missionaries who disputed his parallel claims in a four-part reply they published in *Utayatārakai*.

When Navalar was in his twenties, he spent eight years translating the Bible with Peter Percival (1841–8). This revision was undertaken by the Jaffna Bible Auxiliary at the request of the Madras Auxiliary of the British and Foreign Bible Society. The two Tamil versions available at that time – Fabricius and Rhenius's – had been found to be wanting and, more crucially, were not universally accepted by Tamil Christians. Peter Percival, who was then a Methodist minister in northern Ceylon and a renowned Tamil scholar and educationist, was given the task of producing a version that would unify different Tamil congregations. It was Percival who recruited Navalar, who was his student. This was the time, as Navalar recalled later, when he was agonizingly wrestling with his own faith. It appears that his acquaintance with the biblical texts, especially the temple practices which resembled those of his Saiva tradition, seemed to have clarified his Saiva identity. It was alleged that it was his practice to recite *Tiru-vācakam*, a celebrated sacred Saiva text, before he tackled the translation of the Bible. In a similar vein, he seems to have insisted on maintaining the outward marks of his Saiva distinctiveness by smearing his whole body with dry sacred ashes (*tutulemma*) and having three streaks of ashes on the forehead (*tiri-puṇṭaram*) while rendering the Bible into Tamil. These actions naturally annoyed the pietistic Methodist and Congregationalist missionaries, but when they complained to Percival, he dismissed their protest by saying that Navalar was a good Tamil scholar and that was enough for him. This episode was recounted with relish by Navalar's biographer and nephew Kailasapillai.[9]

The resultant translation, which appeared in 1850, was termed the Tentative Version and later christened by Sapapathy Kulandran as the Navalar Version.[10] It had a tough time in getting approval from the Madras Bible Auxiliary, being dismissed by the South Indian missionaries as 'imperfect, and, as it [stood], unfit to be adopted as a Standard Version'.[11] Its rejection was not Navalar's fault. The more than thirty years of internal and internecine battle that went on between the two Bible Societies need not detain us here, but there are two issues pertaining to Navalar's involvement that merit attention. Besides accusing the Jaffna Version of being 'paraphrasic', the Madras Auxiliary found it loaded with Sanskrit words, and its Tamil style too erudite. The preponderance of Sanskrit words was challenged by the Jaffna Auxiliary, who, for example, pointed out that their Matthew's Gospel had 2,994 Sanskrit terms whereas the proposed Bower's had 2,857. The highly developed literary style was not Navalar's fault, since he was one of the first to introduce the prose style in Tamil and thus did not have a precedent to follow. His literary style was approved by the Jaffna committee, which included missionaries who were formidable Tamil scholars. In fact it got a nod of approval from one of the leading Tamil scholars in Madras, while Jaffna Christian Tamils were very appreciative of this version and told Percival before he set off for his furlough that they had been informed by competent authorities of its 'faithfulness to the Hebrew and Greek originals' and praised its 'simplicity, perspicuity and idiomatic purity'.[12] As Kulandran conjectured, this erudite style was probably aimed at educated Tamils, who represented a high proportion of the Jaffna population at that time. Two hundred years later, another highly educated Jaffna Tamil, Selvanayagam, in his survey of Tamil prose style, praised Navalar for his simple style and referred to the translation of Jesus' conversation with the Rich Man as a fine example of clearness and intelligibility.[13]

The more serious charge was theological and concerned the use of the word '*tēvaṉ*' (heavenly immortals) for God in Navalar's version. In the missionaries' view, this was tantamount to a denigration of the biblical God. The then existing Tamil versions had different words to denote God, such as '*parāparaṉ*' (the most high), '*tam-pirāṉ*' (master, Lord) and '*sarveswaran*' (the omnipotent). Given his notorious anti-Christian feeling, it was alleged that Navalar spitefully introduced the term, probably at the instigation of his mother, to belittle the biblical God. In the Hindu pantheon, '*tēvaṉ*' was 'considered unworthy, and normally used for any minor deity'.[14] There were other troubling aspects of the term, specifically its female form and its caste connotations. It was highly unlikely that the missionaries who lived among the Hindus and who had seen for themselves the images of Hindu goddesses would have let this theological misdemeanour go unchecked. Missionaries were well aware of the female form, 'tēvi', being prevalent among Hindus. Peter Percival himself wrote a book on Hindu gods and their cohorts, like Saraswathi and Lakshmi, both of whom he regarded as 'the active energy of the deity'.[15] Missionaries knew the adverse repercussions in using a caste-sensitive term such as 'tēvar'. Its derivative, tēvar, is identified with a caste in South India, and missionaries who had witnessed the caste tensions in Tamil communities would have been fully aware of the potential adverse repercussions in using such a term. The fact that subsequent Tamil renditions, such as the Bower version, continued to retain 'tēvaṉ' (dispels the notion that Navalar surreptitiously introduced the term.

Interestingly, Navalar, in his letter to the *Utayatārakai*, repeatedly employed the term '*parāparan*' or Jehovah for the biblical God. Remarkably, he used '*kaṭavuḷ*' (one who transcended everything) for Siva in *Caivatūṣaṇa parikāram* and referred to each member of the Trinity as '*tēva*'. It was nearly 100 years after Navalar's version that *tēvaṉ* was replaced by *kaṭavuḷ* in the translation produced by L. P. Larson for the Bible Society. What went unnoticed were traditional Saiva words creeping into the Navalar version, such as *caṅkarpam* (determination, resolve), *naivēttiyam* (offering made to a deity), *cukanta tūpavarukkam* (fragrance) and *kīrttaṉam* (praising and singing a god's name) The insertion of these Saiva words into the biblical texts made the Jewish ceremonies look almost Saivite. But nobody seemed to be concerned about these Saiva characteristics of the Tamil Bible.

In keeping with the true colonial attitude of denying agency to the natives, the contribution of Navalar towards the translation of the Bible rarely gets a mention. His involvement was not acknowledged by the Bible Society or noted in Church records. The records of the Jaffna Auxiliary Bible Society list the names of the missionaries involved, but make no reference to Navalar's contribution.[16] According to the Methodist records, 'the Tentative Version' was a one-man effort, with Percival singled out as the translator of the 'whole Bible'.[17] Percival himself did not mention Navalar in any of his writings or reports.

Relatable Rituals

Navalar's second engagement with the Bible was when he wrote an anonymous letter to *Utayatārakai*,[18] covering a range of subjects. The letter sought clarification from the missionaries, demonstrated his knowledge of the Bible and also the awakening of his Saiva consciousness. Navalar began this sincere and spirited letter by reverently thanking God for sending American missionaries (interestingly omitting the British missionaries with whom he had had earlier contact, as noted above) from a far-away country to raise the local people to a 'noble status' (*uyarnta nilai*-param). He recalled as a professed Saivite how his mind was sensitized by listening to their sermons and stirred by the books that were published by the American Mission Press, a powerful propaganda organ at the time. This experience, he wrote, had prompted him to read the Bible systematically, which had raised serious 'doubts' (*camucayam*) for him about the Christian faith, and, more pointedly, had drawn his attention to the wilful misinterpretation of the Bible by the missionaries. Essentially, the intent of the letter was to seek clarification of these matters from the missionaries.

Frustrated with the missionaries and their abuse of Saivism, especially its temple practices, the letter demonstrated how both the Saiva and Jewish religions extolled and encouraged temple rules and regulations. He cited the books of Exodus (25, 37), Leviticus (17, 24), Numbers (16, 19, 21), Psalms (80) and 2 Samuel (6) to emphasize this point. He noted striking similarities between Saivism and biblical religion, especially the temple practices of the two traditions. While Saivas worship God in the form of *iliṅkam* (a representation of Śiva in stone or another material) the Israelites worship God dwelling in the ark made of wood. The Israelite God lived between cherubims whereas the God of the Saivas dwelt in the image. Shaivites built temples, Israelites made sanctuaries and tabernacles. The Israelites adored the cherubim and a bronze serpent; Saivas revered images made of gold and silver. While the Israelites had shewbread and wine in their sanctuaries, Shaivites had fruits, flowers and *piracātam* (thanks offering). Both used incense and musical instruments in their worship. He legitimized temple worship by reminding the missionaries of the involvement of Jesus and Paul in such practices. Navalar also wondered what was the 'difference between the rites and ceremonies of Saivas and those of the Bible'?[19] It was crystal clear to Navalar that the present-day Christians had given up these temple rituals, which were meant to be performed in perpetuity.

More importantly, Navalar reminded the missionaries that it was their duty to adhere to temple rituals. His question to the missionaries was how could they say these observances were 'loathsome' (*aruvaruppu*) to God when he had ordained them for eternity. If they were as disgusting as the missionaries claimed, he told them that they should admit that these ordinances were invalid (*vīṇ*) and that they had been ordained by God in his 'ignorance' (*aṟiyāmai*). He also remarked that the Israelites were more punctual and observant in performing these 'ceremonies than the Śaivites'.[20] The letter ended with a mild reprimand for the missionaries – that the temple ceremonies followed by Śaivaites were natural acts and not chuckle-inducing gestures for children, as the missionaries claimed. These ordinances were prescribed in the Old Testament for all time, and Jesus and his disciples had continued to observe the rituals involved, hence it was the 'duty' (*kaṭamai*) of the Christians of today to follow them. The fact that they had not done so, Navalar argued, was due to the 'cranky' and unbending obstinance (*viparīta-putti*) of the missionaries.

As in the case of Roy, noted in Chapter 1, the missionaries here were aggrieved by Navalar's exposure of their theological double-standards. They defended the Christian position and published a riposte in the same the journal (*Utayatārakai*), entitled 'Remarks on the Pretended Resemblance between the rites and the ceremonies of the Mosaic dispensation and those of the Sivas, being a reply to the communication in last No. of the Star on this subject'. *Utayatārakai* presented this reply in four instalments over subsequent issues of the journal.[21] Their response was a complicated blend of defence of the already held Protestant position, spectacularly simplistic exegesis and a veiled threat to the Saivites if they failed to embrace the faith missionaries were propagating.

The hermeneutical strategy of the missionaries was to claim an exceptional status for the Bible. This being so, they righteously argued that the Jewish temple practices were ordained by God, whereas there was no such clear divine warrant for Siva temple ceremonies. These rituals were largely the 'craft of deceitful men' and of no value. They also reiterated that the religious ceremonies and rites of Siva resembled the Mosaic practices only in 'form as if they *were copied*', but that in their grand object and fundamental principles they were totally different.[22] The central purpose of the Mosaic dispensation was to teach the unity of God and prevent polytheism and idolatry – the characteristics that marred Saivism.

The missionaries' response also questioned Navalar's insistence that these ceremonies and rites were established 'for ever'. Providing quotes from Hebrew Scriptures, the missionaries asserted that phrases and words like 'for ever' and 'perpetual' had only 'limited significance'. For instance, they artfully argued that when God said to Moses, 'Lo, I come unto thee in a thick cloud, that the people may hear when I speak with thee, and believe thee for ever' (Exod.19.9), it was 'limited to the term of Moses' death'.[23] Further, they argued, it was foretold by the prophets and reinforced by Jesus that the old covenant of ceremonies and offerings would be abolished and that a new spiritual worship would be established. The rituals of the old covenant were mere symbols and lost their validity with the crucifixion of Jesus. The death of Christ abrogated the old dispensation and instituted a '*new and better covenant*'.[24] They quoted suitable passages from Jeremiah and the sayings of Jesus in John to support their deeply held view. They also conjured up a strange and speculative explanation for Paul's observance of the ceremonies while in Jerusalem – that it was a conciliatory act on the part of Paul to avoid communal tension. Paul's preaching had previously infuriated the Jews, such as when he told the Gentiles that they should abandon Moses and that there was no need for circumcision. Paul therefore consented to follow the rituals on the advice of James and other elders as a gesture of conciliation to the Jews and, more importantly, to 'avoid a tumult'.[25]

Along with their passionate defence, the reply of the missionaries contained warnings, threats and injunctions. They cautioned about what would happen to those who indulged in idol worship, quoting Exodus 32 which talks about God rooting out nations which practice idolatry and giving the lands as inheritance to his own people. The subtext is clear: if the Saiva lands did not give up polytheistic worship, they would be taken over and given to the new Israelites – the Christians. It also had a stern warning about apostasy, citing verses from Hebrews 10 which spoke of severe punishment awaiting those who declared the new covenant invalid – punishment that would be worse than for those who had rejected the rules of religious observances given by Moses (10.28, 29).

The reply also had instructions to those who had converted to Christianity about what they should do to people who were fomenting unrest and attempting to lure them back to the old Saiva practices. These people should not be shown any mercy: 'Stone them to death, because they tried to turn you away from the LORD your God, who brought you out of Egypt, out of the land of slavery' (Deut. 13.10).

The implication was that Jaffna Christians should be wary of troublemakers like Navalar.

There was no immediate reaction from Navalar and it was more than a decade later before he addressed another Bible-related matter.

Ritual Resonances

Navalar's third engagement with the Bible occurred when he published *Caivatūṣaṇa parikāram* (Remedy for Invective on Saivism). This was nearly thirteen years after his letter to *Utayatārakai*, when he first established substantial parallels between Jewish and Saiva temple practices. This small but incendiary tract contained twenty-two '*pirakaraṇam* ' (chapters). The first fourteen dealt with the temple ceremonies and worship of a single God, while the rest focused on the lifestyle of Saivites, their dress codes, bodily cleanliness and the invocation of Siva's name, all fundamental to the Saiva faith. This polemical pamphlet was aimed at two very different audiences: one, Navalar's fellow Saivites and the other, his disputants – missionaries and the converted Jaffna Hindus. It had straightforward objectives, Navalar explaining clearly at the outset that he wrote this agitational text partly to refute *tūṣaṇa nūlkaḷ kal* (abusive literature) produced by missionaries and Christian converts against the Saivites. He specifically mentioned such texts as *Kuruṭṭu-vaḻi* (Blind Procedure, 1833), *mu-mmūrtti lakṣaṇam* (The greatness of Hindu Triad, 1832) and *Tur-ācāra viruttam* (An Account of indecent Life), which John Murdoch, the chronicler of book publishing in India, described as 'pungent texts'. *Caivatūṣaṇa parikāram* was partly a defence and response to the reply of the missionaries to the initial open letter Navalar had published in the *Morning Star*. In this pamphlet, his intention was to 'rescue' or prevent himself from falling into the traps set by the missionaries and to 'warn' his fellow Saivites of the 'evils of the enemies', namely the Jaffna Christians, who in their criticism, he believed, went beyond common human decency. The rebuttal had Navalar's customary blunt succinctness.

In the section addressed to his fellow Saivites, he explained how the missionaries, whom he called *pātiri pullar* (padre without character), were the enemies of Siva, and provided his readers with an outline of the drastic action to be taken against them. Ironically, whether by accident or design, Navalar began where the missionaries left off in their *Utayatārakai* reply. There the Jaffna missionaries had warned the Saivites of the punishment that awaited those who failed to embrace the invader's faith, or those who subsequently apostatized. This time it was Navalar's turn to warn the missionaries who abused Siva, Saiva texts and Saiva *ācāriyar* (teachers). These were the three kinds of 'cursers' (*nindithar*) who should be disciplined. If the missionaries quoted from the Bible to admonish Saivites, Navalar drew on *Civa-tarumōttaram*, an Āgamic text on Śaiva Dharma translated from Sanskrit into Tamil by Maṟaiñāṉa-campantar, a Saiva servitor. Quoting from this sixteenth-century Siva text, he informed the missionaries of the chastisement that awaited those who curse Sivan, referring to them as 'Those who hold anything equal to or greater than the teachings delivered by Siva – the incomparable, the one without beginning and end, and who has no equal will burn in hell.' The same fate awaited those who stole (*kaḷavu cey-tal*) the Saivite Scriptures, entertained 'any doubt' about the Tamil sacred writings being the 'word of Sivan', or questioned the diligent interpretations of Siva *ācāriyar*. Navalar's cruel punishment for people who insult Siva and his devotees comes from the traditions of Saiva *nāyanārs*. Tirumullar, a Saiva servitor, said of anyone insulting Siva, that their fate is like 'that of the parrot torn by a cat'.[26]

The second part of the rebuttal was addressed to an unknown *pātiri* for whom Navalar showed utter contempt. It is unlikely that the missionary Navalar had in mind was Percival. The Methodist reports of the time show that Percival was not the typical abusive preacher of colonial times but an 'exceptional' one in that his preaching was emollient and used methods that were 'more akin' to that of Paul addressing the philosophers at Athens.[27] The fact that Percival gave a character reference to Navalar in his case against another Saivite scholar, Ramalinga Swamigal, was indicative of the cordial relationship between these two men. Navalar's principal aim was both to refute the misconception of Saivism by the missionaries and to educate them in their own scriptural tradition, which they seemed to have lost. The strength of Navalar's refutation was in the persuasive parallels he provided from the Hebrew Scriptures for every Saiva theological and temple practice that the missionaries mocked and sneered at. His comparison covered theological issues like polytheistic practices, acts of penance, pilgrimage, invocations and *iliṅkam* worship, their ablutions, oblations and other observances and rites, along with idol worship, temple offerings and matters related to pollution and purity.

Navalar's comparative examples are often the result of forced and surface-level readings of biblical texts. His method was an uncomplicated one – find temple practices in the biblical narratives which were equivalent to those of the Saiva and then taunt the missionaries for mocking the Saiva faith when the same rites and ceremonies are found in the Semitic religion. When missionaries denounced Saivites as being believers in many gods, Navalar turned it around and stated that it was the Christians who worshiped multiple gods in the form of Yahweh, Jesus and the Holy Spirit. For such excess, he called Christians *aññāṉi* – people without spiritual knowledge. He conceded that the Saivites worshiped other gods such as Vishnu, but clung on to the default Hindu position when accused of polytheism that all manifestations were of the same Sivan who had appeared in various forms. The word he often used to indicate the presence of God in various forms was *atiṭṭi*, the Tamilized form of the Sanskrit term *adhi-ṣṭhā* – 'abide in', 'to enter as a divinity in an image'. He noted with relish such examples of worship of the servants of God in the Hebrew Scriptures. The most noteworthy cases are Abraham serving three messengers of God, and Joshua falling down in reverence before the commander of the army of God (Gen. 18.2; Josh. 5.14).

When missionaries sneered at Siva for having consorts, Navalar pointed to the Song of Songs, where the woman and her suitor expressed love for one another. He allegorized the suitor as Christ wooing his bride. Navalar's question to the missionaries was how did they tolerate such flirtations in the Bible and never bother to censure them. He was also able to locate parallels for *iliṅkam* worship, a vexatious issue, both for the biblical writers and the missionaries. While missionaries who had been brought in the puritanical tradition found this phallus-like symbol abhorrent, for Saivites it represented creative power and energy. Navalar enlisted several passages from the Old Testament to substantiate his case. He found a suitable counterpart for *iliṅkam* in the Ark of the Covenant.

To embarrass the missionaries, he cited the cases of biblical heroes paying similar reverence before the ark as the Saivites did before the *iliṅkam*. The examples included Joshua and the elders falling down before the ark after defeat at the hands of their enemies; David sacrificing oxen and fatted sheep and dancing before it; and Solomon offering innumerable sheep and oxen before the ark (1 Kgs. 6, 8). When missionaries mocked the pietistic and personal habit of Saivites uttering *thiru mantiram* (invoking Siva), Navalar saw no difference between this and Jesus urging the disciples to recite the Lord's Prayer, thus designating the Christian prayer as equivalent to the Saivite one.

Navalar located biblical texts touching on temple performances that were comparable to Saiva worship. For the lighting of the lamp, he unearthed passages where Jehovah commanded Moses and Aaron to keep the lamp burning regularly and continually (Lev. 24.1-4; Exod. 27.20-1). He found compelling examples of dancing, singing and the playing of musical instruments in the Jewish temple, equivalent to the Saiva liturgical practices that the missionaries ridiculed. On this matter, he referred to David and all the house of Israel who 'played before the LORD on all manner of instruments made of fir wood, even on harps, and on psalteries, and on timbrels, and on cornets, and on cymbals' (2 Sam. 6.5) He also reminded the missionaries of David's appointment of Levitical and priestly musicians who were skilled in using lutes, lyres and cymbals (1 Chron. 15.14) and cited biblical verses which endorsed such musical activities: 'With trumpets and sound of cornet make a joyful noise before the LORD, the King' (Ps. 98.6). When the missionaries dismissed the observance of auspicious days by Saivites as 'vain activities', he dredged up examples of such practices of sacred times and seasons in the lives of the biblical Jews listed in Leviticus 23, his point being that Jews not only had sacred places, persons and objects but also had dedicated days and times devoted to God.

After seizing upon every comparable Jewish and Saiva temple practice and rite, Navalar took added pleasure in reminding the missionaries that these ordinances were in perpetuity and were to be performed for the generations to come: 'it shall be a statute for ever unto their generations on the behalf of the children of Israel' (Exod. 27.21; see also Num. 10.8 and Lev. 24.3).

Amidst these twenty-two chapters, Navalar inserted two interjections, which he termed *vivēcaṉam* (insight), both appearing to answer the missionaries' refutation in the *Utayatārakai*. He expressed exasperation at the strange logic of the Christians for deserting the practices listed, recognizing that what the missionaries had presented was in fact a simple restatement of the stock defence of the Christians that with the death of Jesus the old temple worship patterns had come to an end. Navalar argued that if Jesus had abolished these temple observances, then Jesus must have had a better perception (*nuṉ-ṉ-aṟivu*) than God, and, if that was the case, then he posed a threat to God. Navalar wondered how able and educated men could accept and worship two discordant personalities – God and Jesus. More to the point, there was no evidence in the New Testament that Jesus *had* abolished these temple observations. He was also not convinced of the answer the missionaries had come up with for Paul's continuing observance of temple rules. Their reasoning was that Paul had followed the rules in order to avoid communal tension. Navalar made the missionaries aware that Paul had prohibited only circumcision (in his letter to the Romans) and sacrifices (in his letter to the Hebrews, accepting the popular assumption that it was Paul who wrote this letter), but had retained the rest of the temple rituals and regulations. He referred to the passages in Acts which record Paul fulfilling these temple rituals. At the same time, Navalar was also refuting the stance of the missionaries that these temple observations were purely symbolic. If so, he argued that there were no clear indications from Jehovah as to the significance of these symbols. Navalar therefore wondered whether Moses and others observed these practices without knowing their real meaning. Elsewhere in the text, he exposed the duplicity of the missionaries. While they interpreted the eating of the bread and the drinking of the wine as symbols of the body and blood of Jesus, they refused to accord such figurative meanings to Saiva practices. He curtly asked them if they thought his God had such an impaired state of understanding (*mati- mayakkam*) that he couldn't differentiate between what was offered to the images and what was offered to God.

Navalar made other forays into the Bible. These included the three booklets (some of which were co-authored) *Viviliya- kurcitam* (Disgusting things in the Bible), *Viviliya- kurcitakantana atikāram* (Confutation of the loathing aspects of the Bible) and *Pātiri-kaluku car-putti* (Noble Advice for the Padres). Unfortunately, it was not possible to trace copies of these booklets.

Navalar made devastating use of his knowledge of the Bible – acquired during his translation work with Percival – to demolish the condescending attitude of the missionaries. Navalar's documentation of the parallel readings posed questions for the missionaries. Since both these traditions engaged in similar temple rituals and rites, why did the missionaries ridicule and sneer at the Saiva temple practices? Why were the Saivites not allowed to read symbolic meanings into their actions, whereas such privileges were accorded to Christians? More crucially, why did the missionaries give up these temple ceremonies when God had ordained them to be performed for generations to come? This last query made the missionaries look like bogus preachers, and their version of Christianity unbiblical.

Navalar's detailed comparison of what went on in the temples of Siva and Yahweh was principally to demonstrate that these religions were essentially similar and had much in common. It had subsidiary aims, too. One was to demonstrate to his fellow religionists that the Christian rituals were nothing but pure Saivite practices, and another was to inform the missionaries, who were hell-bent on defaming Saivism, that their faith was basically Saivite. In other words, he made the biblical faith resemble the Saiva temple practices and showed the biblical Jews to be true Saivites. Unlike the Christian thinkers who read Christianity into Hinduism, Navalar flipped it and read Saivism into Christianity.

Navalar's other aims were to remind his fellow Saivites that they, too, had equally authoritative scriptural texts, and to tutor them in their own textual tradition so that they could challenge the Christian Bible and missionary propaganda. These Saiva texts, he proudly claimed, had sustained them over the years and now had come under threat with the arrival of the 'barbarous missionaries' in *pārata kaṇṭam* (a Vedic term to describe the subcontinent), who had not only introduced a strange (*nūtaṉa*) religion, but had misread the Hindu Scriptures. He urged Saivites to read their own texts and fortify themselves to counter missionary defamation and misrepresentation. He reminded them that these Saiva texts demanded that they oppose the ignorant missionaries and repudiate their despicable Christian doctrines. Such refutations were deemed to be 'incomparable Saiva merits' (*uyar ōppu illā civa puṇṇiyankaḷ*).

Navalar's style all through *Caivatūṣaṇa parikāram* was confrontational and at times impolite. The civility he had shown to the missionaries in the earlier letter, calling them hospitable and charitable, was missing here. In Tamil there are three forms of the second-person singular – you. One is '*niṅkaḷ*' which is a polite form for speaking to elders or superiors. The second is *nīr*, used when addressing an equal. Navalar employed the third form, '*nī*' (you), when dealing with the missionaries – an impolite form addressing a respectable person. He also didn't refrain from using uncomplimentary terms such as 'people of little knowledge' ('*aññāṉikaḷ*') and 'worst criminals' (*atipātakaṉ*). Each chapter ended with grand and incisive rhetorical questions posed to the missionaries, often exposing their double standards, ignorance and childishness.

Navalar was at his vitriolic best when he made sardonic sideswipes at the missionaries. This might have provided entertainment and ammunition for his fellow Saivites, but it caused irritation and embarrassment to the missionaries and to converted Christians. For example, when the missionaries poked fun and asked sneeringly when Siva would come to consume the fruits, milk and steamed or boiled rice cake (*mōtakam*) offered to him, Navalar derisively asked them when their God would come to devour the lamb, ram, unleavened bread, cakes and drinks placed on the altar (Num. 6.14-17).

Compared to the ferocious rebuttal of Navalar's initial letter to *Utayatārakai*, the response to *Caivatūṣaṇa parikāram* by the missionaries was noticeably different, exhibiting a grudging appreciation of the man and his biblical knowledge. The 1855 Wesleyan Mission Report said that Navalar's text was not dismissive of Christianity as 'theoretically illogical' or 'practically weak' and did not claim that the rituals of Saivism were of divine origin and superior to Christianity. What was unpalatable was Navalar's attempt to prove that every one of the articles of Saivite belief and its observances had their parallel in the 'credenda and ceremonials set forth in the Christian scriptures'. The report admitted that the scriptural verses employed to advance the case for these similarities was 'most surprising' and that the 'adroitness with which every possible objection [was] anticipated and repelled belong[ed] only to a first rate mind'.[28] E. J. Robinson, a Wesleyan missionary commenting on *Caivatūṣaṇa parikāram* nearly ten years after of its publication, observed that Navalar displayed an 'intimate and astonishing acquaintance of the Holy Bible' and 'cunningly defended' Saiva temple ceremonies 'on the authority of our sacred writings', conceding that the quality of Navalar's argument 'in favour of Saivism against Christianity cannot be denied'.[29] The general verdict of the Jaffna missionaries was that the book caused 'much mischief'.[30]

Just as William Jones (1746–94), the Western Orientalist who was fond of Sanskrit literature, had used the Hindu puranic flood stories to authenticate biblical deluge narratives,[31] Navalar turned the gaze around and utilized the temple rites in Hebrew Scriptures and the rituals performed by Jesus and Paul to affirm, legitimize and celebrate Tamil temple culture and Tamil Saivism.

One Book, Two Readings

Navalar treated the Bible as the book of a cult, a code of purity, a prescription for temple-centred worship. These temple obligations were not seen as a burden or as otiose, as the missionaries deemed, but a requirement prescribed by Yahweh. He cited nearly thirty-two passages from the Hebrew Scriptures drawing from Genesis, Exodus, Leviticus and Numbers to prove that these were 'eternal ordinances' (*nittiya niyamam*) which had perpetual relevance and obligation. While for Navalar the Bible was the handbook of temple rites and celebrations, for the missionaries it was a book of grace which freed believers from the yoke of works and exterior bodily rituals. The two sides envisioned contrasting ways of experiencing and expressing devotion to God – one through faith and inner renewal, the other through outward bodily rituals and personal efforts.

For the missionaries, the Bible was the primary source of the revelatory witness to Christ and his salvific work on behalf of humankind, but for Navalar it was a repository of texts related to temple practices which had resonances in other scriptures. They had different perceptions of the Bible. For the missionaries, the Bible was the book of the Church and the guardian of its truth, and this being so, they regarded Navalar's stance as one that destabilized the Church and fundamentally misunderstood the Bible's purpose.

For the missionaries, the Bible functioned less as a theological document and more as an identity marker, preserving a safe distance between 'us' and 'them', Christians and Hindus. For Navalar, it was a unifying influence, bringing Saiva and Christian communities together under the rubric of temple ceremonies and worship. While the missionaries stressed the words and actions of Jesus, Navalar turned the debate towards God's ordinances about temple performances and practices.

The missionaries and Navalar had different attitudes towards the Hebrew Bible. Missionaries routinely reiterated the traditional position that the Church had held since the patristic times, that the principal function of the Hebrew Scriptures was to prefigure the advent of Christ and anticipate his salvific work. They did not treat the book of the Jews on its own terms, having its own history and integrity. For them, its charm and charisma rested on its 'Churchly, Christological character'. It was a theological treasure trove to discover Christ, whereas for Navalar it was a code of temple practices and proof that these were not dissimilar to Saiva rites and were not the vain and useless observations that the missionary propaganda made out.

While the missionaries viewed the Hindu and Hebrew narratives as preliminary, unrefined, unfinished and needing much nourishment and renewal through Jesus, Navalar perceived both these Scriptures as complete, wholesome and valid for eternity. He in practice made no distinction between the Old and the New Testaments, perceiving them as an unbroken whole and not as something new and progressive, one superseding the other, as the missionaries condescendingly declared.

Navalar and the missionaries mined two kinds of theologies from the Hebrew Scriptures. To use the categorization of Margaret Barker, who did substantial work on temple-related narratives, one indulged in 'Deuteronomic theology' and the other in 'Temple theology'. The 'Deuteronomic theology' which the missionaries advocated discouraged worship of gods and goddesses such as Baal and Asherah; removed the host of heaven, fire, the ark, the menorah, the lampstand and cherubim; forbade priests from burning incense; and banned the anointing oil, the jar of manna and Aaron's rod. Navalar, in contrast, fervently pursued the 'Temple theology', which involved worshipping with incense, libations of wine and bread as described in the book of Revelation, which was in essence a restoration of the first temple – 'always remembered as the true temple'.

For Navalar, God's presence amidst the Jews was not discerned through the Scriptures or doctrines or through historical events, but through liturgical practices and by obediently performing them in the temple. But for the missionaries, the arrival of Jesus and the destruction of the temple gave primacy to the Scriptures and doctrines of the faith. Ironically, the missionaries who rejected rituals replaced them by resolutely ritualizing the Scripture and making an idol out of it.

Like most upholders of orthodoxy, Navalar had a romantic view of his own Scriptures. The Saiva truths were found only in the Saiva Scriptures and not in traditions or what he termed '*viḷ akkam*' (elucidation, explanation). He regarded traditional practices as secondary to the written authority of the Saiva *ākamam* (Šāstras, Scriptures) and did not invest them with the authority of the Saiva canon. Navalar, being a serial curser, condemned those who held onto traditional practices as committing a sin against the Saiva *agamas* and liable to fall under the curse of Sivan.[32]

Navalar particularly disliked the missionaries' use of the term *Vētākamam* for the Tamil Bible. Combining the titles of the two texts important to the Saivas – *vēṭam* and *ākamam* – the missionaries christened the Tamil Bible as *Vētākamam*, implying that the Christian text superseded the Saiva Scriptures. Navalar regarded this a deception, pointedly asking them 'Where did you steal the title from? Your scriptures, were they really *vethams*? (The Vēdas) Giving Aryan titles to the Christian text was like a hunter camouflaging himself with leaves to attract his prey. Calling your text the Holy Bible was like describing a sex manual as an ethical book.'[33] He advised them that they should use the Bible's original title and simply call it the book (*puttakam*). He also warned the missionaries that for this heinous act they would be caned by Jesus Christ on the Judgement Day. Interestingly, the Tamil Bible in which Navalar had a hand has *puttakam* in its title, '*Vēṭa puttakam*' (Christian Book).

Navalar's exegetical conclusions were deceptively simple. His familiarity with the Bible led him to believe that at the core of the two religions in dispute was temple-centric worship with its attendant and comparable liturgical practices. Navalar's conviction was at variance with the long-standing popular perception of Judaism as the 'religion of the book', as he turned it into a religion of liturgical prescriptions and temple protocols. This being so, the missionaries were plainly wrong when they found fault with Saiva practices, as this was inconsistent with the teachings of the Bible.

Navalar's biblical interpretation is one-dimensional, often the result of cherry-picking episodes in the Christian Bible to match them with his own Saiva temple ceremonies and rites. Like most polemical hermeneuts, he saw only what he looked for in the Bible. In reducing it to mere liturgical practices, he overlooked its prophetical, poetical, historical and ethical content. What was least interesting to the missionaries was what electrified him. Navalar provided often lengthy citations from the Hebrew Scriptures, sometimes citing from his own version and at other times paraphrasing them. Nonetheless, it was his ability to use biblical texts that forced the missionaries to exhibit a grudging admiration for his fertile mind.

Although Navalar and the missionaries often spoke past each other, in their methods they were aligned to each other. Both patched together scriptural verses related to their favoured argument in order to construct and consolidate it. Both worked under the notion that the sacred Scripture is its own interpreter. They sought an association of ideas rather than a specific meaning for biblical terms. Both paid scant respect to the historical context of the text and to the Enlightenment pursuit of inquiring into its formation or the direction in which it was heading.

Navalar distanced himself from the practice of private reading, which Protestants advocated and cherished. He viewed the Saiva texts as too complex and profound and thought they needed initiation and an erudite tutor. He did not emancipate the Saiva devotees from the clutches of priests and gurus. Devotion to God was through outward bodily rituals and not faith alone, as the Protestants claimed.

It was the understanding or misunderstanding of the rituals which caused problems between Navalar and the missionaries. While the Protestants brought to Pauline theology a downplaying of good works and personal efforts, treating them as insignificant and even dismissing them as popish, for Navalar, the 'works' were done by *tīṭcāvāṉ*, the one who was initiated by a Saiva guru.

Both Navalar and the missionaries read the Bible at the redacted level of the texts, without paying much attention to any possible composition history. Searching for the supposed sources of the Bible had yet to be developed. For the missionaries, the Bible exemplified the grand scheme of doctrines beginning with original sin, justification by faith and inward renewal. What was important for them was the wholeness of Scripture which in today's critical scholarship would be seen as Canonical Criticism. Navalar's reading of Scripture outside its ritualized context would have seemed as unnatural as a fish out of water.

Navalar succeeded where the missionaries found it difficult to comprehend the intricate temple system. His cross-textual reading made biblical texts intelligible to his fellow Saivites and in the process made them aware that these temple practices were not as grotesque as the missionaries made them out to be, but were in fact universal. He introduced some of the tenets of Saivism to his readers in an easily assimilable form, comparing some of the Saiva temple practices with the Jewish ones. His catalogue of similarities between Jewish and Saiva temple ceremonies showed Saiva Tamils that they did not differ much from the customs, rites and rituals of the Jews. This process made the Israelites appear as disguised Saivites.

In a way, Navalar initiated Saiva biblical interpretation, paving the way for Ramanathan's (whom we will encounter later) use of *Saiva Siddhdnta* in his reading of the Gospels. Obviously, both men engaged in diametrically opposite hermeneutics. Navalar used analogical liturgical practices while Ramanathan used Saiva philosophical and doctrinal concepts to open up the texts. By doing so, both men all but transfigured biblical religion into a Saivite one.

Navalar reclaimed the counter-texts related to temple tradition, which had almost been forgotten amidst the Protestant fixation with the theology of the word that it might serve as a guard against humanly constructed gods, images and idols. In the colonial context, it was the marginalized who recovered these texts to empower themselves. Navalar excavated the texts to remind Christians of their forgotten hermeneutical history and obligations, and his resolute championing of temple rites demonstrated that the Protestant notion of *sola scriptura* was really a hindrance rather than a help in inculcating the biblical faith. Navalar effectively questioned the missionaries' belief that the Christian faith could be explained as a straightforward story of the Word of God.

Revered Texts, Restricted Readings

Navalar's hermeneutics was both resistant and restrictive. While he battled to establish a place for the Saiva texts which were belittled by both the missionaries and converted Tamil Saiva Christians, he was also intent on sidelining some Saiva texts, practices and voices.[34] He desired a wider readership among the Tamils for his books, the title pages of which stressed that they were meant for all – 'Savites learnt or otherwise'. He encouraged them to read what he called *tiraviṭa vētam* (Dravidian Veda), such as *tēvāram* (a collection of devotional songs in honour of Śiva) and *Tiru-vācakam* (the celebrated poem in praise of Śiva by Māṇikka-vācakar), which established 'Saivism as the true religion'. Navalar promoted serious and detailed study of the Tamil Scriptures, but was less enthusiastic about opening them to certain groups, especially missionaries and low-caste people, despite the commitment to inclusivity noted above.

Navalar justified this restriction when missionaries criticized him for the refusal of the Saivites to make their Scriptures accessible to all – a cardinal principle of Protestantism. When the missionaries goaded him for his reluctance to open up the Saiva texts to scrutiny, he became defensive. He informed the missionaries that there were no written scriptural texts among the early Christians and that the faith had spread through *vāy-moḻi* (oral declaration) or letters written by apostles which explained their religion. Put another way, there was no evidence of the early Christians having access to their religious texts nor reading them. If this were the case, why should the missionaries harass the Saivas, insisting that they share their texts.

Navalar resolutely clung to the idea of divine authorization and upheld the view that there was no permission from Sivan to make their Scriptures available to those who would pervert them. He argued that the Saiva Scriptures could not be taught to those who abused Siva, ate cows' meat and committed heinous crimes (*peru-m-pātakam*). Ironically, he summoned the sayings of Jesus to support his limitation of access to the Saiva texts to a select few. Opening the texts to all, he claimed, would be like giving 'what is holy to the dogs' and casting 'your pearls before swine' (Mt. 7.6).

Navalar posed a further rhetorical question when he asked why Saivas should allow Christians to read their Scriptures when not all Saivas themselves had authority to read them. Only those who had undergone the rite of initiation (*caiva-tīṭcai*) into the Śaiva religion (*samaya*) and had a direct realization of Lord Siva through *Jnana Guru* had the necessary expertise to interpret the texts. In spite of his inclusive gestures, his principal readership was the high-caste *veḷḷāḷars* like himself, an erudite people who regularly read Saiva revivalist literature. In his view the Saiva texts were very complex and profound, requiring initiation and a learned tutor.

Navalar not only restricted the reading to a few scriptural specialists but also advocated an un-Protestant approach – an intermediary, a *caiva-camayācāriyar* (spiritual preceptor or guru), as the interpreter of texts. He did not emancipate the Saiva devotees from the clutches of priests and gurus, but rather reinforced the power of the former. Reading the Scriptures without the help of a guru, he maintained, was like going to the battlefield having had no training in the use of weapons.

Navalar also laid down strict practical instructions to his fellow Saivites as to how they should handle the Scriptures. He firmly believed that the Saiva Scriptures should be read by those who did not eat meat, drink liquor or indulge in countless grievous sins. More importantly, that person should have gone through the Saiva initiation process. He also established a procedure for how a Saiva text should be treated, advocating that it should be placed on a podium, that one should bow before it and should that it should be read with love. No Saiva book should be left on the floor, chair, bed or placed on one's lap.[35] His 'list of great sins' included neglecting Sivan, his books and his preachers and 'trafficking in holy books and placing them in unsanctified places'.

Saiva and Jewish Religions and Their Temple Theologies

In the cause of advancing the temple theology, Navalar has a hermeneutical ally in the contemporary biblical scholar Margaret Barker. The missionaries of Navalar's time worked on the assumption that the nascent Christianity of Jesus' time was profoundly influenced by Greek culture and was in particular a product of the non-sacrificial theology of the synagogue of his day. This consensus view has now come under scrutiny. In her meticulous reading of non-canonical texts such as Enoch and the Dead Sea Scrolls, Barker has identified, as noted earlier, two distinct theologies in the Hebrew Scriptures – temple theology; involved with Wisdom and the harmony of creation; and the Deuteronomic theology, concentrated on Moses and the people of Israel as the chosen people. The Old Testament represents an expurgated version of the religion of ancient Israel by the 'Deuteronomists', who wanted to stress obedience to the law of Moses and to make Israel utterly distinct from its environment. On the other hand, Jesus, as Barker has demonstrated, seemed to have been influenced by the theology and ordinances of the first Jewish temple, the temple as it had existed before the accretions of paganism and the 'reforms' of King Josiah in the seventh century BCE.

This older religion was still around in the New Testament times. It survived only in literature, not in the Old Testament canon but in the books of Enoch, and some of the documents found among the Dead Sea Scrolls – 'one of the most widely used books in the time of Jesus'.[36] It was the religion depicted here that formed the background of early Christian beliefs and which shaped the mind of Jesus himself. Jesus' criticism of the temple was levelled against the second temple, which was beset with pagan elements.

In Barker's reconstruction, Jesus was perceived as a restorer of the temple religion rather than an inventor of something new, as the early Church and later missionaries argued. The rigid trinitarian monotheism that missionaries endorsed, if Barker's thesis is correct, was at variance with both ancient Jewish religion and the religion that Jesus reinstated. According to Barker, 'The gospel as it was first preached by Jesus, and as it was developed and lived by the early church, concerned the restoration of the true temple.'[37] Barker asserts that it was temple theology which provided the basic ingredients of the New Testament, which included invocation of the divine presence, incarnation, the human becoming divine (theosis), the mother of God and the self-offering of the Son of God. Barker has convincingly demonstrated that priesthood, the shape of places of worship, and the imagery of sacrifice and atonement all stemmed from the temple practice. The two temple rituals – 'carrying the blood into the holy of holies on the day of atonement and the eating the shewbread on the Sabbath', which were initially and solely limited to temple priests, were 'combined to become the Christian eucharist'.[38] It was not with the manifestation of Jesus that temple practices came to an end as the missionaries repeatedly argued. Early Christianity looked for the older faith and longed for the restoration of the temple. This is evident in the book of Revelation, which speaks of the Holy of Holies and heavenly thrones, which Navalar quoted with delight in his disputes with the missionaries.

If Barker's assessment is correct, it appears that Navalar was closer to the essence of the biblical vision than the missionaries who professed to know the Bible better than the 'heathen'.

The Twin Reformers: Their Concurrences and Divergences

There are certain affinities between Navalar and Roy, whom we encountered earlier. Both had a troubled relationship with the Bible. While Roy regarded it as containing ideas that defy the 'use of the senses and faculties', Navalar found it an 'abusive book' (*tūcaṉa puttakam prapantham*) or a false book (*poy nūl*). He did not view sympathetically any texts which equalled or surpassed Siva teachings. Roy treated the Bible as a book of moral instructions, whereas for Navalar it was a manual of temple ordinances.

Both were confident that they were better interpreters of the Bible than the missionaries themselves and took great pleasure in pointing out that they had totally misread their own Scriptures by ignoring its obvious sense. Roy's emphasis was on the moral teaching exemplified by Jesus, while for Navalar what mattered was adherence to and observation of temple practices. Roy felt that his non-doctrinal approach placed him in a better position to grasp the meaning of the texts in contrast to the missionaries, who were blinded by their doctrinal bias. Roy counselled that the missionaries should 'confine their instructions to the practical parts of Christianity'. Navalar claimed that his familiarity with temple practices and rituals gave him an advantage in understanding the Bible, which was replete with temple ceremonies.

Faced with the accusation of polytheism, Roy and Navalar constructed a single God out of the plethora of deities found in the Hindu tradition. Roy maintained that the 'doctrines of unity of God are real Hindooism' and went on to affirm that the idea of the singleness of God was 'practised by our ancestors'. Navalar also fashioned his own form of a Saiva monotheism, which provided the standard by which to judge the heathenism in both Saivism and Christianity.

Both Roy and Navalar helped missionaries to translate the Bible. While Roy expressed his frustrations at the failure to find the right Bangla words for biblical terms, Navalar, as we noted earlier, had no qualms about incorporating Saiva words into the biblical texts in spite of their manifestly Saiva connotations.

Roy and Navalar were relentless in their opposition to conversion. They felt that missionaries used the inherent power that came with being part of the colonial enterprise and also tricked the hapless natives by offering material inducements, including jobs in mission schools. Furthermore, the missionaries exploited the theological ignorance of the Hindu priests, so that Roy and Navalar were keen to educate and equip their fellow Hindus to refute missionary misrepresentation of Hinduism.

Roy and Navalar were critical of both Christian and Hindu priests. In addition to his quarrel with Protestant missionaries, Navalar challenged the Roman Catholic Bishop Bonjean to engage in a public debate, which the bishop failed to take up.[39] Navalar called his own Hindu priests 'stud bulls', claiming they were incapable of spelling some of the ceremonial rites that they performed and were too incompetent to quote stanzas from their own Scriptures.[40] Roy's reference to the 'pernicious practices' of the Hindu priests increased their animosity towards him.

Both Roy and Navalar were astute hermeneuts and formidable opponents. When missionaries branded Roy and Navalar as heathens, both flipped the accusation and branded the Christians as heathens because they worshipped many gods in the form of Trinity and adhered to foolish doctrines.

Although the Bengali and Tamil were spiritual siblings, there are a number of ways they differed. The obvious one is that they came from different Hindu sects. Roy was a Vaishnavite, whereas Navalar was a Saivite. On the issue of worship, they had contrasting views. Roy, in his early writings, rejected image worship in 'every form under whatsoever veil of sophistry it may be practised' and urged a 'reformation of popular idolatry', but later mellowed somewhat. Navalar was consistent in upholding image worship. He was not ashamed of the practice, perceived the divinely embodied icons as indicating the presence of Siva. Unlike these Indian reformers, Navalar did not accommodate, redefine or make idol worship fit in with so-called superior Western scientific thinking. He never desacralized it and maintained that *linga* worship was an intrinsic part of Saivism.

Roy and Navalar also diverged in another respect. Roy's hermeneutical cry was to bypass the priests and go straight to the Scriptures, whereas Navalar urged his followers to go to the temple, get initiated by a guru and then read the Scriptures.

They differed too in their attitude to colonial rule. There was no palpable appreciation or admiration of the British on the part of Navalar. He never envisaged the British presence as God's providence or as an instrument of God. He simply thanked God for sending the missionaries in a matter-of-fact way, which any decent Jaffna person would have done it. Roy, on the other hand, thanked the Supreme Disposer of the Universe for the presence of the British, viewing them not as conquerors but as deliverers from Mughal rule. It is hard to imagine Navalar using such self-abasing phrases as 'lowest of your subjects' or ' your dutiful subjects', as Roy did.

Where Roy outshone Navalar was in their literary outputs. While Roy wrote both in English and Bengali, Navalar, though proficient in English, restricted his writings to Tamil. Roy had another advantage, in that he made judicious use of Western critiques of Christianity. He drew on Jewish and Patristic writings which his missionary opponents readily recognized and acknowledged as authoritative. Navalar could not access such textual insights in his critical reading of Christian Scriptures, limited instead to Saiva texts which the missionaries instinctively dismissed as vain writings. According to his biographer, Kailasapillai, this critical literature only became available in Jaffna after 1876. In general, Navalar's familiarity with Protestant theology is uncertain, with a memorial article to him claiming that he was only acquainted with Tamil and Saiva texts.[41]

A Testament of its Time

The nineteenth century, in the view of A. R. Vēṅkaṭācala-pati, a cultural critic, provided halcyon days for the Literature of Refutation (*kaṇṭaṉa ilakkiyam*) in South India and Ceylon. The '*uccam*', or acme, of this phemomenon was Navalar's *Caivatūṣaṇa parikāram*.[42] Two other representative works of the Saiva condemnation writings, which vied with that of Navalar, were those by Tāmōtaram Piḷḷai[43] and Muthukumāracuvāmi Piḷḷai.[44] The former, who referred to the missionaries as *vēta piraṭṭar* (one who uses the Bible deceitfully), found the biblical narratives inaccurate and untrue, implying that the Bible could not be trusted. Muthukumāracuvāmi Piḷḷai, meanwhile, argued that Christian religion was not eternal like Saivism, because it had undergone constant change since its inception. He found discrepancies in the genealogy of Jesus, and made fun of the toilet habits of missionaries. Less sophisticated than Navalar, he too, drew attention to parallels between Saiva and Jewish temple practices and wondered why the missionaries were so sarcastic about Hindu rites and regulations.

There were a number of factors which 'roused' Saivas to safeguard their faith and strike at Christianity. John Murdoch, who catalogued Tamil printed books during the colonial period, identified several reasons for the burgeoning of this particular type of literature. One was the enactment of Lex Loci by evangelically-minded British officials who sought to minimize the influence of Indian religions in opposing conversion. A second reason for the spread of the 'Literature of Refutation' was the formation of the Ashes Society, whose members were encouraged to ridicule missionary proselytisers. A third reason was a reaction to the widespread circulation of anti-Saiva writings, such as 'Blind Alley' (a sarcastic take on the temple worship) and 'The Hindu Triad' (referring to the Hindu three deities – Brahmā, Viṣṇu, Rudra – which were depicted as depraved and lacking divine luminosity). In Murdoch's words, 'the wild bull called Christianity' with its 'two horns was destroying the fair garden of Siva.'[45]

There is relatively little engagement with the life and work of Navalar. His story is very well told mostly in reverential tones by some of his admirers,[46] but even cultural critics who had leftist leaning tendencies, like Kailasapthy[47] and Sivathampy,[48] offer hardly any criticism of Navalar's writings on Saiva texts or his construction of Saivism, which are pietistic, firmly traditional and, even worse, casteist. No critical biography of Navalar exists either in Tamil or English. Foreign interpreters raised on a steady diet of Protestant theology tended to pigeonhole him in Western categories and portray him as a Saiva Luther or a Dravidianized Moses,[49] thus erasing his personality and his extremely incisive reading of the Bible and at times idiosyncratic hermeneutical nonconformities. In these Western portrayals, Navalar emerges as a one-dimensional over-zealous Saiva fanatic who spent his entire life spewing invective against Protestant missionaries in Jaffna. They conveniently overlook his involvement in political and social issues of the day.

True, Navalar was not a firebrand anti-colonialist and did not work to bring down the British regime. Such an idea was non-existent at that time. But he was not reticent about castigating the Government Agents of Jaffna, some of whom behaved as if they were the 'Rajah of the North'.[50] One such was Sir William Twynham, known generally for his corrupt governance but specifically for his failure to bring relief to the Jaffna people suffering from cholera and famine. Leonard Wolf (the husband of Virginia), who served as an Assistant Government Agent in Jaffna, found him to be a 'formidable' character.[51]. Navalar condemned the hardship caused to Jaffna people by the inaction of Twynham. One hundred years before liberation theology took up the cause of the poor, Navalar talked about taking care of the poor, the lame, the deaf, the sick, the old and the young, and organized a rice gruel kitchen to feed the hungry.[52] He was also involved in the formation of an agricultural society to protect farming. Although there was no blatant anti-colonial sentiment in his writing, he did pen a blistering attack on *Utayatārakai* for its colonial bias and support for the colonial regime. He called this newspaper an 'enemy of the people'[53] and was very critical of the missionaries, warning them that if they continued to abuse Saivism, they would be chased out of the country.

Navalar's construction of Saivism was a product of patriarchy and privilege. The temple rituals he was fond of, whether they were Saiva or Jewish, were not liberating for women. Even in the case of men, such practices were restricted to a selected few of the high-caste community. The temple regulations prescribed an inferior status to women, with Navalar noting that temple ritualization reinforced the ascendancy of the Jaffna male. For him, a true Saivite is a male Vellalar, a consecrated, formidably perceptive individual who had taken *tīṭcai* (a one-to-one ceremony where one is initiated by a guru), attended puja and listened to Saiva preaching. This process excluded those who were not part of the hegemonic caste in Jaffna. Navalar did not rationalize or critically analyse the temple rituals, but simply followed them because they were ordinances of Sivan.

Navalar put a high premium on the performative aspects of Saiva rituals but overlooked the fact that the rituals can be acts of extreme fanaticism. *Periyapurāṇam*, a Saiva text, which narrates the lives of sixty-three Saiva saints which he made into prose form so that it could be easily accessible to ordinary people, contains instances of extreme violence that these saints commit to demonstrate their love to Sivan. Navalar recognized that these rituals were essential to spiritual life but failed to note the abusive and gruesome nature of the acts involved. That said, he was not fanatical about all temple rituals. Navalar disregarded animal sacrifices not prescribed in the *Śiva ākamam.* and mockingly posed a question to his fellow Saivites: did you think that Jaffna would not be safe without the slaughter of a goat?

There is an exclusive streak in Navalar. His Sivan has both particularistic and universalistic functions. On the one hand, as his Saiva catechism made clear, the liberation of Buddhists and Christians is contingent upon these religionists being born again as Saivites, following the Saiva Vedas and then fulfilling the prescriptions of Siva *agamas*, such as doing service to Saiva gurus and worshipping Siva.[54] On the other hand, however, he conceded that Sivan would accept all those who perform good service and diligently worshipped their own gods. For Navalar, Sivan will redeem all and indeed the whole world.

Like most religious reformers, Navalar was at heart a moralist and a puritan who insisted on unrelenting personal hygiene. His constant advice to his fellow Saivites was to maintain a high standard of morality by refraining from telling lies and visiting prostitutes and by abstaining from drink. His *Caiva Camaya Vinavidai* prescribed rules as to how to be clean which included hand washing after eating and the cleansing of oneself after encountering a 'low-caste'.

In contrast to some of the Hindu reformers, Navalar rarely ridiculed the biblical texts, viewed them as spurious or made any disparaging or mocking remarks about biblical figures. An exception was Moses, whom he called a deceiver, a crook and a 'heinous sinner' (*paṭu-pātakaṉ*). Unlike his Ceylonese contemporary and Buddhist revivalist, Dharmapala, Navalar did not rail against the biblical God or Jesus. Dharmapala called the God of the Jews 'the savage deity of Horeb',[55] said that Jesus was a rude, intemperate and a hotch-potch preacher, and that his life and teachings were of no 'cosmic usefulness'.[56] While Dharmapala used the Old Testament to ridicule, Navalar found it valuable to strengthen his Saiva claims and to demonstrate that biblical Jews were no less observant of temple rituals than the Tamil Saivites.

Navalar did not even anticipate the dissolution of Christianity or advocate the removal of missionaries from the subcontinent. Neither did he encourage Christian converts to reconvert to Saivism, though he expected them to respect the Saiva faith that they had left behind. His plea to the missionaries was that they should stop abusing his beloved Saivism and cease converting his innocent people by promising material inducements. His chastisements were directed towards missionaries whom he believed were spreading falsehoods about Saivism. He did not hesitate to reprimand them, and encouraged his fellow Saivites to tell the missionaries to 'shut their mouth' (a literal translation of his phrase). He viewed such rebukes as one of the Saiva merits.

Navalar did not use Saivism as a ploy to espouse Hindu nationalism, as some of the Hindu reformers did. In his booklet *Caiva camayam* he clearly distinguished between Saivism and Tamil. He wrote that it was the 'ignorant who treat Saivism as a Tamil religion and Saiva temples as Hindu temples. Tamil is not a name of a religion. It is a language.'[57] He did awaken the Saiva consciousness among the Ceylon Tamils, but it was not turned into an important component in the political quest for self-rule.

The cry of the Hindu reformers in India was to go back to the Vedas, whereas Navalar's call was to go back to Saivagamas. In contrast to the Indian Hindu apologists, he did not feel or yield to the customary and tiresome Orientalist view that that Saivism had moved away from its original purity and fallen into disrepute, and thus it had to regain its ancient cultural glory. Navalar envisioned his task as *neri-p-paṭu-thal* (to be put in order): to be kept within bounds. While some Indian Hindu reformers rediscovered the eighth-century BCE thinker Sankara's *Advaita*, Navalar drew on the Saiva saints. He held the view that the missionaries were there to uplift the people from their moral decadence. He saw the missionaries' role primarily in secular terms – to elevate the people of Jaffna to a 'higher foundation' (*uyarnta nilai-param*).[58]

In his social thinking, Navalar was unapologetically conservative and encouraged caste observation. His *śaiva viṇā viṭai* (Saiva Catechism) is replete with caste discrimination, dismissing the low caste as not worthy of entering the temple and prohibiting them from participating in temple rites. He discouraged eating with them and if ever a high-caste person physically touched a person from a lower caste, he wrote in the *Fourth Pala Padam* that that person should cleanse himself as well as the dress he was wearing. Navalar even had his own hierarchy of Hindu gods. For example, he totally opposed the worship of the goddess kaṇṇaki, a popular deity among the people, because she belonged to the chettyar caste.

One hundred years after the publication of *Caivatūṣaṇa parikāram*, a contributor to the journal *Caiva Kāvalaṉ* (Guardian of Saivism) overstated his case when he remarked that Navalar's pamphlet was not just concerned with the past but that its contents were still relevant and would remain pertinent forever.[59] Navalar mattered for Saivism because Saivism mattered for Jaffna Tamils at that time. Essentially, *Caivatūṣaṇa parikāram* was a pamphlet of its time. In a changed context in Jaffna, Christianity is not as fierce and dominant as it was in the nineteenth century, and more pertinently, it does not pose any threat to Saivism.

Christian churches do not control educational institutions as they once did and they do not have powerful publishing houses. Their political influence is very minimal, although there were a few Christian leaders, like S. J. V. Selvanayagam, leader of the Federal Party, who were involved in politics in a private capacity rather than representing any institutionalized church. Today there is a different adversary in the form of Sinhala Buddhist nationalism and populism. To combat this formidable force, *Caivatūṣaṇa parikāram* has no hermeneutical energy, expertise or effectiveness. To survive and prosper in these different and difficult times, one needs new texts. Navalar, an astute and attentive reader of social and political changes, would certainly have appreciated this point.

Notes

All citations of the Tamil books mentioned here are my own translations.

1. For the life and work of Navalar, see K. Sivathamby, 'Hindu Reaction to Christian Proselytism and Westernization in 19th Century Sri Lanka: A Study of educational and socio-religious activities of Arumuka Navalar (1822–1879)', *Social Science Review: Journal of the Social Scientists Association of Sri Lanka* 1, no. 1 (1979): 41–75. For Christian-centric assessments of the principal concern of the chapter, see Dennis D. Hudson, 'Winning Souls for Siva: Arumuga Navalar's Transmission of the Savia Religion', in Raymond Brady Williams (ed.), *A Sacred Thread: Modern Transmissions of Hindu Tradition in India and Abroad* (Chambersburg, PA: Anima Publications, 1992), 23–51; Dennis D. Hudson, 'Arumuga Navalar and the Hindu Renaissance Among the Tamils', in Kenneth W. Jones (ed.), *Religious Controversy in British India* (Albany: State University of New York Press, 1992), 27–51; Dennis D. Hudson, 'A Hindu Response to Torah', in Hananya Goodman (ed.), *Between Jerusalem and Benares: Comparative Studies in Judaism and Hinduism* (Albany: State University of New York Press, 1994), 55–84. Dennis D. Hudson, 'Tamil Hindu Responses to Protestants: Nineteenth-Century Literati in Jaffna and Tinnvelly', in Steven Kaplan (ed.), *Indigenous Responses to Western Christianity* (New York: New York University Press, 1995), 95–123; Richard F. Young and S. Jebanesan, *The Bible Trembled: The Hindu–Christian Controversies of Nineteenth-Century Ceylon* (Vienna: Institut fur Indologie der Universitat Wien, 1995); R. S. Sugirtharajah, *The Bible and the Empire: Precolonial Explorations* (Cambridge: Cambridge University Press, 2005), 165–75. Tamil biographies on Navalar are largely reverential, the exception being K. Kailasapthy, *Kailasapathy on Navalar* (Colombo: Kumaran Book House, 2006).
2. See the Appendix in T. Kailasapillai, *Arumukanavalar Carittiram* (Madras: Educational Preservation Press, 1955), 119–25.
3. K. P. Rathnam, *Navalar Nianivu Malar* (Chunnakam: Thirmugal Achu Yantrasallai, 1938), 74.
4. P. Saravanan, *Aurtpa Martpa:Kantana tirathu*, Nagercoil: Kalachuvadu Pathippakam, 2010), 61.
5. Rathnam, *Navalar Nianivu Malar*, 84.
6. For the documents related to the debate, see Saravanan, *Aurtpa Martpa*.
7. Kamil Zvelebil, *Lexicon of Tamil Literature* (Leiden: E.J. Brill, 1995), 67.
8. K. Arumukampillai, *Caivatūṣaṇa parikāram* (Remedy for Invective on Saivism) (Madras: Jubilee Press, 1890).
9. Kailasapillai, *Arumukanavalar Carittiram*, 12–13.

10 Sabapathy Kulandran, 'The Tentative Version of the Bible or "The Navalar Version"', *Tamil Culture* 7 (1958): 229-50.
11 *A Brief Narrative of the Operations of the Jaffna Auxiliary Bible Society in the Preparation of a version of the Tamil Scriptures* (Jaffna: Strong and Asbury Printers, 1868), 86.
12 Peter Percival, *The Land of the Veda: India briefly described in some of its aspects, social, intellectual and moral including the substance of course of lectures delivered* (London: George Bell, 1854), 510.
13 V. Selvanayagam, *Thamil Urainadai Varalaru* (History of Tamil Prose) (Colombo: Kumaran Book House, 1957).
14 J. S. M. Hooper, *Greek New Testament Terms in Indian Languages: A Comparative World List* (Bangalore: Bible Society of India and Ceylon, 1957), 86.
15 Percival, *The Land of the Veda*, 206.
16 *A Brief Narrative of the Operations of the Jaffna Auxiliary Bible Society in the Preparation of a version of the Tamil Scriptures* (n.p.p.: Strong and Ashbury Printers, 1868), 8.
17 G. G. Findlay and W. W. Holdsworth, *The History of Wesleyan Methodist Missionary Society in Five Volumes*, vol. 5 (London: Epworth Press, 1924), 34.
18 *Supplement to the Morning Star* 3, no. 2 (1843): 21-3.
19 *Supplement to the Morning Star* 3, no. 2 (1843): 23.
20 *Supplement to the Morning Star* 3, no. 2 (1843): 23.
21 *Supplement to the Morning Star* 3, no. 3 (1843): 33-5; 3, no. 4 (1843): 45-7; 3, no. 5 (1843): 57-61; and 3, no. 6 (1843): 73-8, 83.
22 *Supplement to the Morning Star* 3, no. 2 (1843): 33 (italics in original).
23 *Supplement to the Morning Star* 3, no. 5 (1843): 57.
24 *Supplement to the Morning Star* 3, no. 6 (1843): 74 (italics is in original).
25 *Supplement to the Morning Star* 3, no. 6 (1843): 73.
26 C. V. Narayana Ayyar, *Origin and Early History of Saivism in South India Madras*, University Historical Series No. 6 (Madras: University of Madras, 1939), 214.
27 W. J. T Small (ed.), *A History of the Methodist Church in Ceylon 1814-1964* (Colombo: Wesley Press, 1968), 207.
28 Kailasapillai, *Arumukanavalar Carittiram*, 120.
29 E. J. Robinson, *Hindu Pastors: A Memorial* (London: Wesleyan Conference Office, 1867), 126.
30 Kailasapillai, *Arumukanavalar Carittiram*, 120.
31 William Jones, *The Works of Sir William Jones in Six Volumes* (London: G.G. and J. Robinson, 1799), 134-6.
32 K. Kailasapillai (ed.) *Arumukanavalar Pirapantattiratu* (Collected Works of Arumukanavalar in two volumes (Colombo: Department of Hindu Religious and Cultural Affairs, 1996), 17.
33 Selvanayagam, *Thamil Urainadai Varalaru*, 83.
34 For a refutation of fake inspirational verses, see Saravanan, *Aurtpa Martpa:Kantana tirathu*, 695-713.
35 K. Arumukampillai, *Caiva Camaya Vinavidai* (Questions and Answers About Saivism) (Colombo: Thendral Publications, n.d), 21.
36 Margaret Barker, *Temple Theology: An Introduction* (London: SPCK, 2004), 14.
37 Barker, *Temple Theology*, 11.
38 Barker, *Temple Theology*, 10.
39 S. Thanajeyarajasingham, *Naawalar Panigal* (Activities of Arumuga Navalar) (Colombo: Colombo Tamil Sangam, Colombo, 2011), 63.

40 Kailasapillai, *Arumukanavalar Pirapantattiratu*, 75.
41 Rathnam, *Navalar Nianivu Malar*, 72–3.
42 See his introduction in Saravanan, *Aurtpa Martpa*, 26. For a collection of essays on Hindu refutation, see M. Vaiapuri (ed.), *Coloniya Kala Mathaprasarathil Krisuthuvarkal-Inthukal*, (Christians and Hindus in Colonial Religious Propaganda) (Chennai: Alaigal Achagam, 2011).
43 C. W. Tāmōtaram Piḷḷai, *Vivilia Virtōham* (Enmity towards the Bible) (n.p.p.: Varthamatharangki Press, 1867).
44 Muthukumāracuvāmi Piḷḷai, *Yesumataparikāram* (A Remedy against Jesus Religion), in *Muthukumārac Kavirayar Prapanthatiraṭṭu* (Chunnakam: Pulavarakam, 1952).
45 John Murdoch, *Classified Catalogue of Tamil Printed Books with Introductory Notices* (Madras: Christian Vernacular Education Society, 1865), 143.
46 S. Shivapadasundram, *Arumukha Navalar* (Jaffna: Saiva Paripalana Sabhai, 1978).
47 K. Kailasapthy, *Kailasapathy on Navalar* (Colombo: Kumaran Book House, 2006).
48 Sivathamby, 'Hindu Reaction to Christian Proselytism and Westernization in 19th Century Sri Lanka', 41–75.
49 Young and Jebanesan, *The Bible Trembled*, 117.
50 Leonard Woolf, *Growing: An Autobiography of the Years 1004–1911* (New York: Harvest Books, 1975), 104.
51 Woolf, *Growing*, 105.
52 S. Thananjayarajasingham, *Naawalar Panigal* (Religious Activities of Arumuga Navalar) 2nd edn (Colombo: Colombo Tamil Sangam, 2011), 44.
53 Kailasapillai, *Arumukanavalar Pirapantattiratu*, 184.
54 Arumukampillai, *Caiva Camaya Vinavidai*, 45.
55 Anagarika Dharmapala, *Return to Righteousness: A Collection of Speeches, Essays and Letters of Anagarika Dharmapala* (Colombo: Government Press, 1965), 408.
56 Dharmapala, *Return to Righteousness*, 499.
57 Kailasapillai, *Arumukanavalar Pirapantattiratu*, 101.
58 *Supplement to the Morning Star* 3, no. 2 (1843): 21.
59 *Caiva Kāvalaṉ* (Guardian of Saivism), 15 September 1969, 5.

Chapter 3

UNIVERSAL AND INTUITIVE TRUTHS

Colonial Calcutta was not short of colourful religious personalities. During the 1870s, one such colourful leader headed a procession of singing, dancing and banner-holding devotees to a disused tank in Calcutta. The leader convinced his followers that they were at the River Jordan in Palestine. He wanted them to imagine that they were witnessing the baptism of Jesus. He blessed the river and told them that they had come to the land of the Jews and were seated on the bank of the River Jordan and that it was here the Lord Jesus was 'baptized eighteen hundred years ago'.[1] He anointed himself with oil and, just as Jesus did, immersed himself in the water. The leader was Keshub Chunder Sen (1838–84)[2] and his followers were the members of the New Dispensation Church. He was prone to dreamy devotional acts which were a puzzle to his followers. He was perceived as both charismatic and a charlatan, with little apparent consideration given to the possibility that he was neither. The intention of this chapter is not to resolve these polarizing tendencies but to explore an under-investigated aspect of his life and work – his relationship with the Bible.

Keshub was foreordained to become a religious leader. He himself said that he was 'destined and commissioned by God to be a spiritually-minded, and not a worldly-minded, man'.[3] Though not a brahmin, he came from a rich and influential family from Garifa (Gouripore, West Bengal). Keshub recalled that he was reared 'by a wealthy father and grandfather. Opulence and luxury surrounded my childhood, but as I grew up my mind began to show the spirit of natural poverty'.[4] One of his early biographers notes that at a time when the moral condition of Bengali boys was 'simply frightful', Keshub was rightly regarded as a saint in their midst.[5] He attended the prestigious Hindu College, acted in Shakespeare plays and later worked in the Bank of Bengal at the monthly salary of Rs. 25. Unsatisfied with his secular work, he was determined to dedicate his life to the spiritual regeneration of his country. Recalling this period of his life, he obviously sought God's help. Where should he go to satisfy his spiritual quest? Apparently, the Lord told him in, 'unmistakable language', that he should give up his secular work. Would his family not starve without any subsistence, queried an anxious Keshub? He got a terse reply: 'Talk not as an infidel', and he was assured that all things would be added onto him. Keshub confessed that he felt ashamed of his scepticism.[6] The Lord's assurance resulted in him joining the Brahmo Samaj, a reformist movement within

Hinduism. The rest is Keshub's hermeneutical histrionics. From then on, he would play his anointed role with aplomb.

Possessed of the Bible, Obsessed with the Truth

Keshub, like Roy, genuinely believed that the Bible had a lot to offer to Indians who were 'hungering and thirsting after spiritual comfort'.[7] In a lecture to a British audience in 1870, he said that the Bible had been 'received and studied, and appreciated by the educated natives of India'. He went on to say that however much Indians were proud of their own ancient religious books bequeathed by their forefathers, and attached 'great value' to them, it was a fact that India could not do without the spirit of the Bible. Such words might have been music to the ears of those in the audience who had condescending views of anything Indian. He pronounced confidently that India must read the Bible because there were 'certain things in the Gospel of Christ which [were] of great importance' to his nation, which was passing through a transitory phase. He thundered that 'the spirit of that wonderful book must come into contact with the Indian mind'.[8]

This remarkable endorsement, disappointingly for the missionaries, was not for the view of the Bible they introduced. Their Bible embodied Western ideals, made exclusive claims, spoke of 'one elect' race or contained stock elements of Christian theology such as the creation, the fall, redemption and the final revelation of God. The text Keshub had in mind was the story of the whole of humanity, and how God is related to it. It contained truths which were as 'old as the creation, repeated and more or less purely in every tongue'.[9] It was a depository of universal and intuitive truths which Keshub judged to be God's truth and nature's truth and truths 'tall[ied] with natural reason'. Concerning these truths, Keshub deemed that 'every man has the right to use them, for they are God's truths, and therefore, common to us all'.[10] For him, truth is God's property and found in various sources, such as 'in Socrates, in Confucius, in the Bible, in the Hindu Scriptures, or in the Mahometan Scriptures'.[11] His was the Bible that was not primarily European or Asiatic, biblical or Vedic, Christian or Heathen, but one that came from a 'common property', and everyone had a 'birth right to use them'.[12]

Aligned to this was his idea of the Word of God being a mixture of the East and the West, and not strictly of Semitic origin. For him, the Word of God was not the monopoly of one religious tradition. Rather, it is an alluring mixture of the Occident and the Orient, or as Keshub put it, the 'Scriptures of science' in the West and 'Scriptures of inspiration' of the East 'constitute together the word of God'. Thus the 'mind and strength' of the one and the 'heart and soul' of the other join in the service of one another.

Keshub strenuously maintained that religious truths are learned not through books, as the missionaries insisted, but through intuition. What the Bible contained were the 'intuitive truths'. His standard line was that 'Intuition is our revelation.' He wrote that 'the human mind intuitively, and *"independently of written revelation"*, arrives at the knowledge of God'.[13] For Keshub, the saving truths are not found in books but discerned through revelation. He acknowledged that the books of all religions are 'rich repositories of what is noble, pure and saving'. Though we approach them with 'profound reverence', they are not revelation. Book revelation, as he put it bluntly, is 'self-contradictory and suicidal'.[14] A book is an external object and cannot be scientifically called revelation, because revelation is subjective. Keshub relentlessly reiterated the message that revelation was not a book, nor aimed at the mind, but an appeal to the heart. Or, as he put it in a typical emotion-filled phrase, the Word of God comes through 'holy feelings'.[15]

The Bible that Keshub wanted India to read was the Asiatic Bible with its Oriental manners, figurative images and poetical beauty. 'The Bible abounds throughout in this sacred figurative language,' he claimed.[16] He often spoke of the 'spirit of the Bible' or the 'spirit of the founder of our faith' and not its history, or personalities or doctrines. He never explained or defined what the spirit of the Bible was. To hazard a guess, it could mean the love of God and love of fellow human beings, which he called the 'golden maxim'[17] and which he often referred to in his lectures and writings. Keshub's Bible was a non-doctrinal, non-sectarian, non-denominational and non-nationalistic text. It constituted 'one harmonious brotherhood', in which 'brothers and sisters' were united as one family, rejoicing in the Lord.

The Bible that Keshub espoused was not the inventory of historical information about biblical events, personalities or doctrinal matters, but a work that contained cultural references such as to dancing and singing. He reckoned that it was a book which warmly encouraged dancing, singing and strong aesthetic feelings. Keshub was emphatic that no Scriptures were 'fuller of the accounts of dancing than the Bible'. David, the greatest of the Hebrew prophets, danced before the Lord, and likewise the sons and daughters of ancient Israel danced in the midst of their religious fervour. Dancing was an antidote to 'lifeless rationalism'. Keshub argued that all religions, without exception, warmly encouraged dancing. He cited Shiva's dance on the Himalayas, the Sufis' whirl and the weird, quaint moves of Ceylonese Buddhist Bhikus and the lamas of Tibet.[18] The Bible, in his perception, was not only about spirituality but also about swaying.

Keshub's Bible was not infallible or the inspired Word of God. While the missionaries at the time believed the Bible to be God's oracle, Keshub took a different approach to the question of biblical inspiration. It was not the book as such that was inspired, but the biblical personalities and biblical events embedded in the book that were energized: 'The inspiration lies only in the events which make up the Jewish and the Christian dispensations. Moses was inspired and Christ was inspired, and all prophets and apostles who played subordinate parts in the drama were inspired.'[19] The deliverance of the Jewish nation and 'fresh events' depicted in the New Testament were marks of inspiration and not 'the lifeless traditions recorded on paper'. He maintained that the physical books themselves were not inspired: 'What you read in the Bible *was* inspired. It would be incorrect and wrong to say the Bible *is* inspired. Inspiration dwells in the fact [that] the Bible [is . . .] the living Gospel, not in the letter of the book.'[20]

Keshub not only denied that inspiration was produced in any of these religious texts, but also did not utilize them to establish an ethical principle, settle a doctrinal dispute or support a theological proposition: 'That a book has come down to us from heaven, cut and dry, containing lessons for our guidance and salvation, we do not believe.'[21] His faith was in fresh revelations and 'fresh fields' that God would lead humanity to and not buried in the dead letters of the book.

Ever since the Reformation, the refrain of most Western interpreters had been that one should go straight to the Bible, as if it contained uncontaminated theological truth, and extract from it a textual essence that would be the sole means of defining of the entire book. While the Reformation imposed an abstract theological notion of justification by faith as the essence of the Bible, Keshub reduced the whole message of the Bible into a practical act of love of God and love of fellow human beings, which he termed the 'grand doctrines'. He admitted that he had also 'gone direct to the Bible' to ascertain the genuine doctrines of morality inculcated by Christ, but what he found there was not a European but an Asiatic Christ[22]

Keshub differentiated between the Bible as a book and as a revelation. It is a mere book or a letter when read by those who are spiritually unenlightened and only becomes a revelation when read with the 'inspiration of the Holy Spirit'.[23] He rejected dogmatic certainty and the identification of revelation with human words. Revelation is essentially a personal encounter and not confined to written texts. He professed that 'books [were] not the only enlighteners of mind'. Wonders of nature and beauty, too, edify us. As he put it, every object from revolving 'stupendous orbs in the air to the smallest grain in the sand' discloses God. While the missionaries believed that nature and the created order were there to be exploited and dominated, Keshub viewed them as a source of inspiration which the ancient *rishis* recognized long ago. He was aware of the sanctity of nature before contemporary theologians discovered it.[24] He intoned, 'All nature is aglow with divine radiance.'[25] Keshub urged his followers to find God's truths in 'trees, books in running brooks, sermons in stones, and good in everything'.[26] He claimed that that the sun, moon, stars, clouds, refreshing showers, beasts, fowls, fishes, gentle rill, hills and mountains all spoke of God. In his words, 'The voice of nature is the voice of God.'[27]

Keshub was conviced that no one comes to God through written sources like the Bible or through personalities like Christ. On the contrary, one is influenced and sanctified through the 'inworking Spirit of God' and requires the workings of the Holy Spirit of God. To understand the 'sweet and sacred vernacular' of one's soul, one needs 'the light of God' and without it, the Bible will be a 'sealed book' and one's soul will be a 'dry fountain'.[28] It is the Holy Spirit in its still small voice that exhorts believers.

Given his feelings about written revelation, it is no surprise that Keshub urged his devotees to 'cherish the Bible and not worship it'.[29] He envisioned the Bible as akin to the net described in the New Testament parable, which had gathered 'every kind' of good and bad alike and where the soul should choose good and cast aside the bad. For him, human beings were above the Bible: 'The Bible was made for man, not man for the Bible.'[30] Although Keshub came across plenty of 'marvellous truths' in the Bible, he found 'inner revelation to be superior to all outward books' and to 'all the second-hand derivative revelations'.[31] His scorn for 'book revelations' or 'paper revelations' was largely due to the impact of Theodore Parker, the

American Unitarian minister who had great influence on Keshub. In end, written text had no final authority for him.

Keshub was an unashamed cultural appropriator. He believed that all religious texts should be treated as common property and that humanity should consider itself to be the heir of all the various Scriptures. These are borderless texts, accessible for adaption across cultures. He informed his devotees that 'whether in the pages of the Bible or Koran ... where ever we find the truth we must go and accept it'.[32] Scriptures, whether Christian or Hindu, were for him translations which spoke 'the rude yet the simple vernacular of the heart's language' and the 'same language unto God – language of love, child-like simplicity. There is no creed, dogma, no sect and denominations. What they constitute is one harmonious united family.'[33] Truth, he remarked, was 'confined neither to Jerusalem or Arabia, neither to Jesus or to Mohammed'.[34] In his own inimitable way, Keshub enthused, 'The Vedas and the Bible are mine, the cross and the crescent are mine.'[35] He once described the Bible and the Vedas as 'sisters in sweet accord'.[36]

Given his attitude to the Scriptures, it was inevitable that Keshub found the closed canon something which stifled God's continual revelation. 'Our Scriptures', he announced were not 'closed'. Fresh chapters were being added perennially: 'What the Lord will reveal to us ten years hence who knows save He.'[37] Keshub was convinced that revelation did not end with Vedas, Jesus or with the New Testament, but was a continuing process. Scriptures are works in progress. It would be a betrayal of Christ if one believed that divine revelation stopped with him. Revelation will take us through 'new ways and fresh fields'.[38] To strengthen his argument, Keshub sought scriptural validation in the last words of Jesus, where he said that he would send the Comforter to lead the world into all truth. His solemn supplication was 'Do thou teach us hundreds of thousands of thy new Vedas.'[39] The proof of the ongoing revelation was Keshub's Church of the New Dispensation.

While missionaries presented the Bible as evolving from oral to written form, Keshub reversed the conventional hermeneutical presupposition. He tried to recover the orality of the Bible. For Keshub, the Word of God is not in a written format. It is spoken and not printed. All divine injunctions and precepts begin with *'Thus Saith the Lord and not so it is written.'* It is essentially God's thrilling message heard in the soul. These precepts were not written by God's own hand and therefore should not to be taken as God's 'direct inspiration'. They were only 'instructive narratives' of what God had done in the lives of prophets and saints. 'The original word,' he insisted, 'was spoken, not written.'[40]

Although Keshub wanted the Bible to be introduced to India, he castigated the missionaries for their 'vain' attempts to deluge India with copies of the Bible. His contention was that nothing would be possible unless the Holy Spirit touches the heart. Books and teachers might be helpful mediators but had limited agency. 'It is only the Holy Spirit', he solemnly maintained, that 'can convert outward truth into inward purity'.[41] 'The Bible has never of itself animated or inspired anyone, nor can it. But the spirit of God converts its dead letters into living ideas.'[42] For Keshub, the authority of the Scriptures did not lie in the texts but in the spirit.

Keshub proposed that his New Dispensation Church should have its own Scriptures. His selection was very typical of Keshub – a motley group of subjects, ranging from science to theology. His 'Old Testament' included physics, geology, astronomy, chemistry, botany, zoology, metaphysics, ethics, natural theology and analytical faith, while the 'New Testament' comprised history, biography, eclectic philosophy, baptism, sacrament, inspiration, yoga or communion, Bhakti or love, supernatural theology and synthetical faith.[43] Intriguingly, there was no place for the Christian Bible or the Vedas.

Reading as Introspection, Spiritualization and Visualization

Keshub, a Hindu, first mooted the idea of an Asian reading of the Bible at a time when interpretation was regarded as the sole business of the missionaries. In one of his lectures in England, he appealed, 'Leave us to ourselves and let us study the Bible,'[44] which got rousing reception from his fawning English audience. Like most of his noble intentions, Keshub never explained what he meant by an Asian reading, except to say that the missionaries should let Indians understand the Bible 'in our own way'.[45] It would be a Himalayan struggle to sum up cogently what Keshub had in mind, since it is scattered throughout his voluminous writings. The following points may be the key elements of his Asian approach to Bible, which, as you will note, elevate and ennoble the staple features of Oriental culture.

First, the Asian method was about subjectivity and introspection and converting 'outward facts and characters into facts of consciousness'.[46] The intelligibility of the Scripture is not related to its literal or direct sense but to the intuitive and spiritual meaning. It is the subjective which should be given 'faithful recognition'. What was paramount for Keshub was not logical reflection but 'intuitive appreciation'. Intuition was the *'primary source'* and *'basis of our religion'* and it was 'co-extensive with the truth'.[47]

Second, the Asian reading is about celebration, tolerance and the veneration of diverse Scriptures. Keshub, as a serial respecter of all Scriptures, accorded no pre-eminence to any particular religious writings, especially the Bible, which the missionaries promoted as an exceptional text. He made the Bible resonate with many Indic texts, repeatedly declaring, 'We appeal to all Scriptures.'[48] We have all 'Scriptures and all Saints' and therefore we loathe 'exclusivism'.[49] While the prevailing missionary reading was marked by intolerance and the suppression of all other Scriptures, Keshub opened up the texts as having equal value.

Third, the Asian method is about harmonizing and synthesizing the textual differences, 'our object being to show the harmony and universality of truth'.[50] The scriptural texts of the world, though emerging out of national exigencies, are linked together in the unity of a vast synthesis. The markers that are universally found in all religions are love, reconciliation, holiness and goodness.

Fourth, the Asian approach is about the vivid and imaginative visualization of biblical events and personalities. It is about picturing and imaginatively participating in those ancient events. For example, Keshub declared, 'I am with

Moses near the burning bush; I am with Jesus and his disciples, listening to his Sermon on the Mount.' He called such representational and imaging processes 'the Asiatic study of the Bible!' In his Jeevan *Veda*, a kind of spiritual self-reflection, he wrote, 'The rishis, Nanak, Kabir, Jesus and Gouranga and other saints are in me.'[51] Keshub's Asian reading of the Bible did not mean treating it as the book of the past, but rather seeing its characters and its events as 'living characters and fresh scenes'.[52]

Fifth, the Asian approach is about the spiritualization of the Bible. Keshub told the audience in England that he studied 'Christ ethically, nay, spiritually, and I studied the Bible also in that same spirit'.[53] It is about texts being 'vivified and spiritualized by the living touch of Heaven'. For Keshub, the fundamental truths of faith were the result of 'revelations of Intuition, not the results of Bible-reading, not the conclusions of reasoning deduced exclusively from external data, but truths implanted by God in the mind'[54] – this required being open to the spirit of the Bible rather than engaging in an intellectual exercise.

Sixth, while missionaries were obsessed with the modernist notion of a single meaning, Keshub pointed to the Indian spiritual and Asian aesthetic appeal. His Asiatic reading involved looking for the 'imageries and allegories of the Gospels'. These spoke of Asia's literature as 'sacred poetry' and the language of 'prophetic poetry' without further elaboration. Keshub even provided a Christological endorsement: 'The habit of talking in parables and indulging in the sweet poetry of faith' were, he claimed, learnt at the 'feet' of Christ's 'feet'.[55] Aligned to this is the idea of an ecological reading of the Bible, because Asians have a 'fuller perception of the force and beauty' of the 'natural sceneries' of the biblical world than do Europeans. In a chest-thumping manner, Keshub asked, 'Who on earth is so adoringly fond of flowers as the Asiatic? And who kneels so reverently at the foot of the mountain as he?'[56]

Keshub was at his impulsive best when he proclaimed, 'Do you not know that we Asiatics never read books but converse with them, and that we never study Nature but commune with her?'[57] This sounds attractive and alluring, but also looks vague and hollow without more substantial explanation. Such exaggerated enthusiasm makes Asian reading an intuitive, emotional and introspective process. The trouble with such a reading is that everyone is free to interpret the text however they see fit in order to meet their psychological and spiritual needs. The identification with and visualization of the biblical characters and events say more about Keshub than about the biblical characters.

Two Testaments: Tentative and Tendentious

Keshub's understanding of the relationship between the two testaments is remarkably unique. It was a challenge to the default Christian position which viewed the Old Testament as having no significant disclosure in its own right or that its themes and ideas were made archaic by the New Testament. He did not subscribe to the traditional view that these testaments were initially concerned only with the story of Israel and then with the story of Christians. The New Testament, for him, was not an extension to the Old. 'In God' s work there is no repetition,' he announced, as if it was a divine directive.[58] The world, he professed, did not want 'a repetition of the old story'.[59] The New Treatment was not a radical rewrite of the Old but a 'logical consequence' of it.

Keshub discerned a 'logical unity of idea and method' and 'order and continuity' and a 'secret thread' which connected the testaments. He referred to this connection variously as 'unity in duality' and 'unity in multiplicity'. The two testaments, in his understanding, were a 'concatenated series of ideas, which show[ed] a systematic evolution of thought and development of religious life'.[60] Keshub reckoned that this link was analogous to that of Hinduism and Buddhism.

While in popular perception the New Testament was regarded as the story of how Christians replaced Israel, Keshub interpreted it as a story about Israel and the Gentiles. More significantly, he did not conclude that the Gentiles were the new people of God, the new heirs of God who took the place of Israel. Nor did he view these testaments as tethered to and dominated by Jewish messianic and apocalyptic expectations. Keshub went beyond the prevalent notion of projecting Jesus as ushering in a new people of God.

Keshub viewed the Old Testament as God establishing his hegemony in the material and the animal world, and then his dominion among humanity. Once this was accomplished, the 'volume of the Old Testament was closed'. The New Testament commenced with the birth of the Son of God and ended with the culmination of humanity in the Divine Son. He maintained that the New Testament was not the continuation or fulfilment of or an improvement on the Old. It supplied the 'deficiencies' of the Hebrew Scriptures. What it rectified was the Sonship. The New Testament was about the Son, not about the Father. The two testaments, in his view, represented two aspects of divinity. One sang Jehovah's glory and the other the Son's. One is about the law and the other is about love. Thus, in the New Testament the world had a new illustration of Divine goodness and wisdom, a fresh manifestation of God, not as Godhead but as Godhead living in the Son. It is about the 'heavenly affectionateness of the Son' and the Son's dependency on the Father. The distinctiveness of the New Testament is also due to it not only teaching the Sonship of God but conferring sonship on humanity: 'We are the younger brothers and co-heirs of Christ, and are destined to share with him the crown of divine humanity. That is the new teaching of the New Testament.'[61]

Like the prediction of Ecclesiastes, Keshub argued that there was no end to making testaments – it is a continual process. Just as humankind could not be satisfied with the Old Testament and needed the New Testament, Keshub claimed that it was time for another dispensation: 'A fresh Testament was needed to supplement the Old Testament and the New Testament.'[62] For Keshub, God's dispensation was an ongoing evolution. If the Old Testament was about the Father, and the New was about the Son, then another testament is needed to praise the Holy Spirit. He ased, '[W]here is the Scripture that sings the name of the Holy Spirit?' The answer, he announced, triumphantly was in his new movement:

> Seek it, my friends, in the Church of the New Dispensation, which is in India. Judaism has taught us the Father; Christianity has taught us the Son; the

New Church will teach us the Holy Ghost. The Old Testament was the First Dispensation; the New Testament the Second; unto us in these days has been vouchsafed the Third Dispensation.[63]

He piously declared that 'we are the fulfilment of Moses' and that 'the New Dispensation is the Christ fulfilled' and a 'deduction and corollary from his teachings'.[64] Just as Jesus was the logical consequence of Moses, and Paul was the logical consequence of Jesus, Keshub tacitly suggested that he was the natural successor to Paul.

Intuitive Selections, Emotional Readings

Keshub's writings and lectures are marked by the widespread use of biblical texts and quotes from various Scriptures. In the same sermon or lecture, one may find quotations from the Bible, the Vedas and the Koran, all cited in the same unprejudiced vein and spoken of with equal reverence. But what are these texts actually doing there?

First, the obvious and prosaic explanation: they serve as the text for his sermons. Keshub's published sermons usually have a biblical verse at the top of the text, often serving as a pretext and as a convenient ploy to promote his message. For instance, he marshalled Jesus' words that they shall come from East and West, North and South to sit in the Kingdom to give credence and sanction to his idea of the mutual enrichment of the Orient and the Occident, without paying any attention to Luke's context. In his exposition on the Prodigal Son, he did not draw on the parable of Luke but instead selected a verse from John (1 Jn 4.16) and spoke of God's love and the 'emphatic assurance of God's mercy'.[65] Inevitably, Luke's background and intention were completely shut out.

Second, the Bible acts as a repository from which biblical texts, characters and events can be drawn to bolster his work. He claimed that the Bible bore 'irrefragable testimony to the existence of intuitive truths',[66] a key element in his hermeneutics. He used Romans 2.15-16, which says that the Gentiles who live by their conscience would be declared righteous by God, as biblical approval of the impassioned feelings of religion founded in the God given intuitions.

Third, the texts are often taken out of their original context to settle contemporary difficulties, especially Keshub's own. When his Brahmo Samaj came under attack from Christians and Hindus, Keshub cleverly employed the advice of the Jewish teacher Gamaliel. The Jewish authorities had threatened to kill Peter and the other apostles who continued to preach the Gospel despite being previously prohibited from doing so. Gamaliel urged the Jewish leaders to show caution and leniency, citing the earlier examples of Theudas and Judas and how they went horribly wrong. Gamaliel's hands-off policy and his warning to his colleagues that they should not be seen as God-fighters (Acts 5.38–9) sent a thinly veiled triple message to Keshub's opponents: to oppose Keshub and his movement was to oppose God; history has shown that such hostilities were counterproductive and were doomed; if the movement was part of God's plan, human opposition is pointless. Similarly,

Keshub made use of the phrase 'other sheep I have' – a vague statement by Jesus made in his encounter with local religious leaders – to claim legitimacy for the New Dispensation Church. Faced with hostility from Protestants and Catholics, who branded his movement 'the foes of God', Keshub reframed his Church of the New Dispensation as the 'other sheep'. It was a telling reminder to his Christian doubters that they were the latter-day Pharisees. To rub it in, he sardonically cited the words of Jesus: 'I am the good shepherd, and am known of mine.' His point was that since the sheep knew him, who were these people to question his credibility. This clever recasting of the narratives provided biblical precedents and divine providential sanction for Keshub's life and work and his Brahmo Samaj activities.

Fourth, Keshub authenticated the Bible by claiming that he was the eyewitness to and present in person at some of the significant events in Jesus' life. One such was the baptism of Jesus. As mentioned in the opening paragraph, he took his disciples to a stagnant tank in Calcutta and convinced them they were in the River Jordan in Palestine. He told them, 'Beloved brethren, we have come into the land of the Jews, and we are seated on the banks of [the] Jordan. Let them have eyes, see.' What Keshub wanted for his acolytes was a baptismal experience analogous to that of Jesus had. After blessing the water, just as Jesus did, Keshub immersed himself in it. On other occasions, he convinced his devotees to believe that he was an eyewitness to the transfiguration and the resurrection. His hermeneutical intention was to convert 'eighteen centuries old' historical events 'into a fact of the present moment'. As he put it, 'every figure breathes, every scene lives over again, every historic incident is re-enacted, and the recorded words of wisdom vibrate through the soul as the solemn whispers of living prophets'.[67] His trick was to convince his followers that he had similar experiences to those of the biblical characters. In his words, 'I felt with David in the spirit of his Psalms, and I responded to the exhortations of Christ, and I entered into communion with Paul.'[68] He desired that his followers should have spiritual experiences akin to the ones the biblical characters had. Such comparable identification enabled him to bridge the hermeneutical gap between the ancient texts and contemporary Calcutta.

Fifth, his reading at times clashed and came into conflict with the received and commonly cherished texts. One such was the Golden Rule acknowledged as the very core of the religiosity of all religions. Keshub criticized the Golden Rule, although he readily admitted that it was a 'consistent testimony' found in all scriptural traditions. While feigning respect (I 'bow before the wisdom of these ancient texts'), and with typical Indian flourish, he summarily dismissed this scriptural injunction as a 'low and worldly doctrine' and found it had more utility than moral value. Or, as Keshub put it more memorably, 'This is more John Stuart Mill, not Jesus Christ.'[69] He found the standard of self-love as the benchmark for loving others, as a 'restraint' and fixing of 'a limit'. His quarrel with this axiom was that it called upon people to render generous services to each other up to the extent they serve themselves, and no more. His virtuous proposition was to ask why we should not 'serve our neighbours more than ourselves'? His point was that if love gushes forth ceaselessly and passionately, why then set a limit? He told his audience that he emphatically objected to the Golden Rule because 'heaven teaches us a much higher doctrine of charity'.[70]

Sixth, interpretation for Keshub is a conversation, a personal communication with biblical figures. It is a vocal act. At critical times of his life, biblical figures, such as John the Baptist, Jesus, Paul and of course God, seemed to have direct communion with Keshub. It was the words of John the Baptist – 'Repent, ye, for the kingdom of God is at hand' – that, as he later confessed, stirred him to get on with the Brahmo mission. Jesus' words about not caring about what to eat and what to drink and not thinking about tomorrow led him to live a frugal life. At a time when he had qualms about marrying, it was Paul who told him, 'Let them that have wives be as though they had none.' Keshub had the ability to make his audience believe that these biblical figures were actually communing with him. Hermeneutics was not a wordy exercise – it had a ring of the oracular nature about it, implying that Keshub was in the line of prophets who had received direct messages from God.

Seventh, Keshub neutralized any claims of exceptionalism for the Bible, diluting any special face-to-face encounters that Jewish patriarchs and prophets such as Abraham, Moses and Elijah had with God. He pointed out similar direct communication the ancient *rishis* had with God and noted that there was clear evidence in Hinduism, Judaism and in early Christianity of people seeing God's glorious face. 'More than cold intellectual belief', they earnestly longed for a 'perception of God's fiery presence' and its enkindling effect on the soul. Keshub professed that the theism claimed for the Bible was already found in Vedic texts which pre-dated the Bible.

However, there are conspicuous gaps in Keshub's selection of biblical texts. In his insistence on inner self-transformation, he underplayed the practical ethics and social concerns embedded in the biblical texts. The Hebrew prophets' call for mercy and justice and the subversive message in Mary's Magnificat were noticeable by their absence. Keshub could counter any criticism on this matter by saying that he never looked to the Bible for moral lessons. There was an exception when he used biblical verse to admonish the English for encouraging liquor-drinking among Indians, which was contrary to the logic of the Lord's Prayer, which said 'Lead us not into temptation.' He reminded rulers that it was their responsibility to protect the vulnerable from temptation.[71]

Keshub's reading of the Bible was in many ways an innocent act, often taking the texts at face value. He did not question the authenticity of the Gospels except to say that they had evolved over 1300 years and that there had been additions and deletions by its authors and redactors. On one occasion he was agitated by a Bombay paper which queried the historicity of John's baptism of Jesus. He retorted that for 'natural' eyes, it might be a fiction like *A Thousand and One Nights*, but for spiritual people, it was 'sacred'.[72] As far as Keshub was concerned, the text was authentic because it came from 'men' inspired by God, and his own reading was genuine because it came straight from his heart.

Transgressing and Transcending

Like most interpreters, Keshub too redefined significant scriptural doctrines and special biblical events to suit his interpretative needs. In particular, he reformulated those associated with Jesus, and in the process Indianized them and deprived them of their original content and vitality.

Keshub was dismissive of and differed from the stock Hindu and Christian understanding of the incarnation. In the Hindu perception, the incarnation is seen variously as the Brahman appearing on earth, often in a low creaturely form, or as putting on 'human body, infinite becoming finite in space and time'. Keshub took the view that Christ did not appear on earth as an incarnation of the Father but to represent divine sonship. For Keshub, Jesus' 'mission' was to reveal the harmony of the human and Divine will in the Son, and to 'show us how the Father dwells in the Son and the Son in the Father'.[73] Whereas in Hinduism, God was seen as an avatar on earth, in Christianity it is the Son of God who appears in history not as the Supreme Being but as the First-Begotten Son. Keshub reconfigured Christ as a '*filial* incarnation' of the Father, a 'filial representation of the paternal nature', or better still, the 'Father born and begotten in the form of the Son'. Incarnation is about the divine manifestation of 'corporeity'.[74]

In line with the thinking of most Indian reformers, Keshub did not limit divine incarnation to an event exclusive to Jesus, but as one that happened to all regenerators of religions who enriched humanity in their day. These religious leaders were not only entitled to divine human status but also placed Jesus along with Moses, Mohammed, Nanak and Chaitanya as an incarnated soul, to the outrage of Christians.

Keshub considered baptism to be a 'widespread and time-hallowed' Indian custom and Indians to be 'peculiarly fitted' for such a ritual. It was 'but a prelude to the supernatural and spiritual cleansing' which Christ would introduce among the nations.[75] He distinguished between the ordinary bath, which was a natural ablution, and baptism as a spiritual act. What happened at the Jordan was that the Son of Man went down to the river to cleanse his body, but emerged as a Son of God with a sanctified and purified soul. While biblical commentators rummaged through the books of Isaiah and Psalms to associate Jesus with the history of Israel, Keshub, without providing any references, invoked Indian Scriptures and prophets and implored Indians to do the same as a mark of loyalty to their Indian heritage. As with incarnation, baptism was not a once-in-a-lifetime act. Indeed, Keshub advocated 'progressive baptism' so that one might become 'purer'.

The Eucharist, he assured his devotes, was not a 'foreign custom' or an 'outlandish supper'. Christ's invitation to the feast was 'truly oriental' and one that was 'congenial' to India's 'taste and traditions', since Indians were accustomed to spiritualizing and sanctifying every meal. Keshub divested the sacrificial import of the Eucharist and made every Indian meal a Lord's Supper, thus opening it up to all Indians, urged them to take it up as a 'national feast'. Furthermore, he suggested substituting rice for the bread, and water for the wine, which hardly seems revolutionary today, after many years of indigenization, but was shockingly innovative at that time.

Keshub described the transfiguration as if he was personally present at the event. He reconfigured the metamorphosis that took place as 'one became three; again, the three became identified in one'.[76] His objective was not to 'disunite' Moses, Elias and Jesus and 'enshrine' them in separate tabernacles but to see them as spiritually united. Whereas those engaged in biblical exegesis tend to interpret the event as prefiguring the resurrection, or the second coming, an occasion of eschatological significance with God declaring Jesus to be his son, or in which the temporal and the eternal coalesce in Jesus, Keshub wrested the transfiguration from these restrictive and narrow biblical connotations and allusions and placed it in a religiously plural global context. He did not perceive what happened at the transfiguration as a singularly biblical event but widened it to become a more religiously diverse phenomenon. It was seen as a 'blessed confraternity of disembodied souls' of world figures. In his re-envisioning, besides the presence of Moses, Elias and Jesus, there was Paul and all the apostles, and Indic religious figures such as Sakya Muni, Chaitanya, the Chinese Confucius and the Persian Zoroaster, thus indicating that Jesus was not alone but part of family of world saints and prophets. They were not separate entities but one body. Keshub found a similar celestial vision in the Bhagavad Gita, where the Lord Krishna revealed his universal form to Arjuna. The transfiguration was not an objective event but an 'inward spirit-countenance', visible only to a yogi's eyes. It was a past event but this communion is possible for a present-day Peter, James and John of the Church of the New Dispensation.

Keshub interpreted the Cross as 'the crucifixion of the flesh, the destruction of animal propensities, the annihilation of the old man'. The Cross was an act of 'supernatural moral heroism', an 'honourable and disinterested self-sacrifice' and a 'beautiful emblem of self-sacrifice unto the glory of God'. He described Jesus hanging on the Cross as a 'yogic posture'. This Cross is possible for every one whose senses were dead unto the flesh, whose carnal nature had been 'wholly subdued by communion'. Like all events in Jesus' life, the Cross experience was not unique to Jesus. There were other representatives of this experience, such as the Buddha and Siva, whose slain selves redeemed humanity. Keshub's reappropriation of the Cross stripped away its traditional blood rituals and the sacrificial elements attached to it to leave self-sacrifice as a redemptive act.

Keshub derisively dismissed the resurrection as scientifically 'untenable'. The resurrection was for him the continuity of Christ's humanity. Whereas the disciples saw the body which was unharmed by corporeal corruption or deterioration as fit enough to enter the spiritual world, Keshub spoke of a wounded and decayed body due to the natural processes which forced the unbelieving Thomas to come up with his confessional statement 'My Lord and my God.' The resurrection was the fact that the Father and Christ were indissolubly united. Just as with other major events in Jesus' life, Keshub, in an emotional outburst, claimed that he was personally present at the resurrection scene: 'I am proud to be one of them.'[77] It was a hint to his followers that he was part of the original group of disciples who had witnessed the resurrection. He also assured them that not only had Christ risen, but that everyone could rise with him and 'in his spirit to the highest heaven'.

Keshub extolled the virtues of biblical events and dogmas and at the same time sought to soften their exclusivity by finding analogous examples in the Indic traditions. He further reduced their significance by claiming that they were endlessly recurring and not a-once-and-for-all event that happened to Jesus.

Our Jesus, Our Asiatic Christ

Keshub, who had been studying Christ for a quarter of a century, envisaged his task as making Jesus a source of 'life, strength, and righteousness'. He acknowledged that there was an 'infinite diversity of opinions' about Jesus, and stated that he had 'no desire to enter into a theological controversy on this subject' or get involved with 'the thousand theories which have been propounded about him and his creed'. Ironically, his Christological formulation added to the 'wranglings and disputes' which he wanted to avoid.[78]

Keshub's interest was not in the 'outward and dead Nazarene' – his 'business' was with 'the spiritual, universal, and living Christ'. He posed the question, 'What shall we do with the physical body of Jesus?' and followed it with the default Hindu position: 'By Christ we mean not the person bearing that name, not his form and flesh, but the spirit he embodied, – the spirit of faith, love, righteousness and sacrifice of which he was unquestionably a noble impersonation.'[79]

Keshub described Jesus in glowing terms, such as the 'necessity of the age', 'who by his wisdom illumined, and by his power saved, a dark and wicked world' and left a priceless legacy of divine truth. He recognized Jesus as a the 'greatest and truest benefactor of mankind', a 'tremendous moral force', the 'Prince of Prophets', the 'means of man's renewal' and a 'sanctifying and civilizing influence'. Keshub declared Jesus to be 'above ordinary humanity' and one who did 'infinitely better to the world than others'. He hailed Jesus as the greatest poet who ever lived, the finest example of his bardic talents the expressive words 'Behold the lilies of field.'[80]

The Jesus that Keshub admired was not the Jesus of Davidic lineage or the expected Jewish Messiah, or 'the God of the conquering race' who came with the missionaries. It was the Jesus who was a 'perfect Asiatic' in his 'manners and habits', in his flowing garments, in his features, in his preaching and ministry and in 'his very language and style and tone'. He proclaimed proudly that this Jesus was surely 'Jesus *our* Jesus'. He declared that the Jesus that we read of in the Gospels was 'one of us'.[81] He announced to his audience that the West had come to return 'our Christ, *Asia's* Christ'. Keshub wanted a Christ who was not a 'civilized European' but an Asiatic ascetic whose 'wealth is in communion and whose riches is in prayers'. Jesus was not only an Asiatic but his religion was also an altogether Oriental affair. 'Shall we not magnify our race by proclaiming Christ Jesus as a fellow-Asiatic?'[82] he thundered in one of his famous lectures. He found such a Christ much sweeter than the Bible which the missionaries had introduced.

What Keshub appreciated and honoured was the 'large spirit-Christ' with whom is identified all that is 'true and good' – not 'the little man-Christ of Nazareth' or the 'Smaller Christ' propagated by the missionaries. His is the true Christ with whom all prophets and saints, all devotees and martyrs were identified. This was the inclusive Christ in whom whatever goodness and truth existed outside Christendom was found. He was 'vindicated and magnified by such eclectic principles'. It was Jesus' universality and his placement among the religious saints that made him stand out. Once this 'very ocean of truth and goodness and blessedness' of all humanity was taken away from Christ, he becomes the narrow Christ of the West.

The Christ that Keshub championed was 'Asiatic in race' and 'Hindu in faith'.[83] He declared that 'the picture of Christ's life and character I have drawn is altogether a picture of ideal Hindu life'. The doctrine of absorption in the Deity is India's creed, 'one of the ideas of Vedantic Hinduism', and through this idea, he believed that 'India [would] reach Christ'. He wanted Indians to look upon Jesus as one of the Eastern prophets and honour him just as they would honour Indian sages. His Jesus was not the fulfilment of Jewish Scriptures, but was seen as a devout yogi, a loving bhakta, the fulfilment of India's 'national prophets and Scriptures'. While Roy just hinted at Jesus being Asiatic, Keshub embraced Christ as the fulfilment of India's devotional struggle. He did not regard Christ as the revelation of God in Israel's history and wrap him up in biblical terminology. Jesus, as an Asiatic effectively conveyed to his fellow Hindus that he belonged to the same continent and one of them, while also challenging the missionaries' portrayal of him as the prophesied Messiah from the Hebrew Scriptures.

It was not the manly Jesus that Keshub admired. Jesus for him was a 'union of manly and womanly excellence'. Jesus, he argued, was of 'double nature', which made him attractive to Keshub. Jesus added to the stern manly virtues the 'graces and charms' of a woman. His solicitude for Jerusalem was like a mother's feeling for her children. Jesus' heart often melted away like a woman's heart at the sorrows and weaknesses of others. If Jesus had any divinity, it was not manly divinity but the 'womanly divinity' of Mary. While the West held the view that 'Asia [was] a vile woman', Keshub turned the muscular totemic figure of the West into a tender and caring woman of the East. He confidently proclaimed, 'If the worship of manhood is scriptural, that of womanhood too is scriptural.'[84]

Keshub redefined the biblical Son of Man in Asiatic terms. Jesus' austere poverty, his tender love, self-sacrifice, fasting, temptations, lonely vigils, prayers on mountain tops, self-immersion in the Deity – all these Keshub solemnly maintained 'constituted the Eastern conception of the Son of Man'. This is completely at variance with the biblical and popular understanding of the Son of Man identified in Daniel 7, where he would rule with glory and power.

In Keshub's reading, Jesus turned out to be an exemplary Son. For him, Jesus is *the* Son of God whereas others, like the Buddha, Confucius and Mohammad, were merely sons of God. Each of these 'towering characters' had a 'peculiar and distinctive mission', representing variously the law, self-knowledge and tranquillity, love and so on, whereas Jesus came only to signify sonship. In other words, 'That was *his* mission – to reveal the harmony of the human and Divine will in the son.'[85] 'Christ', he wrote, was 'but an example in history, an objective portraiture of faithful Sonship'.[86] He also stated that 'in the *Christ of the Gospel* we have true Sonship, an example' and a blessing unto the 'world'. To learn about sonship, Keshub urged his followers not to search in sacred books but to look upon Jesus.

Keshub's Jesus did not come to preach the Kingdom of God as routinely claimed by the Gospels, or to teach new theological dogmas, or the principles of a new system of morality. His mission was not the purging of humanity's sins, for he had a 'different errand'. His purpose was to teach 'Divine Humanity'. He was not a moral teacher, as Roy claimed; rather, his objective on earth was to raise humankind upward and make it 'more Divine'. 'It was for this purpose', Keshub assuredly pronounced, that Christ came into this world. Jesus' mission was not satisfied with manifesting one Christ, but to show 'how to make every man Christ'.[87]

The Jesus that Keshub envisaged was not the saviour figure of traditional Christian discourse. He argued that while the Holy Spirit was present and powerful, Jesus himself was powerless to save humanity. Jesus might teach, reveal and show the way, but he could never give humankind the power of 'overcoming sin' and give the strength to 'make us new creatures'. Keshub was convinced that only the Holy Spirit achieve all this. He startled his devotees by declaring that the Holy Spirit was 'our Saviour' and 'Sanctifier', and that Jesus himself depended entirely upon the Holy Spirit. The fact that Jesus was begotten and baptized by the Holy Spirit, as 'the scriptural history testified', was a sign of his dependency on the Spirit that came from outside of him, 'down from above'. Keshub put this in faux Pauline terms: 'We worship the Father, we honour the Son, we are inspired and saved by the Spirit. Our Father is here, our brother is here, our Saviour is here.'[88] It was this Spirit that made Christ, 'otherwise a mere historical character, a sanctifying power within us'. 'Sanctification', Keshub declared, belonged to 'the Holy Spirit alone'. 'National sanctification' was not possible without the Holy Spirit. But the Holy Spirit had another function: the power to make dead souls become altogether new creatures.

In keeping with the thinking of Hindu reformers of the time, Keshub too was reluctant to accord divine status to Christ. It was like having 'Jehovah again in the New Testament' and there was no need for another God, which would be a 'superfluity'. Jesus was 'not another God, but God's spirit', 'God-consciousness not God'. Keshub summoned the support of ante-Nicene fathers such as Tertullian and Justin Martyr, all of whom his missionary adversaries would have readily recognized and acknowledged as having authority, but all these past ecclesiastical giants placed Jesus 'next in rank to God' and 'next after God'. He declared with customary assurance that in the providential arrangements, there was 'no room for two Gods': 'Never say Christ is the very God of the universe, the Father of all mankind.' He warned anyone who claimed that Jesus was 'the very God, the Father Supreme, in human shape' was a 'deceiver', and that such a Christ is a 'fiction of mythology, nothing more'. If he was the 'old God over again in a new form, he [had] nothing new to reveal or teach'. He called for the abandonment of this 'forged "Second God"'. Christ's paramount mission was to 'manifest this divine life in humanity', which he accomplished in a way that no person had done before. His task was to spread the sonship and carry 'all mankind heavenward'. The highest accolade Keshub would accord to Jesus was 'Moses perfected'. His insistence on the human nature of Jesus can be seen as a response to the prevailing pessimistic nature of humanity which was evident in by many of Keshub's missionary challengers.

Keshub defined Christ's nature as 'divine humanity', which was expounded through a kind of kenotic theory largely unheard of and underdeveloped at the time. The text that undergirded this kenotic understanding was not the customary verse in Paul's letter to the Philippians (2.7) but the Johannine verse – 'the Father and I are one'. This, Keshub maintained, was a self-abnegation in a 'very lofty spiritual sense' and the 'highest form of self-denial' on the part of Jesus. He declared that divine humanity was essentially a Hindu doctrine, explaining that the idea of absorption and immersion in the deity was one of the ideas of 'Vedantic Hinduism' and 'India's creed'. Thus, it made Christ approachable for Hindus. Unlike the early Church fathers, he did not envisage this union as a metaphysical or bodily one, but shared Roy's view that it was one of mystical and moral communion.

In summary, Keshub's construals of Christ went through a full circle – from an early excited embrace, to a slight diminishment and finally an unabashed endorsement. In his first lecture on Christ in May 1866, Keshub went overboard and painted him in glowing terms, which provoked controversy among his fellow Indians as well as Christian missionaries. While his 'high view of Christ' was unappreciated by Hindus, the missionaries were alarmed that his teachings might compromise Christian theism. The second lecture, four months later in October, in response to the negative reaction to the first, diluted Christ's role and placed him alongside other great men of India, including Keshub himself. This toning down could have been due to the influence of Dayanada Saraswati, a fierce Hindu reformer who was in Calcutta at that time. Thirteen years later, in 1879, Keshub was at his impulsive best when he spoke of 'My Christ, my sweet Christ, the brightest jewel of my heart, the necklace of my soul',[89] and in a fit of frenzy implored his audience to prepare themselves to receive Christ, the bridegroom, and urged them to put on their best apparel and show the joy and enthusiasm that the 'oriental nations display on such occasions'. The success of Keshub's visit to England and the devotion of his supporters might have emboldened him to take this audacious stance. He genuinely felt the need in India for the self-sacrificial spirit embodied in Christ. The Christ he had in mind was not a 'stern' or a 'stately figure towering ... above all', but a Christ who embodied 'forgiveness, lamb-like meekness, and self-sacrifice'.[90]

Keshub's presentation of the Hindu aspect of Christ's character has to be seen against the background in which it was formulated. It was articulated at a time when there was intense hostility from Hindus towards Christ and Christianity and equal antagonism from Christians towards Hindus. Debendranath Tagore captured the vile mood: 'Let not the name of Christ enter into Adi Samaj. Three hundred and thirty-three millions of Gods and Goddesses have been defeated by Brahmoism. Let us not be intimidated by another infinite God.'[91] Christian missionaries showed equal vehemence, but did not help their cause when they engaged in what Manilal Parekh called 'un-Hindu' or 'anti-Hindu' tirades.[92]

M. M. Thomas's accusation that Keshub paid scant respect to 'the centrality of the historical Jesus'[93] is true only up to a point. Keshub acknowledged the historical Jesus but, like most of the Hindu reformers, he was not overly excited by such a figure. Keshub conceded the fact that there was an earthly Jesus born in the 'boundary line that separates ... Europe and Asia'.[94] Keshub was not enormously attracted by the historical Jesus; for him, the genuine Christ was not the 'Christ of flesh and blood that lived some time ago ... not the visible, but the spiritual Christ'.[95] Keshub's Christological stance was captured in the remark that 'When I read the Gospel of Christ, I do not note the sayings and doings of one who has passed away and is now in his grave, but I see a living man, born of the Spirit, moving about and quickening the souls of those about him.'[96] Ultimately, what counted for Keshub was not the historical Jesus but the spirit and the values that

Jesus represented: 'In the purely human Christ we hardly feel interest' he confided. His belief was that Jesus did not 'present himself to us as an external fact to be believed [as] historical testimony'.[97]

Keshub urged his audience to seek Christ not in the 'sepulchre of books and dogmas, churches and rites', but in the 'simplicity of living faith'.[98] He assured them in his usual enthusiastic manner that 'that grand man, the Christ of history, divinity in humanity, is not far from any of us'.[99] Keshub tutored his devotees as to how they should treat Jesus. Paying homage to Christ did not mean worshipping his 'Divinity', for rather 'we *worship* the Father' while 'we *honour* the Son'.[100] He wanted his followers to 'honour Christ, but never be a "Christian"'.[101]

Keshub was totally opposed to anyone binding themselves as 'slaves to any particular person as the only chosen prophet of God'.[102] Such an attachment would be tantamount to dishonouring those religious leaders who both preceded and would come after Jesus. To drive home his point, Keshub cited the Letter to the Hebrews to assert that God who had revealed himself in the past in diverse manners would continue to speak in the future (1.1).

A Bible-Besotted Bengali

Keshub idealized the principles of Hinduism, spiritualized its sacred texts, advocated Hinduized Christianity and promoted the reconciliation of all the truths of different religions. He worked tirelessly for a constructive understanding of religions which could be forceful vehicles for unity and interfaith harmony at a time when the intrusion of a foreign religion was threatening Indian inclusive tendencies.

Keshub demonstrated a spirit of reverence for all Scriptures. He was charmed by the Psalms of David, taken by the riches of the precepts of Jesus, entranced by the blissful poems of Hafiz and stirred by the spiritual eloquence of the Upanishads. He asked whether a heart which 'lustily thirsted' could reject or be indifferent to such 'noble ideas set forth in such books?'[103] The motto from the Bhagavad Gita which accompanied a selection of theist texts assembled from various sacred writings was a stunning indication of his catholicity: 'As a bee gathers honey from flowers great and small, so does the wise man gather substantial truth from the chaff of all scriptures, great and small.'[104]

Keshub overlooked the fact that the Bible he was so enthused about is a mixture of harshness and kindness. His paean to the poetical excellence of the Bible does not get divine approval. The biblical God threatened those who listened to his words as poetry: 'And, lo, thou *art* unto them as a very lovely song of one that hath a pleasant voice, and can play well on an instrument: for they hear thy words, but they do them not' (Ezek. 32.33).

Keshub resisted giving any intermediary roles to prophets or books. He was certain that one does not find any aid in the Scriptures or prophets unless light, guidance and strength are provided by God: 'The whole Bible would be a sealed book but for the enlightening and guiding spirit of God.'[105] He did concede that when one's inward voice is 'drowned in the tumult of our passions and lusts', one does require 'the auxiliaries of good books and holy influences of spiritual men'; but he warned that it is 'not books or holy men that save us' but rather the redeeming spirit of God,[106] which is revealed intuitively, through direct vision or through nature. Max Müller, who privately urged the Brahmos to become Christians, was dismissive of Keshub's appropriation of the Bible as 'random' and meant to 'give point and emphasis to his own sentiments' – an accusation that could in fact be levelled against any biblical interpreter.[107]

Like Navalar, Keshub introduced some of the tenets of Christianity which were at that time new and incomprehensible to Indians in an easily assimilable form, intriguingly comparing some of them with Hindu images. For example, he found that the doctrine of the Trinity corresponded 'strikingly' to the Hindu notion of *satchitananda*. He also declared that the Trinity was hidden in the images of the Durga, the mother goddess, the Creative Force – the equivalent of the 'Father' in Christian theology. Saraswati is the 'Logos', wisdom, representing the Son, and Lakshmi, the Hindu's 'comforter', stands for the Holy Spirit.[108]

The Christianity that Keshub welcomed was the antithesis of what the missionaries wanted to propagate. It was a Christianity which did not believe in the divinity of Christ or in the infallibility of the Bible, and which rejected the dogmas of hell and eternal punishment and vicarious atonement. He promoted a Christianity which tallied with inner revelation. He claimed that his intuitive knowledge 'existed long before the birth of Jesus and long before the Bible came into existence'.[109]

Keshub's lectures and writings should come with a health warning: they contain extreme demonstrative emotionalism. They are largely rhetorical and filled with flowery language. The theological imagery he employed delighted his admirers but was an irritant to his detractors. His style was a veritable mixture of existential and subjective outpourings; his thinking was chaotic, intuitive and transgressive. What those who attended his townhall lectures and who joined his New Dispensation Church sought was not neat exegesis but oracular truth – of which they got plenty. Townhalls were his temple/church/mandir. He had all the hallmarks of the 'superiority of a sermonizer'.

Like all leaders on a crusading mission, Keshub was a dab hand at giving instructions to the missionaries. He counselled them as to how to present Jesus, urging them to avoid the perception of him as another avatar. He warned them that India was a nation of countless incarnations, and that a new and a foreign avatar would 'plunge a country already darkened with superstition into an abyss of deeper darkness'. He was dismissive of Indian avatars, describing the phenomenon as 'a crude representation of the ascending scale of Divine creation'.[110]

Just as Roy had done, Keshub reminded the Western missionaries that it was pointless parading the miracles as 'the most acceptable credentials of the divine character of Jesus', since 'no part of the world is so full of the miraculous as the East, and especially India'. This type of presentation, he argued, would positively lower and 'compromise his heavenly claims'. The real miracle, Keshub reminded them, was Christ's 'love, holiness, faith, and self-sacrifice'.[111]

Keshub's hermeneutics might be described as divine madness, or what he called 'heavenly enthusiasm'. His aim was to provide an alternative to 'reason', which he regarded as the 'watchword' of modern Christian Europe. Keshub's objective was to replace this 'intellectual belief' with the passion and feeling and that was inherent to the 'songs' and 'poetry' of the ancient Indians. The madness he was talking about is not clinical madness but religious madness, spiritual madness. He saw the difference between philosophy and madness as the difference between 'science and faith', 'cold dialectics and fiery earnestness', logical deductions and the living force of inspiration. He urged that philosophy should be more 'enthusiastic and mad'. If Western reason and philosophy facilitated the evolution of humanity from animality, he reckoned that Eastern madness would allow humans to evolve further and drag humanity to a 'higher stage above the world, far away in heaven, where divinity speaks and rules in man'.[112] Keshub told his rapt audiences that 'all religious men are in some measure Mad' and startled them by describing Jesus Christ as 'the Prince of mad men'.[113]

A notable feature of Keshub's pronouncements is that at times they verge on being self-refuting, best exemplified in his approach to the Bible. He would say that the Christian Bible was a 'wonderful book' and that the Indian mind should come into contact with it, but then quote from Hindu Scripture and proclaim 'that is my Bible, my creed'. He referred to the Bible as 'dumb and lifeless', a 'dead chronicle of facts', but later enthused that 'every page of that book is instinct [sic] with life'. One minute he would announce that he valued all Scriptures and the next he would declare that he 'never wanted to enlighten myself from any other source' than the teaching of the Veda and Vedanta. He would then totally contradict this by saying that 'of all books, the Book of Life is the best' and that the Lord of the Universe had 'made the life of man greater than the Veda and Vedanta'. At times he gave the impression that he had abandoned traditional Hindu and biblical resources for Western science and looked forward to a day when science would be 'your religion' above 'the Vedas, above the Bible'. A similar inconsistency is found in his understanding of Jesus. He would startle his community by declaring the divine nature of Christ, but on a different occasion he might say that Jesus was merely 'Mary's child'. A charitable verdict on these contradictions would be to attribute them to 'impulsive spontaneity'.

Like most of the Hindu reformers, Keshub had a profound belief in Indian spiritual exceptionalism asserting that 'We are nearer the secrets of heaven' and that 'The Indian world is near the holy kingdom of heaven.'[114] He claimed that Indians were blessed with 'peculiar prerogatives conceded by Providence for interpreting the triune nature of the deity',[115] and spoke in vague terms about the 'grand ideas of Eastern countries'. Keshub reckoned that because of their nearness to God, Indians had an intuitive perception and were 'privileged to speak with authority concerning the things of the spirit world, which none can gainsay'.[116]

The Christianity that Keshub emphasized was not that imported from the West. He found English Christianity 'too muscular and hard' and a 'repulsive and foreign form', not 'fit enough for soft, gentle hearts'.[117] What he focused on was the 'Oriental' and 'Asiatic aspect' of Christianity – an idea borrowed from Rammohun Roy but further developed. His refrain had been that in its nascent state Christianity had been Asiatic: 'Christianity in its founder, in its earliest traditions, in its earliest labourers, was Oriental, Asiatic.'[118] Keshub urged the missionaries to preach

Christianity in its Oriental purity, arguing that to understand the Christian faith, they needed to 'get orientalised'.[119]

This leads us seamlessly to the question of conversion. While Roy was against conversions, Keshub had a very different view on this contentious issue. Since Christianity was 'founded and developed by Asiatics', conversion was futile. His message to converts was that if they were following the Asiatic Jesus, reading their Bible in an Asiatic way, appreciating biblical tenets from Hindu perspectives, and practising Christian rituals in Hindu ways, there was no point in embracing this imported faith. As we noted earlier, Keshub was able to provide parallels from Indic sources to demonstrate that there was nothing new to learn from the biblical heritage. He regularly reminded his audience that Jesus was an Asiatic, and that the doctrines which the missionaries claimed were unique had an equivalent in Indian traditions. Hence, there was no need to embrace this foreign religion and 'make themselves alien to their country or race'. They could follow Jesus while staying within the Hindu tradition. After all, what Keshub advocated was a Jesus who was a Hindu in character and manner and a Bible that was Asiatic in content. He often spoke of Christianity as 'our faith', implying it was integral to the Indian religious vision. Since no faith was superior, conversion was pointless or unnecessary.

In line with most of the Hindu campaigners of the time, Keshub had the ambitious and utopian dream of uniting East and West in what he called a 'spiritual union'. He linked this to the themes of 'national unity' and 'national redemption', leading ultimately to 'universal salvation'. Jesus' birth on the border between the East and West was perceived by Keshub to be providential, evidence of God's hand at work. Keshub also devised a division of labour between the two parts, in which the East would tend to the spiritual needs of the West, while the material development of the East would be managed by the West: 'Let then India learn from England practical righteousness; let England learn from India devotion, faith and prayer.'[120] As an antidote to the corruption of Western materialism, Keshub, like other Hindu reformers of the time, offered Eastern sanctity and temperance.

Keshub promulgated the idea of Asia as a single region which could be characterized as catholic, cosmopolitan and a common home for Hindus, Muslims, Christians, Buddhists, Jews and Parsees. He saw it as a uniform composition with clearly defined cultural features and spiritual values: 'a vast home, a wide nationality, and an extended kinship'.[121] His writings were replete with Oriental binary canards in which the East is presented as spiritual and synthetic whereas the West is scientific and systematic.

Keshub was not your typical anti-colonial champion or a resistant subaltern. He was from a 'regal and high-placed caste'. The fact that Queen Victoria was the godmother to his granddaughter further cemented his elitist credentials. On the surface, his lecture on 'Asia's Message to Europe' had all the standard ingredients of anti-imperial rhetoric, with references to the 'slaughter' and 'frightful havoc' of Indian culture and religions and the destruction of the Indian economy caused by colonialism. Yet, he was hesitant to free India from the colonial yoke. In the same speech, while he said that India should 'repudiate' any secular reconciliation or political treaty, he also advocated a 'spiritual alliance' wrought by 'double and perfect atonement' in which the reconciliation of fallen humanity with God is replicated in the unification of the colonizer and the colonized. He perceived colonialism as providential and regarded the British as God's instrument to cleanse India of its idolatry and superstitions. Keshub described himself as a 'loyal subject' of Queen Victoria and saw India and England 'connected by an over-ruling providence'. He predicted that India was destined to 'sit at the feet of England for many long years'.[122] Applying postcolonial analysis, his attitude to colonialism appears to be compliant and cringing.

At the same time, Keshub does not fit the postcolonial trope of a 'mimic man'. He did not simply accept and imitate the missionary version of Christianity. He declared that denominational Christianity presented only one side or one section of the Christian creed, although each sect claimed it represented the whole of it. He perceived Christianity as a 'many-sided religion, and every individual and nation takes in a small portion of the many-sided thing'.[123] Needless to say, Keshub, too, appropriated his share.

Linked to this was his elite status and his espousal of Aryan values. His writings and lectures were strewn with phrases like 'Aryan heart', 'Aryan theology', 'Aryan ancestors', 'Aryan minds', 'our Aryan forefathers', 'Aryan faith', 'Aryan instinct' and 'Brahmanical intuition', which set him apart from the majority of Indians, who are outside this hegemonic system. In these caste-sensitive days, his use of the phrase 'Aryan mind' would be seen as jarring, insensitive and callous.

Keshub sounded messianic on many occasions. Public utterances such as 'I am commissioned to preach certain truths' and 'I am under heaven's injunctions' were evidence of this characteristic. He confidently set himself up as the contemporary Moses or Paul, imagining his New Dispensation Church as the modern-day church of Paul. Just as the Paul of old had been engaged in abolishing race and nationality, Keshub and his organization were involved in breaking the obnoxious distinction between the *brahmin* and the *sudra* (caste). He rephrased the words of Paul to imagine him as the successor to the disciples of Christ: 'What do we see before us in India to-day but the fruit of that tree, whose seed Jesus planted [and that] Paul watered centuries ago?'[124] The Scripture-savvy audience would have got the subtle message – Keshub was God's 'instrument'.

Keshub's self-identification with saviour figures, both biblical and Indic, had a great deal to do with the political and personal harassment he faced at that time. The sole purpose of his bombastic grandstanding and pompous claims to be Moses, David and Sakya Muni was to affirm a natural affinity with these biblical and Indian sages so as to preserve the reverence of his status before his followers and rivals. His exhibitions of prophetic superiority were aimed at the indigenous audience and were not for the benefit of the missionaries. Keshub's identification with Moses and Jesus created an intimacy and heightened communication between him and the ancient figures and between him and his audience. Importantly, it gave the illusion of glorying in and sharing the secrets reserved for the chosen *rishis* and saints of the past. His casting of himself alongside ancient religious figures revealed more about Keshub than it did about the biblical characters. For Keshub, hermeneutics was the embodiment of the Scriptures in one's life. He once told an audience that it was not a sign of reverence to simply hold the Bible in one hand and the Koran in the other. The crucial thing was to enact the essential truths of these Scriptures in their personal lives.

Keshub's writings and lectures were addressed to a culture which was not only saturated with the Scriptures but also knowledgeable about them. His expertise as a scholar of several Scriptures informed and infused his discourse. His public lectures were peppered with biblical texts and phrases such as 'the evidence of things not seen' and the 'substance of things hoped for', but without any references to the biblical books from which they were drawn. In fact, all his quotations came from the King James Version of the Bible and were a reflection of his highly biblically literate Calcutta audience, most of whom were Hindus.

Keshub exhibited the colonial tendency to minimize everything to one, single narrative. Like many of those who favoured what we would now call multiracialism, but inevitably ended up imposing their own worldview, Keshub, too, had his reductive version. While discouraging superficial assimilations such as adding a Madras turban to an English dress, he desired the blending and harmonization of the thoughts and goodness of different nationalities, the 'many types of schools and thought to one truth'. For him, all truths were one truth and that truth was obviously his – the eclectic truth in which all the goodness and beauty of different creeds and nationalities were blended together and harmonized.

Keshub is often judged unfairly in two ways for not meeting the arbitrarily-set requirements of the West. First is the all-too-familiar accusation that he was not systematic. Systematization may be a significant element in Western theological development and might have played an important role in building up and carrying forward the tradition of theological thinking, especially after the devastating impact of historical criticism. Indian Christian thinkers, especially Hindu reformers, were not responding to such conditions and there was no need for them to systematize theological thought. Their question uppermost in their minds was how to make sense of a faith that was totally foreign to the Indian way of thinking. As the writings of Keshub had shown, any systematization at this stage would have stifled their creative imagination.

The second way in which Keshub was judged unfairly was the criticism that his theological inputs did not match up to ancient and orthodox ecclesiastical creeds. Manilal Parekh, one-time disciple of Keshub, faulted him for his failure to measure up to the 'Nicene Creed – bed-rock of all speculation',[125] which meant he was not in accord with the dogmas of the formative years of Christianity. Keshub's critics often employed ancient heresies to label him variously as a latter-day Arian, a Semi-Arian, a Unitarian or an Adoptionist. Such categorizations are based on a lazy notion kept alive by theologians who believe that ancient heresies recur couched in modern terms. The subtext is that the ancient doctrines are definitive, have settled all doctrinal questions and have provided answers to modern questions. Unlike history, heresies rarely repeat themselves and when the originating context no longer exists, the comparison becomes far-fetched. There is also a danger that using these labels mutes critique and debate. The pertinent and perennial question is: why should every Indian thinker, just like the puranic Sita, have to go through the *angina praksha* (ordeal of fire) to prove their hermeneutical purity?

The significance of an interpreter lies not in how he or she matches up to Eurocentrically-devised tests but how they set the tone for the future. In this regard, Roy and Keshub were excellent exemplars. Historically, Keshub was ahead of his time when he came up with a form of kenotic theory (Jesus emptying himself), Jesus as the humanity of God and Jesus as showing maternal instincts. He articulated these ideas well before modern Western scholars engaged in such pursuits. His description of Jesus as someone transparent to God, as he self-abnegated himself, presaged some of the Christological developments in the late nineteenth and twentieth centuries. Keshub introduced the idea into public discourse a decade before *Lux Mundi* – a collection of essays published by Bishop Charles Gore, which popularized the idea of divine kenosis in 1889. In the twentieth century, the idea was further explicated by Paul Tillich, whose description of Jesus as the 'bearer of the final revelation [who] must surrender his finitude – not only his life but also his finite power and knowledge and perfection' is reminiscent of Keshub's views. One could see echoes of it in John Robinson's statement that 'Jesus reveals God by being utterly transparent to him, precisely as he is nothing in himself'.[126] Keshub's articulation of the self-abnegation of Jesus differed from these Western perceptions in that, while Western scholars wrestled with what Jesus had divested himself of, Keshub articulated what Jesus had gained – sonship. The hermeneutical provenance, too, was different. While Keshub did not want to create another God in the form of Jesus, the later Western scholars were responding to the emergence of science and the secular tendencies of the time, and tried to rediscover the real humanity of Jesus. Another example of Keshub's hermeneutical prescience was his idea of Jesus as divine humanity. Karl Barth's Jesus as a 'man from God or of God from man' has resonances in Keshub's thinking. Well before feminists and Shusaku Endo popularized the maternal aspects of Jesus,[127] Keshub came up with the idea in the nineteenth century. Sadly, his accomplishments remain unacknowledged in Western discourse.

Keshub's stellar service to Indian Christian theology was to set the tone for engaging with Indian Christian theology. It was a Hindu like him who promoted the idea of Asian realities as points of reference and anchors for the Gospel rather than fitting Semitic idioms into Asiatic contexts. It is not the Gospel transforming and purifying Asia's ancient wisdom, but rather Asian truths reshaping the biblical message. Keshub's creative-disruptive theology reversed the conditions and parameters of knowledge production, so that Asia was not seen as a passive recipient but as an active participant. He reversed the traditional missionary approach of translating biblical concepts into Indian images, as though the biblical story had the privilege and superior status and the rest should match up to it. As Keshub put it, in his own inimitable fashion, why should India go through Jerusalem to discern the divine, when we have Banaras, Chidambaram and Palani?[128] Sadly, the reconceptualization that Keshub commended has not been heeded by later generations of Indian Christian theologians. Most of them are still stuck with colonial methodologies and their inherent triumphalistic discourse. It appears that some Indian Christian theologians have hardly taken a step out of the Christian compounds created for them by the missionaries.

Notes

1. John Campbell Oman, *The Brahmans, Theists and Muslims of India*, 2nd edn (London: T. Fisher Unwin, 1907), 139.
2. For a competent account of the life of Keshub Chunder Sen, see John A. Stevens, *Keshub: Bengal's Forgotten Prophet* (London: Hurst and Company, 2018). For an analysis of his theological thoughts, see Manilal C. Parekh, *Brahmarshi Keshub Chunder Sen* (Rajkot: Oriental Christ House, 1926). Though dated, this is still a decent work.
3. Keshub Chunder Sen, *Keshub Chunder Sen's Lectures in India* (London: Cassell and Company, 1901), 337.
4. Protop Chunder Mozoomdar, *The Life and Teachings of Keshub Chunder Sen* (Calcutta: Baptist Mission Press, 1887), 82.
5. Mozoomdar, *The Life and Teachings of Keshub Chunder Sen*, 87.
6. Sen, *Keshub Chunder Sen's Lectures in India*, 1901, 345.
7. Keshub Chunder Sen, *Keshub Chunder Sen in England: Diaries, Sermons, Addresses and Epistles* (Calcutta: Writers Workshop, 1980 reprint), 88.
8. Sen, *Keshub Chunder Sen in England*, 88.
9. Keshub Chunder Sen, *Keshub Chunder Sen's Essays: Theological and Ethical*, Part 2, 2nd edn (Calcutta: Brahmo Tract Society, 1892), 92.
10. Keshub Chunder Sen, *Keshub Chunder Sen's Lectures in India* (London: Cassell and Company, 1904), 179.
11. Sen, *Keshub Chunder Sen in England*, 458.
12. Sen, *Keshub Chunder Sen's Lectures in India*, 1904, 179.
13. Sen, *Keshub Chunder Sen's Lectures in India*, 1904, 189. Emphasis in the original.
14. Sen, *Keshub Chunder Sen's Essays*, 145.
15. Sen, *Keshub Chunder Sen's Essays*, 92.
16. Sen, *Keshub Chunder Sen in England*, 241.
17. Sen, *Keshub Chunder Sen's Lectures in India*, 1901, 38.
18. Keshub Chunder Sen, *The New Dispensation or the Religion of Harmony complied from Keshub Chunder Sen's Writings*, vol. 2 (Calcutta: Brahmo Tract Society, 1910), 226.
19. Keshub Chunder Sen, *The New Dispensation or the Religion of Harmony complied from Keshub Chunder Sen's Writings* (Calcutta: Bidhan Press, 1903), 34.
20. Sen, *The New Dispensation*, 35. Emphasis in the original.
21. Sen, *The New Dispensation*, 34.
22. Sen, *Keshub Chunder Sen's Lectures in India*, 1901, 37.
23. Sen, *Keshub Chunder Sen's Essays: Theological and Ethical*, Part 2, 150.
24. Lance E. Nelson (ed.), Purifying *the Earthly Body of God: Religion and Ecology in Hindu India* (Albany: State University of New York Press, 1998).
25. Sen, *Keshub Chunder Sen's Lectures in India*, 1901, 301.
26. Sen, *Sen's Essays: Theological and Ethical*, Part 2, 156.
27. Sen, *Sen's Essays: Theological and Ethical*, Part 2, 152.
28. Sen, *Keshub Chunder Sen's Lectures in India*, 1904, 359.
29. Sen, *Sen's Essays: Theological and Ethical*, Part 2, 85.
30. Sen, *Sen's Essays: Theological and Ethical*, Part 2, 92.

31 Sen, *Sen's Essays: Theological and Ethical*, Part 2, 159.
32 Sen, *Sen's Essays: Theological and Ethical*, Part 2, 157.
33 Sen, *Keshub Chunder Sen in England*, 409.
34 Sen, *Sen's Essays: Theological and Ethical*, Part 2, 158.
35 Sen, *Keshub Chunder Sen's Lectures in India*, 1904, 57.
36 Sen, *The New Dispensation*, 85.
37 Sen, *Keshub Chunder Sen's Lectures in India*, 1901, 278.
38 Keshub Chunder Sen, *The Brahmo Samaj* (London: W. H. Allen and Co., 1870), 36.
39 Keshub Chunder Sen, *Jeevan Veda or Life Scriptures Autobiography of Minister Keshub Chunder Sen*, trans. B. Mozoomdar (n.p.p: n.p., 1915), 140.
40 Sen, *Keshub Chunder Sen's Lectures in India*, 1901, 209.
41 Sen, *Keshub Chunder Sen's Lectures in India*, 1904, 40.
42 *Keshub Chunder Sen's Lectures in India*, 1901, 347.
43 Sen, *The Brahmo Samaj*, 257.
44 Sen, *Keshub Chunder Sen in England*, 92.
45 Sen, *The New Dispensation*, 34.
46 Sen, *Keshub Chunder Sen's Lectures in India*, 1901, 470
47 Sen, *Keshub Chunder Sen's Lectures in India*, 1904, 190. Emphasis in the original.
48 Sen, *The New Dispensation*, 47.
49 Sen, *The New Dispensation*, 36.
50 Sen, *The New Dispensation*, 47
51 Sen, *Jeevan Veda*, 110.
52 Sen, *Keshub Chunder Sen's Lectures in India*, 1904, 114.
53 Sophia Dobson Collet (ed.), *Keshub Chunder Sen's English Visit* (London: Strahan & Co, 1871), 238.
54 Sen, *Keshub Chunder Sen's Lectures in India*, 1904, 189.
55 Sen, *The New Dispensation*, 36.
56 Sen, *Keshub Chunder Sen's Lectures in India*, 1904, 116.
57 Sen, *Keshub Chunder Sen's Lectures in India*, 1904, 114.
58 Sen, *Keshub Chunder Sen's Lectures in India*, 1904, 23.
59 Sen, *Keshub Chunder Sen's Lectures in India*, 1904, 22.
60 Sen, *Keshub Chunder Sen's Lectures in India*, 1901, 460.
61 Sen, *The New Dispensation*, vol. 2, 27.
62 Sen, *Keshub Chunder Sen's Lectures in India*, 1904, 46.
63 Sen, *Keshub Chunder Sen's Lectures in India*, 1904, 43.
64 Sen, *Keshub Chunder Sen's Lectures in India*, 1901, 465.
65 Sen, *Keshub Chunder Sen in England*, 107.
66 Sen, *Sen's Essays: Theological and Ethical*, Part 2, 137.
67 Sen, *Keshub Chunder Sen's Lectures in India*, 1904, 113.
68 Sen, *Keshub Chunder Sen in England*, 211.
69 Sen, *Keshub Chunder Sen's Lectures in India*, 1901, 224.
70 Sen, *Keshub Chunder Sen's Lectures in India*, 1901, 223.
71 Sen, *Keshub Chunder Sen in England*, 171.
72 Sen, *The New Dispensation*, 24.
73 Sen, *The New Dispensation*, 46.
74 Sen, *The New Dispensation*, 27.
75 Sen, *Keshub Chunder Sen's Lectures in India*, 1904, 102.
76 Sen, *Keshub Chunder Sen's Lectures in India*, 1904, 3.
77 Sen, *Keshub Chunder Sen's Lectures in India*, 1901, 421.

78 Keshub Chunder Sen, *Keshub Chunder Sen's Essays: Theological and Ethical Part 1*, 3rd edn (Calcutta: Brahmo Tract Society, 1889), 35.
79 Sen, *Keshub Chunder Sen's Essays: Theological and Ethical Part 1*, 36.
80 Sen, *Keshub Chunder Sen's Lectures in India*, 1901, 302.
81 Sen, *Keshub Chunder Sen's Lectures in India*, 1901, 365.
82 Sen, *Keshub Chunder Sen's Lectures in India*, 1904, 55.
83 Sen, *Keshub Chunder Sen's Lectures in India*, 1901, 388.
84 Sen, *Keshub Chunder Sen's Lectures in India*, 1904, 27.
85 Sen, *The New Dispensation*, 46.
86 Sen, *Keshub Chunder Sen's Lectures in India*, 1904, 40.
87 Sen, *Keshub Chunder Sen's Lectures in India*, 1904, 15.
88 Sen, *Keshub Chunder Sen's Lectures in India*, 1904, 43.
89 Sen, *Keshub Chunder Sen's Lectures in India*, 1901, 391.
90 Sen, *Keshub Chunder Sen's Lectures in India*, 1901, 481.
91 John F. Hurst, *Indika: The Country and the People of India and Ceylon* (New York: Harper and Brothers, 1891), 482.
92 Parekh, *Brahm Arshi Keshub Chunder Sen*, 106.
93 M. M. Thomas, *The Acknowledged Christ of the Indian Renaissance* (London: SCM Press), 69.
94 Sen, *Keshub Chunder Sen in England*, 412.
95 Sen, *Keshub Chunder Sen in England*, 456.
96 Sen, *Keshub Chunder Sen's Lectures in India*, 1904, 113.
97 Sen, *Keshub Chunder Sen's Essays: Theological and Ethical Part 1*, 36.
98 Sen, *Keshub Chunder Sen in England*, 480.
99 Sen, *Keshub Chunder Sen's Lectures in India*, 1904, 4.
100 Sen, *Keshub Chunder Sen's Lectures in India*, 1904, 43.
101 Sen, *Keshub Chunder Sen's Lectures in India*, 1901, 488.
102 Sen, *Keshub Chunder Sen's Lectures in India*, 1901, 87.
103 P. K. Sen, *Keshub Chunder Sen* (Calcutta: Art Press, 1938), 24.
104 Hurst, *Indika*, 480.
105 Sophia Dobson Collet (ed.), *The Brahmo Year Book for 1876: Brief Records of work and life of the Theistic Churches of India* (London: Williams and Norgate, 1876), 6.
106 Sen, *Keshub Chunder Sen's Lectures in India*, 1904, 356.
107 Max Fueller, *Biographicl Essays* (London: Longmans, Green, & Co., 1884), 153.
108 Sen, *The New Dispensation*, vol. 2, 70.
109 Sen, *Keshub Chunder Sen's Lectures in India*, 1904, 192.
110 Sen, *Keshub Chunder Sen's Lectures in India*, 1904, 13.
111 Sen, *The New Dispensation*, vol. 2, 33.
112 Sen, *Keshub Chunder Sen's Lectures in India*, 1901, 313–14.
113 Sen, *Keshub Chunder Sen's Lectures in India*, 1904, 382.
114 Sen, *Keshub Chunder Sen's Lectures in India*, 1904, 5.
115 Sen, *Keshub Chunder Sen's Lectures in India*, 1904, 9
116 Sen, *Keshub Chunder Sen's Lectures in India*, 1904, 9.
117 Sen, *Keshub Chunder Sen in England*, 454.
118 Sen, *Keshub Chunder Sen in England*, 92.
119 Sen, *The New Dispensation*, 26.
120 Sen, *Keshub Chunder Sen's Lectures in India*, 1904, 283.
121 Sen, *Keshub Chunder Sen's Lectures in India*, 1904, 53.
122 Sen, *Keshub Chunder Sen's Lectures in India*, 1901, 324.

123 Sen, *Keshub Chunder Sen in England*, 212.
124 Sen, *Keshub Chunder Sen's Lectures in India*, 1901, 466.
125 Parekh, *Brahm Arshi Keshub Chunder Sen*, 171.
126 John A. T. Robinson, *Honest to God* (London: SCM Press, 1963), 73.
127 Shusaku Endo, *A Life of Jesus* (Tokyo: Charles E Tuttle Company, 1979).
128 Important religious sites of Hinduism.

Chapter 4

A SAIVA CĀSTIRAM

Around 1880 a scantily clad and barefooted guru from South India entered *Sukastan*, a splendid stately home in Colombo in Sri Lanka, then known as Ceylon, which was remarkable for its luxury, ostentation and Western materialism. As the guru entered the premises, the lord of the mansion demanded to know who this trespasser was. The South Indian saint with his commanding enunciation told him, 'I have come to reform you.' The guru was Sri Paranandha Swamigal (real name Illakanam Ramasamipillai) of Tanjore, South India, and the disciple he sought to enlighten was Ponnambalam Ramanathan, the principal focus of this chapter. This story, narrated with great relish by Ramanathan's biographer Vythilingam, has all the hallmarks of the apocryphal story. But like all apocryphal writings, there is a smidgen of truth in it. Ramanathan did meet the Swamigal and, as he admitted later, this encounter led him to a 'higher work' than what he was doing at the Bar or in the Ceylon Legislative Council.[1] He went to great lengths to project his near otherworldly status in getting photographed in sanyasi-like postures. This higher work of piety and spiritual endeavour reached its zenith when a Russian woman married to an English man turned up at the home of Ramanathan and floored him with the words, 'You have the truth that I am seeking.'[2] What had motivated this woman was her reading of Ramanathan's commentary on the Gospels of Matthew[3] and John,[4] which is the immediate concern of the chapter. These expositions were the result of Ramanathan studying Saiva Siddhantha texts like Tayumanavar under the guidance of the Swamigal.[5]

Ramanathan's exegetical works were probably the first modern biblical commentaries in Asia, ironically produced by a Hindu. His hermeneutical efforts included not only eccentric exegesis but his own translations of the texts. His other writings included the two lectures he delivered in the US, which expanded on the themes already sketched out in his Gospel commentaries: *The Spirit of the East Contrasted with the Spirit of the West* (1905) and *The Culture of the Soul among Western Nations* (1906). Both contained a considerable number of biblical references and allusions which complemented what he had already presented in the commentaries. According to the information given in one of his books, Ramanathan was also at work on three further prospective books on biblical exposition: *The Exposition of the Psalms of David (I–XXX) According to Jnana Yoga*; *Lectures on the Sermon on the Mount*; and *Lectures on the Doctrine of the Resurrection* of the Dead, being a commentary on the XVth Chapter of the First Epistle of Paul to the Corinthians. However, my attempts to trace these works have drawn a blank, and it is uncertain whether they were ever published.

Ramanathan (1851–1930), to use a stock phrase often found in Indian matrimonial advertisements, came from a well-connected family which was distinguished for its public and pietistic works. The family's contribution to social, educational and political life is part of the folklore of the island. The Ramanathan clan produced several statesmen and scholars, a number of whom, including Ramanathan, received knighthoods from the British government. Ramanathan himself was the Solicitor-General and entered the Legislative Council at a young age as a member representing both the Tamil and Sinhalese communities. Like all secular, robust male saviour figures, Ramanathan's life and work was complicated. To his admirers, he was the island's 'finest exemplar of the Platonic ideal of the philosopher-statesman, the superman envisaged in the Hindu shastras',[6] whereas for others, his obdurate political stance and reactionary social pronouncements 'caused more harm to Tamil causes'[7] than good.

The Bible: Depository of Spiritual Experiences

Ramanathan called the Bible the 'best book of Christendom' and a 'book of Spiritual Experiences'. It was a record of the spiritual awakening of the great masters like Abraham, the Palmists, Jesus, John and Paul, who were strongly endowed with a sense of divine reality. Like the Vedas of the Indian sages, biblical books were about 'rearing the spirit with utmost care', and helping the soul reach perfection, which in Ramanathan's judgement was the 'greatest work of life on earth'. The sages of India and Judea proclaimed the same message – the different stages through which ripening soul passes, passing from self-love to neighbourly love and finally to perfect love. To reinforce the point that perfect love is love at its full maturity, Ramanathan cited the words of Jesus ('Be ye perfect, even as the father in heaven is perfect', Mt. 5.48) and Paul ('unto a perfect man, unto the measure of the stature of the fulness of Christ', (Eph. 4.13).

Ramanathan did not treat biblical books as biographical or historical works, although they contained some elements of these. They were essentially works of 'Biblical Sages who were men of deep spiritual experience'. The authority and the authenticity of the New Testament did not depend on solving 'historical and literary' problems. Indeed, such an approach would continue to discredit Jesus and the sages of Judea.

Ramanathan devoutly observed that the Bible had two 'intended' meanings – literal and spiritual. Like his contemporary Indian reformers, he bitterly regretted that the Bible had lost its spiritual meaning, especially in the West. Ramanathan never fully explained what this intended or spiritual meaning of the Bible was, making vague claims that the intended meaning could only be conveyed by the people who knew and heard the message first hand from the master or those who have had lives 'precisely similar' to the experience of the master. In this respect, the vast majority in the West had totally 'misunderstood' its spiritual sense and had sadly not moved from the 'oldness of the letter as observed by Paul'. But the correct interpretation of the Bible would continue as long as 'men of deep spiritual experience existed on earth'. The Eastern sages of former times who revealed the truth were the 'surest' and the 'proper teachers of the West'.[8] Ramanathan considered himself to be one of those Indian *jnanis* (sages) set apart to teach the West.

Ramanathan accorded more weight to the oral than to the textual tradition. The oral traditions of Jesus and Paul were not committed to writing for fear that 'dogs' and 'swine' should read them. These traditions were not to be dispensed randomly but only to ripe souls orally 'in the ear' (Mt. 10.25), but they had been lost due to the persecution suffered by the early Christians. Ramanathan did not disparage the written word, but wanted to uphold both the written word and the oral ordinances, the one complementing the other. He echoed the position of Paul: 'Stand firm and hold on to the traditions which we taught you whether by word or what we wrote.' What Ramanathan advocated was that the written word should be complemented by the oral tradition. He reminded his readers that Moses received the oral law to 'complete and interpret the written law contained in the Pentateuch'.[9] But to make the Bible a living force, it had to be perfected by the spoken word. Those who came after the first apostles – that is, the Church councils and Church fathers – had, he sighed ruefully, 'killed' the Christianity taught by the early masters such as Jesus and Paul and replaced it with textualized 'Churchianity'.

Although Ramanathan privileged the oral tradition of Jesus, he was very vague about its shape. It was not clear whether he was referring to the sayings of Jesus prevalent in the Palestinian Church; the verbal testimonies of the Hellenized churches of Paul with their *kerygma*; or the whisper of God's words by Saiva *jnanis*.

Ramanathan bemoaned the fact that from the beginning of the first century, biblical interpretation had fallen into the hands of the 'unlearned' and the 'unstable' and this problem was perpetuated further by the 'spiritual ignorance of those learned in the words of the Bible'.[10] Its reputation had been damaged by unqualified and unprepared persons who, in his customary contemptuous way, Ramanathan called 'unspiritual interpreters' who had discredited the Bible. It was this kind of unsound interpretation that 'killed' the Christianity preached by spiritual masters like Jesus and Paul and produced an 'aggregate of different literary and historical problems full of vain questions and *strifes of words* (1 Tim. 6.4)', incapable of leading human beings to salvation.[11]

The Bible's true meaning is manifested to those who have 'spiritual discernment'. It was not those who loved themselves but those who had moved onto neighbourly love and then onto perfect love who were in a position to appreciate the Bible. In his lecture at the Brooklyn Institute of Arts and Sciences, Ramanathan told the audience: 'The true meaning of the sayings of Jesus and the Apostles are easily understood by those who have wide neighbourly love in them, and the surest interpreters of the Bible are those who have perfect love, and great spiritual experience called knowledge of God.'[12] It is through these enlightened souls that the Gospel of God preached by Jesus and other masters continues to illuminate and emancipate people from their attachments and desires. A mind that dwells on sensual and worldly matters is not in a position to understand the *Jana Shastras*. One has to the realize the supreme *atman* within oneself to properly comprehend the message of the Bible, the implication being that the awakened souls need no theoretical basis for their personal and peculiar method of interpretation. Intuitive realization is enough.

For a correct reading of the Bible, the West needed the assistance of the Eastern sages. Once it had been read with the help of Indian gurus, it could become 'truly the Book of Life', capable of not only solving spiritual dilemmas besetting both individuals and civilizations, but also helping to overcome the cultural divisions between the progressive West and stationary East.

Spiritual Doubles: Matthew and John

Ramanathan's commentaries on Matthew and John were initially private instructions and not for public consumption. They were delivered as a personal tutorial to one R. L. Harrison who took upon herself the task of compiling them. Later she became Ramanathan's wife. The wording of the title pages of Matthew and John simply state that they were 'interpreted to R. L. Harrison' and 'edited by R. L. Harrison'.[13] In presenting these volumes to Cornell University, Ramanathan's handwritten note identified the books as 'my works' and himself as 'the author'. Harrison was Australian heiress who had come to see Ramanathan when she was in a state of religious confusion and uncertainty. What he did was to explicate the Saiva truths enshrined in the very text that had caused her to despair – the Bible. He adopted a similar approach when another of his devotees sought meaning in Eastern spirituality, having become thoroughly disenchanted with the Bible. Harrison wanted him to expound the Bible, but he urged her to first read the Gita. When she asked what was there in the Bible, he advised her that the quickest way to understand the deepest truths of the Gita was to read the Bible again. He was of the view that the truths about God should be made available to people through their own religious tradition. After two years of study, Harrison learnt to appreciate both her precious Gita and the Bible and became an enthusiastic missionary in Australia. Ramanathan envisaged his hermeneutical task to be akin to that of Jesus and Paul. Just like Jesus, he did not want to destroy the traditions in which he had grown up, and like Paul he was willing to adapt himself to become a Jew to a Jew and a Gentile to a Gentile in order to explain the faith embedded in each person's tradition.

Ramanathan's commentaries are not expository sermons, which were a fashion at that time, but made use of three important modern developments – investigation of the Bible in the original languages; the Reformation principle of using the Bible to challenge institutional interpretations; and focusing attention on the text, verse by verse and passage by passage, in order to analyse its history and its literary and philological nuances.

Ramanathan did not delve deeply into the historical details of Matthew's Gospel, such as when it was written or who the intended audience was. He deftly approached the question of its authorship by referring to the writer as the person who wrote the Gospel 'according to St. Matthew'. Similarly, he barely addressed question of the authorship of John. The Gospel contained the recollections of John, first as a disciple and later as an apostle in his old age, long after he had attained Christhood. This double attestation, Ramanathan stated, would have satisfied the popular Jewish expectation of two witnesses to prove the authenticity of the Gospel. He found the fourth Gospel 'wonderfully cohesive and terse', John subtly blending the historical facts of his teacher Jesus with his doctrinal teachings.

If Matthew's was a 'Gospel of Peace', the fourth Gospel was a 'Gospel of the Mystery of Love' or 'the Gospel of the Formation of Christ in Man'.[14] It is essentially a collection of Truth relating to God, the Holy Spirit. Ramanathan identified twelve principles enunciated by John, chief among them being that God is infinite love, God has infinite power called the Holy Spirit, and it is the Holy Spirit which teaches the way to be as pure as God.

Ramanathan reckoned that the Matthew's Gospel really only began at the third chapter. He dismissed the first two chapters, which contained the genealogy and the conception and commission of Jesus, as women's talk, echoing the words of the Pastoral Letter – 'the profane and old wives' fables' (1 Tim. 4.7). He was particularly dismissive of the ancestral list, and reminded his readers of the biblical caution against such family ties (Tit. 3.9). Ramanathan's difficulty with the genealogy was twofold: its historical inconsistencies and its Christological perspective. He found a number of discrepancies in the ancestral lineage which he believed contradicted the accepted chronology. For instance, the gap of nearly 400 years that separated Salmon and Jesse covered only four generations. He also had other reasons for rejecting these chapters, such as their containing 'foolish questions' regarding the genealogy of Christ. In Ramanathan's theological firmament, Christ was the embodiment of the spirit, and just like the sanctified spirits of India, personified righteousness and peace without 'parentage or genealogy'. What was important was not the immaculateness of the parentage of the personalities mentioned in the genealogy, but the spiritual consciousness they possessed. He took a similar view on Thiruvalluvar, a revered figure among the Tamils and the author of *Thirukkural*, who also had a mixed parentage – a brahmin father and a pariah mother. What counted was not the outward body but the spiritual accomplishments such as love and selflessness of spirit that reside within the body.

Ramanathan's contention was that whoever wrote Matthew's Gospel was not responsible for the first two chapters. Matthew's genealogy was included to support what Ramanathan called 'vulgar belief among the Jews' that the Messiah was to come from the house of David. This was disputable on three counts: a) Matthew's prophecies about Jesus were included with a view to making his Gospel acceptable. 'In these days of deep research and enlightened criticism', his argument was that the 'authority of Jesus' did not 'rest on prophecy'; b) attempts to link Jesus with David after declaring that Jesus was not the son of Joseph but born of the Holy Spirit did not make any sense; and c) Jesus himself showed little interest in old family connections, but was keener on forming new family ties which transcended blood and ancestral links. Ramanathan's unwavering belief was that sanctified souls did not have a genealogy.

What did Ramanathan make of the distinctive contributions of these Gospels – the Sermon on the Mount in the case of Matthew and the Logos in the case of John? According to Ramanathan, the Sermon on the Mount was a 'series of lessons of love culture or soul culture'. Jesus' message was a 'marvellously beautiful exposition of the principles, long held secret (Mt. 13.35) of that Infinite Love, Light, and Joy' which characterized God.[15] It is all about the 'blessedness of the spiritual joy which was distinguished from worldly joy', or in the phrase of the Psalmist, the 'greatness of blessedness'. It is about 'spiritual growth and [the] conquest of care and sorrow'.[16]

Ramanathan's Sermon on the Mount was not meant for the masses. It was delivered specifically to people who were spiritually mature enough to hear the truth. He listed eight classes of such persons mentioned in the Sermon. They were the 'poor in spirit', 'they that mourn', 'the meek', 'they who hunger and thirst after righteousness', 'the merciful', 'the pure in heart', 'the peacemakers' and 'they who are persecuted for righteousness' sake'. In keeping with his exclusionary hermeneutical practices, Ramanathan asserted that the principal truths of the Sermon would have no meaning for those were carnally-minded and whose happiness was rooted in worldly pleasures. In this respect, it had a great and practical value to Western nations who were all in thrall to the 'almighty dollar'.

Unlike Gandhi, who successfully utilized the Sermon on the Mount for his political causes, Ramanathan considered it irrelevant for such secular pursuits. It is not about loving friends and enemies alike, but more about 'matters of inner experience' and not 'objective phenomena'. He extolled the authenticity and originality of the message of the Sermon and simultaneously undermined it by pronouncing that its core precepts existed even before Jesus was born.

For Ramanathan, the logos was not a matter of speculation, or a product of the literary imagination of Greek thinkers or an abstract concept. The philosophers and historians of the ancient Greeks and Hebrews had contemplated this for nearly eighteen centuries. For Ramanathan, the logos is not a 'creature of literature at all. *It is a matter of deep spiritual experience.* It is a stern reality attested by the Sanctified Spirits of men who have attained Christhood,'[17] such as Jesus, John and Paul. The logos, in his view, had three additional meanings. It is an 'all-pervading power of Direction, the great Informer of the Universe, the Power that *forms or shapes* every entity, mental or material'.[18] It is the Holy Spirit acting as teacher, with the doctrine or teaching emanating from God through the sanctified spirit called Christ. More than this, Ramanathan reinterpreted the functions of the Johannine doctrine of the logos as doing the work of the Lord Shiva, which included 'creation, maintenance, and destruction; instruction; rewarding and punishing; and redeeming'.[19] This was a clear allusion to the *Saiva Siddhantha* idea of Sivan (one of the deities of Hinduism) being the creator, protector and transformer of the world.

Ramanathan's exegesis did not produce the detached and dry propositions often found in standard Western commentaries, but was enlivened with a series of personalized prescriptions and subjective spiritual meditations amply buttressed by Saiva insights. These were sensitive and respectful and he only showed disdain when the texts deviated from his theological perspective. He regarded the Gospels of Matthew and John as profound Saiva Siddhanta meditations. They were Hindu-biased and Siva-centric expositions and the yearning of a *bhakta* (devotee), a 'stream of scriptural consciousness'. Ramanathan's commentaries were in line with modern day biblical commentaries and demonstrated his familiarity with the latest biblical scholarship. In number of places, he provides his readers with helpful background information, for example his extended notes on the Samaritans. However, his minimal references to the texts and excessive Saiva theological indulgences might have been jarring for traditional Christians.

Ramanathan's commentaries are not simple expositions of the Gospel writings but an attempt to make the Gospels conform to his predetermined Saiva vision. When the Gospel narratives do not meet the already scripted Indian spiritual expectations, they are dismissed as the work of an 'ignorant' copyist. For instance, when the text claimed that Jesus was 'led into the wilderness to be tempted', Ramanathan blamed the writer for misunderstanding the withdrawal of Jesus. He maintained that Jesus was not being tempted but was in a deep yoga – spiritual communion with God. For forty days and nights Jesus retired to the wilderness 'dead to the world and alive to God'. He was also dismissive of one of the supplications in the Lord's Prayer – 'As we also have forgiven our debtors' – a gloss on the part of the writer. Ramanathan's contention is that the conduct of the debtor cannot be an example to God. This verse, in Ramanathan's reading, is more about the egotism of a human being, or in his Saivite terminology – *anava* pride.

Visions of Seers and Outpouring of Souls: Judaean Prophets and Psalmists

Ramanathan distinguished between the Old and the New Testaments, perceiving the former as a manual of rituals and the latter as a guide to spiritual self-realization. He stripped out the stock contents of the Hebrew Scriptures, such as the Covenant and the patriarchal histories, and reduced it to a book of ceremonies around tabernacles, the observance of festivals and pilgrimages to holy places. He redesigned the New Testament not as a book advocating outward performances and works but as a suitable resource for inner spiritual realization. While Moses urged formal worship, Jesus enabled the spiritual actualization of souls, in Saiva terms producing *pakkuva athma* – a ripe soul, ready for instruction.

Ramanathan, who was involved in the colonial politics of Ceylon, did not find attractive or approve of the political interventions of the prophets. He completely sidestepped the social significance of the prophets and turned them into non-politicized figures. He declared that one earned the title of prophet through a mixture of 'gifts of clairvoyance, rhythmic utterance' and austere living and not by drawing attention to people's civic responsibilities or reminding the state of its social obligations. Ramanathan's Hebrew prophets did not speak about justice, peace and mercy or taking care of the widows, but held religious seances, as had been the practice of Elisha, with the aim of imparting 'history and patriotism' and building the faith of the people. More importantly, the prophets wanted to proclaim the 'inutility of sacrifices when divorced from inner faith'.[20]

Ramanathan regarded the prophets as the transmitters of the oral tradition which was once the preserve of the priestly class, who had become corrupt and therefore unable to discern the inner meaning of the Mosaic code. This change of role was largely precipitated by the 'companies of prophets' initiated by Samuel, a key figure in the history of Israel, which Ramanathan, who was prone to describe everything in spiritual terms, called 'schools of spiritual instruction'. His descriptions of these schools resemble that of the *Saiva maṭam* (monastery), where students were taught sacred poetry, music and dance. These students held meetings to build up the faith of their communities and they preached morals and spirituality as opposed to traditional ceremonies or the inculcation of nationalism. Their discourse was in the form of songs and dances, like the Hare Krishna devotees: 'They saw visions and sang them in stirring verse, interpreting the visions by the light of current history and impending events.'[21] Ramanathan's prophets do not tell truth to power. Instead, their chief function seemed be to provide 'edification, comfort, and consolation'.[22] Basically, they dispensed words of advice, support and hope for those who were despondent.

In Ramanathan's graded hermeneutical universe, the prophets do not occupy a high rank. They were not sanctified in spirit, and therefore could not be called saints, apostles, masters or teachers of the true doctrine. They did not even know the truths related to the kingdom of God, and though they desired to hear these truths from the living lips of a master, they had failed to find him, nor had they any 'opportunities to commune with him'.[23]

The prophetic penchant for patriotism and the prediction of the one and only Messiah, limited to the Jewish people, did not endear the prophets to Ramanathan. The prophetic prediction of one Christ for all time and for all the world would not only be a hinderance to those habituated to cherishing many Christs, but was also inconsistent with the teaching of Jesus and Paul, who often spoke about other persons attaining the state of Christhood or the sonship of God. He queried the different prophetical passages which announced Jesus as the one and only saviour of humanity and argued that the redemption of humanity by the Infinite Mercy had gone on for ages before Jesus and would still go on even after the nation that cherished Jesus had passed away. It was an 'error', both on the part of Western nations and the later biblical interpreters, to insist that Jesus and Jesus alone was the Messiah. He told his Brooklyn audience that it was foolish to monopolize God or God's messengers, that God would continue to send apostles as the occasion demanded, and that messianic prophecies were not exclusive to the Jewish people, who were part of what Ramanathan called 'the general Divine Law of the "drawing" or "calling"' of the Spirit to God, which Jesus so frequently taught.

While Ramanathan downplayed the spiritual status of the prophets, he put the psalmists on a pedestal as Indian yogis (seekers of God) or *Jnanis*, who had succeeded in attaining the full knowledge of God. Among the teachings of the Hebrew Scriptures, Ramanathan singled out the book of Psalms as 'truly the highest', describing it as a 'great storehouse, not so much of history as of spiritual wisdom'.[24] The Psalms were the songs of the seekers of God and 'utterances of a *Jnana Guru*'.[25] They were basically the *actual experiences* of the seekers or those who had sought and found God. Psalmists were those who were tired of the corruption of the soul, and, unable to overcome it, appealed to God as the only power who could help them. God responded to such prayers and freed the soul from corruption. The book of Psalms was 'the outpourings' of yogis and contained 'many a doctrine of Truth and Grace, and many an exercise in Godliness'.[26] In effect, Ramanathan made the Hebrew psalmists look like *Saiva Nayanmars* (hounds of Siva).

Saiva Assurances, Biblical Blunders

Ramanathan imposed his idiosyncratic reading on the few radical references found in the biblical verses, thus draining them of their political and social significance. A notable example is the saying in Matthew about neglecting the weightier matters of law: justice and mercy and faith (23.23). He pronounced that the rendition of crisis as 'judgement' and 'condemnation' in the Authorized and the Revised Versions was 'inappropriate'. As the Solicitor General of Ceylon, he took a lawyerly approach and urged an 'intelligent reading of the law', and was wary of ignorant lawyers who might pass unrighteous judgements. In keeping with his idea of oneness with God, he suggested 'separation' or 'differentiation' as possible alternatives to 'judgement'.[27] Justice, for him, was not making resources available to the orphan, the weak and poor, or advocacy on their behalf, or fighting for their protection, but simply reuniting them with the divine. Similarly, he diluted the social and political contents of other weightier matters of law such as love, justice and faithfulness. He redefined mercy in condescending terms as showing pity and not standing in solidarity with those in a hostile legalistic environment, or challenging exclusionary religious, social and economic practices and structures which placed them there. Faith, for him, was enacting ordinary acts in everyday life and not putting one's trust in overcoming obstacles or transforming situations of need. He declared that the more substantive or 'important part of the law' was not concerned with justice, mercy or faithfulness, but rather 'spirit, life, light and true doctrine'. The protection of the poor and the vulnerable – a major scriptural preoccupation – is thus individualized, ignored and suitably spiritualized.

Ramanathan was not slow to point out erroneous translations or inaccurate phrasing by Gospel writers, or the unnecessary additional phrases inserted by bible translators. His most celebrated dispute concerned the translation of one of the pivotal phrases of John, *monogenenes huios*, as the 'only begotten Son', which led the Christian Church to believe in a single Christ, something which Ramanathan found untenable. He claimed that Jesus, Paul and other apostles spoke often of the 'possibility of other persons also attaining the state of Christhood, called also [the] Sonship of God'.[28] Jesus himself taught that others could be as perfect as God in love (Mt. 5.48) and as exceptional as him if they had faith. Ramanathan invoked the words of Jesus to challenge those who said that it was not possible for human beings to achieve such a Christhood, providing a series of biblical texts which 'have proved a stumbling block to those who are wedded to the belief that there is only one Christ for all time in the Universe, and that Christ is Jesus'.[29] Ramanathan provided his own rendition of *monogenenes huios*, which of course was the correct one – 'alone-become'. He explained that the 'alone-becoming' of the soul is known in India as *kaivalya*, a state of aloneness in which the 'soul knows itself and God who is in it'.[30] 'Alone-becoming' is a great spiritual experience 'known only to those have succeeded in *jnana yoga*',[31] namely those who have been emancipated from desires and selfishness and are in constant fellowship with God.

Ramanathan also objected to the Authorized and Revised versions' translation of *ekbellei* as 'bringeth forth' (Mt. 13.52), pronouncing it to be plain 'wrong'. Rendering *ekbellei* as 'bringeth forth', he maintained, was to miss the main thrust of the chapter. Viewed in the context of the narrative, the proper translation should be 'casts out or throws out', meaning giving up the treasures of worldly life in order to enjoy the treasures of the kingdom. This was in accord with his *Saiva Siddhanta* theology of rejecting carnal ties and desires. Similarly, in a lawyerly fashion, he ruled that the translation of *didaskalos* (= teacher) in Matthew 23.8 as 'master' was incorrect. Being a teacher was different from being a master. A teacher is a godly, sanctified servant who teaches in the name of God what has been revealed to him. Teaching implied knowledge or illumination, whereas the term master or lord was suggestive of dominion or superiority, something which Jesus neither had nor claimed.

Ramanathan did not simply criticize inaccurate translations but also provided his own and somewhat peculiar interpretations. He rendered the 'Son of Man', traditionally understood as a corporate figure and an image for an ideal people for the kingdom, into a single 'Son *in* Man'.[32] Jesus not only renounced his parents and kith and kin but also relinquished the name given to his corporeal body by his parents. He used the expression 'Son of Man' made familiar by the Hebrew saints and the prophetical writings. Ramanathan even dared to correct Jesus and suggested that a 'more intelligible' rendition would be 'Son *in* Man' – a sign of making peace within oneself and being acknowledged by the Father as a Son. For Ramanathan, the Son of Man and Son of God are the same, because Jesus had used both expressions to denote Christ.

Ramanathan often questioned the authenticity of the text. Though not trained as a true historical critic, he questioned a number of later additions. For example, he pointed out that the saying 'For many be called but few chosen' was not found in the best texts and did not naturally follow the words 'the last shall be first'. He judged that the statement was out of context in its current redacted setting and that its rightful place was in the Parable of the Wedding Feast (Mt. 22.1-14). Likewise, he found the phrase 'and be baptized with the baptism that I am baptized with' (Mt. 20.22) to be one of a number of 'meaningless interpolations' not supported by the ancient authorities.[33]

For Ramanathan, the unassailability of a biblical text was determined by its potential to yield Hindu meanings. The failure to yield such meaning was a sign that the text was flawed. If the texts cannot be made to yield Hindu senses, Ramanathan declared them unsound. If a translation did not agree with his view, he dismissed the translators as 'not having spiritual knowledge' and for getting it 'wrong on such a deeply mysterious experience of the spirit'.[34]

Biblical materials and contents were convenient conduits for promoting his Saiva ideas and concepts. The parables of Jesus were a means of illustrating and enforcing his Hindu vision. For example, he turned the Parable of the Prodigal Son – one that was very much embedded in the Christian consciousness – into a Saiva story of an awakened soul. He praised the parable as a 'history of civilization', which beautifully outlined human progress from worldliness to Godliness, carnality to spirituality. It was about a spirit which 'strayed away into the mazes of worldliness and returned to Godliness'. The contrite words of the son – 'I will arise and go to my father, and will say unto him, Father, I have sinned against heaven, and before thee' (Lk. 15.18) – expressed the determination of the soul who had realized the folly of a sensuous life and wanted to seek redemption. The prodigal son was analogous to a *jiva* (soul) releasing itself from worldly attachments.

The other parables that Ramanathan used to propagate his Saiva ideas included the Wise and the Foolish Virgins. When the bridegroom arrived, one was ready, or in Ramanathan's parlance, ripe enough, to accept the master whereas the other was spiritually unripe, and so was left outside. The Parable of the Good Samaritan was another perfect vehicle for Ramanathan to validate his main theological thrust: the mercy shown to the Samaritan was a perfect example of how self-love turned into neighbourly love, which in turn grows into spiritual love with the 'corresponding dislike for things corporeal'. While traditional biblical commentators perceived an implied Christology in the parables or allusions to how God's reign operates, Ramanathan treated the parables as illustrations of 'active exercises in Godliness'.

Ramanathan recast and reconfigured biblical concepts such as Messiah, high priest and shepherd, almost making them counterpart figures to Saiva *jnanis*. The Messiah that he came up with did not spring from the 'seed' of David, show up in the 'temple' or manifest on 'Mount Moriah', or rally together the 'dispersed tribes', or vanquish all their 'enemies' and establish a 'universal empire', with Zion as its centre. In Ramanathan's envisioning, the Messiah was not a flesh and blood person but a sanctified soul. He cited Isaiah's words that the Messiah had 'no form or comeliness' (53.2) to reinforce his vision. This Messiah was without any shape or form, yet was found 'transcendingly beautiful'.[35] Similarly, the Royal Priesthood was not about power and authority but about a person attaining the 'fullest maturity or perfection'. The Royal Priest was more like Melchizedek because both had a similar spirit of the high priesthood of God. Neither had a father and mother, or descent or beginning or end.

Biblical teachings on important Christian doctrines were readjusted by Ramanathan to accommodate Saiva philosophy. The atonement, as the bodily sacrifice of Jesus offered as a ransom for many, would have been a repulsive act for a vegetarian Saivite like Ramanathan. He reconfigured this act of sacrifice as Jesus releasing his soul. He perceived that the suffering of Jesus was merely an objective lesson to teach the subjective truth – self-effacement: 'All this figurative language means that in order that "lost" souls may regain the kingdom of God, he had to teach them objectively (by sacrificing his life) the subjective truth that self-effacement, or forsaking all the rudiments of the flesh, was essential to attain God.'[36]

Similarly, Ramanathan dismissed the resurrection, arguably the key belief of Christianity, as a 'vulgar doctrine' and reinterpreted it variously as the 'regeneration of the Spirit', 're-birth', 're-rising', 'second birth', 'awakening with the spirit' and 'the conversion or regeneration of the spirit'. He asserted that the resurrection had nothing to do with the carnal body but had to do with the soul. He was clear that Jesus did not teach bodily resurrection or believe in a general universal resurrection on the one and the same day. The idea was 'ignorantly engrafted' onto their religion by the Jewish people after being taken captive by Nebuchadnezzar, King of Babylon, and deported to Chaldea (in 587 BCE). Furthermore, there was no evidence of the resurrection in the Mosaic Law. Ezekiel had simply utilized the doctrine to revive the despondent Jewish spirit which was very low after the captivity. According to Ramanathan, resurrection is about spiritual communion with God and being dead to the world. It happens when the spirit is freed from the flesh, from captivity, separated from the womb of the flesh and appearing in the glory of God. It is not a once-and-for-all event. After the 'first birth' there are subsequent risings of the soul. Finding Christ and having that spiritual experience is also resurrection. To be resurrected or reborn is to become Christ, and without attaining this Christhood, it is impossible to see God. For Ramanathan, resurrection was not a historical but a metaphorical event, constituting 'the conversion of the worldly spirit into the Godly spirit, by *death* unto the world and *re-birth* unto God'.[37] Resurrection as a purely spiritual experience can be taught. 'I am the Resurrection' thus signifies 'I, Christ Jesus, am the resurrecting agent – I can teach you how to rise to, or attain, a realisation of God.'[38] The unique historical event is now thrown open to all. With a proper spiritual guru, one can attain spiritual resurrection.

Like the Hindu revivalists whom we will meet in this volume, Ramanathan has a tendency to universalize or spiritualize what is peculiar to Israel. For instance, all those wandering souls were likened to the House of Israel seeking the 'ministrations of Christ'. They were the people who had strayed away from the kingdom of God and now 'wish to return to God'.[39] Ramanathan likened the wandering of the Jews to that of his own people being led away from the 'ancient ideals' and losing their souls to Western materialism and civilization. In other words, he spiritualized the Jewish search for Jerusalem.

Similar to Radhakrishnan, Ramanathan made biblical books conform to the doctrine of karma, which he called a 'universal doctrine of judgement according to works'. Both emphasized the chain reaction of events. Ramanathan provided an array of biblical citations from Ecclesiastes, Psalms, Proverbs, Jeremiah and Paul to establish the credentials of the Bible in terms of endorsing the principle of cause and effect. In his exegesis of both Matthew and John's Gospels, Ramanathan constantly emphasized the decisive role of karma in governing one's future prospects. It is not about chance, injustice or unearned increments but about reaping what is due to a person. One is entitled to such reward for the work done for the Lord in one's past life, though the justification for such a reward may not be apparent to human reasoning. Ramanathan claimed that karma had a positive role and was a crucial step towards attaining grace. He also provided clues as to how to avoid bad karma – by peace-making and pacification of thought.

Ramanathan gave an extraordinary explanation for Jesus forbidding his disciples from going to the Gentiles or to the Samaritans. This largely condescending conjecture is derived from the *Saiva Siddhānta* notion of ripe and unripe souls. In this division of humankind, these foreigners were deemed to be 'not ripe enough to receive the gospel'.[40] Such spiritual gifts were reserved for the souls which showed a certain spiritual ripeness, enough to receive the message. This was another important reason for Jesus to speak in parables, because 'the craving of the masses' was not 'commensurate with their intelligence to understand the lessons conveyed'.[41]

Ramanathan regularly offered eccentric exegetical advice, one example being the exemption of the saints from paying taxes as they were above the law and not subject to the requirements of the law. Commenting on the Tribute money incident, he suggested that the saints and the sanctified need not pay taxes. It was a 'misconception' on the part of earthly authorities to impose such taxes on those who had become sanctified in spirit and had transcended the world. What Ramanathan overlooked was the clear instruction of Jesus to his disciples to pay the tax.

The key question is whether in the end these reframings led to constructive changes in the cherished doctrines of the Christians. The simple answer is that they did not, but they did make them safer and more comprehensible for Saiva readers who were confounded by alien Semitic images. Ramanathan's recastings and alternative renditions gave significant new meanings to the Scriptures which would not have occurred to the original authors. His task was akin to Indian sages who engrafted onto earlier texts new concerns which were different to the ancient versions. For Ramanathan, reading the Scriptures did not mean going back to an imagined perfect past, but rather routinely revising and interpreting and dramatically updating texts to meet new spiritual demands.

Ramanathan's interpretative tactics were a reversal of the earlier attempts of the Orientalists, missionaries and some converted Indians like K. M. Banerjea in two ways. Firstly, the latter used Hindu Scriptures as an ancillary to biblical texts and as suitable background material to make the Christian Bible better Scripture. Ramanathan argued that what was hidden in the Hindu Shastras was fully revealed in the Bible. He upended the argument by asserting that it was the Hindu shastras that provided authentication for the biblical message: 'When some of the sayings of Hebraic sages have been sufficiently interpreted, you will see how their conclusions stand corroborated by the teachings of the Eastern Masters whom India adores.'[42] In other words, it was the writings of the Eastern sages which confirm and strengthen the teachings of the Bible. The real facts about the existence of the spirit in the body and the gradual stages the soul goes through from self-love to neighbourly love, and neighbourly love to perfect love, are the basic message which was 'fully recognized' and proclaimed by the sages of India and Judea.

Secondly, Ramanathan was not trying to interpret the biblical text from the perspective of Saiva Siddhanta. When a reviewer of his books commented that it was an exposition from the viewpoint of Siva Siddhānta, the editor of the influential journal *Siddhānta Dīpikā* corrected him, saying that such a reading was 'misleading'. The editor pointed out that what Ramanathan did was to accentuate Saiva teachings embedded in the Gospels based on the deepest spiritual experience and realized in the depths of one's inner being. Such truths are the same all over the world. Agamas, Vedas and Christian texts all speak the same truth to those who have found God.[43]

Ramanathan held the conviction that the teachings of the Indian saints were not foreign to the Judean rabbis.

Sanctified Soulmates: Jesus and Paul

The development of faith, for Ramanathan, depended on two things – a 'qualified teacher and a discerning pupil'. Jesus and Paul neatly fitted the role of teacher due to their spiritual experience. Ramanathan replicated the then prevalent neo-Hindu view, initially popularized by Roy, that Jesus was an 'oriental' and a 'great Eastern Master' whose teachings were draped in allegorical and symbolical language so common among Eastern thinkers.[44] He accorded the same geographical identity to Paul, hailing from 'the East', whose voice went unnoticed.

Jesus and Paul, in Ramanathan's construal, come across as undifferentiated spiritual souls. Both attained the status of Christhood and spoke about sanctification. Jesus defined it as 'perfection' (Mt. 5.48) and Paul as 'maturity' (Eph. 4.18). They believed that human beings could become as perfect as God or, in Paul's words, one could come up to the 'stature of the fullness of Christ' (Eph. 4.13). Both advocated that the tangible body carried within itself, in Jesus' case, the Kingdom of God ('Behold,' said Jesus, 'the kingdom of God is within you' [Lk. 17. 21]) and in Paul's case, the temple of God ('that ye are the temple of God, and that the Spirit of God dwelleth in you' (1 Cor. 3.16)). They were effective teachers of sound doctrines who not only exhorted but also convinced the gainsayers. They both emphasized the orality of the message. Jesus said that 'one heareth my words and loveth the Kingdom of God', while Paul wrote that 'faith cometh by hearing'. Jesus delivered his teaching 'wholly by word of mouth', whereas for Paul the traditions were 'written and unwritten'. Both acknowledged that what they taught emanated from God. Faith for them was not a 'product of credulity' but a realization of love for God. Both were mocked by the people. When Jesus preached and performed miracles, his own countryfolk derisively asked was he not the carpenter's son? When Paul spoke of himself as an 'apostle raised from the dead', he was laughed at by both Jews and Gentiles. Both came to a brutal end – one was crucified and the other beheaded.

Ramanathan's Jesus was not as stern a judge as the missionaries presented him to be, but behaved like a Saiva guru. He did not pass any judgement or castigate those attached to worldly possessions. He showed the way and whispered the message of the 'manifestation' or 'appearance' of Christ within each person (John 14.21; Mt. 24.30). Judgemental sayings attributed to Jesus were all rerendered to fit with the image of the guru as an enabler who frees the soul from bondage.

Jesus in Ramanathan's construction fostered an austere religious individualism. He was an ascetic and not an agitator on behalf of the Palestinian proletariat. He showed concern for the poor, women and widows, but at an individual level he had no concrete plans for the structural remedying of their oppression and rejection. Unless their souls were ripe enough to receive the message, the marginalized had no hope.

The Jesus we encounter in Ramanathan's writings saw nothing of value in the ceremonial laws of his people and constantly clashed with the priestly class over sabbath observation and food laws, those for whom adherence to these very laws constituted the very essence of their peoplehood. This Jesus did not fit in with Schweitzer's apocalyptic assumptions. He was not a suffering servant who stirred people to repentance by suffering, but a serene Saiva guru who whispered God's message into the ears of the bhaktas (devotees) that God was not to be found in the world but in 'resplendent Tillai' (the abode of Lord Shiva) or the region of pure consciousness or atma, a staple feature of Saiva Siddhanta teaching.

The Jesus that Ramanathan projected showed no national or political aspirations. He was a non-messianic Jesus with hardly any interest in restoring the much-anticipated Davidic kingdom. He did not agitate against Roman colonialism. At his trial, Jesus spiritualized his mission. He admitted that he was the king, but a spiritual king who had conquered worldliness and whose dominion was over those who were pure enough and spiritually ripe enough to understand his teachings. He preached a spiritual and not a nationalistic commonwealth. The kingdom that he proclaimed was politically unthreatening. It was 'purely a spiritual existence transcending all names and forms'. Ramanathan employed marriage metaphors to describe it – 'the kingdom of God is like a marriage, or union of the Soul with God, God being the bridegroom and the Soul the bride'.[45] He wrote of 'an energy of obedience to the spiritual guide'.[46] The Kingdom that Jesus declared did not have any social significance and it was not to be established on earth but primarily to be realized internally.

In Paul, Ramanathan found a fellow Saiva stalwart. He perceived him as a religious genius and a 'veteran who warred triumphantly against error and illusion'.[47] He was the one who carried to the extreme some of Jesus's teachings and had the boldness to say to his readers that 'Christ [was] the end of the Law' and that they had been 'delivered from the laws'. Paul, along with the masters of India, enunciated the principles of the Kingdom of God. Like Jesus, Paul was free from Jewish nationalism and lacked any strong ethnic feeling. Ramanathan informed his readers that Paul's references to Jewish people should not be taken literally but symbolically, referring to those who 'were circumcised in heart out of regard for spirituality'.[48]

Jesus and Paul, in Ramanathan's formulation, come across as persons who distanced themselves from the idea of Jewish exceptionalism so ingrained in the consciousness of their people. Jesus and Paul proved to be willing recruits for Ramanathan's hermeneutical agenda of dispensing the message to those who already had a smidgen of spirituality.

Ramanathan reframed Jesus and Paul as Saiva *Jananis* of ancient India who preached the doctrine of true life – God in his immeasurable mercy, sympathetic to the bondage of souls in corruption, did not permit them to wallow in that awful state but invested in each soul instruments of knowledge and action which enabled them to pass from sensuousness to spirituality. This is not the Jesus or Paul constructed by the historical-critical method but figures who came straight out of mystical interpretation. Ramanathan represented Jesus and Paul as idealized versions of Saiva *jnanis*, and as with Saiva *jnanis*, the spiritual vision of Jesus and Paul was introverted and subjective.

Be Like a Saivite and be Saved

Frederic Farrar, the Dean of Canterbury, stated near the end of the nineteenth century that 'The Bible is a book of Eastern origin, and can only be understood by the methods of Eastern literature.'[49] In the theological ecosystem of the time, the 'Eastern' that Farrar had in mind were the Near Eastern nations like Assyria, Babylon, Egypt and Persia. He wouldn't have imagined that a year after he had published his book, a Sri Lankan would bring out the full force of the Eastern Vedic and Saiva literature to illuminate and rescue the Bible for Western Christians.

Ramanathan's interpretative work was undertaken at a time when the Scriptures were perceived as spiritual depositories. They were regarded as suitable instruments for humanity to unite with the divine, transcending their worldly existence and experiencing a higher spiritual consciousness. While most of the missionaries in Jaffna subscribed to every detail of the Bible, Ramanathan understood its mythical and allegorical appeal. He perceived it as flexible and adaptable rather than a set of archaic rules and literal truths that had to be believed. Like a true Saivite, Ramanathan held to the belief that studying the Scriptures alone would not enable a disciple to achieve enlightenment and that the shastras were not a substitute for the experience. He wanted to wean Christianity from its muscular tendencies and discern its mystical bearings.

His approach abandoned the uncommitted neutrality of the interpreter celebrated by modernism, and introduced theological pre-understandings into the process of grasping the meaning of a text. In a sense, his commentaries were a prototype for theologically constructed expositions, in contrast to the earlier commentaries which had focused on dry philological and historical questions. His biblical explanations prefigured Karl Barth's celebrated commentary on Romans, published in 1919, which set the tone for theologically-driven biblical elucidations. His textual analysis was decidedly influenced by his theological interest, which he, unlike modern exegetes, openly admitted.

Ramanathan was unashamedly an elitist both in his hermeneutical and pietistic activities. He limited the interpretation of traditions to those few who had found Christ within their hearts and 'cleansed their consciousness of every trace of worldliness and made their souls as radiant and pure, as "godly," as Jesus' was'. This restriction of interpretation to the few was seen as the 'essential condition of faithful discipleship'.[50] Ramanathan was even more stringent about the amount of truth that should be imparted to those who were who were ripe enough to hear it. Citing Isaiah, he advised that the message should be given 'here a little, there a little', contingent upon the 'intellectual and spiritual' assimilating power of an individual. Invoking Pauline metaphors – 'milk' or 'strong meat' – he suggested that the way the truth should be impartated depended upon one's spiritual status and needs: 'Esoteric truths cannot be imparted to all alike in the same way, but only in ways suitable to each person, for fear that the information conveyed may take the person further away from the goal than he is already.'[51] In other words, the message of Jesus was not for the masses. *Jnanis*, like Jesus, exert their influence only on those individuals when they 'perceive a certain ripeness of the soul',[52] marked by the renunciation of the pleasures of the world and a generous preference towards the interests of others.

Just as interpretation was the exclusive enclave of the few, Ramanathan believed that suffrage was the entitlement of the upper caste alone. He opposed the Donoughmore Commission recommendation of a universal franchise for Sri Lanka and wanted to limit voting rights to the high caste Vellala Tamil men, contending that extending these privileges to women and non-Vellala would lead to mob rule and be 'anathema to the Hindu way of life'. 'The universal suffrage,' he wrote, 'in the hands of the two million of uneducated, undisciplined and reckless people will be the ruin of Ceylon.'[53] One person, one vote – a sacred principle of modern democracy – was, in the words of his obeisant biographer, 'abhorrent' to Ramanathan. The Tamil cause he claimed to have championed, too, was limited to the high-caste Tamils.

Ramanathan's biblical works were an endeavour to make the Gospel teaching corroborate Siddhantha ideals and reconfigure the Gospel as part of Saivism. His goal, as far as the Gospel was concerned, was to absorb it, reinterpret it and make it part of the Hindu system. The way he appropriated Matthew and John's Gospels for his Saiva cause meant that these two Semitic texts almost became two more additions to Meykander's selection of approved Saiva canonical texts.

There is an implicit acknowledgement of the superiority of the Hindu Scriptures in Ramanathan's writings: 'The final or eternal truths' were 'known in the *Vedas* as *Vedanta* and in the *Agamas* as *Saiva Siddhanta*',[54] and it was these books which 'impart a full knowledge of those principles and practices which result in the actual attainment of God'. [55] In correlation with this is the unspoken affirmation that the only religion at present capable of imparting principles and practices which could result in the realization of God was Saivism.

Ramanathan found the Western perception of Christianity to be largely objective and not sufficiently subjective. For this reason, the West had idealized and sacramentalized Jesus instead of truly understanding him. Western thinking had habitually been preoccupied with external and extraneous pegs – an inspired book, an idealized person, or burdensome doctrines – all of which it had to give up to realize the divine within oneself.

Ramanathan's message was simple – spiritual enlightenment is not something one can attain or seize in the external world. It is not knowledge per se, but rather an experience which one had to realize within. Sainthood or Christhood is not a doctrine to be studied but something one should realize in one's life. An ideal saint or Christ has to achieve two things – detachment and the manifestation of the divine. This actualization of saintliness does not mean withdrawing from the mundane affairs of the world or turning away from social relationships, but remaining dispassionate in the world and transcending petty self-interest. In his lecture tour of America, Ramanathan offered Paul-like advice to his audience: 'Adorn worldly life with every comfort, convenience, and luxury, but do not quench the spirit.'⁵⁶ The world, in his view, ceased to have meaning unless we were prepared to vest some spiritual meaning in the seemingly material aspects of our lives.

Ramanathan is part of the long list of Hindu thinkers who initiated and contributed to Christian theological thinking in the subcontinent. His writings demonstrate his vast range of reading of Western literature and his knowledge of biblical languages. He belonged to a group of Eastern thinkers like Rammohun Roy, Keshub Chunder Sen and Swami Vivekananda who had broad convictions about the West at the height of colonialism. Just like them, Ramanathan was not afraid to unleash erudite righteousness against the decadent West. As he put it in his own forceful way, the West had manifestly embraced 'worldliness, materialism, irreverence, and atheism'[57] and was in need of spiritual enlightenment. The Indian spirituality he championed was like the one championed by Indian reformers of the time – imprecise and indistinct.

Just like other Indians, Ramanathan held the view that Western Christians had completely misunderstood the 'spiritual meanings of the doctrines of Jesus,'[58] had made the Bible a 'discredited book' and had become incapable of interpreting their own Scriptures. As such, he arrogantly assumed that only Eastern sages had the spiritual acuteness to rectify these Western weaknesses. As the West had lost 'the unwritten traditional interpretation of the words of Jesus', the only means of restoring the 'spirit' or the true meaning of the words of the Bible was to seek guidance from the Indian sages. They were the only people who could secure the true meaning of the words of the Bible. Ramanathan called them the '"able ministers" from the *East who are now living, and on whom the effulgence of His grace has been shed*'.[59] Indian sages had the advantage because Indian culture had survived many upheavals almost intact because it had got the balance correct between materiality and spirituality whereas all other ancient cultures had perished. Ramanathan further asserted that the 'Spirit of the East is alive unto God' and the East had a 'duty' which it owed to itself and to the living God it served 'not to allow the treasures of the world which moth and rust doth corrupt, to multiply themselves beyond a certain limit and deceive man unto perdition'.[60] While the West knew of 'only one Christ', India knew 'scores in each generation, busy saving seekers from the perils of atheism and materialism, and leading them to God'.[61] They were the *jivanmuktas* (the Liberated Ones) or *jannis* (Knowers of God), the anointed of God – and there were many of them. These were the people whose authority did not rest on the 'historical and literal problems' relating to the books of the Bible, but who relied on their own spiritual enlightenment. They were the experienced ones and 'experience indeed is the touchstone of interpretation'.[62] Ramanathan's fervent hope was that these Eastern *jnanis* would restore to Western nations the 'Key of Knowledge' (Lk. 11.52), the true teachings of Jesus, just as the ancient sages of Judea had done.

Ramanathan imagined himself to be a modern day *jnani* who had the inherited power to provide spiritual instruction to America. In recalling his purpose in visiting the United States, he made a lofty claim that bordered on haughtiness, contending that Americans had not understood the sayings of Jesus and other biblical masters, and that he 'could give them a more satisfactory exposition' than they already had.[63] In his lecture at Brooklyn, Ramanathan quoted Matthew

Arnold who had said that those in the West wanted a ' a *clue* to some sound order and authority'.[64] He assured his American audience that such a clue, which could guide the West away from the mazes of the worldly towards a Godly existence, was to be found not in the Christian Bible but in the oral and the written teachings enunciated by the sages of India in the Vedanta and Siddhanta Shastras. These venerable texts provided a 'great sphere of education in which the soul (*jicama*) is the learner (*Sisya*), and God (*Isvara*) is the teacher'. The lesson the soul has to learn was that it is in bondage to corruption (*malam* or *avidya*) and should break away and attain true freedom (*moksha*).[65]

In Ramanathan's hands, the Scriptures do not call to account the individual or those in power. The Gospel's dissenting views about justice, compassion and loving the stranger and even an enemy were not brought to bear on everyday existence. The Bible was commended for its utility in solving both the spiritual needs of the individual and civilizational questions faced by the advanced West and the static East. While Ramanathan was expounding lofty spiritual truths to the Western rich, he had nothing to offer to the marginalized and those who were left outside. He maintained that simple money-giving was neither a cure nor a balm for the suffering. He urged the rich that, instead of writing cheques, they should give themselves to the poor in order to 'get more in spirit, in light and love'. The poor were only there so that the rich could improve their spiritual prowess. He had good news only for the rich.

Traditionalists will find fault with Ramanathan on a number of counts. He does not let the text speak for itself – a misleading ideal that conservatives hold on to. He imposes his own predetermined theological views, which tend to obstruct the text. Those who hold to the dominant traditional view that the Gospel message was supersessionist will be appalled by his lack of differentiation between the message of the testaments, acknowledging no historical linkage or unity. His writings do not subscribe to the view that the dry legalism and the vengeful God of the Hebrew Scriptures were replaced by a loving and forgiving God. For him, the sages, whether Judean or Indian, were repeating the same message heard from the beginning.

Ramanathan showed a refreshing curiosity and an eagerness to explore different scriptural traditions, but at the same time was a hardcore champion of reactionary social and political causes. Imperious, prudish and unashamedly misogynist and a strict believer in social hierarchy, he started schools for women not to produce leaders but to encourage them to become good Hindu housewives. He condemned the intermingling of higher and lower castes at Kopay Training College. The combination of the individualism of Saivism and social conservatism led him to passionately support conventional social norms.

Ramanathan's biblical expositions became so famous that there were some obsequious American admirers who testified that he had given them back their Bible and made it 'an inexpressible help and inspiration and source of consolation'.[66] These enthusiastic Western reviews were reproduced in Ramanathan's books and published in leading erudite periodicals such as the *Hibbert Journal* and newspapers like the *Manchester Guardian*. His greatest cheerleader was the American Myron Phelps. Back at home the reception was not so frenzied.

Ramanathan's exegetical works were found wanting on two counts: one, his overtly obsessive reading of Saiva concepts into biblical texts, and second, his awkward translations. A. J. Appasamy, the first properly trained Indian biblical scholar, whose doctoral dissertation on John was supervised by B. H. Streeter in Oxford in the 1920s, blamed Ramanathan for reading too much Indian meaning into a text which originated in 'another land and in a different environment' and for going 'against the fundamental laws of historical criticism'.[67] Ironically, Appasamy committed the same crime when he employed the bhakti tradition to read the fourth Gospel. Likewise, Robin Boyd, a pioneer in unearthing the theological writings of Indians, dismissed the commentaries of Ramanathan as breaching the 'permissible methods of Scriptural exegesis'.[68] Boyd made two erroneous statements: that Ramanathan was an Indian and that he was influenced by Vivekananda's *advaita*. Ramanathan's casual attitude to his cherished Christian doctrines was too much for a person like Boyd, raised on a steady diet of Barth's neo-liberal theology.

Substantial criticism came from Gnana Prakasar, a formidable Roman Catholic bishop in Jaffna. He pointed out that the idea of *kaivalya* (aloneness) was quite foreign to Saiva Siddhantha and did not mean, as suggested by Ramanathan, 'isolation of the spirit from worldliness'. It was unwise to associate it with the New Testament word *monogenes*, which meant 'the only begotten'.[69]

Ramanathan was not hostile to missionaries but what troubled him was their hermeneutical hubris. He referred to them as ignorant divines and criticized their 'arrogant assurance' that they 'knew all about God and his ways'.[70] Like all Hindus, he was clearly concerned that the missionaries' proselytization went too far. He was also aware of the dangers of Hindu children losing what he called their 'ancestral faith' in Christian schools. In spite of these reservations, Ramanathan appreciated the benefits of the good English education imparted by the missionaries. He not only donated to Christian schools, but as a member of the Legislative Council also supported grant applications from these schools whenever they came before the Council. He urged his fellow Hindus to join hands with the missionaries 'for the glorification of the one and the same God who is to be found within the pure souls of all human beings'.[71]

Ramanathan's nationalism and patriotism were expressed through being a loyal British subject. His relentless attack on Western materialism did not translate into anti-colonial resistance. He blamed the West for its 'selfish mercantile principles' and its worship of wealth, but in none of his writings did he censure the British for their imperialism and exploitation. While his contemporary, Anagarika Dharmapala – the controversial Buddhist revivalist in the South –profitably mined Buddhism to whip up nationalism, Ramanathan, a knight of the empire, placed his faith in the British and in their sense of fair play. He castigated the West for its accumulation of material goods but not for its predatory colonial ambitions.

Ramanathan gave unequivocal support to Theodore Herzl's idea of establishing a Jewish state or homeland. But the Jerusalem he had in mind had pure Ramanathan written all over it. Jerusalem was not an objective geographical region to which the lost tribes of Israel return, but rather an idealized site – an inner site – a spirit within oneself. He told the Boston Zionist Association that the attainment of the geographical Jerusalem was good, but better still was the realization of the Jerusalem within, by turning away from the tribal attachment to seek God internally, thereby spiritualizing the idea of Jerusalem. In other words, for the Jewish existential problem he offered a Saivite solution – finding God within oneself. As he always insisted, 'the greatest of all discoveries' is 'the discovery of God in the soul'.[72]

Ramanathan could be accused of being one of those upper-class pompous reformers who believed that they could bring about meaningful change by offering a simple message of inner spiritual regeneration without truly understanding the problems of everyday quotidian life. He urged his people to give up worldly possessions and attachments, and reduced the Gospel to austere living, which could lead to hardship for ordinary people who were feeling the weight of the empire. Ramanathan himself was not above a spot of worldliness. He was sustained by his parental fortune, had servants and lived in spacious houses. He delivered the virtues of austere living to American audiences in a costume characteristically his own – 'crowned with a gold laced white turban'.[73] His message of ritual-free, inner spirituality looks hollow when he renovated the temple his father built at an enormous cost to fit in with the Saiva canonical texts.

In contrast to his Jaffna Hindu compatriots, such as C. W. Tāmōtaram Piḷḷai and Muthukumāracuvāmi Piḷḷai, who dismissed the Bible as duplicitous and shallow, Ramanathan treated the Gospel writers as theological interpreters of considerable subtlety and distinctiveness. Instead of rejecting the Bible, he embraced it and made it accommodate Saiva doctrines. He even encouraged, as we saw earlier, those Christians who were spiritually lost to study their own text as the quickest way to grasp the truth. He also made it easier for the Saivites to find their own Saiva teachings in the Bible.

A Christian may not find his or her faith enunciated in Ramanathan's biblical writings. His approach might have been idiosyncratic, but he was never disparaging about the biblical religion. This was in contrast to the missionary literature of the time in Jaffna, which denounced and defamed Hindu texts and their faith. His biblical writings were equally about the redemption of the West and the superiority of Saiva spirituality. Ramanathan's message to the West was very clear and in total contrast to that which the missionaries had been directing against the good people of Jaffna: become great again by becoming more like us – meaning, like Saivites.

Notes

1 M. Vythilingam, *The Life of Sir Ponnambalm Ramanathan in Two Volumes*, vol. 1 (London: Ramanathan Commemoration Society, 1971), 511.
2 R. Līlāvati, *Western Pictures for Eastern Students: Being a description of the chief Incidents of a journey made by that distinguished scholar, statesman, and sage, from Ceylon to the United States of America in 1905-1906* (London: W. Thacker & Co., 1907), 237.
3 Ponnambalam Ramanathan, *The Gospel of Jesus According to St. Matthew as interpreted to R. L. Harrison by the light of the Godly experience of Sri Parananda* (London: Kegan Paul, Trench, Trübner & Co. Ltd, 1898).

4   Ponnambalam Ramanathan, *An Eastern Exposition of the Gospel of Jesus according to John being an interpretation thereof by Sri Parananda*, ed. R. L. Harrison (London: William Hutchinson & Co., 1902).
5   Saiva Siddhantha is the philosophy of the Saiva religion, one of the major traditions within Hinduism. Its central doctrine is that the Sivan is the Supreme Reality, and that the Jiva (individual soul) is of the same essence as Sivan, but not identical, thus running counter to the *advaita* advocated by Sankara. Siddhanta means the final conclusion (reached after taking into consideration all other important views). Tamil Saiva Sithaantham is different from Kashmiri Saivism or Vira Saivism. It is a philosophical system based on Saiva Agamas and ancient Tamil works consisting of devotional books like *Thirumurais, Tevarams Tiruvacakam* and philosophical works like *Sivajnanabodham* and Meykanda *Sastram*. These works are held up as supreme and on a par with Sanskrit sacred texts. For an easy-to-read introduction, see Thomas Thangaraj, *The Crucified Guru: An Experiment in Cross-cultural Christology* (Nashville, TN: Abingdon Press, 1994), 35–58. The earlier works of V. Paranjoti, *Saiva Siddhanta* (n.p.p.: Luzac and Co. Ltd, 1954) and John H. Piet, *A Logical Presentation of the Śaiva Siddhanta Philosophy* (Madras: Christian Literature Society of India, 1952) are also worth having a look at.
6   Vythilingam, *The Life of Sir Ponnambalm Ramanathan*, vol. 1, 19.
7   A Jeyaratnam Wilson, *Sri Lanka Tamil Nationalism: Its Origin and Development in the 19th and 20th centuries* (London: Hurst and & Company, 2000/1981), 58.
8   Ponnambalam Ramanathan, *The Spirit of the East Contrasted with the Spirit of the West, being a Lecture Delivered by Ponnambalam Ramanathan, K.C., C.M.G. before the Brooklyn Institute of Arts of Arts and Sciences at its Opening Meeting of the Season of 1905–1906* (New York: G. P. Putnam's Sons, 1905), 20.
9   Ponnambalam Ramanathan, *The Culture of the Soul among Western Nations* (New York: G. P. Putnam's Sons, 1906), 140.
10 Ponnambalam Ramanathan, 'The Miscarriage of Life in the West', *Hibbert Journal* 7 (1909): 7.
11 Ramanathan, *The Culture of the Soul among Western Nations*, 73. Emphasis in the original.
12 Ramanathan, *The Spirit of the East Contrasted with the Spirit of the West*, 20.
13 The Ramanathan–Harrison relationship is akin to that of Karl Barth and Charlotte von Kirschbaum. It was Charlotte who assisted Barth in producing his monumental *Dogmatics*. See his preface in *Church Dogmatics: The Doctrine of Creation*, vol. 3, Part 3.
14 Ramanathan, *An Eastern Exposition of the Gospel of Jesus according to John*, 299.
15 Ramanathan, *The Culture of the Soul among Western Nations*, 225.
16 Ramanathan, *The Culture of the Soul among Western Nations*, 197.
17 Ramanathan, *An Eastern Exposition of the Gospel of Jesus according to John*, 4. Emphasis in the original.
18 Ramanathan, *An Eastern Exposition of the Gospel of Jesus according to John*, 2. Emphasis in the original.
19 Ramanathan, *An Eastern Exposition of the Gospel of Jesus according to John*, 5.
20 Ramanathan, *The Culture of the Soul among Western Nations*, 137.
21 Ramanathan, *The Gospel of Jesus According to St. Matthew*, 114.
22 Ramanathan, *The Gospel of Jesus According to St. Matthew*, 114.
23 Ramanathan, *The Gospel of Jesus According to St. Matthew*, 113.
24 Ramanathan, *The Gospel of Jesus According to St. Matthew*, 171.
25 Ramanathan, *The Culture of the Soul among Western Nations*, 188.
26 Ramanathan, *The Culture of the Soul among Western Nation*, 171.
27 Ramanathan, *An Eastern Exposition of the Gospel of Jesus according to John*, 132.

28 Ramanathan, *An Eastern Exposition of the Gospel of Jesus according to John*, 34
29 Ramanathan, *The Culture of the Soul among Western Nations*, 210.
30 Ramanathan, *The Culture of the Soul among Western Nations*, 97.
31 Ramanathan, *An Eastern Exposition of the Gospel of Jesus according to John*, 34.
32 Ramanathan, *The Gospel of Jesus According to St. Matthew*, 70.
33 Ramanathan, *The Gospel of Jesus According to St. Matthew*, 176.
34 Lilavati, Western *Pictures for Eastern Students*, 120.
35 Ramanathan, *The Culture of the Soul among Western Nations*, 156.
36 Ramanathan, *The Gospel of Jesus According to St. Matthew*, 177.
37 Ramanathan, *The Gospel of Jesus According to St. Matthew*, 93.
38 Ramanathan, *An Eastern Exposition of the Gospel of Jesus according to John*, 116.
39 Ramanathan, *The Gospel of Jesus According to St. Matthew*, 134. Emphasis in the original.
40 Ramanathan, *The Gospel of Jesus According to St. Matthew*, 82.
41 Ramanathan, *The Gospel of Jesus According to St. Matthew*, 112.
42 Ramanathan, *The Spirit of the East Contrasted with the Spirit of the West*, 20.
43 *Siddhānta Dīpikā* 10, no. 11 (May 1910): 512.
44 For a longer version of Ramanathan's portrayals of Jesus, see R. S. Sugirtharajah, *Jesus in Asia* (Cambridge, MA: Harvard University Press, 2018), 67–94.
45 Ramanathan, *The Gospel of Jesus According to St. Matthew*, 221.
46 Ramanathan, *The Gospel of Jesus According to St. Matthew*, 222.
47 Ramanathan, *The Spirit of the East Contrasted with the Spirit of the West*, 14.
48 Ramanathan, *An Eastern Exposition of the Gospel of Jesus according to John*, 92.
49 F. W. Farrar, *The Bible: Its Meaning and Supremacy* (London: Longmans, Green and Co, 1897), 242.
50 Ramanathan, *The Culture of the Soul among Western Nations*, 49.
51 Ramanathan, *The Gospel of Jesus According to St. Matthew*, 24.
52 Ramanathan, *The Gospel of Jesus According to St. Matthew*, 35.
53 Ponnambalm Ramanathan, *The Memorandum of Sir Ponnambalm Ramanathan on the recommendations of the Donoughmore commissioners appointed by the Right Honourable Secretary of State for the Colonies, to report upon the Reform of the existing constitution of the Government of Ceylon* (London: Vacher & Sons, 1930), 17.
54 Ramanathan, *The Culture of the Soul among Western Nations*, 125. Emphasis in the original.
55 Ramanathan, *The Culture of the Soul among Western Nations*, 126.
56 Vythilingam, *The Life of Sir Ponnambalm Ramanathan*, vol. 1, 518.
57 Ramanathan, *The Culture of the Soul among Western Nations*, 73.
58 Ramanathan, *The Culture of the Soul among Western Nations*, 67.
59 Ramanathan, *The Culture of the Soul among Western Nations*, 81. Emphasis in the original.
60 Ramanathan, *The Spirit of the East Contrasted with the Spirit of the West*, 28.
61 Ramanathan, *The Culture of the Soul among Western Nations*, 81.
62 Ramanathan, *The Culture of the Soul among Western Nations*, 38.
63 Vythilingam, *The Life of Sir Ponnambalm Ramanathan*, vol. 1, 532.
64 Ramanathan, *The Spirit of the East Contrasted with the Spirit of the West*, 18. Emphasis in the original.
65 Ramanathan, *The Spirit of the East Contrasted with the Spirit of the West*, 19.
66 Vythilingam, *The Life of Sir Ponnambalm Ramanathan*, vol. 1, 522.
67 A. J. Appasamy, *Christianity as Bhakti Marga: A Study of the Johannine Doctrine of Love* (Madras: Christian Literature Society, 1926), 19.
68 R. H. S. Boyd, 'The Use of the Bible in Indian Christian Theology', *Indian Journal of Theology* 22, no. 4 (1974): 146.

69 N. M. Saverimuttu, 'Relations between Roman Catholics and Hindus in Jaffna, 1900–1926: A Study of Religious Encounter', PhD thesis, University of London, 1978, 132
70 Vythilingam, *The Life of Sir Ponnambalm Ramanathan*, vol. 1, 533.
71 Vythilingam, *The Life of Sir Ponnambalm Ramanathan*, vol. 1, 254
72 Ramanathan, *The Culture of the Soul among Western Nations*, 212.
73 T. Muttucumaru, *Sir Ponnambalam Ramanathan, Kt., K.C., C.M.G., All-Ceylon Leader and Educational Seer* (Jaffna: Saiva Manakaiyar Sabai, 1961), 11.

Chapter 5

A WORLD-RENOUNCING GOSPEL

The year was 1886. In a suburb of colonial Calcutta, a venerable sage was dying of cancer. His devotees were at his side. His constant thought was what would become of these ardent followers after his demise. He was suffering intensely and couldn't speak. So, he scrawled on a piece of paper the following words: 'Narendra will teach others.'[1] This was seen to be a passing-on of the mantle of management of the 'great spiritual empire' which he had built by conquering two treacherous invaders – lust and gold. Earlier, he had told this precociously spiritual child, 'I leave them to your care.'[2] The sage was Sri Ramakrishna Paramahamsa, his chosen successor, Narendra, or to give him his full name, Narendranath Datta. This Narendra would later be known to the world as Swami Vivekananda (1863–1902). When this quasi-anointing took place, he was only twenty-three years old.[3]

Colonial Calcutta used to produce spiritual luminaries just as the Indian cinema is wont to manufacture blockbuster heroes. Vivekananda was one such saint-in-waiting. His master saw him as a 'nitya-siddha, perfect in realization even from his birth'.[4] His father, a famous high court lawyer, wanted him to follow his profession. But the son had other ideas. His education and the vibrant culture of Calcutta forced him to seek out his own philosophy. Faced with a mixture of opinions which ranged from strict orthodoxy to meaningless rebellion against ancient traditions and to the agnosticism of the Western variety of rationalism espoused by Herbert Spencer, he was on an intellectual and spiritual quest. He tried Brahmo Samaj, which at that was time examining its own teachings, and worse, was beset with quarrelsome leaders. In a fortuitous meeting with Ramakrishna, he found a guru who changed his life, and for that matter, Hindu India.

The mention of Vivekananda immediately conjures up a turban-clad sannyasin and his speech at the 1893 World Congress of Religions in Chicago. Even if Vivekananda had not done anything else in his life, this speech alone would have ensured a lasting legacy for him. In his address, he looked at America through his version of a spiritual India and offered a devastating critique of Western materialism. One hundred years after this visit, another Narendra went to America. Unlike the earlier Narendra who had critiqued America from his invented Hindu spirituality, offering it as a deliverance from the decadent West, the later Narendra viewed India through the prism of the sybaritic Silicon Valley and persuaded the Indian middle class to imbibe its capitalist corporate world values. A Trumpian style self-publicist, Vivekananda lectured to large audiences in India and abroad. If reality TV had existed at that time, he and Keshub would have had their own show.

A Veiled Vedanta: Fitting the Scriptures

Although Vivekananda's work largely involved the exposition of Advaita Vedanta, the Bible remained an inescapable part of his hermeneutical world. Sadly, Anantanand Rambachan's admirable work on Vivekananda's use of the Scriptures does not feature Vivekananda's considerable references to biblical texts.[5] As the writings of Roy and Keshub have shown, these Hindu thinkers were not only interacting with the Bible – thanks to their colonial education – but were also addressing an audience well-versed in the biblical stories and its traditions.

Vivekananda's Bible knowledge was considerable, ranging from something as trivial as identifying (erroneously) the colour of Solomon to be same as that of Krishna, to something as important as the division between the houses of Israel and Ephraim and their different theologies and temples. The Bible suited his Hindu ideals, especially as it could be counted on to reinforce Advaitic philosophy, Hindu ideas of renunciation, reincarnation and devotion to God as a servant (*dâsya bhakti*), or as a master, spirituality, or the pre-existence and transmigration of souls, and the Bhagavad Gita's spirit of complete self-surrender. Vivekananda perceived the Bible as embodying Hindu values, chiefly ascetic values and saw no difference between what he understood to be the religion of the Bible and the teachings of Advaita.

Among the biblical books, Vivekananda's favoured one was the Song of Solomon, which he considered one of the 'most beautiful parts of the Bible'.[6] Invoking the gender binaries that men are philosophical and analytical whereas women are devotional and emotional, he found the language of the book to be affectionate and akin to the spiritual outpourings and prayers of countless Hindu women saints. Unlike the conventional interpretation which viewed the Song of Solomon as a prophecy symbolizing Christ's love for the Church as his bride, Vivekananda's regarded the book to be about a woman's 'wonderous love' for God, couched in a demonstrative language which came from her heart and not from her mind. His interpretation was reminiscent of the third-century theologian and biblical scholar Origen's reading of the book as that soul's longing for God, rather than the eschatological union between Christ and his bride, the Church. The 'frenzy of religious fervour' and 'extreme emotions' found in this poetry, he pointed out, was challenging for people who were reared in a country where the thermometer reads 40 degrees below zero. It was this type of extremely emotional love of God, he claimed, that was found in India. What this book indicated was that the 'absence of the thought of self is the essential characteristic of the love for God'.[7] Even in this sapiential literature, Vivekananda was able to detect the ideal of self-abnegation which he avidly promoted. Another reason he liked the book, which he never explicitly stated, might have been the absence of stock features of the Hebrew Scriptures – the God of Israel, the law, the Covenant and patriarchal history.

Like most of the Bengali reformers, Vivekananda, regarded the Bible as an Oriental book. The following quote from him could have been written by Keshub:

> All the similes, the imageries, in which the Bible is written – the scenes, the locations, the attitudes, the groups, the poetry, and symbols – speak to you of the Orient: of the bright sky, of the heat, of the sun, of the desert, of the thirsty men and animals; of men and women coming with pitchers on their heads to fill them at the wells; of the flocks, of the ploughmen, of the cultivation that is going on around; of the water-mill and wheel, of the mill-pond, of the mill-stones – all these are to be seen today in Asia.[8]

A biblical story which exemplified and reinforced Oriental characteristics was the Story of the Woman at the Well. Vivekananda was enchanted by it because of the idyllic image of village India it presented – a woman coming to draw from a well, a 'monk' asking for water and doing a 'little mind-reading', she being taught by him and going back to the village to talk about the new mendicant preacher. Vivekananda called it an 'Indian story' depicting 'Indian life'.[9]

For Vivekananda, the Bible was a battleground between different Jewish tribes who vied with each other to establish their god as supreme. One of Vivekananda's examples of this struggle was how Moloch-Yahweh, who was the god of the tribe called Israel, conquered and destroyed other deities and was declared to be the Supreme Moloch of all the Molochs. He reminded the audience of the amount of bloodshed, tyranny and brutal savagery that was a consequence of these religious conquests. He was aware of a similar struggle in India, but that it was the 'great good fortune of this country and of the world' that amidst this confusion there was a saner voice which declared, 'That which exists is One; sages call It by various names.' It was this pluralistic approach that enabled various sects to live in harmony.

Vivekananda viewed the Bible as a depository of progressive and graded spirituality akin to that of Vedic teaching appropriate for people at various stages in their faith journey. One of the claims of Hindu reformers was the capacity of Hinduism to cater to different spiritual needs. Vivekananda perceived a similar quality in the Bible. Just as a Hindu goes through different phases before he or she reaches unity and identity with Brahman, Vivekananda claimed that Bible also offered a gradual process. Initially, the masses were taught something tangible to take hold of, and then were slowly led to the 'highest ideal'. Vivekananda provided the most appropriate sayings of Jesus, naturally quoting out of context to support his wildly contentious claims. For the 'masses' who could not conceive of a personal God, Jesus taught them, 'Pray to your father in heaven.' But for those who were slightly more advanced spiritually, Jesus assured them, 'I am the vine, ye are the branches.' But to those who had reached spiritual maturity, Jesus offered a 'more elevated teaching',[10] proclaiming the highest advaitic truth: 'I and my Father are One.' Vivekananda saw in the teachings of the Bible a gradation similar to the one that led a disciple through the stages of *dvaita* (dualism) to *Visistadvaita* (Qualified Non-dualism) and ultimately to *advaita* (non-duality). For Vivekananda, the Bible was a book which embodied suitable spirituality for all, from the masses to mature disciples.

In spite of making grand statements about the Bible, Vivekananda had a condescending attitude towards it. He accorded a low status to the Christian text and ranked it along with the Hindu *puranas* – literature consisting of legends, myths and folklore. There are eighteen *puranas* which are viewed as having lesser standing than the Vedas. These *puranas* are largely about Hindu gods, thus reducing the status of the Christian Bible to a book of one of the Gods, albeit a Christian God. His designation of the Bible as *puranas* was based on two of his hermeneutical judgements: first, like the *puranas*, the Bible contained historical details, and second, unlike the Vedas, the Christian texts were human-made. Christian Scriptures were *puranas* because they dealt with historical matters rather than principles. The Bible, or, for that matter, Buddhist Scriptures record the stories of the flood and histories of kings and ruling dynasties, and document and record the lives of 'great men'. 'This', Vivekananda, claimed is 'the work of the Puranas'.[11] As long as the Scriptures of other nations which have moral teachings in them comply with the Vedas, they are 'perfectly good', but when they disagree they have 'the authority of the Puranas, but no more'.[12]

The Bible, for Vivekananda, was a mimetic text – a reproduction of various sources ranging from the surrounding cultures to those of South Asia. He felt that the Bible, in spite of the inflated claims made by the missionaries, was nothing 'but a collection of little bits of Indian thought', a 'very, patchy imitation'[13] with 'a few doctrines of the Advaita ... grafted' upon it.[14] Echoing the newly emerging History of Religions School viewpoint, he stated that the Bible was a composition of theological ideas borrowed from Middle Eastern countries. The ideas of the soul, of life after death and of Satan exclusive to Persian religion found their way into the Bible. Other borrowings included Babylonian cosmology and flood narratives which had been 'incorporated wholesale into the Bible'.[15] Vivekananda alleged that the foundation of these civilizations could be traced back to the Sumerians who were impacted by the Tamils of South India.[16] He boldly pronounced that 'almost all Christianity was Aryan' and that 'Indian and Egyptian ideas met at Alexandria and went forth to the world, tinctured with Judaism and Hellenism, as Christianity.'[17] Thus, in positing biblical narratives as borrowed and incorporated from various traditions, Vivekananda drained the Bible of its authority and weakened the superior status claimed for it by Christians.

The biblical texts provided the sources to expose the hypocritical position of Christian missionaries and to draw attention to texts in the Bible which resembled Indian texts, but which were ridiculed by the missionaries. When the missionaries denounced images of deities, Vivekananda, like Navalar though not as nuanced or devastating as the Jaffna thinker, was able to expose their double standards. When Hindu idols came under attack, his biblical learning enabled him to note that the Jerusalem temple built by the Israelites had an image of Yahweh consisting of male and female figures preserved in an ark and a big phallic column at the door. In Ephraim, he informed his readers, Yahweh was worshipped in the form of a gold-covered bull. One can detect a sarcastic tone in the following lines, of which Navalar would have approved:

If God is represented in any beautiful form or any symbolic form, said the Jew, it is awfully bad; it is sin. But if He is represented in the form of a chest, with two angels sitting on each side, and a cloud hanging over it, it is the holy of holies. If God comes in the form of a dove, it is holy.[18]

Vivekananda found the Bible unsuitable for those raised with different desires and goals. Whereas in the East, people aspired to the lofty ideals of austere and frugal living, those in the West adored wealth and prosperity. He claimed that the books of the Bible were sharply at variance with the aspirations of the 'cold-blooded Western nations', who were more 'apt to worship the almighty dollar'. Their love for God and their prayers were tainted by a selfish attitude and selfish requests.

Like most of the Hindu interpreters, Vivekananda did not hesitate to correct biblical doctrines and offer alternatives based on Advaita. One such doctrine was that of original sin. He felt, on the whole, that the Christian tradition placed excessive emphasis on human depravity and sinfulness. Unlike Augustine, who spoke of everyone being born of sin, Vivekananda insisted on the Advaita understanding of the inherent purity of the *âtmân*. This view was consistent with Irenaeus' notion of sin as a human failure to be perfect rather than a falling away from past glories, as orthodox theology asserted: 'When Adam fell, he fell from purity. Purity is our real nature and to regain that is the object of all religion.'[19] The first human being, in Vivekananda's view, was 'pure' and 'perfect' and although this purity was destroyed by evil deeds, the Bible shows the possibility, nay, the certainty, of reclaiming that original state: 'This is the whole history of the Bible, Old and New Testaments together.'[20] His view was that 'The Perfect never becomes imperfect.'[21]

Vivekananda acknowledged that human beings and religions need a book, and that despite the rise of rationalism, humanity was still attached to religious texts. He dismissed the Bible, the Vedas and the Koran as 'only words, external arrangement, syntax, the etymology, the philology, the dry bones of religion'.[22] Since he accorded a secondary role to Scriptures, he did not consider it important to gain sufficient command of languages, grammar and the development of words to grasp the essential meaning of any Scripture. Sacred books, for Vivekananda, were only a guide, providing 'only the maps, the experiences of past men, as a motive power to us to dare to make the same experiences and discover in the same way, if not better'.[23] For Vivekananda, what should be sought in the Scripture is not eloquence but truth: 'Each part of the scripture is to be read with the same spirit wherewith it was written.'[24]

Vivekananda criticized Christians for their over-reliance on a book, denouncing it as 'book-worship' and the 'worst kind of idolatry'. He made fun of Christians' veneration of the Bible, remarking that 'Every man in Christian countries has a huge cathedral on his head and on top of that a book.'[25] He urged Christians to emulate the sages of the Vedas, who were not only 'preachers of principles' but themselves 'became illustrations of the principles they preached'.[26] His said to Christians, 'You have to *become* the Bible, and not to follow it, except as paying reverence to it as a light on the way, as a guide-post, a mark: that is all the value it has.'[27]

Vivekananda's aversion to book knowledge as a means of understanding religion came not from his admirable Vedic saints, but rather was imbibed from the Buddha, whom he viewed as 'more brave and sincere than any teacher'. He asserted that it was the Buddha who said, 'Believe no book; the Vedas are all humbug. If they agree with me, so much the better for the books. I am the greatest book; sacrifice and prayer are useless.'[28]

Vivekananda was not always prejudiced against books. Interestingly, he did urge his followers to read a book; however, not the Bible but a medieval text, *The Imitation of Christ*, written by the Catholic monk Thomas à Kempis. His recommendation was based on two factors. First, it carried a Bhagavad Gita-like message. The ideas contained in the book – renunciation, total surrender and dependency on the will of God – reminded Vivekananda of the Bhagavad Gita's teaching: 'Give up all Dharmas and follow Me.'[29] Second, in its representation of Christianity, Vivekananda believed he saw the true spirit of the Christian faith, which would eradicate the 'ugly impression left on our mind by the ultra-luxurious, insolent, despotic, barouche-and-brougham-driving Christians of the Protestant sects'.[30] He particularly encouraged those Indians who refused to read any book written by a Christian to read the *Imitation of Christ*, urging them to 'read this great book with the attention it deserves'.[31] To support his argument that it was acceptable to read mlechchha's (a derogatory term for foreigners) books, he quoted the Sanskritic aphorism *Vaisheshika Darshana*, which implied that the teachings of *Siddha Purushas* (perfected souls) have a 'probative force' and quoted Rishi Jaimini, the commentator who said that '*Apta Purushas* (authorities) may be born both among the Aryans and the Mlechchhas.'[32]

For Vivekananda, religion was not to be learnt through any books or from prophets but to be found within oneself. As with his master, Ramakrishna, religion was about self-realization. He claimed that 'Religion is in us. No books or teachers can do more than help us to find it, and even without them we can get all truth within.'[33] He also said:

> We are the living books and books are but the words we have spoken ... We are the light that illumines all the Bibles and Christs and Buddhas that ever were. Without that, these would be dead to us, not living. Stand on your own Self.[34]

Once 'the inner light' has flashed, his advice was to 'let the books go, and look only within. You have in you all and a thousand times more than is in all the books.'[35]

Vivekananda was unyielding in his conviction that the Vedas had a number of advantages over the Scriptures of other nations. First, they are eternal and remained the same throughout all ages. Their authority and application extended to all ages, climes and persons. In contrast, the Bible was only provisional and never final; contextual and time-bound. Second, the Vedas were not the creation of human beings: 'There is no man or woman who can claim to have created the Vedas.' Vivekananda believed that they were the 'embodiment of eternal principles; [that] sages discovered them'.[36] Linked to this was idea that the Vedas were 'never written' and 'never came into existence'. The Bible, on the other hand, was historical and made by human beings. According to Vivekananda, the 'non-historicity' of the Vedas was something 'in their favour', but also claimed that they were 'the best-preserved scriptures in the world'. Their principles had never been 'tarnished' and none dared to diminish them, a veiled reference to critical questions raised by the historical critics and rationalists of the time about the authenticity of the Bible. Compared to other books, there were 'no interpolations, no text-torturing, no destroying of the essence of thought in them'.[37] Third, their teachings are in 'harmony' with modern scientific investigations: 'the conclusions of modern science are the very conclusions the Vedanta reached ages ago'.[38] Fourth, 'Vedanta was not based on a book' and does not acknowledge the authority of any book, refuting 'emphatically that any one book can contain all the truths about God, soul, the ultimate reality'. He reminded the regular readers of the Upanishads of its repeated message: 'Not by the reading of books can we realise the Self.'[39] Whereas he pitied the Christians who were stifled by the 'tyranny of the Protestant Bible'.[40] Finally, Vedanta is superior because it could encompass and embrace the truths which are hidden in other scriptural texts. The tripartite spiritual progress within the biblical narratives, *dvaita*, *visistadvita* and *Advaita*, leading to the ultimate goal is a pure Vedic scheme of things. Additionally, the Vedas offer guidance for everyday life, a metaphysical framework for social concern and a universal religion in which different faiths could be harmoniously integrated.

Vivekananda explained the apparent dualistic and monistic tendencies embedded in the Vedas as not 'contradictory' but 'necessary' for the evolution of the soul – one for children and the other for grown-ups. The Vedas embodied the first class of truths and he was certain about its position among Indians: 'Whatever be his philosophy or sect, everyone in India has to find authority in the Upanishads.'[41] Vivekananda's mantra was 'Let the Upanishads shine in their glory.'[42]

Having spoken eloquently about Scripture-less inner realization, an inner light that leads one to the ultimate goal, Vivekananda, in characteristic fashion, discarded what he had advocated and placed the Upanishads above other Scriptures, calling them 'the Bible of modern India'.[43] All other books were 'useless' and are 'good' only in so far as 'they confirm our book'.[44] Vivekananda asserted, 'So far as the Bible and the scriptures of other nations agree with the Vedas, they are perfectly good, but when they do not agree, they are no more to be accepted.'[45]

Let's Eat Mango

Vivekananda had a healthy contempt for exegesis, dubbing it a 'sort of grammatical twaddle'.[46] He found the 'various methods of explaining the dicta of the scriptures' were done for 'the enjoyment of the learned', who produce a 'three-volume book on its origin and use'. For Vivekananda, exegesis was a way of showing one's learning and gaining praise. No one attains perfection through sophisticated exegesis and he claimed that none of the great leaders of the world engaged in such 'text-torturing'. He used a story told by his master Ramakrishna to explain the futility of the work of exegetes. It is like going to a mango orchard and counting the twigs and branches and admiring the colour of the leaves and the sizes of mangos but not having the sense to eat the fruit. His advice was to forget the 'leaf-counting' and 'eat the mangoes'.[47]

Vivekananda criticized Western exegetes for reading their own perspectives into the texts they studied, thus destroying their essence. One of the texts he used as an egregious example of textual 'bending' was the saying of Jesus 'Sell all that thou hast, and give to the poor.' He interpreted this statement as explicitly encouraging 'practical equality' and urged Christians to take the truth as it is and not twist its meaning or weaken its applicability. He observed that one of the spurious tactics employed by Christians to negate the injunction in the saying to 'level' society was to restrict its application to the handful of Jews who were immediately present when Jesus uttered these words. He noted that the saying trampled on every privilege and was aimed at bringing 'the feeling of sameness towards all mankind'.[48] He challenged Christians to face the truth as it is. Even if they could not enact Jesus' words in their lives, they should confess their weakness rather than attempt to destroy the ideal of creating an equal society.

Vivekananda was uninterested in the historicity of the biblical records. He admitted that he was not anxious to discuss how much of the New Testament is 'true', or how much of the life described there was 'historical' or whether it was written within 500 years of Jesus' birth. What mattered for him was something that lay behind these writings – the marvellous manifestation of spiritual power which he wanted people to 'imitate'.

He maintained that the Bible had been in preparation for a long period stretching back 500 years before the Common Era and for several centuries after the coming of Jesus. 'The Bible', he stated was 'a mass of literature of different ages; different persons are the writers, and so on. It is a collection.'[49]

Vivekananda was familiar with the work of the emerging school of historical criticism known as higher criticism. He echoed the view propounded by historical critics and doubted the authenticity and the originality of the Gospels. He declared John's Gospel to be 'spurious'[50] and the other three Gospels simply copies of some ancient book, though the name of that book he never revealed. He did, however, subscribe to the idea that these Gospels were produced long after Jesus' time. Reflecting the accepted hypothesis of that time, Vivekananda reckoned that the Epistles were older than the Gospels, but erroneously placed the Acts of the Apostles earlier than the Synoptics. He expressed confidence in Paul's writings, even though he was not an eyewitness and Paul's obsession with saving souls by any means irritated him, saying this overzealous conversion activity was akin to 'Jesuitry'.[51]

Vivekananda's plea not to 'torture texts' did not mean that he objected to their serious investigation. He conceded that there was a place for such study but that it should be done in 'the spiritual realm'. Texts were plain and became easier to understand when one applied the doctrine of *adhikari-bheda* – whereby all are deemed to be qualified and have the right to know the truth, irrespective of spiritual status.

Vivekananda made a few attempts at exegesis, for example his reading of John's Gospel. He noted that the first five verses of John contained the 'whole essence of

Christianity' and that each verse was full of the 'profoundest philosophy'. True to his character, he never spelt out what this profoundest philosophy was. A similar under- explained verse was 'In the beginning was the Word, and the Word was with God, and the Word was God.' While for the Jews, the Word meant creative and sustaining power and for the Greeks it suggested reason, Vivekananda simply added a Hindu perspective and called it Mâyâ, the manifestation of God, because it is the power of God. His view on Mâyâ is a complicated one. Put crudely but not inaccurately, it is about 'cosmic illusionism'. Transferred to the Johannine narration, it has implications for the physicality and personality of Jesus, making him an apparition. Then Vivekananda jumps to the twenty-ninth verse, 'taketh away the sin of the world', which he interpreted not in the traditional Christian pietistic sense, of Jesus cleansing the sins of humanity, but rather how Jesus showed humanity the way to realize perfection.

Vivekananda was also not keen on the contemporary practice of comparative exegesis. He was wary that such exercises were undertaken to compare non-Christian religions with Christianity and expose the theological inadequacies of the former. For instance, Christian interpreters compared the morality of the Sermon on the Mount with the ethical teachings found in Hindu and Islamic texts. Vivekananda called this 'book-fighting' and believed that books were inadequate judges in matters related to the comparison between religions. He argued that there was something more universal and more ethical than these books and that the 'proof of religion' depended on the 'truth of the constitution of man', something which varied from nation to nation. After all, these books were made by 'men', while 'We are yet to see the books that made man.'[52]

Unlike Roy and Gandhi, Vivekananda was not much enamoured of the Sermon the Mount. Whereas for Roy and Gandhi, the sermon was principally about morality, for Vivekananda it was about renunciation and self-abnegation. He had no doubts that this Sermon was by Jesus, but he made no attempt to study it in a sustained way. He haphazardly made references to a few verses in his speeches and writings and this random selection elicits a mixture of polite recognition, gentle condescension and mild puzzlement about the sermon's moral precepts. Like the Gita, he recorded that the sermon's great hallmark was its 'simplicity', with the truth so clearly and directly revealed that even a streetwalker could understand it. He found the beatitude 'Blessed are the pure in heart' attractive because it is this purity that leads to renunciation, something which he heartily endorsed. He contemptuously dismissed the opening of line of the Lord's Prayer, one of the components of the Sermon the Mount – 'Our Father which art in heaven' – as intended for the 'uneducated'.

There are two vital textual units nestled within the Sermon on the Mount which Vivekananda found wanting. One was the Golden Rule, which, like Keshub, he was not a great fan of. Acknowledging that the saying was as old as the earth itself, he derisively dismissed it as 'exclusively vulgar' and 'a horrible, barbarous, savage creed'.[53] He found fault with it because of its attachment to the self, a particular Christian failing: 'Always self! always self!' As he put it, 'all self is bad' and 'all non-self is good'.[54] His contention was that one should transcend attachment to the soul and achieve oneness with the absolute. But being an Advaitin who acknowledged and recognized different levels of spiritual stages in people, Vivekananda did not totally disparage the Golden Rule. He regarded its principles as a stage in one's spiritual growth. Of all the great religious teachers the world had known, he praised Lao-tze, the Buddha and Jesus, who transcended the Golden Rule and said, 'Do good to your enemies', 'Love them that hate you.' The other statement he found confusing was the saying 'Ask, and it shall be given [to] you; seek, and ye shall find; knock, and it shall be opened unto you.' Vivekananda had difficulty in knowing who was doing the asking and what was being asked. In contrast, Roy in his reading of the same passage, saw a heartfelt petition as an effective means of obtaining salvation rather than going through intermediary agencies.

Though Vivekananda was dubious about book learning, he conceded that one is 'safe in taking the teachings of the Sermon on the Mount as a guide'.[55] He regarded the sermon as an aspiration and an ideal to be achieved. One who realized the ideals of the sermon would be a 'perfect' person, but he lamented that even among Christians it would be difficult to find 'a real Christian' who had fulfilled the expectations of the sermon.

Vivekananda's reading of biblical texts used the 'final form' of the text, with no interest in the dates or the history of the development of various biblical books. He was not motivated to investigate 'whether Christ was born in Jerusalem or Bethlehem or just finding the exact date on which he made the Sermon on the Mount'.[56] Similarly, he was unconcerned whether the New Testament was 'true' or if the life of Jesus was 'historical'. It did not matter, he said, 'whether the New Testament was written within five hundred years of his birth, [or] how much of that life was true'.[57] What he really cared about was the feel of the passage, 'the spirit of the scriptures' and the 'lovable' features of characters like Christ and Krishna. As he put it in on another occasion, one had to take from the text 'what appealed to our inner spirit'.[58] For someone to understand the Scriptures, there was no need to know the historical data and details of any Scripture. There was no need to know the particulars of Krishna or Jesus' life: 'You only require to *feel* the craving for the beautiful lessons of duty and love in the Gita.'[59] Similarly, if one wanted to be a Christian, the only requirement was to 'feel the Sermon on the Mount. It is not necessary to read two thousand words on when it was delivered.'[60] However, the trouble with doing exegesis at the redacted level is that once you situate the text in its narrative context, it loses the intended meaning it had for the original readers/hearers.

Two of Vivekananda's favourite texts employed to establish his advaitic ideals – 'I and Father are one' and the 'Kingdom of God is within you' – lose their shine when they are read in their original context. Whereas Roy believed that this unity was a 'perfect concord of will', Vivekananda saw in the Johannine saying an unmistakable proclamation of unity and equality of Father and Son. But what he overlooked was that the same Gospel contained a number of other passages that point to the secondary nature of the Son. What is equally prominent in the fourth Gospel is the Son's dependence on the Father, and the 'sentness' aspect of Jesus's career. The Johannine prologue that Vivekanand loosely referred to clearly states that the Son was sent by the Father, that he was different from him and that his function was to reveal the Father (1.18).

The other saying – the 'Kingdom of God is within you' – reads differently if placed within Luke's context. This utterance was in direct response to the question posed by the Pharisees, whom Jesus regarded as hypocrites. 'He answered *them* and said ... For indeed, the kingdom of God is within you.' Contextually, it would be incredible if Jesus had said that the Kingdom would be in the Pharisees, his sworn opponents. Jesus was speaking to a crowd of Pharisees, who had come to question him about the Kingdom of God (Lk. 17.20). The addressees were a crowd. 'You' in this situation is plural. Then there is the troublesome Greek word *entos*, which the King James Version translated as 'within', a reading used by Vivekananda. Recent Bible revisions have rectified this erroneous translation and often use 'amidst' (RSV) or 'among' (ISV). Vivekananda's mobilization of biblical texts for his Vedantic cause looks bare when set against a particularly difficult and nuanced reading.

This was the era when exegetes introduced historical questions about the Gospels, asking when and where these stories happened. In contrast, Vivekananda asked no questions about the history of these stories, but simply wondered whether the stories themselves were historical. Supernatural and rational interpretations did not attract him. He judged the biblical narratives to be unconscious mythologies and allegories, asserting that Judaism and Christianity depended upon such mythologies and that 'the patriarchs such as Abraham, and Isaac, and Joseph are proved to be mere allegories'.[61] As far as Vivekananda was concerned, the real, highest religion 'rises above mythology; it can never rest upon that'.[62]

Vivekananda was aware of the newly emerging historical criticism which he called the 'new science of research', and he knew of its stringent criticism of historical texts. His hope was that Christian interpreters who mercilessly tore apart the Hindu and other Scriptures would show the same moral vigour and courage to investigate the Bible.

Vivekananda's work is rarely exegetical in the explicit sense of the word. What he accused Shankara of – resorting to 'sophistry' in order to prove that his philosophical ideas were upheld by the texts – could well be have been levelled against him.

Jesus the Renunciant

Vivekananda was a great admirer of Jesus but as completely overwhelmed by him as Keshub was. But he, too, could manufacture equally emotionally-drenched sentences to match his fellow Bengali, such as: 'Had I lived in Palestine, in the days of Jesus of Nazareth, I would have washed his feet, not with my tears, but with my heart's blood!'.

As might be expected, the Jesus that Vivekananda admired was not the historical personality but the principles he preached and the ascetic life he lived. Like most Hindus, Vivekananda was decidedly averse to what he called religions built around 'historical men'. The standard argument was that any religion based on historical facts and figures was bound to be shaken 'if that rock of historicity' proved to be unreliable. Once the whole edifice was 'shaken and shattered', it would never regain 'its lost status'. Hence, Vivekananda maintained that our 'allegiance is to the principles always, and not to the persons. Persons are but the embodiments, the illustrations of the principles.'[63] There were two further reasons for his reluctance to place too much faith in any religious figure: first, such a faith in personality had a tendency to produce idols out of these saviour figures;[64] and second, given the diverse nature of humanity, it would be 'vain' to 'gather all the peoples of the world around a single personality'.[65]

The quest for the historical Jesus was in its infancy at the time that Vivekananda was engaging with the Bible. He dismissed Renan's *Life of Jesus* as 'mere froth',[66] doubted the likelihood of discovering something of the real historical Jesus from the written sources. He was also aware that there was no reference to the historical Jesus in the writings of historians such as Josephus and Philo, who were renowned for recording even 'petty sects'. Vivekananda claimed that he had never doubted the historical personality of Jesus, but also asserted that, according to Hindu philosophy, the 'completeness of an idea' is more important than the 'question of historical authenticity'. So, it was not important whether Jesus lived at a certain time. What the spiritual figures of the past do is 'urge us onward to do the same, to experience religion ourselves'.[67]

Vivekananda's scepticism about historical figures did not prevent him from acknowledging a certain trueness in the life of Jesus. He conceded that Jesus' public life lasted only a little more than eighteen months, a life for which he had been silently preparing himself for thirty-two years. He identified the historical juncture at which Jesus appeared: when Jews were caught between two waves – a wave of tiredness and conservatism and a wave urging them to move forward, 'towing ahead'. He summarily dismissed the theory which was popular at that time, that Jesus had visited India and studied with Brahmins at the temple of Jagannath, as fraud, because the temple was originally Buddhist and was 're-Hinduised' only later.

Unlike Keshub who was prone to use florid and emotional language to describe Jesus, Vivekananda confined himself to detached secular, generic and sectarian terms. His Jesus was an 'unselfish man', 'an Oriental of Orientals', 'the true son of the orient' and a 'Sannyâsin', 'the God of the Europeans', 'the great one of Galilee'. All Vivekananda asked of Christians was to show the same appreciation of Indian sages as they did of Jesus.

Vivekananda was wary of Western interpreters appropriating Jesus for their various vested causes and projecting him as a 'patriotic Jew', a 'great politician' and a 'great military general'. He discarded such portrayals as unendorsed by the Gospels. While rejecting these ideologically inspired constructs, he came up with his own philosophically-fuelled images based on Jesus' own words and the life he lived. Indeed, he contended that the best commentary on Jesus' life was the way he lived, captured in Matthew 8.20: 'The foxes have holes, the birds of the air have nests, but the Son of man hath nowhere to lay his head.'

Vivekananda's construal of Jesus makes the latter appear very unoriginal. His teachings were not his own; they were taken from Rabbi Hillel. Vivekananda declared that 'On the whole, I think old Rabbi Hillel is responsible for the teachings of Jesus.' Even the teachings of Jesus that Vivekananda most admired and enthused about – 'go thy way, sell whatsoever thou hast, and give to the poor' – was somewhat diminished by remarking that the ideal of renunciation was preached by 'all great prophets of the world', who had lived it out in their own lives. He even summoned a Vedic statement to prove how common this teaching was: 'Neither through wealth, nor through progeny, but through renunciation alone, is immortality to be reached.' 'All great Masters teach the same thing.'[68]

For Vivekananda, Jesus remained an Oriental. He routinely told the missionaries that they often overlooked the fact that that 'the Nazarene himself was an Oriental of Orientals'. However much they painted him with 'blue eyes and yellow hair, the Nazarene was still an Oriental'.[69] He complained that in Western portrayals of the Last Supper, Jesus sat at the table, which was not Oriental custom. Instead, Jesus, like the people in India, would have squatted with others on the floor. Also, Jesus and others had a bowl in which they dipped bread and shared among themselves. He attributed this European misrepresentation of the Oriental custom of sitting on the floor and sharing food to centuries of Greek and Roman influence and corruption.

Vivekananda's Jesus has all the ingredients to be one of the Vedic saints. The strength of Jesus was not the healings he enacted or the miracles that he performed but the Vedic-like message of purity and asceticism that he preached: 'Blessed are the pure in heart.' How did Jesus make a person pure? Vivekananda's answer was by renunciation. This was found in Jesus' instruction to the rich young man: 'Again and again did he preach renunciation as the only way to perfection.'[70] But Jesus did not come for all humankind. Vivekananda argued that the religion Jesus preached was essentially fit for Sannyasins only. His teaching '"Give up" – nothing more – being fit for the favoured few.' He lamented that Europeans never took these words of Jesus Christ 'seriously', and even provided the reason for this negligence: the West's love of the mighty dollar.

Vivekananda's Jesus was a preacher of the non-dualistic idea of oneness, exemplified in his sayings 'I am the Father are one' and 'I in you, you in me, and all is God.' This, Vivekananda claimed, was 'the teaching of Christ'. His Jesus believed in reincarnation, Vivekananda citing two of the sayings of Jesus as proof, though they are taken out of context: 'Before Abraham was, I am' and 'This is Elias who is said to have come.'[71]

For Vivekananda, there were two kinds of manifestations of God. One, a general one through nature, and the other, a special manifestation through the great revelatory figures such as Krishna, Buddha, Jesus and Ramakrishna. While Keshub was sceptical about using the Hindu understanding of incarnation, it was the doctrine of multiple manifestations that provided Vivekananda with the hermeneutical framework to grasp the meaning of Jesus. Christ was the special manifestation of the Absolute. The absolute cannot be known. One cannot know the Father, except through the Son. What the incarnated Christ did was to show humankind what the Father looked like. It was through Christ's 'tint of humanity'[72] that one saw the Absolute.

Vivekananda distinguished between two types of Christs – the Trinitarian Christ, who was elevated above humans; and the Unitarian Christ, who was merely an ethically good human being. According to Vivekananda, it was the Trinitarian Christ who was the Incarnation of God, who had not forgotten his divinity and who could help humans. It was this Christ who showed humanity its true nature – 'that we too are God. We are human coverings over the Divine; but as the divine Man, Christ and we are one.'[73] It is this Christ who rescued the 'jewel of truth' from the clutches of the priestly class and 'gave it to all the world.'[74]

Like many contemporary and later Hindu interpreters, Vivekananda clashed with Christians who made claims of exceptionalism for Jesus and blamed Paul for creating a 'mythic personality' as a centre of worship.[75] His message to the missionaries was that Jesus was 'a manifestation of God; so was the Buddha; so were some others, and there will be hundreds of others'. His plea was, 'Do not limit God anywhere.'[76] Vivekananda's point was that restricting God's manifestation to a once-and-for-all event would undermine God's power to manifest multiple times and put a limit on God's love. Vivekananda urged Christians to recognize the numerous avatars of God, both in ancient times and in revelations of the future: 'Let us, therefore, find God not only in Jesus of Nazareth but in all the great ones that have preceded him, in all that came after him, and that are yet to come. Our worship is unbounded and free.'[77] Jesus took human form just to do good to mankind.

Vivekananda had very little to say about the crucifixion, death and resurrection of Jesus – what the early ecclesiastical figures called 'the inviolable archives'. When asked whether he believed in Christ's crucifixion, Vivekananda gave a classic docetic answer: Christ was God incarnate and as such the authorities could not kill him and 'that which was crucified was only a semblance, a mirage.'[78] He claimed that Christians believed that Jesus Christ had died to save people, but that this doctrine had 'nothing whatever to do with salvation'. The event was more about what Jesus demonstrated on the cross than the salvific efficaciousness of his action. It was about Jesus' refusal to use the power to summon angels to help him out, and a sign of his endurance and humiliation. Misleadingly, he appended to his argument what Jesus said in his early ministry, as if it had been uttered on the cross: 'Come unto me, all ye that labour and are heavy laden, and I will give you rest.' On one occasion, he casually described the Christian cross, one of the foundations of Christian faith, as nothing but two Shivalingas (a symbolic representation of the Hindu deity Shiva) made into a cross. As was his habit, Vivekananda further reduced the significance of the event for Christians by saying that the cross existed in other cultures, such as those of the Aztecs and Phoenicians, and that crucified saviour figures were known to almost every nation. For Vivekananda, the cross was a 'universally prevalent symbol'. He also took a very offhand approach to one of the founding events of Christianity – the resurrection, likening it to a 'spring-cremation' practised by rich Greeks and Romans.

One of the few events associated with Jesus that Vivekananda gave serious thought to was the transfiguration. He perceived it as an occasion when radical change happened in the life of Jesus. He observed that Jesus went to the high mountain as Jesus of Nazareth and came down as Jesus Christ. He described the change this way: he went to the mountain as a child, and returned as an 'old experienced man'. This experience was unique to Jesus but was also 'possible for everyone of us'.[79]

Vivekananda, as we saw earlier, was suspicious of any comparative study but this did not stop him engaging in a similar pursuit. He saw a 'great deal of similarity' between the lives of Jesus and Krishna: their birthplace was a manger; there were tyrannical kings when both were born and all the boys born in that year were killed; both were saved by angels; and their childhood was the same. In the end, both were killed. Krishna was killed by an accident but he took the man who killed him to heaven. Jesus, too, was killed, but 'blessed the robber and took him to heaven'.

Similarly, Vivekananda saw parallels between the Buddha and Jesus: one was a Buddhist and the other a Jew, but both exercised enormous spiritual control over humanity. Both were calm and non-resisting, poor beggars who possessed nothing and had no money in their pockets. They were despised all their lives, called heretics and fools. Both sacrificed their lives for humanity, but Buddha went further and gave his life for an animal. Neither preached anything new. Shakya Muni, like Jesus, came to fulfil and not to destroy. Both were the logical development and conclusion of their respective traditions. Both were misunderstood by their own people. As the Jews did not understand the fulfilment of the Old Testament, so the Buddhists did not comprehend the completion of the truths of the Hindu religion. Their own disciples did not realize the importance of their teaching. While the Jews rejected Jesus Christ and crucified him, the Hindus had accepted Shâkya Muni as God and worshipped him. Buddha was a 'working Jnâni', whereas Jesus was a Bhakta. Both had a similar goal – to free the soul from the bondage of attachment. Both antagonized the principal religions of the time. 'Christ and Buddha were Gods; the others were prophets.'[80]

Once Vivekananda claimed that his particular 'fancy' was that the Buddha later became Christ. One of the astonishing claims he made was that it was not the Hebrew prophets who anticipated the coming of Jesus, but it was Buddha who foretold: 'I will come again in five hundred years', but not as a royal, kingly personality but as a 'calm and non-resisting', penniless mendicant owning nothing.

As to who was the greater religious figure between the Buddha and Jesus, for Vivekananda, Buddha comes first and next to him is Jesus. Buddha was the first human being to give to the world a complete system of morality and 'was more brave and sincere than any teacher'. What distinguished Buddha from Jesus was his kindness and civility. Buddha's 'words were full of blessings: never a curse came from his lips, nor from his life. So were Zoroaster and Confucius' – an indirect reference to the curses of Jesus recorded in the Gospels.

In the final reckoning, although Buddha and Christ were the two biggest 'bubbles' the world has produced, they were in Vivekananda's estimation inferior to Krishna. What these religious figures do is to urge us on to have the same experience as them: 'Whatever Christ or Moses or anybody else did' was 'to urge us on'. 'These great children of Light, who manifest the Light themselves, who are Light themselves.'

Vivekananda's playing down of certain features in Jesus' Jewish background is not so much an oversight in relation to Jesus' Jewishness as a yearning to see him as more like a Vedant. Vivekananda's Jesus was far from the apocalyptic and eschatological Jesus envisioned in the lives of Jesus popular at that time.

Vivekananda had no qualms about acknowledging Jesus' divinity or accepting the exclusive claims made on behalf of Jesus. He confessed that the 'Truth came to Jesus of Nazareth, and we must all obey him.'[81] He went on to say that as an Oriental, if nothing was left for him, he would worship Jesus as God. These Christocentric confessions might warm the hearts of a certain generation of Indian Christian interpreters, who viewed every Hindu reformer as a potential convert to Christianity, but these Christians should closely read Vivekananda's often-quoted statement: 'I pity the Hindu who does not see the beauty in Jesus Christ's character. I pity the Christian who does not reverence the Hindu Christ.'[82] His concession to Christ should be seen against the advaitic understanding of God, in which a personal God is lower than and superseded by a superior impersonal reality which Vivekananda called an 'Impersonal Personal God'.[83]

A Suitable Scripture

Faced with antagonism and the impact of Western culture and Christianity, the chief aim of nineteenth-century Hindu reformers was to make Hinduism a singular, unified, rational and ethical religion, relevant not just to India but to the whole world. They had few illusions about the superiority and supremacy of Vedantic Hinduism. Vivekananda was at the forefront in this reimaging and provided impetus for later thinkers like Radhakrishnan, who will feature in this volume.

Vivekananda found an able ally in the Bible for his acetic, advaitic and philosophical-mystical Hinduism. His approach to the Bible, and even to Jesus, was largely shaped by a formidable degree of historical mistrust and an excessive obsession with Vedanta. This scepticism is a mixture of the influence of the Christmyth movement of the time, which viewed biblical narratives as mythological, and the Hindu aversion towards religious personalities rather than the principles they propounded. For Vivekananda, the ultimate benchmark was *Advaita Vedanta*. 'It is,' he said, 'the Vedanta, and Vedanta alone that can become the universal religion of man and that no other is fitted for that role.'[84] He was emphatic that 'The philosophy of the age is Advaitism.'[85] The West might talk contemptuously of Hinduism, but Vivekananda saw his task as demonstrating that the books and philosophies of the West, including the Social Darwinism of Herbert Spencer, contained the elements of Vedantism. He even called Max Müller a 'perfect Vedantist'.[86] His lofty hope that Vedanta would become the faith of the world did not happen. Nor did it stimulate such a faith.

Like Keshub, Vivekananda had the habit of making positive statements about the contents of the Bible and the austere life of Jesus. But in the next breath what seems to have been acknowledged and approved was taken away by diluting its significance. This was achieved by claiming that everything was universal or practised by various cultures.

Since Roy's time, it had become habitual for the Hindu reformers to take upon themselves the task of saving Christianity from Christians. Vivekananda followed his fellow Bengalis in this respect and had the audacity to tell Christians to look at their lives, and especially the ascetic practices of Jesus, and change their lifestyle: 'You are not Christians. No, as a nation you are not. Go back to Christ. Go back to him who had nowhere to lay his head. "The birds have their nests and the beasts their lairs, but the Son of Man has nowhere to lay his head."' His simple advice was 'Better [to] be ready to live in rags with Christ than to live in palaces without him.'[87]

Vivekananda was aware of the need to overcome the antagonism towards Christianity generated by missionary denunciations of Hinduism and aggressive proselytization. But he did not engage in a vitriolic attack on Christianity and denounce its texts as some of the later twentieth-century Hindu thinkers did, some of whom we will meet later in this book. Instead, he chose one of the orthodox schools of Indian philosophy – Vedanta – to make his argument. In doing so, he subsumed all that the Christian Gospels claimed as exceptional and unique within the Vedanta framework. In a polite way, he made it clear that Christianity is imperfect without Vedanta. He was always courteous but ruthlessly dogmatic.

Vivekananda's message to Indian Christians was 'Have your own Bible. Have your own Christ.'[88] What he meant was that the Indian Christian should recapture the Oriental characteristics, such as inclusiveness, diversity, detachment and tolerance, encapsulated in the Bible and enacted in the life of Jesus. Indian Christianity was so entrenched in a mission-field mentality and had delivered little more than reiterations of mission theologies while maintaining their exclusivist claims and Christo-centric views. Even liberation theology, which was supposed to have radicalized the thinking of the Church, could not get rid of the exceptionalist claim for Christ and his Church as the new chosen people of God. The current Indian theological scene is so sterile and dull that there doesn't appear to be the aptitude, aspiration or acumen to work out a more adventurous form of Christianity.

The positive attitude shown towards Jesus and the Christian Gospel by Vivekananda and other Hindu religious thinkers, although founded on their own Hindu-biased interpretation, was rarely reciprocated by the missionaries of the time. In other words, the missionaries did not demonstrate a comparable understanding and appreciation of Hinduism. There were some exceptions but this was confined to isolated individual scholars rather than the efforts of the institutionalized Christianity. G. U. Pope's translation of *Thiruvasagam* (Sacred Utterances), an iconic anthology of *Tamil Saiva Siddhanta* and Francis Whyte Ellis's *Thirukural* (The Sacred Verse), a great secular work on ethics, are the examples from Tamilnadu.

At a time when Bengal was awash with Hindu reformers, it is natural to identify Vivekananda as one such, something from which he himself would demur. He conceded that there was a need for an adjustment to and modification of Hinduism, but while admitting that these reformers were 'good', 'well-meaning' and 'laudable', he found them wanting in three respects – they were denunciatory concerning their ancestral faith, imitative of Western models, and interested in reforming 'only little bits'. The end result was of 'no practical' value. He envisioned his hermeneutics as 'growth, expansion, development',[89] whereas the method of these reformers was one 'of destruction', in contrast to his method 'of construction'.[90] His popularity was due to the fine balance he struck between an aggressive defence of Hinduism and a vociferous call for its re-envisioning.

Like his Bengali compatriots, Vivekananda did not oppose the presence of missionaries. What he complained about was the wrong type of missionaries working in India – those who did not live out the life of Jesus. He found these Church workers to be more concerned about attending champagne parties with British officers and getting their wives into high society. He criticized them for wasting their time building churches instead of saving people from hunger, arguing that it was 'an insult to a starving man to teach him metaphysics'.[91] He saw 'no hope' for large scale conversions, viewing proselytization as dangerous and a mark of destruction for all religions. Coalescing people around a 'oneness of mental temperament' would spell death for religious diversity. 'Nature', he said, was 'too wise to allow such things'.[92] His solution was that each religion must assimilate the spirit of the others and yet preserve its individuality and grow according to its own law of growth.

There are a number of standout criticisms of Vivekananda's work which equally apply to other Hindu thinkers of the time. One, levelled by Christian theologians, was that he was prone to read his Vedantic presuppositions into the Bible. This was an often-repeated criticism of most of the Hindu reformers – that they marshalled biblical texts to fit a theological agenda which was foreign to the biblical view. Vivekananda's selections of biblical texts prove that his reading of the bible was rooted in his hermeneutical demands, fuelled by Vedantic tendencies and ascetic compulsions. His opponents accused him of 'putting Vedantism into the Bible',[93] and Vivekananda openly acknowledged that Vedanta philosophy did buttress his hermeneutical effort. What Vivekananda did was not that different from the appraisal of Hinduism by Christians, who insisted on viewing Hindu Scriptures and traditions through the prism of Jesus. Vivekananda's 'crime' was that he reversed the process. But Vivekananda never claimed that he was engaged in proper exegesis nor did he show any aptitude for or interest in value-free exegesis. He saw religion in terms of advaitic faith and consistently interpreted the religion of the Bible in this light.

The other criticisms related to his highly polarized and simplistic dual divisions which smacked of Oriental binaries, his unsystematic thinking and his limited respect for history. He presented Asia, and especially India, with its intrinsic religiousness, as the antithesis of the highly mechanicalized but characterless West. He had a weakness for inconsistent thinking. We saw a flagrant example of this earlier. On the one hand, he would say, 'No book, no person, no Personal God. All these must go' but on the other hand, he would furiously pronounce that anyone who denied the authority of the Vedas is a *Nâstika* (atheist). He did not regard his vision as systematic but as praxis and accessible even to a child:

> The dry, abstract Advaita must become living – poetic – in everyday life; out of hopelessly intricate mythology must come concrete moral forms; and out of

bewildering Yogi-ism must come the most scientific and practical psychology – and all this must be put in a form so that a child may grasp it. That is my life's work.'[94]

As Nalini Devdas concluded in her insightful study of Vivekananda, his genius lay not in the 'systematization of his thought' but in his presentation of a 'wide range of ideas and suggestions under a broad metaphysical framework'.[95] He was not rigorous in substantiating his assertions and could make astonishing statements without providing any historical or documentary evidence. For example, he claimed that both Eastern countries like China and the Western nations like Greece and Rome were indebted to ancient India for their philosophical insights and spiritual beliefs, without substantiating this with hard facts.

Underdogs fighting against oppressive power can themselves wield power in disturbing ways. Vivekananda was no exception. Just as Christians insisted that the Bible was unique and the Christian Gospel was universal, Vivekananda resolutely maintained that 'the Upanishads is the primary authority',[96] that 'the Vedanta only can become the universal religion'[97] and is the 'highest authority'.[98]

With the emergence of Vivekananda, Brahmoism – an amalgamation of Hindu and Christian tenets and texts – which Keshub advocated lost its appeal. In its place, Vivekananda's Advaita Vedanta emerged as a combative counter-narrative to the Gospel message. While Brahmos advocated a supine Hinduism, Vivekananda's construction of a nationalistic Hinduism addressed the needs of the colonial period. Vivekananda worked out a patriotic form of India's ancient faith at a time when Hinduism was under heavy attack from missionaries who had tacit support from the British rulers. In more modern times, without the support of colonial power and the passing of draconian laws restricting foreign funds, the threat became much weaker. Vivekananda's construction of Hinduism was basically a Hinduism for its time. What he couldn't have predicted was that this rear-guard Hinduism he reimagined would one day be mined for majoritarian Hindu upliftment that would cause great distress and anxiety among minority religious groups. To this vilification of marginal communities, Vivekananda would certainly not have extended his support.

Notes

1 *The Life of Swami Vivekananda by His Eastern and Western Disciples*, 6th edn (Calcutta: Advaita Ashrama, 1960), 147.
2 *The Life of Swami Vivekananda by His Eastern and Western Disciples*, 132.
3 This chapter deals exclusively with Vivekananda's use of the Christian Bible. For other facets of his life, see Amiya P. Sen, *Swami Vivekananda* (New Delhi: Oxford University Press, 2000). Though dated, still a competent introduction is Makarand Paranjape (ed.), *The Penguin Swami Vivekananda Reader* (New Delhi: Penguin Books, 2005).
4 *The Life of Swami Vivekananda by His Eastern and Western Disciples*, 62.

5   Anantanand Rambachan, *The Limits of Scripture: Vivekananda's Reinterpretation of the Vedas* (Honolulu: University of Hawaii Press, 1994).
6   Swami Vivekananda, *The Complete Works of Swami Vivekananda*, Mayavati Memorial edn, vol. VIII (Kolkata: Advaita Ashrama, 2006), 202.
7   *The Complete Works of Swami Vivekananda*, VIII, 203.
8   Swami Vivekananda, *The Complete Works of Swami Vivekananda*, Mayavati Memorial edn, vol. IV (Almora: Advaita Ashrama, 1948), 138.
9   Swami Vivekananda, *The Complete Works of Swami Vivekananda*, Mayavati Memorial edn, vol. IX (Kolkata: Advaita Ashrama, 1997), 378.
10 *The Complete Works of Swami Vivekananda*, IV, 144.
11 Swami Vivekananda, *The Complete Works of Swami Vivekananda*, Mayavati Memorial edn, vol. III (Kolkata: Advaita Ashrama, 2007), 333.
12 *The Complete Works of Swami Vivekananda*, III, 333.
13 *The Complete Works of Swami Vivekananda*, III, 275.
14 Swami Vivekananda, *The Complete Works of Swami Vivekananda*, Mayavati Memorial edn, vol. VI (Calcutta: Advaita Ashrama, 1963), 270.
15 Swami Vivekananda, *The Complete Works of Swami Vivekananda*, Mayavati Memorial edition, vol. VII (Calcutta: Advaita Ashrama,1958), 351.
16 *The Complete Works of Swami Vivekananda*, VII, 331.
17 *The Complete Works of Swami Vivekananda*, IX, 377
18 *The Complete Works of Swami Vivekananda,* III, 218.
19 *The Complete Works of Swami Vivekananda,* VII, 418.
20 Swami Vivekananda, *The Complete Works of Swami Vivekananda*, Mayavati Memorial edn, vol. II (Calcutta: Advaita Ashrama,1968), 193.
21 *The Complete Works of Swami Vivekananda*, VII, 3.
22 *The Complete Works of Swami Vivekananda*, IV, 22.
23 *The Complete Works of Swami Vivekananda*, VI, 14
24 *The Complete Works of Swami Vivekananda*, IX, 297.
25 *The Complete Works of Swami Vivekananda*, VII, 30.
26 *The Complete Works of Swami Vivekananda*, III, 183.
27 *The Complete Works of Swami Vivekananda*, IV, 43.
28 *The Complete Works of Swami Vivekananda*, VII, 41.
29 *The Complete Works of Swami Vivekananda*, VIII, 160.
30 *The Complete Works of Swami Vivekananda*, VIII, 160.
31 *The Complete Works of Swami Vivekananda*, VIII, 160.
32 *The Complete Works of Swami Vivekananda*, VIII, 161.
33 *The Complete Works of Swami Vivekananda*, VII, 85.
34 *The Complete Works of Swami Vivekananda*, VII, 89.
35 *The Complete Works of Swami Vivekananda*, VII, 85.
36 *The Complete Works of Swami Vivekananda*, III, 183.
37 *The Complete Works of Swami Vivekananda*, III, 280.
38 *The Complete Works of Swami Vivekananda*, III, 185.
39 *The Complete Works of Swami Vivekananda*, VIII, 124.
40 *The Complete Works of Swami Vivekananda*, VII, 30.
41 *The Complete Works of Swami Vivekananda*, III, 229.
42 *The Complete Works of Swami Vivekananda*, III, 439.
43 *The Complete Works of Swami Vivekananda*, III, 394.
44 *The Complete Works of Swami Vivekananda*, VII, 89.

45 *The Complete Works of Swami Vivekananda*, III, 333.
46 *The Complete Works of Swami Vivekananda*, III, 397.
47 *The Complete Works of Swami Vivekananda*, IV, 24.
48 Swami Vivekananda, *The Complete Works of Swami Vivekananda* Mayavati Memorial edn vol. I (Calcutta: Advaita Ashrama, 1965), 429.
49 *The Complete Works of Swami Vivekananda*, III, 512.
50 *The Complete Works of Swami Vivekananda*, IX, 378.
51 *The Complete Works of Swami Vivekananda*, IX, 378.
52 *The Complete Works of Swami Vivekananda*, I, 369.
53 *The Complete Works of Swami Vivekananda*, III, 500.
54 *The Complete Works of Swami Vivekananda*, III, 500.
55 *The Complete Works of Swami Vivekananda*, I, 328.
56 *The Complete Works of Swami Vivekananda*, IV, 23.
57 *The Complete Works of Swami Vivekananda*, IV, 142.
58 *The Complete Works of Swami Vivekananda*, I, 328.
59 *The Complete Works of Swami Vivekananda*, III, 50 (emphasis is in original).
60 *The Complete Works of Swami Vivekananda*, IV, 23.
61 *The Complete Works of Swami Vivekananda*, VII, 369.
62 *The Complete Works of Swami Vivekananda*, VII, 50.
63 *The Complete Works of Swami Vivekananda*, III, 280.
64 *The Complete Works of Swami Vivekananda*, VII, 85.
65 *The Complete Works of Swami Vivekananda*, III, 184.
66 *The Complete Works of Swami Vivekananda*, IX, 378.
67 *The Complete Works of Swami Vivekananda*, VI, 99.
68 Swami Vivekananda. *The Complete Works of Swami Vivekananda*, Mayavati Memorial edn, vol. V (Calcutta: Advaita Ashrama, 1964), 193.
69 *The Complete Works of Swami Vivekananda*, IV, 138.
70 *The Complete Works of Swami Vivekananda*, II, 100.
71 *The Complete Works of Swami Vivekananda*, I, 321.
72 *The Complete Works of Swami Vivekananda*, VII, 3.
73 *The Complete Works of Swami Vivekananda*, VII, 4.
74 *The Complete Works of Swami Vivekananda*, VIII, 94.
75 *The Complete Works of Swami Vivekananda*, IX, 379.
76 *The Complete Works of Swami Vivekananda*, IV, 27.
77 *The Complete Works of Swami Vivekananda*, IV, 148.
78 *The Complete Works of Swami Vivekananda*, I, 328.
79 *The Complete Works of Swami Vivekananda*, IV, 176.
80 *The Complete Works of Swami Vivekananda*, VIII, 181.
81 *The Complete Works of Swami Vivekananda*, III, 283.
82 *The Complete Works of Swami Vivekananda*, VIII, 219.
83 *The Complete Works of Swami Vivekananda*, III, 249.
84 *The Complete Works of Swami Vivekananda*, III, 182.
85 *The Complete Works of Swami Vivekananda*, V, 222.
86 *The Complete Works of Swami Vivekananda*, V, 222.
87 *The Complete Works of Swami Vivekananda*, VIII, 213.
88 *The Complete Works of Swami Vivekananda*, II, 474.
89 *The Complete Works of Swami Vivekananda*, III, 195
90 *The Complete Works of Swami Vivekananda*, III, 213.

91 *The Complete Works of Swami Vivekananda*, I, 20.
92 9/660 Ramakrishna Vedanta Society of Boston's website version Volume 9 contents, netdna-ssl.com.
93 V, 222. See also M. M. Thomas, *The Acknowledged Christ of the Indian Renaissance* (London: SCM Press Ltd, 1969), 120–6; and Balwant A. M. Paradkar, 'Hindu interpretations of Christ from Vivekananda to Radhakrishnan', *Indian Journal of Theology* 18, no. 1 (1969): 65–7.
94 *The Complete Works of Swami Vivekananda*, V, 104.
95 Nalini Devdas, *Svāmi Vivekānanda* (Bangalore: Christian Institute for the Study of Religion and Society, 1968), 224.
96 *The Complete Works of Swami Vivekananda*, III, 333.
97 *The Complete Works of Swami Vivekananda*, III, 182.
98 *The Complete Works of Swami Vivekananda*, III, 229.

Chapter 6

BAPU'S BIBLE

During colonial days colporteurs employed by the British and Foreign Bible Society used to promote the Bible for its non-spiritual prowess. The popular reports of the Bible Society were peppered with examples of the clever sales technique employed by these indomitable Bible sellers. To impress the unsuspecting buyers, these hawkers would make outlandish claims such as this is the book that cures your sun stoke or whooping cough. It was in a similar vein that the Bible was introduced to one Mohanlal Karamchand Gandhi.[1]

Towards the end of 1889, before Gandhi was seen and revered as the Mahatma, he happened to meet a missionary in a vegetarian boarding hostel in Manchester, UK. In the course of the conversation, Gandhi told of his experience in Rajkot – which caused him so much pain – where he had seen Christians drinking wine and eating meat, and, to his horror, had justified these habits by quoting the biblical verse 'call thou nothing unclean'. The troubled stranger allayed Gandhi's feelings with these soothing words, 'I am a vegetarian; I do not drink. Many Christians are meat-eaters and drink, no doubt; but neither meat-eating nor drinking is enjoined by Scripture. Do please read the *Bible*.'[2] It was from this stranger, whom he assumed was a Bible salesman, that Gandhi first obtained a copy of the Bible – not for its rich spirituality but for its expected secular characteristics regarding the likes of the non-consumption of meat and alcohol.

Thus began Gandhi's lifelong involvement with the Bible, which he called the 'spiritual dictionary' of the Christians.[3] As has been told countless times, his initial reactions were not that positive. The Old Testament patently bored him to death. He especially disliked the book of Numbers and wondered whether what was described there was Christianity. Being a *satyavan* (a man of truth) and to honour the promise that he gave to the salesman that he would read through the Bible, he trudged through it until he hit upon the Sermon on the Mount when he 'breathed a sigh of relief and joy'. The sermon, he noted, gave him 'great peace and consolation'.[4] The rest, to use a trite cliché, was hermeneutical history.

Gandhi's take on the Bible, like his political and social views, is complex and as it was undertaken over a period of forty years, it was bound to be varied and subject to change. This lengthy period gave him the confidence to discard obsolete ideas, to incorporate new ones to suit new occasions and, in the process, to contradict himself.

The temptation is to see Gandhi's reading of the Bible as some sort of minor addition to his interfaith interests. But it needs to be treated as a separate and distinct matter for several reasons. Firstly, the Bible was one of the scriptural sources that authenticated his pivotal ideas regarding political struggle – namely, non-violence and the ideal of renunciation. Secondly, the Bible was part of his Scriptures: 'The Bible is as much a book of religion with me as the Gita and the Koran.'[5] Thirdly, he was not only a keen student of the Bible but also a teacher of it. He ran Bible classes at the Gujarat Vidyapith National College and also taught the Bible to Chinese prisoners when he was in South Africa. Fourthly, he utilized biblical vocabulary to challenge both Christianity and the practices of his own faith. Lastly, he brought scriptural awareness to the public domain, in which the Bible and other religious texts featured prominently.

Gandhi seems to have read the Bible daily along with the Gita, but there is no record of him studying it systematically. It is public knowledge that his biblical expositions were influenced by non-biblical specialists like Tolstoy, whose New Testament elucidations which divested Jesus of his divinity and miraculous power made an impact on Gandhi. An additional reason for his attraction to Tolstoy was that the Russian's views were wholly consistent with Hinduism. Gandhi was candid enough to acknowledge that Tolstoy was his 'source of inspiration'.[6]

Much is made of the impact of commentaries by nonconformists on Gandhi, such as Joseph Parker's *People's Bible: Discourses upon the Holy Scriptures*. He seemed to have attended the Thursday lunchtime services of Parker when he was in London. But Parker's commentaries were full of phrases like Jesus' 'blood cleanseth ours from guilt' and 'the blood of Jesus Christ thy Son is the answer to thy fierce law',[7] and the concept of a reconciliatory process between God and humans founded on human sacrifice would have been detestable to Gandhi as well as to most Hindus. Gandhi's biblical knowledge was mostly self-acquired and influenced by his reading of Hindu Scriptures, while his usage was principally determined by the social, cultural and political issues that concerned him.

Testaments as Records of the Soul

There is a common misconception that Gandhi had an aversion to the Old Testament which was largely fuelled by what he had said in his autobiography. Here he wrote that the reading the book of Genesis sent him to sleep and that he plodded through the rest of the Hebrew Scriptures without interest and without understanding them. Gandhi did not give up after reading the book of Numbers as he claimed, but delved further into the Old Testament and made use of several passages and personalities from the nine books of the Hebrew Scripture to authenticate his political activism and asceticism. These included two books from the Pentateuch (Genesis and Exodus), the historical narrative of 1 Kings, the Wisdom Literature (Job, Psalms and Proverbs) and the Prophetical writings (Isaiah, Daniel and Jonah). He would use these studies to help advance his various agendas, ranging from vegetarianism to non-resistance.

Gandhi called the Old Testament a 'venerable book' and admitted that it had some 'deep truths', but he was unable to accord it the same status as the New Testament. He regarded the New Testament as an 'extension' and in some matters a 'rejection' of the teachings of the Old Testament.[8] The Old Testament gave humankind what it could 'then digest', but the New Testament went further, similar to the way 'the Upanishads fulfilled what the Vedas left incomplete'.[9]

In his Bible class at the National College, Gandhi told the students that if they thought the Old Testament was 'useless' they were 'wrong'. As the title indicated, it was an 'old thing' and it contained some 'incomprehensible' and 'disgusting' things – though for that matter, both testaments had 'germs' – but his advice was that Hindus should know the Old Testament to understand the New.

Gandhi did not fall prey to the stringent Christian binary view of these testaments as one being good and the other bad. His position was somewhere in between. For Gandhi, both testaments were about the 'history of man'. This did not mean that they were simply a record of events, but rather records of the soul, specifically the rise and fall of the human soul. Therefore, there was no need to cling to 'every detail in every word and every comma' but instead extract the essence of the religion that the biblical writers presented to the world. Gandhi perceived that both testaments were 'closely' connected; if not conceptually then genealogically. The early chapters of Matthew traced Jesus' ancestry to David to show that he belonged to the dynasty of David and was part of patriarchal history.

Gandhi did not subscribe to the conventional Christian notion that the Old Testament was a book of harsh rules. He was of the view that Jesus did not come to give a new law but to 'tack something onto the old Mosaic law'. Instead of 'an eye for an eye, and a tooth for a tooth', he urged people to receive two blows when one was given and to go two miles when asked to go one. Despite the cruelty and coldness of the injunctions of Moses, Gandhi found in them real kindness by the moral standards of the day. He clarified the difference between Mosaic laws and the injunctions of Jesus. Those who believed the law of Moses held the view that it was their duty to beat the person who has beaten them, but the law of Jesus said that it is only a 'weakness if we beat the man who beats us, such a conduct casts a slur on humanity. That principal is the quintessence of the New Testament. We shall read the New from that point of view.'[10]

Gandhi had a strong conviction that all Scriptures were 'revealed' and 'inspired', but at the same time he diminished their authority by declaring them to be the 'imperfect word of God'.[11] He added a caveat that these sacred writings suffered from what he called 'double distillation' – once when they were mediated through human prophets, and then again through commentaries and interpreters: 'nothing in them comes from God directly'.[12] For Gandhi, sacred books were an 'imperfect human medium' and likely to 'suffer distortion'.[13] These religious books basically propagated 'the thoughts and the deeds of virtuous men and women' and they did not become a 'religious treatise' until they were backed by actions and deeds. He was certain that the truth was 'the exclusive property' of no single text.[14] As imperfect human beings, it was impossible to understand 'the word of God in its fullness'.[15]

Gandhi was uninterested in the historical veracity of these Testaments, especially the Gospels, which he maintained were written from a 'religious' and not from a 'historical point of view'. Indeed, if one read it from the historian's angle, 'we shall find ourselves caught in a maze'.[16] Moreover, the biblical history is full of gaps, for example Matthew's skipping of thirty-two years of Jesus' life.[17] When asked whether Jesus did teach what was recorded in the Gospels, Gandhi's response was that he did not accept 'everything in the Gospels as historical truth'.[18] He claimed that the biblical writers wrote 'in a mood of exaltation'[19] and that the Bible was a work in progress, hence their writings 'are still being corrected'.[20] He took a similar view of his own Scriptures: 'Judged by historical test, Ramayana would be fit for the scrap heap.'[21]

Babu's Personal Preoccupations and Biblical Expositions

If Keshub introduced the Bible in his Town Hall lectures, Gandhi was responsible for making it known to a wider audience at his press conferences, public prayer gatherings and in village meetings. Gandhi, himself an amateur when it came to biblical criticism, developed his own method based on his idea of truth and non-violence, which enabled him to make bold judgements on biblical texts. He declared clearly that as an outsider, his articulations were 'not bound by Christian principles' and was admitted that he had no 'difficulty in reading into the text a satisfactory meaning',[22] which was anathema to biblical scholars brought up on a high-carb diet of neutrality and objectivity. This exegesis was a harmless act as long as Gandhi remained faithful to the text and approached his task with a 'prayerful and open mind'.[23]

Gandhi's writings, speeches and press conferences are strewn with striking biblical phrases and allusions, such as the 'Still, small voice', 'the pillar of fire in front of us', 'He is a jealous God', 'our forefathers did not betray us for a mess of pottage', 'you cannot save yourself unless you are prepared to lose yourself' and 'a house divided against itself must fall'. He often lobbed bits of biblical verses into his discourse without explaining them or bothering about the actual contexts in which they occurred. These out-of-context citations reflected the distinction Gandhi drew between biblical text and biblical truth. While missionaries were focused on the text, Gandhi was keen to emphasize the truth. This phenomenon was also a sign of the high level of biblical literacy at that time.

Gandhi used a number of biblical passages to support his political and personal preoccupations, such as his non-cooperation with the British government. When his detractors claimed that his anti-government activities were not biblical, Gandhi cited the example of Jesus' refusal to cooperate with power, hence his refusal 'to co-operate with the British Government',[24] also implying that his mission was as divinely approved as that of the Galilean. He also referred to Jesus' rebuke to Satan to 'get behind me' and his calling Pilate a fox as further textual warrants for not complying with the authorities. Gandhi's Jesus was at the forefront of non-cooperation, the one who uncompromisingly challenged the powerful lobby of

Pharisees and Sadducees, and who for the sake of the truth did not hesitate to divide sons from their parents.

Gandhi's non-cooperation did not rely solely on the Christian Bible. He characteristically co-opted all the Scriptures of the world to support one of his most important political acts. He reframed the Bhagavad Gita as the Gospel of non-cooperation between the forces of darkness and light and provided examples from the Hindu puranic tradition in which Prahald disassociated from his father, and Mira disassociated from her husband. The Zend Avesta, in Gandhi's reading, represented a perpetual dual between Ormuzd (light and embodiment of good) and Ariman (spirit of darkness), while non-cooperation was a duty enjoined by world religions. Gandhi claimed that the Scriptures of the world even went beyond non-co-operation by preferring 'violence to effeminate submission to a wrong'.[25] Furthermore, Gandhi's Jesus was not a mere passive bystander to these political and social upheavals – he could not imagine Jesus standing aside or doing nothing when bombs were being dropped or shots were being fired.

Gandhi employed biblical figures as exemplars of civil disobedience and a willingness to face the consequences. For example, Joseph disobeyed the authorities and was prepared to go to jail. Gandhi maintained that the refusal to do so would be uncivil and lead to anarchy. Gandhi himself was prepared to go to prison after many of his political protests. Tyrants and oppressors could control the body but not the soul, because civil disobedience is founded on soul-force. In Gandhi's view, the non-compliant did not hand over the soul but only his/her body to the authorities.

Public fasting was another political act that Gandhi practised on many occasions. When C. F. Andrews and some of his Christian friends raised objections to his frequent public fastings, Gandhi compared his action to the biblical fast: 'Even so was my fast, if I may compare it to the Biblical fast.'[26] He pointed to the Book of Jonah and the public fasting undertaken by the king and people of Nineveh when the prophet foretold the impending disaster, citing nearly five verses from Jonah – the largest portion of biblical text he had ever quoted – and commenting that 'This fast of the king and the people of Nineveh was a great and humble prayer to God for deliverance.'[27]

Gandhi utilized biblical texts to pursue personal objectives and to wage moral crusades against social vices. He had plenty of personal obsessions, one of which was vegetarianism, a cause he championed before it became an ecologically laudable practice. To substantiate his case, he quoted Genesis:

> And God said: behold, I have given you every herb bearing seed which is upon the face of all the earth, and every tree in which is fruit of a tree yielding seed; to you it shall be for meat. And to every beast of the earth, and to every fowl of the air, and to everything that creepeth upon the earth, wherein there is life, I have given every green herb for meat; and it was so.[28]

This supported Gandhi's claim that humankind had been vegetarian before the Fall and that the future eschatological Kingdom of God would have a radically different relationship among and between humanity, the animal world and the ecological order:

> The wolf also shall dwell with the lamb, and the leopard shall lie down with the kid; and the calf and the young lion and the fatling together; and a little child shall lead them.... And the lion shall eat straw like the ox.... They shall not hurt nor destroy in all my holy mountains; for the earth shall be full of the knowledge of the Lord, as the waters cover the sea. (Is.11.6)[29]

Incidentally, when some of the Christian vegetarians sought to ingratiate themselves with Gandhi by insisting that Jesus had also been a vegetarian, he was not fooled. He dismissed their claim and referred them to the incident in which Jesus seemed to have eaten broiled fish after the resurrection.[30]

Another of Gandhi's personal beliefs was that one must work hard to earn food and that those who ate without work were thieves. He generously acknowledged that his idea of 'bread labour' had been inspired by Tolstoy and his reading of Ruskin's *Unto this Last*. Again, he found a suitable biblical verse to validate his cause, this time from Genesis – 'In the sweat of thy face shalt thou eat bread' (3.19) – and, in keeping with his practice, identified a comparable verse in the third chapter of Bhagavad Gita for the same purpose. He wrote that if all laboured for their food, then there would be enough for all; it would be a labour of love, a common good that would lead to the levelling of society: 'There will then be no rich and no poor, none high and none low, no touchable and no untouchable.' Gandhi felt that such bread labour would be the 'highest form of a sacrifice'. But what about those who earned their bread through intellectual labour? For Gandhi, mental labour was work for the soul and should never require payment. In an ideal world, doctors, lawyers and the like should work solely for the benefit of society, not for themselves, but Gandhi was shrewd and practical enough to admit that such an ideal was 'unattainable'. Nonetheless, he urged his followers strive for it.[31]

Gandhi also found biblical support for another cause he promoted, namely socialism. He claimed that he had been a socialist before his contemporaries had declared their belief. Gandhi's socialism was not the result of any books he had read, but had come naturally to him in association with his commitment to non-violence. For Gandhi, socialism meant 'even unto this last', a reference to Jesus' Parable of the Vineyard, where he says 'Take that thine is, and go thy way: I will give unto this last even as unto thee.' However, this parable is arguably more about the complicated relationship between the employer and the employed and the agreed payment than about the distribution of wealth.

Mahatma and his Hermeneutical Manoeuvres

There is an acute hermeneutical intelligence at work in Gandhi's writings. If he had any methodology, it was implied rather than articulated in his thinking. Gandhi resorted to a number of hermeneutical ploys. One such was the hermeneutics of reverence. His approach to any sacred text was habitually marked by phrases such as 'sympathetically', 'friendly' or 'respectfully', recalling that he drew great solace from all them. Gandhi's view was that this compassionate approach should be the 'sacred duty' of every cultured person. He claimed that this approach had enhanced his reverence for the Scriptures, enabled him to better understand obscure passages in his own Hindu texts and, more importantly, made him to be 'equiminded towards all these faiths'.[32] However, this reverential reading did not mean that he agreed with everything in the texts. His experience of aggressive missionary preaching, which not only ridiculed Hindu religious practices but also presented a sterner version of the Gospel teachings, helped lead Gandhi to this position, as he counselled others, 'Do not read the book with a malignant eye'[33] – an injunction principally aimed at those missionaries who ridiculed the puranic stories as irrational and absurd.

Very much related to this inclusive approach was Gandhi's claim to possess multiple religious identities. His oft-repeated claim to be a Hindu, Christian, Mohammedan and Parsee was a hermeneutical strategy to be inclusive and not aggressive. He claimed that by nature he was not 'competitive or antagonistic', captured in the legal maxim *Sic utere tuo ut alienum non laedas*, which means 'Use your property in such a way as not to damage that of others.'[34]

Gandhi's hermeneutics was resonant of those who espoused identity hermeneutics. He claimed that it was 'through my own life'[35] that he interpreted Hinduism, frequently drawing on his own experience as a Hindu and referring to himself as a 'staunch sanatani Hindu',[36] implying that this gave him such a deep understanding of his ancestral faith that he had a right to declaim on it. This further implied that his interlocuters lacked this experience and should therefore defer to his interpretations. The problem with this position however, is that it prioritizes private and personal intuitions above facts and objective scrutiny.

Gandhi's other ploy was a complete reversal of that just described, now presenting himself as an unfit interpreter. He often claimed that he was not 'fit to interpret Hinduism', that he had no 'first-hand knowledge of these wonderful books' and that he was a simple 'lay, humble student of Hinduism'. His self-effacement was carried even further when he described himself as 'a humble seeker after the truth' and 'not the final word on non-violence', emphasizing his own 'littleness and ... limitations'.[37] His writings are saturated with heavy doses of unpretentiousness, yet these statements were often followed by confident textual pronouncements. Ultimately Gandhi's justification for making these assured observations was that he himself knew what truth was and therefore declined to be 'bound by any interpretation, however learned it might be'.[38] This sounds haughty and of course sits awkwardly with his attempts at self-abasement.

Another of Gandhi's hermeneutical methods was to juxtapose equivalent texts from different Scriptures. Indeed, he was a serial raider of these texts. Gandhi discerned striking parallels between Jesus' birth and the puranic figure Karuna, whose mother Kunti was given a boon to conceive a child with the Sun God. His other comparative examples included the temptation of Jesus, for which he found similar traditions in Hindu texts, such as when the sage Vishwamitra overcame the pleasure of the palate and Narada conquered lust. Gandhi conceived himself to be a weaver of different scriptural traditions.

He did not limit himself positive parallels. Whenever he referred to any negative narratives in the Bible, he would point to similar instances in Hindu texts. This might have been a consequence of frequently finding himself at the receiving end of the fulminations of missionaries concerning his own texts. When he commented that the Hebrew Scripture was full of 'blood and thunder', he also remarked that there was enough 'blood and thunder' in the Ramayana.[39] Just as he was dismissive of the historicity of the Bible, he found the Mahabharata to be 'hopeless as history', recording the 'eternal verities in an allegorical fashion'.[40] Gandhi was certainly not blind to the weaknesses of his own tradition.

Gandhi's constant comparisons with other Scriptures was not intended to denigrate or dilute the message of the Bible, but was in fact an attempt to universalize what claimed to be culturally particular and exclusive. His purpose was to show that no one owns the story. This approach provided a useful reminder of the linkages between civilizations, cultures and texts. What he advocated was an emphasis on their 'good points and the beauties' embedded in them, which had a transformative effect on those believed in them.[41]

Gandhi's hermeneutical accomplishment was to establish several tests by which to judge Scriptures – tests naturally arranged to suit his own interpretative intentions. In order to arrive at a proper estimate of a book, it was important to establish that a text was compatible with reason and conscience. He was prepared to reject a scriptural authority if it was found to be in conflict with 'sober reason or the dictates of the heart'.[42] Then he advanced the idea of checking for truth, ahimsa and non-violence – Gandhi's cardinal principles: 'I apply the test of Truth and Ahimsa laid down by these very Scriptures for interpretation. I reject what is inconsistent with that test, and I appropriate all that is consistent with it.'[43] He claimed that Hinduism had produced an 'admirable foot rule' to measure the shastras – namely, the truth. If they were not consistent with the truth, then shastras were 'irrelevant',[44] adding that 'the spirit of nonviolence alone will reveal to one the true meaning of the shastras'.[45] Gandhi argued that the true test of a text lies in its figurative and not its literal meaning: 'One should not stick to its letter, but try to understand its spirit, its meaning in the total context.' Any 'mechanical observance' would be 'futile'.[46] He also suggested internal and external tests. An internal test concerns the desirable effects texts have on their readers. An external test involved judging a text as whole and not in portions – a hint at canonical criticism, which became popular in the 1970s. On this basis, he judged the Ramayana to be a 'book par excellence'.[47] Having stipulated these tests, Gandhi almost negated them by saying that to determine whether a book was good or bad was not to consider the text itself but rather the sum total of the religion it produced.

Gandhi not only set his own hermeneutical rules for interpreting shastras, but also, like Navalar, he outlined the sort of qualities an interpreter should have in order to discern the meaning of texts. At a time when our knowledge of these books was 'most chaotic', he advanced the ideal qualities one should acquire, such as innocence, truth, self-control and renunciation, in order to discern the meanings of the Scriptures. On another occasion, he wrote that for the purpose of interpreting a text 'one must have a well-cultivated moral sensibility and experience in the practice of their truths'.[48] Evidently, Gandhi set very high, arguably unattainable, hermeneutical standards for those in the business of interpretation.

One of Gandhi's hermeneutical maxims was that one should read the religious text as if one came from within that textual tradition. He told the missionaries that simply reading the Gita or Koran was not enough, but that it was vital for them to 'read the Koran with Islamic spectacles and the Gita with Hindu spectacles', just as the missionaries would expect non-Christians to 'read the Bible with Christian spectacles'.[49] His point was that reading as an insider would help one grasp the meaning of the text more fully rather than ridiculing the awkward bits. For instance, the Christological significance of the first chapters of Matthew, which point to the Virgin Birth of Jesus, would not make sense unless one read with the eye of a Christian.[50] Gandhi's repeated question was 'have you read the Gita as reverently as I have or even reverently as I have read the Bible?'[51]

Gandhi did not dismiss outright those biblical narratives that did not meet his own personal hermeneutical ground rules. At times, he tried to explain them away. One such concerned the divine birth of Jesus. He admitted that he did not believe a similar puranic story either. But at the same time, he could not dismiss it as 'absolutely impossible'. He saw in these stories the 'overfondness' of the writers – that the authors were not 'cheating' the readers and that exaggeration of this kind was 'excusable and even proper for an ardent devotee'.[52] Matthew must have written about the birth of Jesus in this vein. He must have felt that Jesus' birth was not an ordinary event, hence he allowed his imagination to run riot. Gandhi's view was that the divine birth in Matthew could be taken as an 'interpolation' and was not to be dismissed as 'senseless, wild talk'. Gandhi's advice for anyone who found an awkward portion in the Bible was to read it with respect and with the eye of a poet: 'Faith has the poet's eye and the poet should be given full freedom.'[53] The incomprehensibility of the text might be due to the intellectual ability of the reader at that time, but over the years one should be able to overcome these baffling elements. In other words, the fault does not lie in the texts but in the intellectual and spiritual capacity of those who attempt to expound them.

Gandhi often claimed that he was 'not a literalist'. What was important to him was 'the *spirit* of the various scriptures of the world'.[54] He regarded any excessive veneration of the Bible, the Koran or the Gita as 'idol worship'[55] and wanted to avoid what he called the 'trap of literalism'. His mantra was that the letter 'killeth' life and the spirit 'giveth' life. He accused the missionaries of unthinking literalism.

While the Reformation introduced a single meaning to the text, Gandhi drew on and exploited the Indian genius for typological reading. He insisted that the texts should not be taken literally and sought to understand and 'catch the drift of the Bible'. He applied typological strategies to biblical events, treating the miraculous birth of Jesus and his death on the cross as an 'eternal event in this stormy life . . . Living Christ means a living Cross.'[56] These are ever-recurring events which could be 'enacted in every life'. He treated his own Scriptures in a similar fashion, interpreting the Mahabharata not as a history of two families but as 'the history of the spiritual struggle of man', an eternal struggle that goes on within a human being.[57]

Gandhi had an aversion to any authoritative interpretations which emerged from the religious establishment or from 'experts', dismissing them as not representing the masses nor conveying the real meaning of the Scriptures as he understood it. He questioned whether Shankaracharyas, pundits or Church authorities could provide a correct interpretation of the Scriptures. For Gandhi, the interpretation of a text was not necessarily correct simply because it had been 'handed down for generations'.[58] Gandhi had no faith in professional pundits either, writing that if he wanted to determine the meaning of a text he would not go to a person who had 'studied the shastras with the desire to be called a pundit'. For this reason, he would not 'seek the assistance of the books written after laborious study by such scholars as Max Müller'. He found that people who professed themselves knowledgeable in the shastras were 'ignorant and conceited'.[59] For Gandhi, it was not the meaning that religious authorities or religious scholars give to a text that mattered, but 'what meaning a prayerful reading of it yields to the reader'.[60]

Long before liberation theology emerged, Gandhi advocated some of its basic tenets. First was the need to re-read the biblical narratives in terms of what was 'happening around us' and be shaped by 'direct experiences',[61] which included current political upheavals, the discoveries of modern science and the spiritual experience common to all faiths. Second, the real meaning of the text is realized by enacting it: 'We cannot realize Rama by reading the Ramayana or Krishna by reading the Gita, or god by reading the Koran, or Christ by reading the Bible; the only means of realizing them is only by developing a pure and a noble character.'[62] For Gandhi, the perusal of shastras did not 'lead to an awareness of the true spirit of religion'.[63] The truth had to be translated into action.

A Sermon for a Spinning Brigade

What is often overlooked is that in the midst his busy life, Gandhi held Bible classes and delivered expositions on the Sermon the Mount. This teaching was carried out at the National College, Ahmadabad, as a result of popular demand by the students, but the sessions were open to all. According to one of the participants, the walls of the classroom were adorned with pictures of scenes from the New Testament. There were flowers in brass pots, and smelling tapers and Eastern music that set the mood for listening to Gandhi's Gospel elucidations.[64] Unfortunately, Gandhi was unable to cover the entire Sermon on the Mount, ending abruptly after having studied with the class chapter 5 and sixteen verses of chapter 6. The exposition remained incomplete, which Gandhi said caused him pain.

At the outset, Gandhi made it clear that his interpretation of the Bible would not be like that of the Christians, and would not be from the missionaries' standpoint. What his listeners would 'imbibe' was its 'general principles'.[65]

Gandhi lionized the Sermon on the Mount as encapsulating the 'whole of Christianity', regarding it as the 'pivot of the New Testament'. According to his interpretation, Matthew had revealed Jesus' full heart. Gandhi stated that in the event of fire destroying these biblical materials, if these Gospel maxims remained intact, they would be enough for humanity's needs. He dismissed the rest of the Gospel accounts as merely an expansion of the same theme with added 'verbosity'.[66] The Sermon on Mount, in Gandhi's mind, went a long way to dispel the stereotypical image of a Christian: that of having a 'brandy bottle in one hand and beef in the other'.[67]

Gandhi impressed upon his students that as lovers of the Bhagavad Gita they should be able to see the similarities between these two texts. On an earlier occasion, he had reportedly told Joseph Doke, his first biographer, that there was 'no distinction between Hinduism, as represented in the *Bhagavad Gita*, and this revelation of Christ; both must be from the same source'.[68] This assertion was consistent with some of the Hindu reformers, who were prone to make flippant hermeneutical judgements, lacking substantiation. Gandhi was not interested in probing which text came first or which influenced the other. His view was that only persons of a purified mind could have produced such sublime thoughts. His key distinction between the Bhagavad Gita and the Sermon on the Mount was that 'What the Sermon on the Mount had done in a graphic manner, the Bhagavad Gita had reduced to a scientific formula.'[69] Inveterate religious pluralist that he was, Gandhi claimed that the Koran, too, had similar thoughts, because it was the work of the Prophet, who had such deep knowledge.

The Sermon on the Mount offered impeccable justification for Gandhi's agenda of anti-covetousness, hostility to commercialism and resentment of self-glorification. What we find in these expositions is a host of strained interpretations and desperate attempts to fit the Sermon into a predetermined hermeneutical agenda, at times even validating some of the injunctions that were at variance with his very idea of ahimsa and non-violence. It was a clear case of the exegetical tail wagging the scriptural dog. For Gandhi, some of the verses – especially 'do not possess things', 'do not beat a man who beats you' and 'give away whatever somebody demands from you' – encapsulated his idea of non-possession. These verses were the 'climax' of the sermon and key to the life of Jesus, but more pertinently they provided the briefest commentary on ahimsa. Gandhi declared that in these sayings Jesus had given a 'definition of perfect dharma'.[70]

Gandhi's attitude to the harsher elements of the Sermon on the Mount was a mixed one. He found that some of the verses 'jarred' his mind and were 'inconsistent with the ahimsa of Jesus'. One such was 'That whosoever is angry with his brother without a cause shall be in danger of the judgment' (Mt. 5.22). Gandhi was genuinely confused by the phrase 'without a cause', so he consulted various translations such as Moffatt and Weymouth for clarification but found them unhelpful. He feared that this clause might give the impression that there were circumstances in which one could be justified in getting angry, and more worryingly, that it could be misused. An inglorious example was General Dyer. Gandhi sarcastically commented that General Dyer, who had mercilessly attacked unarmed Indians at Jallianwala Park in Amritsar, probably had his reasons for what he did, although he found these words of the Sermon on the Mount to be inconsistent with the ahimsa of Jesus.

At the same time, Gandhi did not criticize all the injunctions that did not measure up to his cherished idea of not harming. He did not flinch when he came to the extreme part of the Sermon on the Mount, which said, 'And if thy right eye offend thee, pluck it out' and 'And if thy right hand offend thee, cut it off.' Jesus, who would not stone the woman who committed adultery, took a harsh view of those who committed mental adultery. Uncharacteristically, Gandhi endorsed the severe measures sanctioned by Jesus even if they were opposed to the principle of non-violence. He had preached that all life was sacred and urged that animals be treated humanely and not prodded with blunt instruments, but now supported the aggressive intent in Jesus' saying. He regarded looking at a woman, even one's wife, with lust to be a sin and requiring punishment. For him, a wife is a fellow pilgrim and the partner in the performance of dharma. A wife should be treated as a sister and anyone who deviated from this and looked upon her lustfully was a 'profligate'. His against-the-grain reading of these verses was probably prompted by letters he received in South Africa, from both young men and white women. Young men wrote to him to say that their eyes and thoughts never ceased to wander when seeing women, and a few white women complained to him that men made passes and stared at them. Hence, he upheld these strictures and pronounced that there was 'nothing wrong in following the commandment even to the letter'.[71] This was the same Gandhi who accused the missionaries of their insensitive literal reading of the texts. But it was no surprise that these harsh injunctions of Jesus had Gandhi's support, who tested the most demanding of vows, that of sexual abstinence, in his old age.

For a moment we must digress. Ahimsa for Gandhi meant not merely being inoffensive but actively showing love – even for an evildoer. This did not mean extending support to or acquiescing in the evil ways of the miscreant – quite the opposite. Vigorous love and ahimsa necessitate resistance to the bad person by distancing oneself from him or her even though it may cause harm. This withdrawal showed true love, but it seems to be a perverse way of showing affection and care. Reading in this vein, Gandhi saw the parable of the Prodigal Son in a somewhat odd way. For him, true love meant withdrawing support for the errant son until he repented and mended his ways, but that same love would then prompt him to embrace the son once he had shown remorse. In his inimitable self-confident, even self-righteous, way, Gandhi proclaimed that this was 'the moral of the story of the Prodigal Son'. In the same *Young India* piece, Gandhi persuaded himself that true ahimsa or love meant that he should support General Dyer in his shooting of the innocent people at Jallianwala Bagh – but that would not be the right thing to do. If Dyer repented, Gandhi said, then he 'would nurse him back'.[72]

Gandhi did not hesitate to comment on two injunctions which were critical but personally embarrassing for him: one regarding taking solemn promises; and the other concerned with making a show of public prayer and fasting. Vows played an important role and were imposed on those who joined his ashram at Sabarmati. There were at least twelve of them which took on a spiritual quality. For Gandhi, as long as one takes these oaths in the spirit of dedication to God, these vows were fine. He regarded them as 'purely' religious acts to be taken only with a mind purified, with God as witness.

Since he regarded open communal prayer and fasting to be both political and spiritual acts, Gandhi might have found awkward Jesus' instruction that these acts should be done discreetly. Gandhi was accustomed to performing prayer and fasting openly and so dismissed these recommendations as wholly inapplicable to public prayers, carefully distinguishing between personal and communal prayer. His conviction was that there was nothing in the sayings of Jesus 'against collective prayer'.[73]

Gandhi was not interested in placing the Sermon on the Mount in its historical and political context and so did not provide any background to its origins except to say that Jesus was fed up with the crowd which had besieged him and therefore fled to a mountain where he sat down with the disciples and gave the sermon. It was delivered 'not merely to peaceful disciples but to a groaning world'.[74]

Gandhi treated the Beatitudes as if they were concerned with emotions and personal qualities, failing to appreciate that meekness and mourning could be the consequence of the political, social, religious and economic policies of Roman imperialism, which caused such personal distress. His interpretation of the 'poor in the spirit' had echoes of the standard irrational Christian belief that time will eventually rescue the destitute and cure all their ills. What was seen in its original context as an assurance to those who were economically poor in the Roman world, Gandhi turned it into 'desireless renunciation'. At surface level his explanation looks pious and paternalistic, seeming to imply that those who were humbled before God would be rewarded eventually. Gandhi was not in the least interested in the original context of these sayings. His main focus was on the college students to whom these expositions were directed. He feared that these undergraduates who would earn large salaries would be exposed to Western luxury goods, therefore he wanted them to avoid what he called 'artificial needs' or 'exaggerated needs'. He cautioned them not to be dazzled by Western goods, but learn to live on Rs. 2 and 8 annas per month and imagine themselves living in Indian villages.[75] The aim was to steer them away from the notion that a person's life was essentially about the enjoyment of material goods.

Gandhi's interpretation of the Sermon on the Mount was characteristically his own. In reading into the texts his own political and cultural preoccupations, he offered a different perspective from the prevailing interpretations. The Christianity which came with the missionaries was more of a world-affirming religion characterized by progress in science and technology, social reform and political advancement. Gandhi preached a religion of renunciation, passivity, withdrawal from material benefits, and non-violence. The Sermon on the Mount provided textual legitimacy for such causes. What Gandhi did was to read into the Semitic text the ideals of Indic traditions. But in over-emphasizing non-violence, he left unnoticed a great deal of violence in both the Bible and the Koran.

Gandhi would also be disappointed to know that 'do not resist evil' – the pivotal statement for him – was not found in the original Q version on which Matthew was based, but was a later addition by the redactor. Obviously, Gandhi was not interested in the complexities of textual history, nor did he pay any attention to the history of textual tradition.

At a time when questions were raised as to whether a society could be governed by the principles of the Sermon on Mount, Gandhi interpreted the texts as if they could provide standards for normal relationships between individuals. For some of the missionaries, the Sermon on the Mount did not 'apply to mundane things' and was 'meant for the twelve disciples'. Gandhi disputed this and told them that the sermon had 'no meaning if it was not of vital use in everyday life to everyone'. In Gandhi's view, the eternal principles embodied in the Sermon – truth and non-violence – were applicable 'in courts, legislatures and other spheres of human endeavour'.[76] He urged his followers to 'become worthy of the message that is embedded in the Sermon on the Mount, and join the spinning brigade'.[77]

Mahatma Waiting for the Messiah

Gandhi claimed that he paid 'attention to every word ascribed to Jesus in the New Testament', but the Jesus that emerges is not the familiar one who proclaims the kingdom of God, but a preacher of ethical rules (yamas), of which there were five – *ahimsa* (non-violence), *satya* (truthfulness), *asteya* (non-stealing), *brahmacharya* (moderation of the senses/right use of energy) and *aparigraha* (non-greed). Gandhi's Jesus did not come to preach a new religion but a 'new life', and this life meant doing the will of the Father.[78]

Gandhi regarded Jesus as a 'great teacher of humanity' who, though not perfect, came as 'near to perfection as possible'. To claim that Jesus was perfect would have been to deny God's superiority. Jesus was limited by the bonds of the flesh, and perfection is only possible after the dissolution of the body. Jesus was basically a 'servant of the people or a spiritual aspirant'. He was also a 'supreme artist' because he expressed the truth. Gandhi admitted that Jesus was a 'factor in the composition' of his 'undying faith in non-violence'.

The message of Jesus was a response to 'human want', as were the messages of Krishna, Buddha, Muhammed and Zoroaster. Though these spiritual giants delivered their teachings at different places, they have a 'universal value'.[79] Gandhi did not differentiate between Jesus and other religious figures, repeatedly stating that he had not 'seen any fundamental distinction between him [Jesus] and the other great teachers', hence he paid 'equal homage to Jesus, Muhammad, Krishna, Buddha, Zoroaster and others that may be named'.[80]

Like most of his fellow Indians, Gandhi was uncomfortable in holding on to the conventional views of Jesus held by orthodox Christianity. He could not accept that Jesus was the only begotten Son of God. Such a claim was both theologically and rationally untenable for Gandhi, especially the idea that God could marry and have a son. He commented that the adjective 'begotten' had a deeper and possibly grander meaning, implying 'spiritual birth', and in his own time he was 'nearest to God'.[81] He could not ascribe 'exclusive divinity to Christ', only seeing him as 'divine as Krishna or Rama or Mahomed or Zoroaster'.[82] Gandhi regarded the descriptions

'Father', 'the Holy Ghost' and 'Son' as 'figurative expressions',[83] while 'Son' can also be taken metaphorically, since everyone is a begotten son of God.[84]

Gandhi did not subscribe to the idea that Jesus was God incarnate, and interpreted the stories of the immaculate conception and Virgin Birth 'mystically'. He wrote that it was hard for him to believe in the literal meaning of these stories. He also rejected one of the cardinal creeds of Christianity – 'the doctrine of appropriation of another's merit'. He viewed the sacrifice of Jesus as a 'type and an example' for humanity and encouraged everyone to go through the 'crucified' process for their own salvation.[85]

Gandhi maintained that he needed neither the prophecies nor miracles to establish the greatness of Jesus, arguing that what was 'miraculous' about Jesus was his three years of ministry. Indeed, he was sceptical about Jesus' miracles, including the feeding of the 5,000 and raising the dead to life. Gandhi wondered whether those who were raised had in fact been dead. He claimed that he himself had raised a child who was supposed to have been dead. Gandhi did not deny that Jesus had certain 'psychic powers', but this was not as important as the fact that Jesus was 'filled with the love of humanity'.[86] He valued the 'ethical teaching' of Jesus much more than his performance of wonders.

Gandhi was not unduly perturbed by the claims of exclusivity made on behalf of Jesus, or indeed Jesus own claim that 'I am the way'. He softened such triumphalist pronouncements in a number of ways. He interpreted it figuratively, citing Paul's words that the 'letter killeth'. Gandhi believed that any teacher who had attained purity and dedicated their life to the service of others was justified in making such claims, noting that the Gita itself permitted this type of contentious affirmation. He was not concerned with belief in the person of Jesus as such, but in doing 'the right thing' which the Galilean demanded. Gandhi diverted attention from Jesus the person to the dharma he preached and practised. The enactment of dharma was crucial to a proper understanding of Jesus, rather than veneration of his personality.

Those familiar with Gandhi's thoughts are aware that he had little interest in the historical Jesus: 'If you mean historic Jesus, then I do not feel his presence. But if you mean a spirit guiding me ... then I do feel such a presence. ... Call it Christ or Krishna, that does not matter.' He cared less about whether the man called Jesus lived than that the message recorded in the Gospel might be a 'figment of the writer's imagination'.[87] Similarly, he had minimal interest in the historical Rama, concerned only that the facts of Rama's life might 'vary with the progress of new historical discoveries and researches'.[88]

While admitting that we do not know the 'whole life of Jesus' and that he was not versed in the critical study of Jesus, Gandhi engaged in his own quest for the historical Jesus independent of Western authorities who had reached a dead end at that time due to the historical critical methods they employed. Gandhi identified three distinct kinds of Jesus: the historical Jesus, the Jesus of 'Christian England and Europe' and the 'mystical Jesus of the Sermon on the Mount'. Of course, he thoroughly disapproved the Jesus who came with colonialism. It was the Jesus of the Sermon on Mount that Gandhi admired, but lamented that this Jesus had 'still to be found'.[89]

Gandhi's Jesus, like Gandhi himself, was a non-cooperationist. His attitude to power was defiant. Jesus' preaching and practice 'unmistakably' point to non-compliance, including non-payment of taxes. Gandhi saw Jesus as unyielding to the authorities and to popular demand. When Satan asked him to 'bow and obey me', he refused. Similarly, when the crowd wanted to make him king, he refused to agree because their motives were dubious.

Although Gandhi was sceptical about the historical Jesus, he was not reluctant to comment on historical events associated with Jesus. He interpreted the baptism of Jesus as the Eastern practice of being initiated by a guru, showing Jesus' respect for the age-old custom of being initiated before embarking on a mission to spread knowledge. The fact that Jesus had a 'soul far more advanced than John' and that he was willing to participate in this ceremony showed his humility.[90] His baptism was an act of self-purification which many people shared in at the river Jordon. Gandhi also claimed that this was an act of self-identification with the people, an interesting conjecture that is not in the Gospel narratives or suggested by biblical commentators. This self-identification tempted Jesus to align himself with the millions who expected him to be the long-awaited messiah, but then he heard the voice from within saying 'Run away from here'[91] – a sentence not found in the Gospels. While removing all supernatural manifestations associated with the baptism, such as the spirit of God descending on Jesus like a dove, or a voice publicly declaring him to be God's son, Gandhi here conjured up an inner voice whispering these words to Jesus. While biblical commentators over-read the event, talked about the manifestation of God's presence and Jesus' role in the divine plan of salvation, Gandhi simply turned a public event into a personal and private experience.

Similarly, Gandhi illuminated the temptation of Jesus using his own experience and illustrations from puranic figures. He interpreted the first temptation – the temptation of the palate; a temptation Gandhi must have faced on numerous occasions when fasting – as the mastery of the senses. In resisting the offer of the 'tasty food' by Satan, Jesus gained mastery over his physical needs. The second temptation by Satan sought to excite a desire for power and dominion in the mind of Jesus – but Jesus remained unmoved. The third temptation was to use the miraculous powers (*siddhi*) acquired as a result of mastery over fleshly desires and personal ambition. When Satan asked him to use his supernatural powers, Jesus refused to do so and said that he wanted to serve people. In Gandhi's re-reading, Jesus emerges as a person without inward vulnerability and a non-cooperator with his tempter, much like Gandhi himself. Gandhi's Jesus did not seek solace in scriptural sentences, as the Gospel Jesus did, but from his inner strength. What shines through in Gandhi's treatment of this episode is not Jesus' humbleness but his firm resolution in the pursuit of truth.

At a time when Western studies of Jesus presented him in nationalistic and ethnic terms, such as the Aryan Jesus that some German scholars portrayed; or in abstract terms, such as the Christ of faith of dialectical theologians; or the mystical risen Jesus of Indian Christian thinkers, Gandhi perceived him in secular terms and admired his political and economic teachings. He envisioned Jesus variously as the 'prince among politicians', the 'greatest economist of the time' and ' perhaps the most active resister known to history'. While Westerners saw passive resistance as Jesus' weakness, Gandhi claimed that there was no textual justification for such an opinion, stating that he found 'no passivity, or weakness about Jesus as depicted in the four gospels'.[92]

Gandhi dissociated Jesus from English nationalism. He found the national anthem of England anti-Christian and at odds with the very passive nature and teachings of Jesus. The Jesus who asked his followers to love their enemies as themselves could not have said of his enemies, 'Confound their politics / Frustrate their knavish tricks.'[93]

Like the Bengali reformers, Gandhi believed that Jesus was an Asiatic, but that those Asiatic credentials had been 'disfigured' when the Roman Empire took power, followed later by the West. These Asiatic characteristics were further diluted when Jesus was imbued with values that were alien to Asia, such as authority and power. Jesus, a man from the 'East' with a message of 'love force' was gravely tarnished by the West presentation of his message as 'the religion of kings'.[94] From that point, Christianity became an 'imperialist faith' and remained so ever since.[95] While Bengali reformers used the word Asiatic as a metonym for Indian masculinity, Gandhi employed it positively to highlight truth and non-violence as the common principles of all Asiatic faiths.

While Radhakrishnan denounced the biblical Jesus for acting badly and being judgemental, Gandhi was reluctant to engage in such criticisms. He conveniently overlooked Jesus' fiercest fulmination aimed at the spiritual leaders of his time and his refusal to show leniency to those who speak against the Holy Spirit. Gandhi sought to explain that while Jesus castigated the scribes and Pharisees for their wickedness, he did not hate them. This has echoes of Gandhi's attitude to empire – what he hated were the evils of the Raj but not the English who implemented them: 'That Emperorship must go and I should love to be an equal partner with Britain.'[96]

Finally, however much Gandhi had affection and admiration for Jesus just as the other Hindu reformers studied here, he still placed him in an inferior position to the Buddha. What Jesus lacked was love and compassion towards all living creatures, both humans and animals, or in his words, 'the crawling things of the earth'. Whereas Jesus' atonement used the imagery of a slain lamb, Buddha actually rescued a lamb about to be sacrificed by the Brahmin priest.[97]

Peripheralizing and Praising Paul

Apart from Jesus, Gandhi had little to say about figures in the New Testament. The exception was Paul, for whom Gandhi had a mixture of misgivings and much admiration. Paul was a Greek, had an 'oratorical' and 'dialectical mind' and of course 'distorted Jesus'.[98] Gandhi was not attracted by Paul's abstract, philosophical interpretation of the teachings of Jesus, and drew a distinction between the Sermon the Mount and the letters of Paul, which he found to be a 'graft of Christ's teaching, his own gloss apart from Christ's own experience'.[99]

Gandhi found that the Gospel that Jesus preached was 'subtle and fragrant' and needed no intermediary like Paul: 'If the rose needs no agent, much less does the Gospel of Christ need any agent.'[100] He observed that Paul's salvation by grace was at odds with Jesus' Sermon on the Mount, which prescribed holiness through personal effort. He preferred the original version of Jesus, which was summed up simply as love of God and love of neighbour. It was the very Jewishness of Jesus' teaching that appealed to Gandhi. He posed the question to his readers, 'What should we accept, Christ words, or Paul's? When there are sayings of Jesus himself, where is the need for reading Paul's exposition?'[101]

Though Gandhi had reservations about Paul in public, privately he showed a 'greater appreciation' of him. He placed Paul's teachings on love on a par with truth: 'For me truth and love are interchangeable terms.'[102] He drew on the famous passage from Paul's First Epistle to the Corinthians (1 Cor. 13) to express his gratitude to the Danish missionary Esther Faering who admired his work. As a New Year's gift, he sent his own Gujarti translation of Paul's love poem to his nephew Manilal, expressing his own inadequacy in showing love but observing that if one had love, one had everything.

Make me a Better Indian

Conversion was a sore point between Gandhi and the Christian missionaries. Gandhi felt that Jesus' saying 'Go Ye unto All the World' had been somewhat narrowly interpreted and the spirit of it misdirected – aiming at the stomachs of potential converts rather than their souls. Christian missionaries feared that Gandhi's work among the Harijans could thwart their chances of winning the souls for Jesus. S. K. George, one of the few Indian Christians to join the Gandhian movement, observed that the missionaries were troubled by Gandhi's work among the untouchables since it 'would stop the flow to the Christian churches'.[103]

To say that Gandhi was against conversion is too simplistic and does not reflect the complexity of his position. He supported the inalienable right of the individual to convert, regarding it a personal matter between the individual and their God, but he would not have dreamt of converting others to his own faith. What he opposed was the methodology and the motive of the missionaries. For him, conversion was regarded as the 'price of [missionary] service' and had become a 'matter of business, like any other', with budgets and targets.[104]

Gandhi's opposition to conversion was founded on a mixture of his theological convictions, nativistic impulses, nationalistic tendencies and paternalistic inclinations. His theological hostility to conversion was premised on several factors. Conversion created, especially among those doing the converting, a pecking order of religions which inevitably placed Christianity at the top. This was contrary to his notion of the equality of all religions. He also feared that conversion would lead to a single religion, which would result in the suppression of other faiths and be detrimental to Indian diversity. 'Personally', he confided that the world as a whole would 'never have, and need to have a single religion'.[105]

Conversion, in Gandhi's view, was the result of an insufficient understanding of the spiritual properties of those who wanted to convert. Gandhi's solution was that if one found the indigenous religions 'defective', instead of embracing a new faith, one 'should serve it by purging it of its defects'. He also argued that the transference of faith would not only lead to mutual hatred between religions but also to the abuse of their ancestral faith by the newly converted, which could hurt those who continued to adhere to their original religion.

Besides these theological objections, Gandhi was convinced that the idea of conversion was not in keeping with the swadeshi spirit, which restricted one to one's 'ancestral religion' and their 'immediate religious surroundings'.[106] In other words, the swadeshi spirit discouraged movement to other faiths, as encouraged by Ambedkar, Gandhi's nemesis. He perceived conversion as a sign of 'greater dedication to one's own country, greater surrender to God, greater self-purification'.[107]

Gandhi feared that conversion would open the way for 'denationalization' and break down India's 'social superstructure'. He therefore urged Indian Christians to lead a 'life of greater dedication to one's own country', revert to its 'original simplicity' and serve the nation. He bluntly asked potential converts whether they really wanted to completely cut themselves 'adrift from the nation in whose midst they have to live?'[108] Gandhi feared that conversion would destroy the social cohesion and cultures which sustained his ideal image of village India. He was apprehensive of the disruption of communal harmony that could result from what he called this 'clumsy' method of proselytization.

Gandhi's anti-conversion stance also had an element of condescension. He held the view that the harijans were not sophisticated enough to distinguish between the relative merits of Islam, Hinduism and Christianity. The question he posed to R. C. Mott, who dedicated his life to the conversion of the heathen world, was an egregious illustration of Gandhi's tendency to patronize: 'Would you, Dr. Mott, preach the Gospel to a cow?'[109]

When asked whether his future swaraj would permit Christians to engage in their proselytizing activity without any hindrance, his reply was predictable: 'No legal hindrance can be put in the way of any Christian or of anybody preaching for the acceptance of his doctrine.' Gandhi then muddied his case by coming up with his own version of conversion, involving 'self-purification, self-realization', which he contended was the 'crying need of the times'.[110] For Gandhi, the matter of conversion lay within one's own faith: 'My effort should never be to undermine another's faith but to make him a better follower of his own faith.' His goal and 'our inmost prayer should be that a Hindu should be a better Hindu, a Muslim a better Muslim, and a Christian a better Christian'.[111] His deep theological belief was that all religions were true, hence there was no need for any transference of faith.

For Gandhi, 'India's faiths [were] all-sufficing for her' and there was no need for another imported religion. He encouraged friendly contact between faiths, but without the assertion of superiority by any one and without bidding for converts. Gandhi's consistent message to the missionaries was for them to confine their 'activities to humanitarian services without the ulterior motive of converting India'.[112]

Scriptures as Common Cultural Property

Gandhi's views on the Bible were never constant. His initial enthusiastic endorsement slowly diminished over the years. The early fervent approval at the turn of the last century, embodied references to the 'Bible [being] part of my scriptures' and to the teachings of Jesus as being complementary with the Bhagavad Gita, gave way to a conscious emphasis on indigenous Hindu texts, marked by statements like 'I find the Hindu scriptures . . . satisfy the needs of the soul',[113] and that 'the Gita opened to me, a new life'[114] and had 'become for me the key to the scriptures of the world'.[115] Likewise, his initial fondness for the Sermon on the Mount and for Jesus became dulled and slowly made way for his embrace of Hinduism and the Bhagavad Gita. At a missionary conference in Calcutta in 1925, Gandhi told his audience that it was Hinduism which 'entirely' satisfied him and that he found 'solace in the Bhagavad Gita and Upanishads', something the Sermon on the Mount could not offer.[116] The often-repeated accusation that he was 'leaning towards Christianity' was effectively refuted by confessional statements, such as the explanation that when he was haunted by doubts and when disappointments stared him in the face, he turned to Bhagavad Gita to 'find a verse to comfort'. It was the Gita that allowed him to 'smile in the midst of overwhelming sorrow'.[117]

This change of attitude might have been due to the impact of what Gandhi called 'swadeshi spirit' and his regret at his 'fatal departure' from it.[118] It was this spirit that prompted him to confine his 'attention to the land'[119] of his birth. While the swadeshi movement of the time encouraged the use of goods produced in India, Gandhi applied the same principle to the use of indigenous texts. However, in contrast to the swadeshi movement's advocacy of the burning or boycotting of foreign goods, Gandhi did not reject imported books but urged that they be reread, reinterpreted and cured 'of their proved defects'.[120] Ultimately, it was adherence to the swadeshi spirit that prevented Gandhi from following any other religion or changing his own.

Like Roy before him, Gandhi stressed that the texts rather than the gurus were the source of authority – a common hermeneutical trait of those raised on reformation ideals. He encouraged going directly to the Scriptures because the 'gurus [were] rare in this age'. For those who knew no Sanskrit, in which some of the Hindu Scriptures were written, his advice was to engage in 'regular study of books in regional languages which are steeped in the spirit of devotion'.[121] He differed from the Western reformers on two counts. When reformers talked of the primacy of 'scripture only', what they were referring to was the Christian Bible only, whereas for Gandhi the focus was the Scriptures of the world. Gandhi once told a visiting missionary that he would present to some the Koran, to some the Gita, to some the Bible and to some Tulasidas' Ramayana, like a 'wise doctor prescribing what is necessary for each patient'.[122] He firmly believed that it was the 'duty of every cultured man or woman to read sympathetically the scriptures' of others rather than just one's own. This study of and reverence for other Scriptures, was for Gandhi 'wholly consistent' with his being a 'staunch Sanatani Hindu'.[123] His other difference with the Western Reformers was that while they reduced the biblical message to faith through grace, Gandhi made 'saved through non-violence' the principal message of the Bible as he had understood it.

Gandhi took the Bible and Jesus totally out of Christian control. While the church reformers wrested the Bible from the institutional church and placed it in the hands of the Christian communities, Gandhi went further and made it available to all communities of faith. He told the jailor at the Naini Central Prison that 'Jesus and the Bible were not the sole property of the Christians' but 'the joint estate of humanity at large'.[124]

While modern biblical criticism was obsessed with speculative history behind the biblical texts, Gandhi focused on what we really know – their afterlives in the communities. Thus, Gandhi read the Bible to meet the cultural and political demands of the day. Indian Christian theologians of the time did not find the Bible a useful tool for such purposes. Pandipeddi Chenchiah, one of the key Christian thinkers, who defended Gandhi against those Christians who were uneasy about his adoption of Christian ethics without the acceptance of dogmatic Christianity, took the a slightly unconventional stance position that 'apart from the Sermon on the Mount and a few sayings of the Lord, we cannot get any guidance for our social, economic and political problems from reading the Bible.'[125] Chenchiah found the Bible 'not of much use' when it came to seeking guidance concerning the 'problems of our day'. Instead, he advocated personal and living experience with the risen Jesus in order to find new directions. A similar view was held by A. J. Appasamy, his contemporary, who wrote that the Scriptures were 'full of problems' and had no intrinsic life in themselves. Instead of seeking in vain for guidance 'among the mazes of an ancient revelation' and the 'difficult ancient writings', he opined that it would be more beneficial to hear 'directly the pronouncement of the Lord on particular issues'.[126] While Indian biblical exegetes perceived the Bible to be a validating source for the direct experience of God/Jesus, through which most of them embraced Christian faith, the institutional churches took a more hard line. An English commentator lamented that the Anglican clergy in India serving 'in the suburban Gothic style churches' were 'expounding the authorized version of the Bible, in the light of the Thirty-nine Articles'.[127]

At a time when missionaries believed that the Gospel message was universal and applicable everywhere irrespective of culture or context, Gandhi insisted on its contextual nature. In his talk to the missionaries at the United Theological College in Bangalore in 1927, Gandhi told the missionaries that the contents of the richest word of God were not 'the same' for everyone. It would mean 'one thing to Santhal and another to Rabindranath Tagore'. It took another forty years for this stolid seminary to implement a contextual approach to theological studies, prodded by the World Council of Churches.

Gandhi showed a keen interest in all matters relating to the Bible, such as Bible translation. He thoroughly disapproved of the Guajarati version, finding its language poor and certainly inferior to the King James Bible which was hailed as a 'masterpiece in English literature'. For the sorry state of the Guajarati version, he put the blame squarely on the missionary translators, who turned a book that had reached a 'towering height in spirtualty' into a 'parody of the original'. He also castigated fellow Gujaratis for not making any effort to translate the Bible. Incidentally, when a missionary taunted Gandhi by saying that Bible was the most translated book in the world, his responded by saying that the true test of the superiority of a religious text had little to do with how many versions it begat but to what extend it helped to 'fructify' the truth. [128]

Gandhi exhibited pre-critical, modern and postmodern tendencies in his usage of the Bible. Pre-critical exegesis was evident, as we saw earlier. when he applied literal, anagogical, typological and spiritual readings. He subscribed to the Romantic and Enlightenment notion that 'the Bible was a greater power when the Early Fathers preached it than it is today'[129] which is not true. His minimization of the role of the author, as one who wields enormous power in determining the meaning of the text, predates the mid-twentieth-century literary theory of the death of the author.

Gandhi thoroughly disapproved of using the Bible for non-spiritual purposes, for example as a tool to learn English, which was a prevalent practice in colonial India. He recalled how he was encouraged to read McMordie's English *Idioms and How to Use Them*, which carried the subtitle *Explaining Common Allusions to Persons and Incidents in the Bible*. Gandhi regarded the idea of learning the Bible as a way to acquire English to be a 'lower view'.[130] Similarly, the prevalent view was to study Job in order to learn philosophy, and to study Judges in order to understand politics, but Gandhi held on to the conservative notion of reading the Bible for its spiritual message – though this did not prevent him from employing the King James Version to help a certain Mr. Fortoen, a Chinese prisoner, learn English.

Gandhi was a pioneer in bringing the Bible to the masses. While Indian biblical scholarship of the time was dominated by high-caste converts who sought to relate the Bible to the Sanskritic tradition or got involved in Christological issues, Gandhi took the Bible to ordinary people. Interpretation was a personal conversation within himself coupled with the social act of communicating with the people outside. It was through this social engagement with the self and the world that he conveyed and practised the truth he preached all his life.

Yet while Gandhi took the Scriptures to the masses, he was unsure whether they were capable of interpreting them. He wanted to open up the Scriptures to all, irrespective of caste, but was reluctant to allow them to expound on these texts. He found the high-caste injunction regarding the sudras studying the Vedas to be 'not altogether unjustified', but he reinterpreted the sudras not in the conventional caste terms but metaphorically as a 'person without moral education, without sense and without knowledge'.[131] At the same time, he was pained to hear that the pundits, supported by the authority of the texts, were reluctant to teach the Scriptures to the sudras. He said that as a staunch Sanatana Hindu he was of the firm opinion that even if there were texts which prohibited low-caste people from reading the sacred text, one should not kill the spirit of the religion by literal interpretation. Such Vedic texts should be rejected if they were 'repugnant to reason and contrary to experience'.[132] There were, however, principles for the guidance of the common man, too, but Gandhi did not explain further.

Gandhi was attracted to the Christian message not because it was special but because it resonated with his own beliefs embedded in Hindu texts. He found that 'all that is permanent in ancient Hindu culture' was also to be found in the teachings of Jesus, Buddha, Mohammed and Zoroaster. He used the 'Bible for the British people' to agitate, to provoke, to shame and to galvanize. In other words, he utilized the Bible in his cultural and political strategies.

Gandhi's ideal of non-violence and love of one's enemy was not, as was mistakenly assumed by some Christians, learned from the New Testament but from Shamal Bhatt, a medieval Gujarati poet whom he had discovered before he was introduced to the Bible. Gandhi admitted that it was from Bhatt that he 'first learnt the principle of winning over even an enemy with love'.[133] He said that non-violence was 'common to all religions' but had found its 'highest expression and application in Hinduism'.[134]

Gandhi did not simply look upon the Scriptures as religious texts, but claimed that the Scriptures of the world were 'far safer and sounder [as] treatises on the laws of economics than many of the modern books'. The 'economics' that Gandhi referred to were the general remarks Jesus made about wealth and salvation in his dialogue with the Rich Man recorded in the Gospels. For warning about the detrimental consequences of acquiring wealth, Gandhi called Jesus 'the greatest economist of his time'.[135]

Like most of the Hindu reformers we have studied in this volume, Gandhi pointed out the 'continuous contradiction between' what Christians professed and the way they lived their lives. He believed that Christian institutions did not 'always express Christ's life in action' and that Christianity had 'practically rejected Christ's teaching'. What Europeans brought to India was Western civilization and 'not the life of Jesus'.[136] In his lecture at Colombo YMCA, he said that much of which passed as Christianity was a 'negation of the Sermon on the Mount'. He often wondered whether the Christianity he witnessed was the real one, and gave a Vedic-sounding waggish answer: 'Neti, Neti' (Not this, not this).[137] His message to Christians was that they should 'live Christian lives, and not annotate them'.[138] He was not afraid to take on a pedagogical role – since the message of Jesus of Nazareth had been 'little understood in Europe', then 'light from the East may have to be thrown upon it'.[139]

Ultimately, for the Hindu reformers studied here, it was the Hindu Scriptures that mattered most. Their choice varied from the Upanishads to Saiva texts, but for Gandhi the Bhagavad Gita was the focus – a 'pure religious discourse given without any embellishment. It simply describes the progress of the pilgrim soul towards the Supreme Goal.'[140] He once asked a class, 'Which is the one book that can be to the Hindus what the Bible is to the Christians or the Koran to the Maussalmans?',[141] answering that it was not the Vedas or Devipuranas or Bhagavata, but the Gita, which with its 700 verses encompasses the quintessence of 'all the Shastras and the Upanishads'. He argued that this text exhorted its readers to leave all 'isms and take refuge in the Lord alone'.[142] and claimed that the 'Gita is ever presenting me with fresh lessons.'[143] In the same speech at the Hindu Banaras University, he said, 'Today the Gita is not only my Bible or my Koran; it is more than that – it is my mother. I lost my earthly mother who gave me birth long ago; but this eternal Mother has completely filled her place by my side ever since.'[144]

Just as the King James Version became the book of the empire, Gandhi made the Gita the 'Global Book' which embraced everyone. He made it a book for all, including those outside the Brahmanical caste. The Gita verse that encapsulated this spirt for Gandhi 'O son of Prtha, those who take shelter in Me, though they be of lower birth – women, *vaishyas* [merchants] and *shudras* [workers] – can attain the supreme destination' (9.31).

Gandhi was not in favour of the critical study of the Bible, or for that matter any Scriptures, claiming that he did not approach Scriptures with a 'critical mind'. What he meant was that he was not that keen on using the various types of biblical criticism, such as historical investigation, which could 'vary with the progress of new historical discoveries and researches',[145] in order to arrive at a simpler meaning of the text.

This does not mean that he refrained from criticism of or commenting on what he called the 'sinful institutions'[146] embedded in the scriptural texts, such as the caste system, stoning for blasphemy, slavery and the fostering of warfare. When some Hindus quoted the *Manusmriti* in support of a rigid separation of the castes, Gandhi dismissed such textual approvals as 'apocryphal' and 'meaningless'.[147] He was equally critical of the stoning sanctioned in the Koran. For example, he questioned the morality of the stoning to death of two members of the Ahmadiyya sect in Afghanistan, arguing that this particular form of penalty could not be 'defended on the mere ground of its mention in the Koran'. He contended that whatever was permitted at the time of the Prophet had to be submitted to 'the acid test of reason and universal justice if it is to ask for universal assent'.[148]

Gandhi did not spare Christians in his comments on Scripture, questioning their moral authority to deploying biblical passages in support of their views and telling them in uncompromising terms that they carried a 'double sin on their shoulders, the sin of India's subjection and the subjection of the Negroes and African races'.[149] While his personal experience of the hurtful criticism of non-Hindu commentators taught him not to launch a general attack on 'Islam or Christianity and their founders', he saw it as both his 'right and duty to point out the defects in Hinduism in order to purify it and to keep it pure'. As he remarked, 'Every true scripture only gains by criticism.'[150]

Like many of Gandhi's dreams, his hermeneutical hope remained unfulfilled. At the turn of the last century he had harboured the optimistic belief that the time had passed when the followers of one religion might say that theirs was 'the only true religion and all others [were] false'.[151] This has not only proved to have been a false hope, but in fact the situation has got worse, with many religions asserting their superiority and exhibiting supersessionistic impulses.

In his writings, Gandhi preferred to use the term 'Christian Indians' rather than 'Indian Christians'. Among Hindu reformers, it was Gandhi who urged Christian Indians to get rid of the contentious label 'Christian' and become more Indian. Even before postcolonial discourse began to speak about identity, estrangement and mimicry, Gandhi portrayed Christian Indians as mimic men and women. He found fault with Christian Indians for their 'indiscriminate and thoughtless imitation', which reinforced that idea that 'Asiatics are fit only to copy everything that comes from the West.' He urged them to go through 'the fire of suffering and to resist any unlawful encroachment upon [their] own civilization'.[152]

Gandhi's religious tolerance and intertextual readings might seem of utility and even sensible to certain Hindus but look heretical to Hindutva ideologists, Muslims and Christians, when he called into question the 'premier position' of their religions.[153]

Gandhi left two monumental challenges for Indian Christians. First, his constant cross-textual referencing offered them a choice – either they could uphold the Bible as a single and secluded story, or make it part of the 'Ocean of Streams of Story'. He could not accept that religious texts were closed worlds, to be studied in isolation. He was a compulsive appropriator of world Scriptures and said it would be 'an evil day' if the reading and interpreting of religious books was undertaken in isolation and without cross-referencing with other scriptural texts.[154]

His second hermeneutical challenge for Indian Christians was his willingness to discard Hindu texts which had the potential to hurt people of other faiths. In a speech delivered in Jaffna, he said that if he found 'anything in Hinduism wherein the ancients agreed that [was] repugnant to my Christian brother or my Mussalman brother', he would begin to 'fidget and doubt the ancientness of that claim'.[155] But of course the Bible has plenty of repugnant and reprehensible statements about other faiths, so the challenge for Indian Christian whether they will be bold enough to advocate the jettisoning of such defamatory and triumphalistic content lodged in the Bible.

Notes

1 Literature on the life and work of Gandhi is legion. For the central purpose of this chapter, the following books might be of interest: William W. Emilsen (ed.), *Gandhi's Bible* (Delhi: ISPCK, 2001); Margaret Chatterjee, *Gandhi's Religious Thought* (London: Macmillan, 1983); and James D. Hunt, *Gandhi and the Nonconformists: Encounters in South Africa* (New Delhi: Promilla & Co, 1986).
2 M. K. Gandhi, *The Message of Jesus Christ* (Bombay: Bharatiya Vidya Bhavan,1964), 2.
3 Due to Covid19 and library restrictions, I have depended on online versions of Gandhi's works. All citations are from the Gandhi Sevagram Ashram version unless otherwise stated: https://www.gandhiashramsevagram.org/gandhi-literature/collected-works-of-mahatma-gandhi-volume-1-to-98.php. Hereafter, *Collected Works of Mahatma Gandhi*, 69/340.
4 *Collected Works of Mahatma Gandhi*, 5/39.
5 M. K. Gandhi, *Christian Missions: Their Place in India* (Ahmedabad: Navajivan Press, 1941),170.
6 *Collected Works of Mahatma Gandhi*, 43/7.
7 Joseph, Parker, *The People's Bible: Discourses upon Holy Scriptures. These sayings of mine, revealed in the Gospel of Matthew*, vol. 1 (New York: Funk and Wagnalls, 1888), 32.
8 *Collected Works of Mahatma Gandhi*, 29/90.

9. Mahadev H. Desai, *Day-to-Day with Gandhi: Secretary's Diary*, vol. VIII, 3 January to 30 December 1926 (Varnasi: Sarva Seva Sangh Prakashan, 1973), 228.
10. Desai, *Day-to-Day with Gandhi*, vol. VIII, 229.
11. *Collected Works of Mahatma Gandhi*, 40/117.
12. M. K. Gandhi, *What Jesus Means to Me* (Ahmedabad: Navjivan Publishing House, 1959), 32.
13. Raghavn Iyer (ed.), *The Moral and Political Writings of Mahatma Gandhi*, vol. 1: *Civilization, Politics and Religion* (Oxford: Clarendon Press, 1986), 182.
14. Gandhi, *Christian Missions*, 34.
15. *Collected Works of Mahatma Gandhi*, 40/117.
16. Desai, *Day-to-Day with Gandhi*, vol. VIII, 230.
17. Desai, *Day-to-Day with Gandhi*, vol. VIII, 232.
18. Gandhi, *The Message of Jesus Christ*, 30.
19. Gandhi, *The Message of Jesus Christ*, 46.
20. *Collected Works of Mahatma Gandhi*, 79/255.
21. *Collected Works of Mahatma Gandhi*, 32/336.
22. *Collected Works of Mahatma Gandhi*, 48/483.
23. *Collected Works of Mahatma Gandhi*, 79/255.
24. *Collected Works of Mahatma Gandhi*, 26/372.
25. *Collected Works of Mahatma Gandhi*, 21/116.
26. *Collected Works of Mahatma Gandhi*, 60/380.
27. *Collected Works of Mahatma Gandhi*, 60/380.
28. *Collected Works of Mahatma Gandhi*, 1/310.
29. *Collected Works of Mahatma Gandhi*, 1/310.
30. *Collected Works of Mahatma Gandhi*, 1/310.
31. *Collected Works of Mahatma Gandhi*, 67/207.
32. Gandhi, *Christian Missions*, 5.
33. Desai, *Day-to-Day with Gandhi*, vol. VIII, 231.
34. *Collected Works of Mahatma Gandhi*, 15/164.
35. *Collected Works of Mahatma Gandhi*, 40/290.
36. Gandhi, *Christian Missions*, 48.
37. M. K. Gandhi, *Non-violence in Peace and War* (Ahmedabad: Navjivan Publishing House, 1942), 44.
38. Roland Duncan (ed.), *Selected Writings of Mahatma Gandhi* (London: Fontan/Collins, 1972), 178.
39. Gandhi, *Christian Missions*, 275.
40. *Collected Works of Mahatma Gandhi*, 29/91.
41. *Collected Works of Mahatma Gandhi*, 38/425.
42. M. K. Gandhi, *In Search of the Supreme*, vol. I, ed. V. B. Kher (Ahmedabad: Navjivan Publishing House, 1961), 112.
43. *Collected Works of Mahatma Gandhi*, 32/335.
44. M. K. Gandhi, *Hindu Dharma* (Ahmedabad: Navjivan Publishing House, 1950), 22.
45. *Collected Works of Mahatma Gandhi*, 33/86.
46. *Collected Works of Mahatma Gandhi*, 33/85.
47. Gandhi, *Hindu Dharma*, 23.
48. *Collected Works of Mahatma Gandhi*, 33/85.
49. Gandhi, *Christian Missions*, 203.
50. Gandhi, *Hindu Dharma*, 234.
51. Gandhi, *Christian Missions*, 203.

52 Desai, *Day-to-Day with Gandhi*, vol. VIII, 230.
53 Desai, *Day-to-Day with Gandhi*, vol. VIII, 231.
54 *Collected Works of Mahatma Gandhi*, 32/335.
55 M. K. Gandhi, *The Selected Works of Mahatma Gandhi*, vol. V: *Selected Letters* (Ahmedabad: Navjivan Publishing House, 1968), 370.
56 *Collected Works of Mahatma Gandhi*, 54/310.
57 Gandhi, *Christian Missions*, 273.
58 *Collected Works of Mahatma Gandhi*, 79/255.
59 *Collected Works of Mahatma Gandhi*, 16/138.
60 *Collected Works of Mahatma Gandhi*, 69/340.
61 Gandhi, *Christian Missions*, 159.
62 M. K. Gandhi, *A Guide to Heath. Translated from Hindi by A Rama Iyer* (Madras: S. Ganesan Publisher, 1921), 146.
63 *Collected Works of Mahatma Gandhi*, 16/138.
64 Muriel Lester, *Entertaining Gandhi* (London: Ivor Nicholson and Watson, Strand, 1932), 3.
65 Desai, *Day-to-Day with Gandhi*, vol. VIII, 242.
66 Desai, *Day-to-Day with Gandhi*, vol. VIII, 265.
67 *Collected Works of Mahatma Gandhi*, 54/308.
68 Joseph J, Doke, *M.K.Gandhi: Indian Patriot in South Africa* (Rajghat: Khil Bharat Sarva Seva Sangh Prakashan, 1909), 34.
69 *Collected Works of Mahatma Gandhi*, 40/455.
70 Desai, *Day-to-Day with Gandhi*, vol. VIII, 309.
71 Desai, *Day-to-Day with Gandhi*, vol. VIII, 299.
72 *Collected Works of Mahatma Gandhi*, 21/199, 200. For a detailed study of how Gandhi's personal relationships, and especially his relationship with one of his sons, affected his reading, see Alex Damm, 'Gandhi and the Parable of the Prodigal Son', *Biblical Interpretation* 29, no. 1 (2021): 90–105.
73 Iyer, *The Moral and Political Writings of Mahatma Gandhi*, vol. 1, 564.
74 *Collected Works of Mahatma Gandhi*, 21/169.
75 Iyer, *The Moral and Political Writings of Mahatma Gandhi*, vol. 1, 354–5.
76 *Collected Works of Mahatma Gandhi*, 71/173.
77 Gandhi, *Christian Missions*, 292.
78 *Collected Works of Mahatma Gandhi*, 71/340.
79 Iyer, *The Moral and Political Writings of Mahatma Gandhi*, vol. 1, 550.
80 *Collected Works of Mahatma Gandhi*, 36/321.
81 *Collected Works of Mahatma Gandhi*, vol. 13 (New Delhi: Publications Division, Ministry of Information and Broadcastings), 334; Collected Works Of Mahatma Gandhi, vol. 13: Gandhi, Mohandas Karamchand: Free Download, Borrow, and Streaming: Internet Archive.
82 Gandhi, *Christian Missions*, 170.
83 *Collected Works of Mahatma Gandhi*, 29/90.
84 Gandhi, *Christian Missions*, 171.
85 *Collected Works of Mahatma Gandhi*, 29/90.
86 *Collected Works of Mahatma Gandhi*, 71/132.
87 Gandhi, *The Message of Jesus Christ*, 36.
88 *Collected Works of Mahatma Gandhi*, 32/336.
89 Iyer, *The Moral and Political Writings of Mahatma Gandhi*, vol. 1, 506.
90 Desai, *Day-to-Day with Gandhi*, vol. VIII, 235.

91 Desai, *Day-to-Day with Gandhi*, vol. VIII, 242.
92 Raghavn Iyer (ed.), *The Moral and Political Writings of Mahatma Gandhi*, vol. III: *Non-Violent Resistance and Social Transformation* (Oxford: Clarendon Press), 1986, 26.
93 Gandhi, *What Jesus Means to Me*, 32.
94 Louis Fischer, *Gandhi: His Life and Message for the World* (New York: New American Library, 1954), 131.
95 Gandhi, *What Jesus Means to Me*, 33.
96 *Collected Works of Mahatma Gandhi*, 54/89.
97 Iyer, *The Moral and Political Writings of Mahatma Gandhi*, vol. 1, 504.
98 Fischer, *Gandhi: His Life and Message for the World*, 131.
99 Gandhi, *The Message of Jesus Christ*, 30.
100 *Collected Works of Mahatma Gandhi*, 71/130.
101 Mahadev H. Desai, *Day-to-Day with Gandhi: Secretary's Diary*, vol. VII, 23 May to 28 December 1925 (Varnasi: Sarva Seva Sangh Prakashan, 1972), 36.
102 *Collected Works of Mahatma Gandhi*, 15/436.
103 S. K. George, *Gandhi's Challenge to Christianity* (London: George Allen and Unwin Ltd., 1939), 61.
104 Gandhi, *What Jesus Means to Me*, 23.
105 *Collected Works of Mahatma Gandhi*, 13/154.
106 *Collected Works of Mahatma Gandhi*, 15/159.
107 Gandhi, *Christian Missions*, 121.
108 Gandhi, *What Jesus Means to Me*, 26.
109 Gandhi, *Christian Missions*, 240.
110 Gandhi, *What Jesus Means to Me*, 23.
111 Robert Ellsberg (ed.), *Gandhi on Christianity* (Maryknoll, NY: Orbis Books, 1991), 57
112 Gandhi, *Christian Missions*, 78.
113 Gandhi, *Christian Missions*, 48.
114 Doke, *M.K. Gandhi: Indian Patriot in South Africa*, 29.
115 Gandhi, *Christian Missions*, 61.
116 Gandhi, *Christian Missions*, 51.
117 Gandhi, *Christian Missions*, 52
118 Duncan, *Selected Writings of Mahatma Gandhi*, 138.
119 Duncan, *Selected Writings of Mahatma Gandhi*, 141.
120 Duncan, *Selected Writings of Mahatma Gandhi*, 136.
121 *Collected Works of Mahatma Gandhi*, 33/85.
122 Gandhi, *Christian Missions*, 233.
123 Gandhi, *Christian Missions*, 48.
124 Duncan, *Selected Writings of Mahatma Gandhi*, 159/
125 P. Chenchiah, 'Christian Message in a Non Christian World', in G. V. Job et al. (eds), *Rethinking Christianity in India* (Madras: Hogarth Press, 1939), 175.
126 A. J. Appasamy, *Christianity as Bhakti Marga* (Madras: Christian Literature Society, 1928), 156.
127 Arthur Hirtzel, *The Church, The Empire, and the World* (London: Society for Promoting Christian Knowledge, 1919), 32.
128 *Collected Works of Mahatma Gandhi*, 30/311.
129 *Collected Works of Mahatma Gandhi*, 30/311.
130 Desai, *Day-to-Day with Gandhi*, vol. VIII, 226.
131 *Collected Works of Mahatma Gandhi*, 33/85.

132 D. G. Tendulkar, *Mahatma: Life of Mohandas Karamchand Gandhi*, vol. 2: *1920–1929* (Bombay: Vithalbhai K. Jhaveri and D. G. Tendulkar, 1951), 361.
133 Tendulkar, *Mahatma*, 33/84.
134 Tendulkar, *Mahatma*, 40/291.
135 M. K. Gandhi, *Speeches and Writings of Mahatma Gandhi* (Madras: G. A. Natesan, 1930), 351.
136 *Collected Works of Mahatma Gandhi*, 13/440.
137 Gandhi, *The Message of Jesus Christ*, 25.
138 *Collected Works of Mahatma Gandhi*, 12/ 81.
139 *Collected Works of Mahatma Gandhi*, 15/160.
140 Gandhi, *The Message of Jesus Christ*, 47.
141 *Collected Works of Mahatma Gandhi*, 64/254.
142 *Collected Works of Mahatma Gandhi*, 64/256.
143 *Collected Works of Mahatma Gandhi*, 64/256.
144 *Collected Works of Mahatma Gandhi*, 64/255.
145 *Collected Works of Mahatma Gandhi*, 32/336.
146 *Collected Works of Mahatma Gandhi*, 30/311.
147 *Collected Works of Mahatma Gandhi*, 16/139.
148 *Collected Works of Mahatma Gandhi*, 30/ 311.
149 *Harijan* 9, no. 23 (21 June 1942): 194.
150 *Collected Works of Mahatma Gandhi*, 30/336.
151 *Collected Works of Mahatma Gandhi*, 4/391.
152 *Collected Works of Mahatma Gandhi*, 39/370.
153 *Collected Works of Mahatma Gandhi*, 4/392.
154 *Collected Works of Mahatma Gandhi*, 79/255.
155 *Collected Works of Mahatma Gandhi*, 40/451.

Chapter 7

A VARIANT OF THE VEDAS

Nearly one hundred years after Thomas Babington Macaulay's both celebrated and censured Minute of 1835 on Indian education, there appeared a cloned version. A. G. Hogg (1875–1954), a Scottish missionary who worked in colonial India as an educator, wrote about the impact of Christian schools on the subcontinent:

> The Indian who has had years of instruction in such a school or college is no longer a typical Hindu. His outlook upon life has been modified; he has imbibed many Christian ideas; he has become uncertain or even sceptical about many Hindu doctrines. In mind and soul, he has gone part of the way to meet the missionary, and so the missionary does not need to go all the way to meet him.[1]

The condescending sentiment expressed here was in the same league as that of the famed Minute of 1835, but with a difference. The class of cultural intermediaries that Macaulay hoped for were anglicized Indians, whereas Hogg expected Christianized Hindus to serve as brokers between Western missionaries and India. To the horror of Hogg, one Hindu who did not fit this bill was his favourite student. This individual did not harbour any doubts about his Hindu faith and spent his entire life confidently representing and defining Hinduism. His name was Sarvepalli Radhakrishnan (1888–1975), the philosopher and the second President of the Republic of India. There is a massive critical industry around his work, but the principal concern here is an often-overlooked aspect of his writings – his appropriation of the Bible for his Vedantic cause.[2]

Like the Hindu reformers of the colonial era, it was the misrepresentation of Hinduism, especially by his missionary teachers, that led Radhakrishnan to take a serious look at his religious tradition. As he reiterated in his numerous autobiographical reminiscences, he was particularly depressed by a slew of accusations levelled against Hinduism – concerning its intellectual incoherence, ethical unsoundness and 'unprogressiveness or stationariness'.[3] Radhakrishnan was particularly irritated by the condescending attitude of Edwin Greaves (who worked in North India), who remarked that the better-behaved Hindus were 'nominal Christians'.[4] Such comments 'disturbed' Radhakrishnan's faith and 'shook the traditional props on which [he] leaned'.[5]

Linked to this misrepresentation were a couple of other factors. One was Radhakrishnan's realization that Indian political stagnancy was due to the ineffectiveness of Hinduism. The political crisis was thus a 'sign of an inward crisis, a loss of faith, a weakening of our moral fibre'.[6] The other factor was the Mohammedan conquest and its propagandist work, which shook the 'stability of Hindu society'.[7] As Radhakrishnan recalled later, these matters 'forced' him to undertake a 'critical study of the Hindu tradition'.[8] He saw such a study of Indian scriptural classics as a national and noble duty for every Indian: 'For us Indians, a study of the Upanishads is essential, if we are to preserve our national being and character.'[9]

In this pursuit, two towering figures of Indian renaissance helped to rouse his Hindu pride. As those familiar with Radhakrishnan's work know, he greatly benefitted from 'the enterprise and eloquence of Vivekananda', while he also acknowledged the importance of Rabindranath Tagore in the same essay in which he paid tribute to Vivekananda.[10]

What is often overlooked by scholars is that Radhakrishnan's writings on Hinduism contained many references to the Christian Bible as well as his acknowledgement of its importance. When asked what books influenced him, Radhakrishnan listed on various occasions the Bible, the works of Shakespeare and the writings of Kant.[11] He told one audience that British civilization was a composite symbolized by 'the cricket bat, the ballot box, the limited liable company and the Authorized Version of the Holy Bible'.[12] Like the students who attended the missionary schools in colonial India, he, too, memorized biblical passages. According to his son Gopal, Radhakrishnan planned to write a commentary on St John's Gospel but had to shelve the idea because of his involvement in producing the Gandhi centenary volume.[13]

Scriptures: Beyond Words

Radhakrishnan acknowledged that 'the great scriptures [were] the records of the sayings of the prophets, *āpta-vacana*'.[14] They were 'endless' and the knowledge acquired from them was 'immense', but one needed to be circumspect in choosing which Scriptures to focus on and then 'study them even as the swan takes in only the milk which is mixed with water'.[15] Radhakrishnan had his own chosen canon, which included the Vedas, the Bhagavad Gita, the Upanishads and the Dhammapada. For Radhakrishnan, these were the real Scriptures, what he called 'our classics'[16] and 'the absolute standard for the Hindu religion'.[17] He maintained that these books had 'done more to colour our minds than we generally acknowledge' and were 'life-giving and elevating'.[18]

For Radhakrishnan, the sastras or Scriptures were registers of the 'intuitions of the perfected souls'[19] and the 'experience of the seers'[20] who had 'grappled with the problem of reality'.[21] Acceptance of these sastras was not dependent on their positions on God or their historical validity. Like Keshub Chunder Sen, Radhakrishnan was conscious that any such claims might be undermined by subsequent scientific or historical discoveries.

A Variant of the Vedas

Although an inveterate user of scriptural texts, Radhakrishnan did not give them any 'exaggerated respect'.[22] He was also careful not to ascribe divine authorship or inerrancy to the Scriptures, points which were believed by only a few fundamentalists in each religion.

Radhakrishnan consistently maintained the Enlightenment stance that the Scriptures were 'human documents, written by human hands liable to error'. They were the 'products of history' and some of their content were 'forgeries'. He even went so far as to say that he could not claim that any of these Scriptures were the word of God: their inspired character did not imply their 'alleged divine dictation', but rather their value lay in the 'nature of their contents'.[23] The Scriptures were residues of 'crude, imperfect and undeveloped images',[24] which needed to be refined and improved on the in the light of our present knowledge. As Radhakrishnan advised his readers, 'It will not be wise to look upon ancestral wisdom as infallible.'[25]

Radhakrishnan speaks of the Scriptures in contradictory or opposing ways – as 'eternal and imperishable' and 'temporary and perishable', and as 'context bound' yet 'transcend[ing] time and culture'. He treated the Scriptures as records that were special and specific to each religious tradition: the message was universal but the medium was local. He cited a number of biblical verses such as John 16.12 and Acts 10.34 to support the view that God had chosen to speak in diverse ways, a 'divine self-manifestation' that is mediated through humans. They are a fixed entity, 'the same for nearly fifty centuries',[26] but also a process, a tradition that is growing. Since the Scriptures are tentative and inconclusive, Radhakrishnan cautioned his readers not 'to close the door to future revelations'.[27]

Radhakrishnan gives the impression of being the champion of all Scriptures but such a judgement does not stand up to scrutiny. He maintained that all Scriptures were testimonies to the same truth: that 'all prophets *are* one' and that there is '*one* Bible in all'.[28] Yet the same person who stated that there was no 'dogmatic exclusiveness'[29] in any of the Scriptures of the world, insisted on the pre-eminence of the Vedas, and declared proudly that the other Scriptures 'sink to silence when the Vedānta appears even as foxes do not raise their voices in the forest when the lion appears'.[30] His espousal of Hindu texts comes out clearly in his prescription of Scriptures to be taught in Indian universities. Characteristically, he began with an even-handed approach and encouraged graduate courses to the select from Gita, the Dhammapada, the Zend Avesta, the Old Testament, St John's Gospel and the Guru Granth Sahib. He recommended that only texts which were of 'universal character' should be studied, but the same report, which was largely his own work, identified the Vedantic essence *tat tvam asi* (thou art thou) as the goal of education. This Vedic essence could be possible if one is taught to 'look within'. According to Radhakrishnan, the purpose of education is to 'awaken the pupil to this fact, enable him to find the spirit within and mould his life and action in the light and power of the inner spirit'.[31] Yet the same Radhakrishnan who quoted a Roman senator to enhance the argument that 'it is impossible that so great a mystery should be approached by one road only'[32] also singled out Hindu texts which advocated Vedantic values. Ironically, to substantiate his case for the

Vedantic ideal of finding the spirit within, he cited extensively from Christian biblical texts: 'The spirit of man is the candle of the Lord' (Prov. 20.27) and 'Know you not that you are the temple of God, and the spirit of God dwelleth in you' (1 Cor. 3.16).[33]

Radhakrishnan advocated that the Scriptures of all traditions should be subjected to historical and critical investigation. He wanted to use scientific criticism and historical knowledge to expunge the large mass of myths and legends which were not the inspired word of God and to place the Scriptures in their historical context. Radhakrishnan was of the view that interpretation must be in 'conformity with the findings of science'[34] and should be subjected to 'rational scrutiny'. At the same time, he warned against 'rationalistic self-sufficiency'.

Although Radhakrishnan respected scriptural texts, he did not allot much value to the texts themselves, believing that spiritual truths could not be contained or compressed within the pages of a book. He wrote that there was 'no one way by which spiritual rebirth is attained'[35] and that the essence of truth could not be reduced to writing. Written words are not the sole or exclusive vehicle for experiencing the divine, conveying only partial truths, and mostly only 'feebly', and are 'vain attempts' to validate and defend the meaning of that experience. Such experience transcends all forms, images, concepts and texts. In Radhakrishnan's opinion, Vidya, or knowledge, is not necessarily acquired through 'textual learning'. The experience of a direct relationship with the divine could be achieved through visions and even through silence. The written word was 'utterly futile' compared to the experience of a vision of the divine. Seeing the divine is not an intellectual exercise or a matter of logical understanding, but rather a mysterious wisdom attained through 'dreams and divination'.[36]

Radhakrishnan describes such an experience as a 'reception of the spirit', an 'illumination', a 'deification'. He often said that the knowledge of God comes not through texts but through 'beatific vision'. The ṛṣis are not so much the authors of the truths recorded in the Vedas, as the seers who are able to discern the eternal truths by raising their life-spirit to the plane of universal spirit. Such visions and trances were granted to savants like Moses, Isaiah, Ezekiel and Paul, whose religious awaking was based on an inner vision and not an external revelation. Radhakrishnan cited a range of passages from the Acts of the Apostles and the Corinthian correspondence to establish that ecstatic visions and voices sustained Paul's missionary endeavours. For Radhakrishnan, the experience of the ultimate mystery is an intuitive insight, a *darshan*. Those who had the vision were the people who 'walk[ed] by sight not by faith'.[37] Such visions warm the heart and negate the 'appeal of the "Thus saith the Lord"'.[38]

Another way of experiencing the supreme reality that Radhakrishnan advocated was through silence. The Scriptures have shortcomings in terms of conveying the truth, which is eternal, as opposed to texts, which are temporal and transient. This issue has prompted the greatest religious seers to choose silence over speech in order to communicate the Truth. Radhakrishnan cited the example of Lao Tze, who stated that attainment meant non-discussion; the Buddha, who maintained silence when questioned about the nature of Nirvana; and Jesus, who remained silent when Pilate questioned him about the nature of truth. This silence is an indication of the 'inexpressibility of certain truths of spiritual life'.[39] When the Scriptures deal with this silence, the language is not literal but allegoric and symbolic.

For Radhakrishnan, 'texts' alone were not supreme and certainly did not exhaust the truth. Visions, voices and even silences were sources of things unutterable and testimony to the ineffability of the experience. As he pointed out, 'When one knows the truth there is no need for the *Vedas*.'[40] Radhakrishnan held the view that 'spiritual truth is a far greater thing than the scriptures'[41] and that '[t]he eternity of the *Vedas*', 'the timelessness of the of the *dharma*' of the Buddhists, and 'the eternity of the Divine word of the Christians refer not to the texts but to the truths enshrined in them'.[42] The proper attitude towards the Scriptures is therefore 'not only to reverence them, but to acquire their spirit'.[43]

What was important for Radhakrishnan was not the texts but the truth enshrined in them. His mantra was that the 'spiritual truth is far greater thing than the scriptures'.[44] Texts were not only unreliable but could be 'dated', whereas truth is eternal and timeless. The hermeneutical prescription was that one had to be emancipated from the 'dead letter'.

The Bible: An Upanishadic Book:

Radhakrishnan clearly treated Hindu and Christian Scriptures as crude polarities. The sacred Scriptures of the Hebrews and the Christians were 'more religious and ethical' but those of the Hindus were more 'spiritual and contemplative'. Biblical religion was 'severe, militant, uncompromising, and intolerant', whereas the texts of mystic religions like Hinduism was 'renouncing, other-worldly, peaceful'.[45] He conceded that while the Hindu Scriptures commended non-violence as the supreme duty, there were occasions when a departure from a pacifist approach was 'permissible'.

A significant difference between the Hindu Scriptures and the Christian Bible was that the great Indian texts had no '*ex cathedra* character'. The Christian Scriptures derived their authority from the Church, whereas the Hindu sacred writings derived their authority from the inner certitude and intuitions of a believer. The authoritativeness of Christian texts is marked by strident words such as 'Thus saith the Lord', while in the Bhagavad Gita, Krishna offered counsel without imposing his will, as exemplified by his repeated words 'This is my opinion.' Whereas the biblical writings were developed and preserved by the Church for the 'instruction of its members and the continuity of doctrine',[46] the Hindu Scriptures were registers of the 'intuitions of the perfected souls'. They are not so much 'dogmatic dicta' as records of the 'spiritual experiences of the souls strongly endowed with the sense of reality'.[47] While Christians treated the Bible as a theological touchstone and commended 'mechanical adherence' to its authority, the Hindus perceived their sacred texts as the products of 'spiritual intuitions'. Their utterances are not grounded in fleeting observations, but rather in a 'continuous experience of resident life and power'.[48]

For Radhakrishnan, the Vedas are about 'trust' whereas the Bible is about 'certitude'. One is about the integral experiences of the seers 'ever the same yet changing ever', while the other is about the assurance of the absolute authority of Jesus and his ability to save souls. One is universal and inclusive, the other is about the particular and the exclusive and appeals to those who place their faith in Jesus. Christian Scriptures are dogmatic and ecclesiastical, whereas the Hindu texts are pragmatic and people oriented. The Hindu texts are 'dressed up in myths and stories' to reach the ordinary person, and their prime task is to make the multitude interested in metaphysics.[49]

The openness and the undogmatic stance of Hindu texts places them above other Scriptures. For instance, the experience of Christian seers was a closed one, centring on Jesus and tending to dismiss other experiences as 'illusory' and 'imperfect'. Hindu texts, on the other hand, remain faithful to their 'experimental basis' and are a 'Godward endeavour of the human spirit' as they have continuously developed. They are a 'tapestry of variegated tissues and almost endless diversity of hues', a 'vast, complex, but subtly unified mass of spiritual thought and realization'.[50] In contrast, Christian texts are essentially provincial and vernacular.

Radhakrishnan's choice of the Christian Scriptures was limited to the extent to which they supported his hermeneutical project of espousing the Upanishadic ideals. He even envisioned Jesus and Paul as exemplifying this Upanishadic tone and tenor (but more of that later). He marshalled a number of biblical texts to reinforce the teaching of the Upanishads – the eternal is in oneself, thou art that, *tat tvam asi*. For Radhakrishnan, what distinguished Hinduism from other religions was the divine spark in human beings: 'There is a religious view for which the East has stood, and which is unknown in the West, that man with his sense of values is the most concrete embodiment of the divine on earth.'[51] He listed various biblical texts to reinforce this Upanishadic vision: 'So God created man in his own image; in the image of God he created him' (Gen. 1.27), and from the book of Jeremiah: 'I will put my hand in their inward parts, and in their heart will I write it' (31.33). Another text which Radhakrishnan used quite often was from the wisdom literature: 'The spirit of man is the candle of the Lord' (Prov. 20.27). He habitually referred to the sayings of Jesus, such as 'I and the Father are one', 'All that the Father hath are mine', as examples of God's indwelling presence in the world. For Radhakrishnan, 'Be ye therefore perfect as your heavenly father is also perfect' summed up Jesus' various ethical demands. The example of Jesus demonstrated that the difference between God and a human being was 'only one of degree'. Radhakrishnan envisioned Jesus like the Buddha, Socrates and Zoroaster, revealing the 'divine possibilities of human nature and giv[ing] us the courage to be ourselves'.[52] He declared that 'the point of Jesus' life and teaching is that each one of us can become the Son of God'[53] and that 'we are all fragments of the divine, sons of immortality, *amṛtasya putrāḥ*'.[54] Such divine manifestations were 'not an infringement of man's personality', but, on the contrary, were the 'highest possible degree of man's natural self-expression, since the true nature of man is divine'.[55]

What appealed to Radhakrishnan about the Bible was that it embodied one of the 'the central features of the Upanishads' – *ahimsa*. The exhortation in the book of Exodus to return the straying donkey or the ox of an enemy, the magnanimous behaviour of Joseph towards his brothers depicted in the forty-fifth chapter of the book of Genesis when he forgave them, and Paul's writing to the Romans, using quotes from the book of Proverbs, taking care of the hunger and thirst of an enemy, are examples of the Upanishadic *ahimsa* at work.

Another Upanishadic concept that Radhakrishnan identified in the Bible – the law of karma – did not commend itself to the majority of Christians. Radhakrishnan reminded Christians that karma was not 'peculiar to Oriental creeds'[56] and was frequently referred to in the Christian Scriptures. Radhakrishnan's Jesus appeared to have endorsed the doctrine of karma in the Sermon on the Mount: 'Judge not, that ye be not judged. For with what judgment ye judge, ye shall be judged: and with what measure ye mete, it shall be measured to you again.' Jesus' words to the paralytic, 'Courage my son, your sins are forgiven', and to the sick man, to 'sin no more, lest a worse thing come unto thee', were presented as further proof of Jesus' approval of the law of karma – that past actions have repercussions. Radhakrishnan believed that the parables of the tares, the thief, the hidden treasure, the pearl, the lost sheep, the talents, the ten virgins and the wedding garment all conveyed the lesson that one is saved by one's deed. The five virgins were a conspicuous case in point, having botched their opportunities and wasted their chance.

Just like Jesus, Paul was reframed by Radhakrishnan as an advocate of the Hindu doctrine of karma: 'whatsoever a man soweth, that shall he reap'. This Pauline saying was regularly deployed as an affirmation of the responsibility of each individual. Radhakrishnan found a comparable verse in Ezekiel: 'The soul that sinneth, it shall die' (18.20). Furthermore, the Hebrew story of sorrow and suffering as a consequence of sin and stupidity was seen as confirmation of the Hindu view. If Ramanathan turned the Christian Bible into Saiva Siddhantha sastras, Radhakrishnan reshaped it as a Vedic text: 'Christian teaching in its origin, before it became externalized and organized, was about awakening from sleep through the light shed by the inner wisdom.'[57]

Texts and Testaments

Besides turning the Bible into an Upanishadic text, Radhakrishnan's foray into biblical texts veers from deep appreciation to scepticism of their utility value. He admired the emphasis the Hebrew prophets placed on the simplicities of religion. Amos, for example, did not care for religious ceremonies but only for justice and righteousness. Micah added love to this list and Hosea summed up all these elements: 'He hath shewed thee, O man, what is good; and what doth the Lord require of thee, but to do justly, and to love mercy, and to walk humbly with thy God?' (6.8). Similarly, Radhakrishnan admired the 'pure and simple teachings of Jesus' recorded in the Gospels – it was about 'love and sympathy, tolerance and inwardness'. At the same time, he lamented how this 'simple code' of Jesus lost its clarity and integrity though subsequent doctrinal developments and the formalism that crept into the Christian faith, an example of which was Jesus' last meal, which later acquired a 'magical significance'.[58]

Radhakrishnan's attitude to the biblical texts simply reflected the stock scholarly practice of the time, which, under the intrusive influence of form criticism, viewed them as myths and metaphors and downplayed their historical value and authenticity. He stated that the narratives in Genesis should not be treated as a 'literal account' and treated the Gospels not so much as 'facts of history' as the 'fancies of the devout'. They were works of fantasy: 'The historical facts were soon covered over by the accretions of imagination.'[59] The Gospels were 'historically quite untrustworthy', having been shaped by the 'devotional needs and spiritual experiences of the early Christian communities', with the result that they 'tell more of the faith of the church than of what Jesus actually said and did'.[60] This did not mean that Radhakrishnan dismissed the Gospels as unreliable historical records but that he advised caution in using them. He observed that even if they were 'the products of fervent devotion', there must have been a historical conviction that 'those who lived with Jesus felt that they had been in contact with a personality so superior to them as to deserve divine honours'.[61]

It was not the unhistorical nature of the biblical narratives that concerned Radhakrishnan but their judgemental tone, antiquity and irrelevance. The Christian Scriptures, he estimated, fell into two contradictory lines of thought – 'pacific' and 'militarist', the latter being undeniably prominent. The image of the biblical God varied between a 'loving father, a severe judge, a detective officer, a hard schoolmaster and the head of the clerical profession'.[62] Yahweh of the Hebrew Scriptures was 'essentially a national deity' despite the efforts of prophets like Hosea and Isaiah to make this God the God of the whole earth. Still, Yahweh remained 'provincial'.[63] This God of the Bible, Radhakrishnan asserted, sanctioned wars and wholesale massacre:

> The judgement of God is the dominating note of the Bible. From the sentence upon Adam and Eve and the condemnation of Cain, down to the closing vision of St. John's Apocalypse, we have the emphasis on the sovereignty and judgement of God ... The Christian Church, in the spirit of the Hebrew prophets, often appeals more to the terror of judgement and the wrath of God than to the sense of guilt and the grace of God.[64]

The Parable of the Strong Man (Lk. 11.21-2) and God's harsh treatment of Dives were shocking examples of the biblical God behaving badly. When Jesus was elevated to the status of God, he continued to be judgemental and pronounced sentence on those who offended him. The magnanimity and non-resistance found in the sayings of Jesus, such as turn the other cheek, in Radhakrishnan's observation, were largely meant for personal use for a small group of people in a hostile environment and not for organized society, which had to use coercion to maintain law and order. Radhakrishnan pronounced that 'the real Jesus was not the one who bade us to turn the other cheek, but the one who used the scourge in the temple'.[65] His verdict was that 'Armed resistance is not contrary to the Gospel of Jesus'[66] and that 'Jesus, the saint of the non-resistance, is a fiction of the theologian.'[67]

Radhakrishnan saw the biblical books as products of their time and, as such, had neither universal appeal nor spoke to contemporary times. Replicating the views of C. K. Burkitt, a leading English form critic at that time, he regarded the Synoptics as 'Jewish books, occupied with problems belonging originally to first century Judaism', and as such had no 'meaning for us'. Since large parts of these texts were difficult to use, they forfeited any claim to be 'books of universal religion'.

Radhakrishnan's harshest criticism of the Bible was its lack of originality. Its lack of creativity was exemplified by the presence of echoes, allusions, references and resonances to other Scriptures. The law code laid out in Deuteronomy was 'largely a degraded version of the Hammurabi Code', while the book of Proverbs and considerable parts of the Psalms were based on older Egyptian literature. Likewise, Christian texts had drawn from Greek metaphysics and mystery religions. He found in the sayings of Jesus 'affinities' with Hindu texts, such as Jesus's words concerning his divinity – I am the truth – which has a 'family resemblance' to I am Brahman, '*aham brahmasāmi*', of the Vedic seers. Similarly, Radhakrishnan claimed that the ascended Christ's saying 'I will make him a pillar in the temple of My God, and he shall go out no more' – especially the expression 'he shall go out no more' (Rev. 3.12) – had a 'family likeness to the Hindu view that the saved does not return to the struggle of *samsara*'.[68] Another example of the Indian influence is the phrase 'wheel of birth', found in the Epistle of James. Influences of Alexandrian Judaism, the Book of Wisdom and the writings of Philo could be detected in the Epistle to the Hebrews. Radhakrishnan found an endorsement for these outside borrowings and influences in Paul: 'I am debtor both to the Greeks, and to the Barbarians' (Rom. 1.14).

The hermeneutical ploy that Radhakrishnan employed to undermine anything unique in the Bible was to universalize it and make it commonplace. For instance, he reduced one of the key foundational elements in the formation of Christian faith – the cross – to a routine event experienced within other faith traditions. With his characteristic confidence, Radhakrishnan pronounced that Hindu and Buddhist stories have a number of instances where Rishis and Buddhas had 'sanctified tapas (penance) and suffered more than they deserved for the sake of the world'. The cross, he claimed, was not a 'stumbling block to the Hindu but a great symbol of self-sacrifice and the redemptive reality of God'.[69]

Moreover, Radhakrishnan downplayed the Semitic roots of the New Testament, especially the epistles of St Paul and the Johannine letters, declaring that they did not 'belong to the Palestinian tradition' and that the Judaic basis of their chief theological propositions was 'wanting'. He maintained that the teaching of otherworldliness and the mystical elements found in John the Baptist, Jesus and Paul could not be accounted for by their 'Jewish background', but that there was sufficient justification for regarding them as 'Indian'.

Radhakrishnan further weakened the potency and integrity of the Gospels by saying that the birth stories of Buddha, Krishna and Jesus had 'striking resemblances suggestive of mutual borrowing'.[70] He also asserted that the 'evangelists were unconsciously influenced by the cult of the Buddha'.[71] and that Krishna and Christ were one because there were similarities in their teachings. He reduced the value of some of the signature events of the New Testament, such as the transfiguration of Jesus and the vision of Saul on the road to Damascus, as 'akin to the vison of Arjuna',[72] the charioteer to Lord Krishna.

Radhakrishnan fundamental point was that Christianity was an 'organic' part of the development of world religions and, as such, did not 'come into the world as a readymade supernatural system'. His case was made easier by Friedrich Heiler, German theologian and historian of religion, who argued 'There is not a single central doctrine of Christianity which does not have an array of striking parallels in various non-Christian faiths.'[73]

Moving Beyond the Canon

Radhakrishnan's use of the Christian Scriptures was not confined to the stock canonical books. He delved into the texts that were excluded from the Jewish and Christian Scriptures (in popular parlance, the non-canonical Scriptures), such as the book of *Enoch* and the Acts of Thomas. Unlike some Hindu nationalists, whom we will meet later and who employed these very texts to expose the contradictions in, and unreliability of, the Gospels, Radhakrishnan cites them entirely for different reasons: first, to detect Hindu/Indian traces in them; second, to prove Christianity's indebtedness to the Jewish apocrypha, thus diminishing its uniqueness – a particular interest of his; and third, to establish the presence of Indian Christians from the beginning of the first millennium.

Radhakrishnan's Indian/Hindu-centric method was applied with thoroughness to the non-canonical Scriptures. He ascribed Indian influences to the tenets of the Essenes and to the book of *Enoch*. Themes such as the Kingdom of God, life eternal, the ascetic emphasis and even the ideas about the future presented in the book were seen as departures from the Jewish tradition and closer to Hindu and Buddhist thought. Though *Enoch*'s teaching was 'historically continuous with Judaism, it did not develop from it in its essentials'.[74]

Radhakrishnan attributed 'some of the central features of Jesus' consciousness and teaching' to the book of *Enoch*, which he called 'a remarkable Hebrew work'. He noted that 'the predicates which are attributed to Enoch's God' were 'found in the Upanishads'. In the same book, he uncovered Christological titles such as the Christ, the Righteous One, the Elect One and the Son of Man which could be traced to 'the Aryan East'. Based on the work of Rudolf Otto, a Lutheran and a comparative theologian, Radhakrishnan advanced the theory that Enoch's portrayal of the conflated figure of the Son of God/Son of Man was 'certainly not from Israel' and indeed was found only 'among the Aryans'.[75] While Otto contended that Enoch's primitive deity was quite Indian, Radhakrishnan went further and asserted that the attributes of Enoch's God were found in the Upanishads. He contended that Jesus' identification as the Son of Man and Son of God was linked to an ancient Hindu tradition which Enoch exemplified and Jesus conserved and extended.

Radhakrishnan utilized Jewish and apocryphal writings to prove that Indian Christians were integral to the general Indian community, for example using the narrative in the Acts of Thomas to connect the existence of Christians in India to the mission of the reluctant apostle Thomas, who had been cajoled by Jesus to undertake this work. This text, along with the discovery of the coins of the Indo-Parthian King Gondophares in 1834, was proof of the existence of Indian Christian communities from ancient times. Radhakrishnan's claim that Indian Christians were a constituent part of Indian society disrupted the mainstream and nationalist narratives that represented Christians in India as the products of Western imperialism. Radhakrishnan regarded Christianity as part of India's religious landscape, with a pedigree traceable to the second century CE. Therefore, Christians did not 'merely [have] the rights of a guest but the rights of a native'– a conclusion that was at odds with the views of Hindu nationalists.[76]

Jesus an Eastern Seer, Paul a Vedic Rishi

Jesus' emphasis on intuitive realization, non-aggressive virtues, universalist ethics, non-dogmatic tolerance, in Radhakrishnan's opinion, marked him as a 'typical Eastern seer'.[77] What Jesus taught had nothing in common with the approach of the militant and hierarchal Church. Radhakrishnan's thesis was that the whole life and teaching of Jesus was so distinctive that it could not be regarded as a natural development of Jewish and Greek ideas; that the heart of Jesus' preaching was Eastern in origin.

Radhakrishnan's Jesus resembles the seers of the Upanishads or the Buddha. Just as the seers 'protested against Vedic ceremonialism', Jesus challenged 'Rabbinical orthodoxy' and tried to rid the Jewish religion of its impurities – as he would have done with Hinduism had he been born a Hindu. To Radhakrishnan, Jesus was a reformer who was keen to enlarge and purify his tradition rather than deny or belittle it.

As with the Indian seers, Radhakrishnan portrayed Jesus as someone who experienced a total transformation, going 'through inner doubts and discords, temptations and battles' and gradually advancing in 'wisdom and stature'. This transformation was not the usual penitence or regret for the past but a total self-realization and change of heart and mind, resulting in the 'displacement of ignorance, avidyā, by knowledge, vidyā'. From that point on, Jesus' teachings sprang from this 'transfigured consciousness'. This new orientation enabled him to grow beyond being a 'Jew, a child of Israel' and transcend 'the exclusivist atmosphere of the Hebrews' and their 'idiom and thought'. Striking evidence of this earlier restrictive thinking was the callous way he had treated the Syrophoenician woman. Jesus' refusal to help was expressed very stridently in Matthew's version of the story: 'I was not sent to any except the lost sheep of the house of Israel' (15.24). Now the changed Jesus had grown into 'a regenerate being' who permitted the 'currents of universal life to flow through him'.[78]

One of the consequences of the transformation was Jesus' new perspective on the Kingdom of God. It was no longer a Kingdom 'ranged against the kingdom of this world' or something that materializes on earth or as an abode after death, but instead signified a 'change of consciousness, an inner development, a radical transformation'. For Radhakrishnan, it meant the attainment of truth, an inward revolution, a kind of metanoia (change of mind), raising 'one's consciousness beyond normal dimensions'. It was personal, private and within oneself, an indwelling presence – 'The Kingdom of God is within you.' Like other Hindus, Radhakrishnan contended that Jesus believed that changes to the world were not the result of the occasional interference of God from outside, but were regular events of divine revelation. The central achievement of Jesus was that, like a Vedantin, he undermined the 'false antithesis between man and God'. Jesus was an example of a man who had become God and 'none can say where his manhood ends and divinity begins. Man and God are akin. "Thou art thou", "tat tvam asi."'[79] For Radhakrishnan, this was 'the teaching of Christianity'. Jesus had asked us to bring about this rebirth, the second birth, to become a new man: 'The change takes place by inner contemplation, not outer life.'[80]

In Radhakrishnan's judgement, the mystical experience of realizing the Kingdom of God within oneself is an Indian idea, whereas the notion of a messianic kingdom has its origin in the Palestinian tradition. He cited Rudolph Otto to support his argument: 'Jesus' preaching of the kingdom contains elements which are certainly not of Palestinian origin, but point definitely to connections with the Aryan and Iranian East.'

Radhakrishnan's Jesus appears in various Eastern guises, including as an Eastern seer. Like the seers of old, Jesus passed on the secret – *rahasya* – of spiritual wisdom: 'Thus, I have explained to you this knowledge that is more secret than all secrets. Ponder over it deeply, and then do as you wish' (Bhagavad Gita 18.63). However, this wisdom was not to be shared by all, but only with discrimination: 'Give not that which is holy unto the dogs, neither cast ye your pearls before swine, lest they trample them under their feet, and turn again and rend you' (Mt. 7.6) At other times, Jesus appeared like a Buddha, condemning later doctrinal developments which obscured the simplicity of his personality and teaching: 'But in vain they do worship me, teaching for doctrines the commandments of men' (Mt. 15.9) On other occasions, Jesus manifested as the avatar promised in the Bhagavad Gita, who appears as the spirit of truth whenever there is chaos, when righteousness is diminished and when decadence is fostered by the growth of materialism. Radhakrishnan regarded these appearances as a 'second coming of the Son of Man' and felt that, like those avatars, Jesus restored the 'disturbed harmony of righteousness'.[81]

In Radhakrishnan's reckoning, Jesus was one of those who had evolved, who had realized their latent potential, who are reborn and who serve as examples and guides for others to follow. His ultimate verdict on Jesus was mixed: 'We can pity him but not admire him; we can love him at best but not worship him.'[82]

Radhakrishnan saw Paul as thoroughly Jewish originally, but who, like Jesus, gave up exclusivism and ritualism. Typical of a member of any subjugated people,

Paul embraced the Greek language and culture as this admitted him to Roman citizenship and social equality. Paul's understanding of Jesus grew over time. Initially he focused on the historical reality of Jesus, which was evident in his early preaching about the crucified one. Then he began to see Jesus as 'the image of the invisible God' and the 'divine wisdom God decreed before the ages'. Pauline statements such as 'All our fathers all drank of the spiritual rock Christ' and 'God can be formed in each one of us' (Gal. 4.19) were illustrative of, and a warning against, 'over-estimating the historical Jesus' and looking upon him as the 'symbol of metaphysical truth'. The point is reinforced by what Paul wrote to the Corinthians: 'Even though we have known Christ after the flesh, yet now we know him not' (2 Cor. 5.16). Radhakrishnan attributed the change in Paul's thinking to the influence of Eastern mystery religions, which were pervasive in the Roman Empire, and to the Neo-platonic idea of Logos, which 'reduce[d] the human life of Jesus to a mere illusive appearance'.[83]

Radhakrishnan now began to see Paul in the same way that he perceived Jesus – as an Upanishadic or a Buddhist sage. Radhakrishnan's Paul wrestles with the futility of achievements and the restlessness of this temporary life, seeking an answer to the question of who would deliver him from the last enemy to be faced – death: 'For we know that the whole creation groans and travails in pain together until now ... waiting for the manifestation of the sons of God'. Paul's idea of resurrection is based on the Hindu and Buddhist teaching of *dvitī yam janma*, or second birth. Just as a grain dies and is reborn as a plant, a human being is capable of changing his or her human nature. Radhakrishnan was convinced that Paul borrowed this central teaching of the Eastern religions when he talked about resurrection: 'It is sown a natural body, it is raised a spiritual body' (1 Cor. 15.44). The metaphor of garments that recurred in Paul's eschatology reminded Radhakrishnan of 'the radiant body made of the element of the pure (*Śuddhasattva*) of the Hindu mythology'.[84]

Radhakrishnan even turned Paul into a Vedantist, propagating divine immanence within oneself, and presented an array of quotes from Paul to support his argument: 'Your body is the temple of Holy Ghost which is in you God'; 'Know ye not that ye are the temple of God and that the Spirit of God dwelleth in you'; 'You are the temple of the living God'; and 'For in him we live, and move, and have our being; as certain also of your own poets have said, for we are also his offspring.'

Paul's direct experience of God, his teaching based on an immediate, 'divine, environing presence', and his claim that the servants of Christ were the 'stewards of the mysteries of God' were all credited by Radhakrishnan to the Eastern mystery religions. He stripped Paul of his Jewish background and attributed his mystical theological thinking to the influence of these Eastern religions, which were prevalent in the Roman Empire at that time. In essence, Radhakrishnan viewed Paul as a closeted Hindu thinker.

Hermeneutics: Rehearing, Revisioning, Re-enacting

Radhakrishnan's hermeneutics were a mixture of rectification and recreation. He wanted to rectify the misrepresentation of Hinduism perpetuated by some missionaries and Western Orientalists. One such slander was that Hinduism was indifferent to the problems of the world – what Radhakrishnan called the 'guilt of indifference': 'We cannot lose ourselves in inner piety when the poor die at our doors, naked and hungry. The *Gītā* asks us to live in the world and save it.'[85] The function of liberated souls is not to isolate or withdraw from the world, but to 'take upon themselves the burden of the redemption of the whole world'. Radhakrishnan's hermeneutical mission was to prove that Hinduism was not otherworldly and did not lack social concern: 'Modern attempts to improve the general condition of the community, to transform society so that hope and happiness might be brought within the reach of the needy and the down-trodden, are not inconsistent with Hindu religion but are demanded by it.'[86] Hermeneutics, he affirmed, that was not an 'abstract study remote from the life of man … The civilization of India is an effort to embody philosophical wisdom in social life.'[87]

Radhakrishnan counselled against simply repeating ancient wisdom, advocating instead that all should follow the path of the rishis, who 'desired not to copy but to create'. The solutions of the past cannot simply be copied, because the questions and experiences of the past were different from the present, or to put it another way – history never repeats itself. What the rishis did in their generation and time need not be replicated: 'We have to keep our eyes open, find out our problems and seek the inspiration of the past in solving them. The spirit of truth never clings to its forms but ever renews them.'[88] The Vedas could not have 'anticipated all our needs' or provided for every future 'conceivable' case. Rather, they laid out only certain general principles and urged us to use our own judgement. As Radhakrishnan emphasized, the 'vital thing for us is not to hold the creed but enter into the experience out of which it was developed'.[89] In an ever-changing world, the aim should be to seek 'fresh fields for truth'.

Radhakrishnan's hermeneutical vision was to make the Scriptures 'a living force in the present'. In the preface to the *Brahma Sūtra*, he advised that the scriptural texts should be 'understood by each generation in relation to its own problems'. Truth had to be 'continually re-created'; it was not something 'already possessed' but had to be 're-transmitted'. 'In every generation, it [truth] has to be renewed', while '[t]radition should be a principle not of conservatism but of growth and regeneration'.[90] Radhakrishnan sought to build a 'fresh scheme with originality and freedom in the strength of the legacy of the ancient wisdom'.[91]

Scriptural truth had to be interpreted by each new generation, but since these texts are expressed in human language and are formed by human thinking, the resulting awareness should lead to a 'continual clarifying and fuller understanding of the truths'.[92] The fatal error of the human mind in Radhakrishnan's opinion was to assume that it had full possession of final truth, embodied and standardized, and all that was now required was to 'reproduce feebly' precious features of the old wisdom. Instead, what is needed is a 'change of consciousness, a rebirth, an inner-evolution, a change in understanding'.[93] The scriptural truth has to be constructed again because the faith that is practised today is starkly different to that of Vedic times. An interpreter *must* keep in mind the problems of the age in which he or she is living. While doing justice to the old Indian tradition, one has to formulate a reasoned faith to meet the demands of the modern age. Radhakrishnan reminded his readers that theories, speculations and dogmas 'change from time to time as the facts become better understood'. Fundamental to reinterpretation is that the present generation should not be denied its inquiring spirit. He contended that 'however valuable the testimony of past ages may be, it cannot deprive the present age of its right to inquire and sift the evidence'.[94] Just as the revelation of God is an ongoing process, so is hermeneutics. Radhakrishnan was anxious that the present generation should not try to avoid, or be deprived of, the task of interpreting God's truths: 'Precious as are the echoes of God's voice in the souls of men long ago, our regard for them must be tempered by the recognition of truth that God has never finished the revelation of his wisdom and love.'[95]

Radhakrishnan narrows the gap between ancient texts and existential historical reality by personalizing and universalizing scriptural events. The past of biblical events is connected to the present not by quoting or repeating the texts but by experiencing them: 'By the free use of reason and experience we appropriate truth and keep tradition in a continuous process of evolution.'[96] Important biblical events become meaningful when they are re-enacted in personal life. Incarnation is not merely an historical event that happened 2,000 years ago but a renewal 'in the life of everyone who is on the way to the fulfilment of his destiny'.[97] It wasn't only the 'historic Jesus, but the whole race' that 'will have the gifts of the incarnation'.[98] Likewise, the 'cross becomes significant when we make it our own, when we undergo crucifixion',[99] while the resurrection is not simply an event that happened in the past, but denotes an awakened spiritual consciousness when Christ is risen in the hearts of people. Radhakrishnan sounded like an evangelical preacher when he wrote that 'Jesus is risen in the hearts of men.' It is a kind of born-again experience *á la* Nicodemus. For Radhakrishnan, the truth of the sayings of the sages and prophets did not depend on the historicity or honourable nature of the seers but on one's own experience of them in life. To emphasize his point, Radhakrishnan cited the Buddha: 'Accept my words only after you have examined them for yourselves; do not accept them simply because of the reverence you have for me.' In short, 'It's our duty to live in the spirit of the verse.'[100]

For Radhakrishnan, hermeneutics was not simply about trusting what is said in the sastras or giving unthinking obedience to or trust in a teacher, but should combine reverence for the text and devotion to the teacher with the 'most unrestricted right of free examination and inquiry'.[101] The truth is not confirmed by demonstrating that the author was a historical figure or a respectable person. The authenticity of the truth lies in one experiencing it within oneself. For Radhakrishnan, 'spiritual values are realized on earth through empiric means of family love, of love and friendship, of loyalty and reverence'.[102] The only test for the spiritual truth is provided by the Mahabharata: 'not birth, not learning but only conduct'.[103]

Exaggerated Exegesis

Exegesis may seem like the mechanical recuperation of ancient texts, but for Radhakrishnan it was more than that. It is about actively seeking Hindu parallels, allusions and resonances in the various Scriptures of the world. It is an imaginative and often incongruous placement of mostly biblical and at times Buddhist, Koranic and Confucian texts within the whole Vedic textual continuum. It is a valiant attempt to bring these diverse, ancient and alien texts to life in an Indian religious context. Such textual placements are a sign that the meaning of the text is not confined to the original intention of the author. Radhakrishnan did not make lengthy exegetical comments on any specific texts and it is only through incidental and indirect remarks that one can glean his idea of hermeneutics.

Radhakrishnan's exegesis has much to do with the promotion and celebration of subjective reading, the very thing that traditional exegesis eschews and is scornful of. He is unapologetic about giving intuition a role in interpretation. Reading meaning into text is not new, and many modern and mainstream form critics engage in the practice, though they are not open about it. Radhakrishnan was like a puranic warrior, traversing the testaments and cherry-picking the texts without paying any attention to their history or theology. Though he derided literalism, he himself at times was a literalist.

Though Radhakrishnan insisted that texts should be placed in their historical context, he honoured his own instruction more in the breach than in the observance. He who claimed that the Hindu sacred texts grew 'out of vital urges and under the pressure of a concrete historical situation'[104] did not accord the same significance to the historical background out of which the biblical texts emerged. His reading could be characterized as acontextual: a reading in which the text stands apart from its immediate textual surroundings and is invested with its own meaning and given maximum agency. A noticeable example is his harnessing of biblical references to Christ's or the believer's union with God in order to uphold the Upanishadic ideal of God indwelling within oneself. Luke's saying that 'the kingdom of God is within you' (17.21) could be variously rendered in Greek as 'within you', 'in your midst', 'among you' and 'in the midst of you'. Like Vivekananda, Radhakrishnan misread the context. Reading the narrative as it stands, 'within you' – Radhakrishnan's preferred reading – seems an unsuitable translation. Here Jesus is speaking to the Pharisees, with both showing a mutual dislike. The continuous disputes the Pharisees had with Jesus made him use disparaging language about them, such as 'whitewashed tombs' and 'hypocrites' (Mt. 23.27). In the light of this antagonistic background, it seems highly unlikely that Jesus would have told the Pharisees that the kingdom of God resided within their hearts. A more credible translation would be 'in your midst' or 'among you'. There is a stark difference between saying 'the kingdom of God is within you' and 'the kingdom of God is among you', with the latter clearly at odds with Radhakrishnan's thesis.

Another notable example of Radhakrishnan's acontextual reading is his use of biblical texts to support his idea of karma as an integral component of the biblical message. An obvious case is the words of Jesus to the paralyzed man at Capernaum: 'Courage my son, your sins are forgiven.' This episode is recorded in Mark (2.1-5) and Matthew (9.1-8). As was his habit, Radhakrishnan not only failed to provide any biblical reference but also conveniently overlooked the context. These texts are totally silent about the sin committed by the man, and a close reading of the episode reveal that the sin and the miracle recede into background as the text focuses on Jesus' pronouncement of forgiveness without elaborate rituals of atonement. In his other healings, Jesus did generally link illness to sin, as in Luke 13.1-5 and John 9.2. In both cases, Jesus was very clear that that any attempt to correlate present suffering and past sins was unsustainable. In John's narrative, when the disciples asked whether the man was born blind because he or his parents sinned, Jesus' response was an emphatic – 'No, it wasn't' – but the healing of Jesus was seen as an opportunity to do God's work.

The other biblical statement Radhakrishnan employed to support the presence of karma theory was taken from Paul: 'Whatsoever a man soweth, that he shall reap' (Gal. 6.7). This is only a partial quote, indicating that a selective elision has been used. In fact, Radhakrishnan omitted next verse, which was important contextually: 'For he that soweth to his flesh shall of the flesh reap corruption; but he that soweth to the Spirit shall of the Spirit reap life everlasting' (Gal. 6.8). The phrases 'soweth to his flesh' and 'soweth to the Spirit' are critical to an understanding of what Paul was saying here, forming part of his argument. For Paul, sowing to the flesh means doing the works of the flesh, such as adultery, fornication, uncleanness, lasciviousness, idolatry, witchcraft, hatred, variance, emulations, wrath, strife, seditions, heresies, envyings, murders, drunkenness, revellings (Gal. 5.19-21). To sow to the spirit of is to produce the fruit of the spirt: love, joy, peace, longsuffering, gentleness, goodness, faith, meekness, temperance (Gal. 5.19-23). The other Scriptures, in Radhakrishnan's reading, are variations of the Vedantic ideal: 'We will find the Supreme, and the only Supreme, which it is possible for us to know, when we are taught to look within. The spirit of man is the candle dwelleth in you' (Prov. 20.27); 'Know you not that you are the temple of God and the spirit of God dwelleth in you' (1 Cor. 3.16). These are variants of the famous text *tat tvam asi*, 'that art thou'.

Some Texts are more Equal than Others

Like Hinduism, and India itself, Radhakrishnan's writings are erudite and popular, unifying and exclusionary, polite and strident. Unlike the current Hindu nationalists, he believed that 'the golden age is in the future vision and not in a fabled past'.[105]

Radhakrishnan wrote in a culture which was familiar with sacred texts, both biblical and Hindu. On a number of occasions he did not provide references to the biblical texts he was quoting, assuming that his audience would have been familiar with them. He did the same thing with his own Hindu texts, often quoting them in Sanskrit without providing any translation and often without any references.

Radhakrishnan was not a trained biblical scholar, but he was well aware of biblical criticism, a formidable force at time, which was divided into higher and lower criticism. He was fairly well acquainted with the Synoptic problem and the existence of sources like M, L, and Q, which went on to form the Gospel narratives. He believed that with the advent and advancement of higher criticism, the biblical message could be shown to be Vedanta in origin. He made use of the works of those biblical scholars who deviated from orthodoxy and applied penetrating historical-critical methods to expose inconsistencies and unscientific content embedded in the Bible. Radhakrishnan was especially interested in the works of scholars like Rudolf Otto, C. K. Burkitt, Kirsopp Lake and Martin Dibelius, who demonstrated interconnections between the nascent Christianity and the Roman, Greek and Indian religious and philosophical traditions. But unlike these scholars, he did not analyse the composition of the texts nor interrogate them. He was simply looking for biblical parallels and allusions that would fit with and reinforce his Upanishadic ideals.

Unlike Ramanathan, Radhakrishnan did not engage in detailed exegesis. The Sri Lankan often queried, challenged and corrected the translations of the Authorized Version of Bible, but Radhakrishnan made no attempt to engage in such activities or to scrutinize the philological nuances of the biblical terms or to trace the etymologies and semantics of the biblical languages. His use of textual parallels and correspondences were proof enough for him of the wide-ranging openness and comprehensiveness of his own tradition.

For Radhakrishnan, religious texts were permeated with allusions, quotations, influences and references to other texts, showing that they were 'interconnected' and were not closed entities. Seeking scriptural parallels involves the radical simplification of texts, which was Radhakrishnan's practice. He often wrote about the similarities, resemblances and mutual borrowings between different textual traditions, but was reluctant to talk about the ancestry of these ideas, except to say that if religion was the 'natural outcome of the human mind, it would be strange if we did not find coincidences'.[106] These texts were 'expressions of one great spiritual movement', revealing 'the impressive unity of religious aspiration'.[107] Or, as he put it more colourfully, these aspirations and hopes are 'the same on the banks of the Ganges as on the shores of the Lake of Galilee'.[108] Nonetheless, Radhakrishnan failed to show the complexities of the texts he worked with.

Though he had a lot of respect for the pivotal role the Bible played in the Jewish and Christian traditions, Radhakrishnan studied these texts more as cultural literature than as sacred writings tied to the holy or the supernatural. He was also irritated by the fact that his studies helped to emphasize a distinction between the heathens who had many gods and many lords and Christians who had only one God – the Father – and one Lord – Jesus Christ.

While his fellow Hindu reformers mined scriptural texts profitably for various political, ideological and identitarian causes, Radhakrishnan perceived them in conventional terms as depositories of spiritual truths. To his mind, Scriptures were essentially transmitters of spiritual insights rather than treatises on political reform, and he was very averse to using texts for political purposes. While Radhakrishnan embraced the hallmarks of liberalism – higher criticism and historical consciousness – he strangely shunned another of its virtues – the social gospel. He questioned the use of the Bhagavad Gita by his fellow Hindu thinkers, like Vivekananda, Tagore and Gandhi, for social and political purposes and similarly disapproved of Christians using the Gospel of Jesus for championing 'the programme of Moscow'. He reminded them that 'in essence religion is spiritual redemption and not social reform'.[109] He was also reluctant to run a secular state on a scriptural basis, regarding the Sermon on the Mount as a 'counsel of despair, applicable, if at all, to individuals and not to states',[110] and citing Bismarck, who said that a state run on the lines of the Sermon on the Mount would not last twenty-four hours. This did not mean that Radhakrishnan was not politically astute. Along with the damage caused by territorial colonialism, he was equally worried about the 'cultural imperialism' of the British and the resulting spiritual deterioration in the countries colonized. He considered 'political subjugation', which interfered with inner freedom, to be a 'gross humiliation', while the cry for swaraj was the 'outer expression of the anxiety to preserve the provinces of the soul'.[111]

Unlike the current Hindu nationalists, Radhakrishnan was very reluctant to seek, and glory in, alleged scientific and medical inventions and knowledge in the ancient texts. He made it clear that he was not looking for the 'scientific thought of those days' but for 'the suggestions about the ultimate questions of philosophy and religion which they set forth with philosophic depth'.[112] The value of these texts lay not in their scientific or social content, but in the emancipation they provided from the 'transient preoccupations of the current hour'.[113]

Radhakrishnan did not subscribe to the post-Enlightenment notion that modern people were different or 'in some ways better' and 'superior to the ancients in spiritual depth or moral strength'.[114] He maintained that 'We must not judge ancient writings from our standards'.[115] He castigated Christians for approaching the Bible with modern questions such as how to resolve the divergencies in the life of Jesus, how to reconcile the creation accounts with modern science, how to make sense of the Trinity or the biblical miracles, or how to discern whether the Hebrew prophecies had been fulfilled. He argued that Christian hermeneutics had largely been a 'traffic with the past'. As he put it, 'miracles, faith in an infallible book or an infallible church, do not appeal to the modern mind steeped in the spirit of science'.[116]

Radhakrishnan bemoaned the fact that the biblical texts had been reduced to a human level, thus subjecting them to 'power and profit, the flesh and the devil'. He provided some examples of what biblical texts really meant and how they had been twisted to suit modern needs. The old saying 'Thou shall not kill' had been turned into 'Thou shall kill except animals for food, birds for sport, and men in battle.' 'Thou shalt not covet' had been changed to 'Thou shall not covet except on a large scale as in trade and imperialism.' While 'Thou shalt not hate' had been warped into 'Thou shall not hate except the backward races, the enemy nations and the weak of the world.'[117]

Radhakrishnan's hermeneutics resembles that of a puritan preaching on the salvation of the soul. In the puritan's case, the soul moves from a sinful state to new life and an eternal life in Christ. In Radhakrishnan's Vedantic version, the spirit is delivered from its attachment to matter and the world of sensuality and is absorbed into the eternal being, the Brahman. It is the inward growth of a person from the 'physical to the spiritual mode of existence'.[118]

Radhakrishnan was averse to gurus or institutions that would distance the followers of Hinduism, Christianity or Islam from their faith. He refashioned

Hinduism as a faith which eschewed any fanaticism or sought any outside authority for its legitimacy. He ruled out 'Sastris and the pundits, the Mualvis and Maulanas, the Missionaries and clergymen of the conventional type' as being of no help of in our present condition. What he said about Hindu monasteries would not endear him to traditionalists: 'The mutts have outlived their function. They have ceased to learn and to teach, to inspire and to illumine. Initiative and improvement appear to have deserted them.'[119]

Radhakrishnan's commentaries on the Hindu texts resembled those of the biblical commentaries which came out of modern criticism. Though he modestly observed that his works were not the 'product of purely scholarly interests', he skilfully adapted the methods of the biblical commentaries for his own purposes. Like the biblical commentaries, his study of the Hindu texts placed them in their context, taking note of their provenance and the gradual evolution of ideas. When he found that the Bhagavad Gita contained extraneous materials which impaired its meaning, he set himself the ambitious goal of gathering whatever was valuable and placing it in its 'proper setting'. Where he differed from his Christian counterparts was in paying so much attention to intertextual relationships, especially pointing out the parallels in Christian, Jewish, Buddhist and Taosist texts. Radhakrishnan's commentary on the Bhagavad Gita contained many biblical cross-references. It would have been rare for a Western commentary on John to contain quotes from Vedic or Saiva texts, but Radhakrishnan regarded both texts and the commentators to be products of their time, with the associated limitations.

Spurred on by the Christian theology of the time, Radhakrishnan spoke of Hinduism in Christian eschatological terms and turned Vedanta into a religion which primarily spoke to humanity in its crisis. Just as some of the biblical interpreters, influenced by Schweitzer, espoused an apocalyptic Jesus with his message of the impending arrival of the kingdom and the ensuing eschatological judgement, Radhakrishnan refashioned Hinduism as a faith for the end time. The opening lines of his preface to the *Brahma Sūtra* carried a stark warning: 'We are in the midst of one of the great crises in human history, groping for a way out of fear, anxiety and darkness, wandering in search of a new pattern in which we can begin life over again.'[120] During the two great world wars, Radhakrishnan offered the 'Hindu solution' as a remedy for the mess the world was in: 'the Hebrews gave the world the conception of the unity of the Godhead and the Christians that of the Fatherhood of God, the Hindus will help to make these truths effective in life and thus to achieve the brotherhood of man.'[121] He was not advocating a political role for Hinduism, but the exhibition of 'spiritual power and presence'. Just as Indian mystical and ascetical elements influenced the formative years of Christianity, almost two millennia later he felt that Hinduism offered a similar 'formulative influence on the world'. He proudly claimed that even today 'Japan, China, Tibet and Siam, Burma and Ceylon look to India as their spiritual home.' At a time when it was thought that 'nothing move[d] in this world which was not Greek in origin', he challenged this Eurocentric and almost racist claim by declaring that 'half the world move[d] on independent foundations which Hinduism supplied'.[122]

Unlike some current Hindu thinkers, Radhakrishnan was of the conviction that scriptural knowledge, creeds and theology were insufficient for the attainment of religion's true ends. Mere knowledge was a 'decoration, an exhibit without roots'. He cited the example of Narada, in the Chandogya Upanishad, who confessed that all his scriptural learning had not taught him the true nature of the self. In spite of studying the Scriptures for a prescribed period, Svetaketu, a character from the same Upanishad, was said to be merely conceited and not well instructed. Radhakrishnan observed that 'Spiritual attainment is not the perfection of the intellectual man, but energy pouring into it from beyond ... It is seeing with the spiritual eye of the pure in heart, who have overcome the passions of greed and envy, hatred and suspicion.'[123]

A cursory reading of Radhakrishnan's writings might give the impression that they were littered with simplified binaries, such as the West is rational and logical, while the East is spiritual and mystical. It might look as if his characterizations of East and West embraced and perpetuated eighteenth- and nineteenth-century portrayals, but he was much more assured and intellectually sophisticated than these characterizations implied.

There are significant differences between the nineteenth-century Orientalists' employment of the ancient texts and Radhakrishnan's usage. He did not see these textual troves as historical curiosities to be studied and analysed and then left in their historical context. He envisaged his task as relating 'them to their environment, to bridge the distances of time and space and separate the transitory from the permanent'.[124] While Western Orientalists saw the ancient Indian texts as a 'dreary scene of discord, folly and superstition' and wanted to replace them with Western and Christian writings, Radhakrishnan argued for the refinement of age-old Indian wisdom to reflect contemporary spiritual yearnings and the scientific temper.

He spurned the Western Orientalist habit of simultaneously glorifying ancient heritage and denouncing modern culture as decadent. He wanted to make ancient Indian wisdom one of the 'formative elements in human progress, by relating the immensely increased knowledge of modern science to the ancient ideals of India's philosophers'.[125] While Western Orientalists privileged written Scriptures, Radhakrishnan emphasized the oral, aural and visual nature of Vedic tradition as a way of knowing the truth. Though his obsessive use of the ancient texts might look as if he too was prioritizing the written text as a form of religious expression, he gave equal attention to the role of visions and dreams in discerning the truth.

The Christian hope of the eventual triumph of Christianity in India, Radhakrishnan believed, would remain a 'remote vision'. He blamed its lack of progress largely on the dogmatic inflexibility of the church. Unlike the early church, which was open to ideas from the Greek and Roman religions and cultures, Radhakrishnan bemoaned the fact that the current denominationally-obsessed Christianities adopted an 'attitude of unbending self-sufficiency', resulting in the church losing the 'features of teachability and tolerance which characterized it in its early days'.[126] He even offered a solution – Hinduize it. Christianity's success, he claimed, had depended upon its 'gradual adaptation of an Eastern religion to the Western spirit'.[127] His advice to Indian Christian theologians was very specific – recover the Upanishadic spirit embedded in the biblical texts:

> Students of Christian religion and theology, especially those who wish to make Indian Christian thought not merely 'geographically' but 'organically' Indian, should understand their great heritage which is contained in the Upanishads.[128]

With his characteristic composure, Radhakrishnan reminded Indian Christians that Christianity had originated in Western Asia but later got blended with Greco-Roman culture and so might find her rebirth in the 'heritage of India'.

He prescribed the same Vedantic ideals for the rest of humankind: what the world needed was Hindu morality and spirituality encapsulated in the Vedanta, which is both ancient and modern. Hailed as an advocate of the cross-fertilization of ideas between East and West, Radhakrishnan concluded that 'The fate of the human race hangs on a rapid assimilation of the qualities associated with the mystic religions of the East. The stage is set for such a process.'[129] Other religions can gain universality only by 'bringing them nearer to the religions of India'.[130]

This leads us to another point about Radhakrishnan's writings. These give the impression that he is ecumenical and egalitarian in his thinking and outlook, but this is to ignore the strand of Hindu exceptionalism contained in his discourse. He repeatedly wrote that the truth speaks to us in varying dialects across continents and over the centuries, but the perennial wisdom, the eternal religion behind all these religions, is *sanātana dharma*. He was adamant that Indic religions such as Buddhism, Sikhism and Jainism were variants of Vedanta and subsumed them under his advaitin vision. He was also persuaded that the fundamental principles of the Buddha had 'their roots in the Upanishads'.[131] Radhakrishnan traced the mystic elements and the truths of inner life in Semitic faiths such as Christianity and Islam to the Indian spiritual tradition and claimed that the illustrious representatives of Sufism Attar, Sadi and Rumi had a 'close approximation to the philosophy of Adivaita Vedanta'.[132] He was even convinced that Chinese thoughts were Vedantin, asserting that 'Confucianism stressed the karma aspect, Taoism the mystical or the jnana side.'[133] He credited 'the critical ideas of Taoism' to the Upanishads: 'The contingency of the world, and the reality of the absolute are common to both and developed on more or less the same lines.'[134] He asserted that a Confucian sage was akin to a *sthita-prajna* (one who had divine consciousness), of which the Bhagavad Gita spoke. These appropriations strengthen Radhakrishnan's image as a serial incorporator of other peoples' texts and concepts. He turned Vedanta into a weapon of mass of assimilation.

Although he counselled against thinking that 'our religion is the only true religion, our own vision of Reality is the only authentic vision, that we alone have received a revelation and we are the chosen people, the children of light and the rest of the human race live in darkness',[135] Radhakrishnan ended up espousing and enshrining santana dharma as the true religion. Having frequently advocated 'the spirit of catholic comprehension', he seemed to be constricted by his preoccupation with Advaita Vedanta. Radhakrishnan blatantly exploited Hinduism's endless adaptability in order to accommodate and even annex competing thoughts, helping advance the Vedantic cause.

Radhakrishnan's vision of a Vedantic world did not materialize nor did it provide any impetus for global change. He had envisaged a spiritual community in which the 'Scriptures of all religions have a claim to our allegiance'[136] in so far they are not confined to 'any age or race' nor limited by geography or bounded by ecclesiastical rules. In all his writings, he professed that all religious texts were products of the experience of the seers, but only a few of these texts remained faithfully attached to that experience, namely the Vedas, the Bhagavad Gita and the Upanishad. Ironically, as someone who staunchly acknowledged that God's revelation was 'larger than any single book or set of books'[137] and who was sceptical of any scripture being final or infallible, Radhakrishnan ultimately came to the conclusion that some Scriptures were more authentic than others in communicating the truth. These Scriptures are seen to be superior because they conform to the 'findings of science' and are 'logically coherent' and, more pertinently, because they express Vedantic values. This is entirely subjective and privileges one set of texts over all others. Orwellian before Orwell: 'Some texts are more equal than others.'

Notes

1   A. C. Hogg, *The Christian Message to the Hindu: Being the Duff Missionary Lecturers for Nineteen Forty Five on the Challenge of the Gospel in India* (London: SCM Press, 1947), 13.
2   For the life and work of Radhakrishnan, see Robert N. Minor, *Radhakrishnan: A Religious Biography* (Albany: State University of New York Press, 1987); S. Gopal, *Radhakrishnan: A Biography* (London: Unwin Hyman Ltd, 1989); and Satchidananda Murty and Ashok Vohra, *Radhakrishnan: His Life and Ideas* (Albany: State University of New York Press, 1990).
3   S. Radhakrishnan, *Indian Philosophy*, vol. 1 (London: George Allen and Unwin Ltd, 1923), 53.
4   S. Radhakrishnan, 'Hindu Thought and Christian Doctrine', *Madras Christian College Magazine*, January 1924, 19.
5   S. Radhakrishnan, 'The Religion of the Spirit and the World's Need: Fragments of a confession', in Paul Arthur Schilpp (ed.), *The Philosophy of Sarvepalli Radhakrishnan* (New York: Tudor Publishing Company, 1952), 9.
6   S. Radhakrishnan, 'The Spirit in Man', in S. Radhakrishnan (ed.), *Contemporary Indian Philosophy* (London: George Allen & Unwin Ltd, 1936), 260.
7   S. Radhakrishnan, 'Indian Philosophy: Past and Present', in Robert A. McDermott (ed.), *Basic Writings of S. Radhakrishnan* (Bombay: Jaico Publishing House, 1972), 99.
8   Radhakrishnan, 'The Religion of the Spirit and the World's Need', 9.
9   S. Radhakrishnan (ed.), *The Principal Upaniṣhads edited with Introduction, Text and Translation* (London: George Allen & Unwin Ltd, 1953), 9.
10 S. Radhakrishnan, 'My Search for Truth', in Virgilius Ferm (ed.), *Religion in Transition* (London: George Allen & Unwin Ltd, 1937), 15.
11 Gopal, *Radhakrishnan*, 367.
12 S. Radhakrishnan, 'Indian Culture', in *Reflections on our Age*, Lectures delivered at the opening session of UNESCO held at the Sorbonne University, Paris (New York: Columbia University Press, 1949), 121.
13 Gopal, *Radhakrishnan*, 362.
14 S. Radhakrishnan, *Occasional Speeches and Writings October 1952–February 1959*,

Combined edition (Delhi: Publications Division, Ministry of Information and Broadcasting, Government of India, 1960), 308.
15 S. Radhakrishnan, *The Brahma Sūtra: The Philosophy of Spiritual Life. Translated with an Introduction and Notes* (London: George Allen & Unwin, 1960), 21.
16 Radhakrishnan, *The Principal Upaniṣhads*, 9.
17 S. Radhakrishnan, *The Hindu View of Life* (London: George Allen & Unwin, 1927), 23.
18 Radhakrishnan, *The Principal Upaniṣhads*, 9.
19 Radhakrishnan, *The Hindu View of Life*, 17.
20 S. Radhakrishnan, *Indian Philosophy*, vol. 1 (London: George Allen & Unwin Ltd, 1923), 51.
21 S. Radhakrishnan, *The Present Crisis of Faith* (New Delhi: Orient Paperbacks, 1970), 35.
22 S. Radhakrishnan, 'Indian Philosophy: Past and Present', 103.
23 S. Radhakrishnan, *An Idealist View of Life* (London: George Allen & Unwin, 1932), 39.
24 Radhakrishnan, *The Brahma Sūtra*, 115.
25 Radhakrishnan, *The Principal Upaniṣhads*, 10.
26 S. Radhakrishnan, *The Heart Sūtra of Hindusthan* (New Delhi: Rupa & Co., 2002), 18.
27 Radhakrishnan, *The Brahma Sūtra*, 113.
28 Radhakrishnan, *Occasional Speeches and Writings October 1952–February 1959*, 382.
29 Radhakrishnan, *The Brahma Sūtra*, 250.
30 Radhakrishnan, *The Hindu View of Life*, 23.
31 *The Report of the University Education Commission December 1948–August 1949*, vol. 1 (Simla: Government of India Press, 1949), 300.
32 Radhakrishnan, *Brahma Sūtra*, 250
33 *The Report of the University Education Commission December 1948–August 1949*, vol. 1 (Simla: Government of India Press, 1949), 300.
34 Radhakrishnan, *The Hindu View of Life*, 19.
35 S. Radhakrishnan, *Occasional Speeches and Writings October 1952–January 1956* (Delhi: Publications Division, Ministry of Information and Broadcasting, Government of India, 1956), 277.
36 S. Radhakrishnan, *Eastern Religions and Western Thought* (Oxford: Clarendon Press, 1939), 202.
37 Radhakrishnan, *The Present Crisis of Faith*, 36.
38 S. Radhakrishnan, *The Reign of Religion in Contemporary Philosophy* (London: Macmillan and Co., 1920), 5.
39 S. Radhakrishnan, 'The Teaching of Buddha by Speech and By Silence', *Hibbert Journal* 32, no. 3 (1933–4): 352.
40 Radhakrishnan, *The Brahma Sūtra*, 245.
41 Radhakrishnan, *Occasional Speeches and Writings October 1952–February 1959*, 320.
42 Radhakrishnan, *The Brahma Sutra*, 115. Italics in original.
43 Radhakrishnan, 'Indian Philosophy: Past and Present', 98.
44 Radhakrishnan, *The Brahma Sutra*, 320.
45 Radhakrishnan, *Eastern Religions and Western Thought*, 66.
46 Radhakrishnan, *Eastern Religions and Western Thought*, 273.
47 Radhakrishnan, *The Hindu View of Life*, 17.
48 Radhakrishnan, *An Idealist View of Life*, 90.
49 Radhakrishnan, *Indian Philosophy*, vol. I, 25.
50 Radhakrishnan, *The Hindu View of Life*, 21.
51 S. Radhakrishnan, *East and West: Some Reflections. Beatty Memorial Lectures* (London: George Allen & Unwin, 1955), 120.

52 S. Radhakrishnan, *Recovery of Faith* (Delhi: Hind Pocket Books, 1956), 12.
53 Radhakrishnan, *Recovery of Faith*, 165.
54 S. Radhakrishnan, *Religion and Society: Kamala Lectures* (London: George Allen & Unwin Ltd, 1947), 66.
55 S. Radhakrishnan, 'The Heart of Hinduism', *Hibbert Journal* 21, no. 1 (1922): 9.
56 Radhakrishnan, *An Idealist View of Life*, 275.
57 S. Radhakrishnan, *Religion and Culture* (Delhi: Hind Pocket Books, 1932), 14.
58 S. Radhakrishnan, *Occasional Speeches and Writings July 1959–May 1962* (Delhi: Publications Division, Ministry of Information and Broadcasting, Government of India, 1963), 244.
59 Radhakrishnan, *Eastern Religions and Western Thought*, 187.
60 Radhakrishnan, *Eastern Religions and Western Thought*, 164.
61 Radhakrishnan, *Eastern Religions and Western Thought*, 164.
62 S. Radhakrishnan, *East and West in Religion* (London: George Allen & Unwin, 1933), 62.
63 S Radhakrishnan, 'Hindu Thought and Christian Doctrine', *Madras Christian College Magazine*, January 1924, 21.
64 Radhakrishnan, *The Heart of Hindusthan*, 70.
65 Radhakrishnan, *The Reign of Religion in Contemporary Philosophy*, 9.
66 Radhakrishnan, *Religion and Society: Kamala Lectures*, 207.
67 Radhakrishnan, *The Reign of Religion in Contemporary Philosophy*, 9.
68 Radhakrishnan, 'The Heart of Hinduism', 79.
69 Radhakrishnan, 'Hindu Thought and Christian Doctrine', 33.
70 Radhakrishnan, *East and West in Religion*, 35.
71 Radhakrishnan, *Eastern Religions and Western Thought*, 187.
72 S. Radhakrishnan, *The Bhagavadgītā: With an introductory essay, Sanskrit text, English Translation and notes* (Bombay: George Allen & Unwin, 1948), 271.
73 Radhakrishnan, *Occasional Speeches and Writings October 1952–February 1959*, 382.
74 Radhakrishnan, *Eastern Religions and Western Thought*, 176.
75 Radhakrishnan, *Eastern Religions and Western Thought*, 160.
76 Radhakrishnan, *East and West: Some Reflections*, 35.
77 For an extended study of Radhakrishnan's understanding of Jesus, see R. S. Sugirtharajah, *Jesus in Asia* (Cambridge, MA: Harvard University Press, 2018), 167–97.
78 Radhakrishnan, *Occasional Speeches and Writings October 1952–February 1959*, 306.
79 Radhakrishnan, 'Hindu Thought and Christian Doctrine', 23.
80 Radhakrishnan, *Occasional Speeches and Writings October 1952–February 1959*, 306.
81 Radhakrishnan, 'The Heart of Hinduism', 8.
82 Radhakrishnan, *The Reign of Religion in Contemporary Philosophy*, 9.
83 Radhakrishnan, *Eastern Religions and Western Thought*, 220.
84 Radhakrishnan, *Eastern Religions and Western Thought*, 161.
85 Radhakrishnan, *The Bhagavadgītā*, 67. Emphasis is in original.
86 S. Radhakrishnan, 'My Search for Truth', in Robert A. McDermott (ed.), *Basic Writings of S. Radhakrishnan* (Bombay: Jaico Publishing House, 1972), 42.
87 Radhakrishnan, 'My Search for Truth', 42.
88 Radhakrishnan, *The Heart of Hindusthan*, 106.
89 Radhakrishnan, *Occasional Speeches and Writings October 1952–February 1959*, 332.
90 Radhakrishnan, *The Brahma Sūtra*, 8.
91 Radhakrishnan, 'Indian Philosophy: Past and Present', 103.
92 Radhakrishnan, *The Brahma Sūtra*, 11.
93 Radhakrishnan, *Occasional Speeches and Writings October 1952–January 1956*, 232.

94   Radhakrishnan, *The Hindu View of Life*, 18.
95   Radhakrishnan, *The Hindu View of Life*, 18.
96   Radhakrishnan, *The Brahma Sūtra*, 8.
97   Radhakrishnan, *Recovery of Faith*, 117.
98   Radhakrishnan, *East and West: Some Reflections*, 78.
99   S. Radhakrishnan, *Indian Religious Thought* (Delhi: Orient Paperbacks, 2006), 26.
100 Radhakrishnan, *The Bhagavadgītā*, 381.
101 Radhakrishnan, *The Bhagavadgītā*, 169.
102 Radhakrishnan, 'My Search for Truth', in Robert A. McDermott (ed.), *Basic Writings of S. Radhakrishnan* (Bombay: Jaico Publishing House, 1972), 42.
103 Radhakrishnan, *Indian Religious Thought*, 68.
104 Radhakrishnan, *The Brahma Sūtra*, 7.
105 Radhakrishnan, *An Idealist View of Life*, 19.
106 Radhakrishnan, *Eastern Religions and Western Thought*, 184.
107 Radhakrishnan, *Eastern Religions and Western Thought*, 186.
108 Radhakrishnan, *Eastern Religions and Western Thought*, 184.
109 Radhakrishnan, *An Idealist View of Life*, 73.
110 Radhakrishnan, *Religion and Society: Kamala Lectures*, 207.
111 Radhakrishnan, 'Indian Philosophy: Past and Present', 102.
112 Radhakrishnan, *The Brahma Sūtra*, 11.
113 Radhakrishnan, *The Brahma Sūtra*, 11.
114 Radhakrishnan, *The Brahma Sūtra*, 12.
115 Radhakrishnan, *The Principal Upaniṣhads*, 6.
116 S. Radhakrishnan, 'Reply to Critics', in Paul Arthur Schilpp (ed.), *The Philosophy of Sarvepalli Radhakrishnan* (New York: Tudor Publishing Company, 1952), 807.
117 Radhakrishnan, *Indian Religious Thought*, 58.
118 *The Report of the University Education Commission December 1948– August 1949*, 578.
119 Radhakrishnan, *Religion and Society: Kamala Lectures*, 119.
120 Radhakrishnan, *The Brahma Sūtra*, 7.
121 Radhakrishnan, *Eastern Religions and Western Thought*, 75.
122 Radhakrishnan, *The Hindu View of Life*, 12.
123 Radhakrishnan, *Eastern Religions and Western Thought*, 23.
124 Radhakrishnan, *The Principal Upaniṣhads*, 6.
125 S. Radhakrishnan, *Indian Philosophy*, vol. 2 (London: George Allen & Unwin, 1923), 780.
126 S. Radhakrishnan, *East and West in Religion* (London: George Allen & Unwin Ltd, 1933), 64.
127 Radhakrishnan, *Eastern Religions and Western Thought*, 271.
128 Radhakrishnan, *The Principal Upaniṣhads*, 9.
129 Radhakrishnan, *Eastern Religions and Western Thought*, 259.
130 Radhakrishnan, *Eastern Religions and Western Thought*, 304.
131 S. Radhakrishnan, *India and China: Lectures delivered in China in May 1944* (Bombay: Sangam Press Ltd, n.d.), 37.
132 Radhakrishnan, *East and West: Some Reflections*, 32.
133 Radhakrishnan, *India and China*, 17.
134 Radhakrishnan, *India and China*, 97; see also 106.
135 Radhakrishnan, *Occasional Speeches and Writings October 1952–February 1959*, 368.
136 Radhakrishnan, *The Brahma Sūtra*, 117.
137 S. Radhakrishnan, *The Religion We Need* (London: Ernest Benn Limited, 1928), 25.

Chapter 8

FANATICAL AND FRAUDULENT

Interpreters are like pirates, pillaging whatever pleases them from others, shaping these looted goods for their own purposes. This is a rephrase of what Jorge Borges, the Argentinian writer, said on a different occasion, which could very well apply to the Hindu protagonists featured in this chapter. Their lifelong mission was to raid Christian texts and make regular disparaging comments about the Bible, Jesus and Christianity in general. The people who will feature in this chapter are Kahan Chandra Varma, Dhirendranath Chowdhuri, Sita Ram Goel, Ram Swarup and N. S. Rajaram. Some of them, like Varma and Chowdhuri, were polemically active in colonial India, whereas the rest engaged in their anti-Christian offensive after the Indian independence. They belonged to various Hindu organizations – Arya Samaj, in the case of Varma; Sadharan Brahmo Samaj, a mission-oriented splinter group from Brahmo Samaj, in the case of Chowdhuri; while Goel, Swarup and Rajaram were sympathizers with and mouthpieces for the RSS (Rashtriya Swayamsevak Sangh), a right-wing Hindu nationalist organization. They all followed secular professions, some quite prominently, and their writings had a wide appeal.

The aim of this loosely-knit group was to recover the glorious cultural essence of Vedic civilization. The main factor that runs through their disparate discourse is that of the Veda as the foundation for Indian nationalism and civilization. They invoke it when claiming cultural autonomy, for critiquing social practices and for providing cultural codes for Indian nationalism. What is paramount is the assertion of Hindu primacy and its priority in all matters related to India. A secondary but nonetheless important objective was to protect their fellow Hindus against the predatory tendencies of Christianity. Varma spoke for all when he proclaimed that 'This is a battle for truth.' The group also had a perverse pedagogical motive in wanting to educate Christians about the damage done to the Christian faith by new discoveries like the Christian Apocrypha and the Dead Sea Scrolls, an impact that the church authorities had kept hidden. Rajaram patronizingly claimed that even educated Christians knew only the 'sanitized version' of their history.

Hindu Sceptics, Christian Scriptures

The general perception of these Hindu apologists was that the Bible was a human document and as such had no spiritual value. Rajaram distinguished between two types of scripture – *apaurusheya* (literally not of a human), as not of human origin; and *paurusheya*, of human origin. The Vedas belonged to the former category and the Bible and the Koran to the latter. In this context, Rajaram cited the words of thirteenth-century philosopher Madhava: 'Never accept as authority the words of any human (*purusha*); they are subject to ignorance and deception.'[1] The implication was that his Hindu readers should avoid the Christian Scriptures because they were shallow and duplicitous.

Varma disputed the divine status of the Bible on two counts – its spurious morality, and the lack of antiquity for the origins for the New Testament writings. He cited two shocking examples of the unethical nature of the biblical God: first, the failure to punish the daughters and spouses who committed adultery (Hos. 4.14), and second, God's approval of the acquisition of 32,000 virgins (Num. 31.35). Scriptural revelation, in Varma's view, had to date from the beginning of creation, hence the Christian Scriptures, especially the New Testament, failed to measure up to the criteria he had set. For Varma, the Gospels emerged much later in time and therefore lacked canonical status and significance, but acquired these attributes only in the fourth century as a result of the bizarre and controversial methods of voting practised at various Church Councils. In Varma's opinion, this was not the way to give sacred credence to a religious book

Even by the ruthless standards of his fellow commentators, Varma's assessment of the Bible was harsh. He argued, disparagingly, that the Bible 'indeed [was] a revelation of the ignorance of the uncultured brains of those who compiled this curiosity'.[2] It was a 'hotchpotch' and a 'collection of unconnected books revealing a want of taste and culture in its compilers'. He called the Bible a 'budget of blunders', a 'storehouse of obscene and indecent narratives' and a 'jumbling together of a mass of superstitious legends', recording 'barbarous legislation and a crude moral code'.[3] Chowdhuri described the Christian Scriptures in derogatory terms in order to negate their importance, calling them a 'scrap of paper', a 'confused mass of writings', full of 'misquotations and misinterpretations' and 'mistranslations and errors'. Going much further, Geol declared that the Gospels were the 'first Nazi manifesto', providing a blueprint for Hitler and for all the European imperial atrocities.[4] In the same vein, Rajaram, declared the book of Revelation to be 'the most bloodthirsty book of the Bible'.[5]

The basic conviction of these Hindu commentators was that the Bible, especially the New Testament, was a contrived and fraudulent construction. Its authors had borrowed from various writings, such as the Jewish Scriptures and the Qumran documents, and turned them into a new literature called the Gospels, and in the process invented the figure of Jesus. The composition of the Gospels was depicted not as an act of reverent commemoration, but as a theft of other peoples' texts. As Ram Swarup put it in his own inimitable and cynical style, the Gospel writers 'went on a spree of unacknowledged borrowing and stealing'[6] to produce what were 'little more than fairy tale fabrications' based on Qumran texts. Borrowing from Ian Wilson's critique of Strauss, Goel claimed that the Gospels were basically materials which had been freely constructed from the 'garbled traditions about Jesus' which circulated in the early Church. Varma did not accord any originality to the Gospels, arguing that 'most of the best teachings in the Gospels' were 'either a copy of Buddha's [sic] dissertation or of the Gita'.[7] The final paragraph of Rajaram's book could have been written by any of the group, dismissing the Bible writers as owing 'more to forgery and plagiarism than to any divine inspiration'.[8]

Drawing on the work of Western historical criticism, all of the Hindu apologists took great pleasure in highlighting the inner contradictions of the Gospel narratives. For Goel, the important features of the life of Jesus – namely, the date and place of his birth, his ancestral heritage, his ministry, his trial, and his death and resurrection – contradicted one another and tended to 'cancel out each other.'[9] Furthermore, the names attached to the Gospels were attributions and did not refer to the actual authors. The authors themselves were ignorant of the geography of Palestine and Jewish customs, as evidenced in the writings of Mark and John. Chowdhuri asserted that as the result of higher criticism, the idea that the Gospels were written by the contemporaries of Jesus was now 'disbelieved.' Different accounts of the same events in the life of Jesus narrated in the different Gospels further undermined their authenticity. The Gospel writers, 'modified the texts, added, alerted, revised, and cancelled' at their discretion. Chowdhuri's conviction was that the 'Bible was written by mixed hands'.[10]

For these Hindu apologists, the Gospels also served as an add-on and accessory to Paul's writings. Rajaram dismissed them as 'Pauline Christianity's propaganda literature',[11] written to support the work of Paul and his followers, with the specific intention of strengthening and circulating widely his doctrine of faith. The achievement of the Gospel writers was to 'complement and complete the mythical Jesus of Paul's fertile imagination'.[12] While he disparaged the Gospels as 'fantastic and fable-like', Rajaram surprisingly regarded the Acts as 'history'. Chowdhuri held the same general view – that the Gospels were 'manufactured to fill the gaps' missing in the Epistles.

To their own delight, these thinkers exploited to the maximum the findings of biblical criticism which exposed the errors and inaccuracies in the biblical accounts. The Enlightenment-driven historical approach eroded traditional belief and made the Bible a vulnerable document. Work which emerged from Europe's rationalistic and liberal constituencies was put to use to further the Hindu nationalist cause and discredit the Bible. Ever since the nineteenth century, distortions, superstitions and forgery in the Gospels have all become familiar themes within biblical studies, with continental scholars like Lessing, Semler, Strauss and Reimarus discarding the Church's supernatural beliefs to study the Gospels using literary and scientific methods. Internal criticism within biblical studies – a testament to the robustness of its approach – was made use of by these Hindu exponents as an effective anti-Christian or an anti-Bible instrument to smear and slander the foundational document of Christians. For instance, Géza Vermes' comment that Bultmann and his followers had 'their feet off the ground of history and their heads in the clouds of faith'[13] was welcomed by the Hindu critics as a sign of weakness and disunity among biblical scholars.

In addition to Jesus, the biblical God came in for severe criticism. According to Swarup, the Bible's' monotheistic ideal should not be seen as a spiritual vision but as an ideological goal to emphasize superiority, wage wars, conquer nations and consolidate empires. The trouble with monotheism was that it was a 'rigid, stiff form which cannot take on and reflect other forms'.[14] Varma and Rajaram exploited the numerous triumphalist and belligerent sayings in the Hebrew Scriptures, such as 'There is no other Gods beside me', by presenting them to their readers as an indication of what type of God the Christians worshipped. The god of the Bible was seen as a 'compulsive chooser' who arbitrarily selected Abel, Isaac and Ishmael over Cain, Jacob and Esau and could discard them in a similar arbitrary fashion. The biblical God was a jealous god who always demanded loyalty and obedience to the exclusion of other gods and denounced rival prophets, apostles and doctrines. As well as citing suitable verses from Hebrew Scriptures in support of their thesis, the Hindu scholars utilized Paul's warning to the Galatians to prove their case: 'should anyone preach to you a gospel contrary to that which we preached to you, let him be accursed'.[15] For Swarup, this was an indication of the nature of the Bible. He and his colleagues relished the task of identifying biblical passages that legitimized violence, especially violence done in the name of God.

Another aspect of the Christian deity that these Hindu nationalists found questionable was its anthropomorphic nature. In their view, the regular references to the eyes, feet and ears of the biblical God and the attempts to humanize Yahweh had endowed God with human passions and weaknesses, something diametrically opposed to the Hindu view of God as formless and ineffable.

For Swarup, both the Old and New Testaments were filled with denunciations. In general, the Hindu apologists contrasted the strident, strict, local and colonial nature of the biblical God with their own Brahman who was a 'cosmic truth and consciousness, not an imperialistic creator, intolerant, jealous and seeking to impose his will on all'.[16] Unlike the biblical God, the God of the Gita is portrayed as the one who is less disturbed if one worships another god, Swarup plucking a verse from the Gita to illustrate the point: 'Those endowed with true faith, even when they worship other Gods, verily worship me' (Gita 9-23). Whereas the Semitic tradition thinks in terms of deity, the Eastern religion speaks of *dharma*. In an exclusive tradition like Christianity, God is invoked not to seek answers to questions related to existence but as a means to exercise authority. The Christian God is not seen as a cosmic being but as a source of authority and control. Whereas in Hindu thought, as in the case of ancient Greece, the search is about the 'meaning of the universe and of existence'. [17]

Varma and Chowdhuri scoffed at the unrefined nature of New Testament Greek. They claimed that it lacked the 'style and diction' of Xenophon, Demosthenes and Plutarch. They had justification in lamenting the fact that it was not in the language of the people – Aramaic, Syriac or Chaldean – but their conjecture that it must have been produced after the extinction of these languages was driven by ideological motives. For the Hindu commentators, the fact that the New Testament abounded with Latinisms, Hebraisms, Greek phrases and dialects, and foreign idioms, proved three things: that it was not a) the work of Jews but by Romans; b), that it was written at a time when Greek had become corrupted and was not as 'pure and elegant' as in the time of Jesus; and c) that it was not antique in origin – as was claimed by Christian scholars – because of its impure and unchaste language.

Not all of the Hindu scholars were totally dismissive of the biblical texts – Swarup stood out as an exception. He both censored and celebrated the Bible, condemning its vindictiveness but conceding that it had literary quality: it was 'eminently readable and quotable' and had passages of 'beauty and power' in spite of its 'ferocity and cruelty'.[18] Swarup acknowledged that the Bible eloquently reflected the deep personal emotions – such as hatred, revenge, sorrow and pity. The book of Proverbs was singled out as the 'best part of the Bible' and an 'exception in the Bible'[19] which speaks about humanity in general. He appreciated that a woman had contributed to it. Swarup's preference was based as much on what was absent from Proverbs as on what was in it. The book of Proverbs is notorious for not mentioning the prominent ideas of the Pentateuch and the Prophetic tradition of the covenant, the election of a special people who were God's witnesses. What fascinated Swarup was the willingness of the sages to learn from the unfathomable intricacies of the universe. Proverbs' ethics, too, was of a 'different spiritual tradition', emphasizing self-knowledge which corresponded to Swarup's Hindu idea. More to the point, the book had minimal reference to the God of the Bible. Swarup was particularly interested in the figurative and symbolic functions of animals, birds, reptiles and fish used in the book, which served a didactic purpose in teaching about God and human behaviour.[20] Since it was so unlike the rest of the Bible, Swarup wondered how Christians could possibly draw inspiration from this source.

The general view among these Hindu apologists was that the Bible was too restrictive and did not allow Christians to look beyond its pages. The Hindu Scriptures did not carry such authority, leaving Hindus free to seek divine knowledge through self-effort, while the Bible tried to control believers through human agents like prophets and the son of God, who claimed to have exclusive access to divinity. It is this 'freedom of thought and choice' that lies at the heart of the Hindu tradition and differentiates it from the Bible.

Calibrated Christ, Maligned Messiah

These Hindu apologists reserved most of their invective for Jesus, the revered figure of Christians. They were the Hindu counterparts of the Jesus deniers who were popular in the West at that time. They disputed the very existence of the historical Jesus, especially so Varma and Chowdhuri. Utilizing the work of the Jesus Myth theorists of the time, both scholars declared that a 'person like Jesus has never lived' and denied that there was any evidence of a 'personal Jesus'. Rajaram grudgingly conceded that there was a historical figure called Jesus, but made him a nonentity, an 'obscure and unimportant figure' until he was elevated to a lofty status. More importantly, even if he was a historical figure, there was no sign that his generation 'regarded him as divine'; his divinity was in fact based on the votes of bishops, without any supporting evidence presented. Jesus was simply one among many and not even an important teacher in an extreme Jewish sect obsessed with a messianic vision. In Rajaram's view, Jesus was an 'unimportant brother of James', but was invested with all the characteristics of the Messiah so that Paul could use them for his propaganda. The apologists' objective was to make Jesus an inconsequential and insignificant personality. Goel's description of Jesus as an historically and doctrinally 'flimsy figure' and a 'non-descript Jew from Galilee' encapsulated the group's warped thinking.

In Rajaram's imagination, Jesus was essentially a 'fundamentalist Jew' in the mould of Mattathias Maccabaeus, who led the revolt against the Greek empire. The mission and the message of Jesus could be credited to Mattathias and his followers as part of the Zealot tradition. Rajaram cited the Matthean saying of Jesus that he did not come to destroy the law or the prophets but to fulfil them as a sign of Jesus' ultra orthodoxy. He regarded Jesus not as a radical revolutionary but as an avowed defender of the law and the prophets against the abusive Romans and Herodians. Jesus' resistance to the Roman occupation and its collaborators was not an anti-imperial stance but an attempt to preserve the purity that was being defiled by the corrupting Roman influence. The harsh message that he had come not to bring peace but a sword was aimed at his fellow Jews, who were leading a 'fast and loose lifestyle' under Herod and his successors.[21] Swarup pronounced Jesus to be a 'stern judge' and a staunch upholder of orthodoxy rather than the proponent of a radical doctrine, as the Christian churches made him out to be.

If you look for the character of Jesus in the writings of these Hindu scholars, you will find only negative traits. Goel turned him into both a puranic Hindu villain, in the manner of 'Vritra or Rāvaṇa or Kamsa', and a modern-day totalitarian ideologue like Lenin, Stalin or Hitler. He maintained that the parallel between Hitler and Jesus was so 'striking' and there was not much difference between the Christian and the Nazi creeds.[22] The Hindu apologists listed attributed many character defects to Jesus – 'intolerant', 'short-tempered', 'foul-mouthed', 'stark mad'. He was a 'junk', an 'inflated ego', an 'anti-social', someone who encouraged his disciples to leave their parents, who disowned his mother and set son against father and brother against brother, and one who encouraged 'anti-work' and did not want his followers to engage in any productive labour. Chowdhuri pictured Jesus as an 'ignorant enthusiast' and a 'gloomy puritan' who looked after his own. Swarup denounced him as 'gluttonous and a wine bibber'.

In these pen-portraits, Jesus emerges as a nationalist and a racist. Durga Prasad portrayed him as a person who grew up as a 'bigoted Jew' and so proud of his own Jewish origins that he referred to foreigners as dogs. Chowdhuri labelled him a 'narrow tribal patriot'. But at the same time, Jesus was accused of initiating anti-Jewish sentiments. Goel blamed Jesus for his 'intemperate denunciation' of Jews, which led to 'shrieking anti-Semitism down the ages'.[23] Jesus' sexual orientation was also questioned. Based on the dubious document supposedly discovered by Morton Smith, Goel alleged that Jesus could have been a homosexual.[24] In truth, these portrayals of Jesus reveal more about these Hindu advocates, their motives and their times than they do about Jesus himself.

In the view of the Hindu polemicists, Jesus was a composite figure based on a number of prototypes. Drawing on the works of various Western authors, such as Arthur Drews, Adolf Harnack, J. M. Robertson and Dean Inge, Chowdhuri identified a number of ancient figures, such as Job, Isaiah's Suffering Servant, Phrygian Attis and Mithra, as providing the model for Jesus. He was made to fit into these characters, or as Chowdhuri put it, Jesus was a 'fusion of many personalities',[25] the sum of 'mythical amalgamations' drawn from the characteristics of the saints and prophets of both Jews and Gentiles. He claimed that the lives of Job and Jesus resembled one another in that both were honourable men, both were tormented by Satan, both endured agony and humiliation but were later reinstated to their righteous status. Similarly, the Gospel depiction of Jesus as the Suffering Servant owed its existence not to the historical Jesus but to 'Isaiah of the prophetic fame'. Jesus' focus the poor, his meekness, his complete surrender to God, and his stoicism in the face of his enemies' abuse and cruelty were all drawn from chapters 42 and 61 of Isaiah. Isaiah was the source for the suffering, death and resurrection, but also for the description of the character of Jesus, his miraculous power and his teaching in parables. In other words, the Gospel Jesus was moulded in the form of Isaiah's Servant of God. Chowdhuri dismisses the idea of Jesus as the friend of the poor and downtrodden as marks of Bolshevism 'pure and simple'.

Swarup, too, contended that it was the founder of Mithraism – a mystery religion which originated in Persia but which was practised widely in Rome at the time Christianity was emerging – who provided the prototype for Jesus. Mithra, too, was born on 25 December, from a virgin mother in a cave. He had a band of twelve disciples and baptism was practised as an entry ceremony. He died and rose again. Swarup claimed that Jesus was made to match Mithra's life and work. Like his fellow Hindu nationalists, he concluded that Jesus was a 'pious invention' or someone retrofitted to meet the missiological needs of the time.

Two major events which Jesus was associated with – the incarnation and the resurrection – were treated with a mixture of malicious mockery and a mild modification. Drawing on the work of the rationalist Walter Jekyll, Varma derided the doctrine of incarnation: 'While the Second Person of the trinity [sic] is in heaven with the First Person, the Third Person is alleged to have had intercourse with the Virgin Mary, and the resultant birth is the Second Person.'[26] Swarup wondered what Jesus was incarnated into, speculating that he may have incarnated a new intolerance, since with the coming of Jesus 'bigotry and arrogance descended on the earth on a large scale and with a new power'.[27]

All of the Hindu commentators rejected the physical resurrection of Jesus and emphasized the Gnostic understanding which favoured the spiritual resurrection, in line with Hindu thinking. They imputed a political and predatory motif to the resurrection – a principal platform on which Christian faith is based and built. For Chowdhuri, the resurrection was not about a man risen from the dead, but about the 'rise of monotheism to conquer the world'.[28] It was invented as a 'stop gap for this failure of the messianic mission'.[29]

Praising Paul, Pillorying Paul

While these Hindu campaigners showed utter contempt for Jesus, they were ambiguous about Paul. On the one hand, they were quite happy to put him on a pedestal, but on the other, they unceremoniously pushed him off if he did not fit in with their malicious and destructive agenda. Rajaram conceded that Paul was a historical person, while Chowdhuri regarded him as neither mythical nor historical but as a 'legendary personage'. Both agreed that Paul was an arch-propagandist.

For Rajaram, it was not Jesus but Paul, the 'urbane, cosmopolitan citizen of the Roman empire' who was the true 'revolutionary'. It was Paul who brought Jesus to prominence, when he was an obscure figure. The elevation of Jesus by Paul, according to Rajaram, was the 'real resurrection of Jesus'. Paul needed Jesus in order to give his doctrine of justification by faith a divine sanction. He was more of a politician than a 'religious figure' – it was the imperial majesty of the Roman Empire which spurred Paul on to work out his own theocratic and imperialistic ideology. Rajaram contended that in Paul's expansionist vision, the strict and inflexible Jewish sects with their restrictive laws had little attraction. It was Paul who radically reshaped an 'inward looking puritanical sect of messianic expectations' into an 'outward-looking expansionist ideology'.[30] In order to further his imperial impulses, Paul wanted an easy-to-understand doctrine which would be readily acceptable to the Gentiles. Realizing that the Jewish laws were irrelevant to the Gentiles and that Jesus himself was 'cursed by law' (Gal. 3.4), Paul came up with a new doctrine of faith in which Jesus was not a central figure and therefore not prominent in the preaching of early Christianity. In Rajaram's analysis, Paul's new teaching made him the 'first Christian heretic'. When Paul called himself the 'foremost of all sinners', Swarup said he had made sinning fashionable. Any praise Paul received from these scholars was always tempered with criticism of his expansionist goal or for being the progenitor of the imperial and predatory nature of modern Christianity.

Paul played another vital role in the thinking of these Hindus. He was used as evidence of the non-existence of the historical Jesus. The lack of any reference to Jesus or any mention of his message in Paul was taken as a confirmation that he knew 'no man-Jesus'. Chowdhuri points out that the important teachings of Jesus, such as the 'fatherly goodness of God, the love of neighbour, the fulfilment of the law, the emphasis on meekness and mercy, and the warning against too much desire of worldly goods – all these are conspicuous in Paul by their absence'.[31] The message that Paul preached did not come directly from the historical Jesus but was revealed to him mysteriously 'from within'. Echoing the words of K. C. Anderson, a Congregational minister, Chowdhuri claimed that what Paul desired for his converts was that 'Christ must be formed within them.' The subtext was clear to a Hindu audience: Paul was replicating what Hinduism had always taught – that the divine must be born within, and he urged his converts to seek out this experience. Paul was a prime case of someone who veered between being an icon and being ignominious.

Embracing the Enemy of My Enemy, Enlarging the Textual Spectrum

These Hindu commentators went beyond the conventional, canonical texts to embrace a whole gamut of late Jewish and early Christian literature, such as the Dead Sea Scrolls and the Apocrypha, which Christians officially categorized as Non-canonical Gospels. These two sets of manuscripts were discovered at more or less the same time, but had very different origins. The Dead Sea Scrolls consisted of parts of the Hebrew Bible and other sectarian writings of the communities which lived at Qumran and were dated to between the mid-third century BCE and the mid-first century CE. The Dead Sea Scrolls are important in the sense that they tell the story of another Jewish sect, but do not throw light on early Christianity. The Christian Apocrypha, or Gnostic Gospels, comprise fifty-two texts, which have a different provenance to that of the Dead Sea Scrolls. They were discovered at the Egyptian town Nag Hammadi (hence the collection is also known as the Nag Hammadi Library). They tell a powerful alternative version of the story of the orthodox Christian tradition, including its schisms and the types of spirituality within the early Church. While both Qumran and early Christianity represented apocalyptical and millennial versions of the faith, the former was more about the historical and charitable, whereas the latter was focused on the spiritual and the spartan way of life.

Chowdhuri gave equal weight to the canonical and the apocryphal Gospels, since to give 'greater credit' to the accepted Gospels was to impute some mysterious intuitive power to those who selected them. As far as he was concerned, the canonical and non-canonical Gospels were 'equally factual and fictitious'. Varma also stressed the validity of the non-canonical Gospels, considering them 'essentially of the same character as those in the four Gospels' and accepted by the early Christians 'as the word of God'.[32] While Varma and Chowdhuri accorded an identical status to the canonical and non-canonical Gospels, Swarup went further and identified echoes of Upanishadic teachings in the non-canonical Gospels, such as the Gospel of Philip, the Second Apocalypse of James and the Acts of John. In essence this made these Jewish and Christian texts simple manifestations of the Upanishadic ideals.

Swarup and Rajaram excitedly assured their readers that the discovery of the Qumran and non-canonical texts was a death knell for the Christian Gospel, the textual equivalent of weapons of mass destruction. Both claimed that these texts would 'undermine the church's position', 'shatter the picture of an imagined earlier Christianity' and expose Christianity to be a 'forgery' and the 'greatest deception' in history. Rajaram regarded the discovery of the Dead Sea Scrolls as further evidence of the 'doctrinal fragility' of a human-made religion like Christianity, which was as impermanent as the human being on whose authority it rested.

Their support and enthusiasm for the Christian Apocrypha was negatively motivated. First, the omitted Scriptures provided plenty of scope for discrediting the favourable image of the biblical God that the Christians were keen to uphold and project, and at the same time these texts presented a corrective view of what a true God should be. The descriptions of the biblical God as 'accursed', 'malevolent', 'blind', 'arrogant', 'foolish' and 'ignorant' in the Gnostic writings were useful weapons with which to diminish the biblical God. God being represented as the 'mother of all' instead of as a father figure allowed the Hindu campaigners to argue that the Christian God was limited, almost one-dimensional deity. Furthermore, as Swarup was keen to point out, the non-canonical depictions of God as a 'God beyond God', 'the ground of being', 'invisible' and 'incomprehensible' resonated with the Upanishadic description of God as *neti, neti*. Second, these texts provided easy ammunition to attack the Christian Church and its leadership. They used them as an anti-institutional invective. The Apocalypse of Peter's description of the Church leaders as 'messengers of error', 'blind guides' and 'thieves and robbers' was the sort of anti-institutional criticism that bolstered the mission of the Hindu critics.[33] Third, the advocates for Hinduism marshalled the Gnostic Gospels, with their open, pluralistic vision, to emphasize the narrow and exclusive character of the canonical writings. For instance, John's 'I am the Way, and the Truth and the Life' was contrasted with a passage from the Gospel of Thomas which says, 'There is light within a man of light, and it lights up the whole world.' Fourth, the discarded Gospels supplied materials that weakened the central doctrines of Christianity, Swarup noting how the Gnostics dismissed the bodily resurrection as the 'faith of the fools' and the 'doctrine of a dead man', and described those who subscribed to it as 'dealers in bodies'.[34]

What the Hindu enthusiasts for the Gnostic writings did not seem to realize was that the diversity of this literature makes it difficult to reduce into a single, neat narrative. These omitted texts were disparate and at times contradictory, with Irenaeus acknowledging in frustration that it 'was hard to describe their views'. This is very much the case with regard to baptism and the resurrection. While Swarup eagerly jumped on a verse from the Gospel of Philip which ridiculed the people about to be baptized as those who 'go down into the river and come up without having received anything', he failed to note that the same Gospel says that 'Baptism includes the resurrection and the redemption.' While some Gnostic literature advocated spiritual resurrection, others affirmed the physical rising, as in a verse from the *Treatise on the Resurrection:* 'Do not think the resurrection is an illusion. It is no illusion, but it is truth! Indeed, it is more fitting to say that the world is an illusion rather than the resurrection which has come into being through our Lord the Savior, Jesus Christ.' The Hindu campaigners claim that for the Gnostics, the enlightenment alone was the true resurrection, is not easily sustainable. These texts do not have a singular view of Jesus. While one Gnostic text, The Acts of John, stated that Jesus was a strictly spiritual being, yet the aforementioned the *Treatise on the Resurrection* recorded that Jesus, as the 'Son of Man', died a human death, while as the 'Son of God', his divine spirit transcended suffering and death.

Swarup's claim that the Gnostic Gospels showed political rivalry among the apostles does not bear scrutiny. They were mostly independent missionaries, not rivals. Paul, Peter, John, Thomas and James had theological and missiological differences, but their aim was the same – to preach about Jesus. And whatever their rivalry, Peter, Paul and James all ended up as martyrs to their common cause.

Rajaram was the only one of the Hindu scholars to produce a book – though not a very impressive one – entitled *The Dead Sea Scrolls and the Crisis of Christianity: An Eastern View of a Western Crisis*. In it he claimed that the New Testament and the Qumran texts were intimately connected, the former drawing heavily on the latter. He also contended that many incidents which originated in these texts were projected into the life of Jesus to make him a more credible Messiah figure. There were not only literary but also extensive doctrinal and liturgical borrowings as well, including the Lord's Supper and the Lord's Prayer. Even Paul's justification by faith was lifted from the Habakkuk Commentary.

Rajaram's claim that the ministry of Jesus was concurrent with the existence of the Qumran community is extremely dubious. The significance of the Scrolls is that they record the story of another Jewish sect and had hardly any impact on early Christianity. None of the Scrolls refer to Jesus nor do they mention any of his followers, as described in the New Testament. The closest textual resemblance is between the list of miracles found in Luke 7.21–2 and the Dead Sea Scrolls text known as the Messianic Apocalypse (4Q521), written nearly 150 years before the third Gospel. In Luke's version, Jesus tells the disciples of John the Baptist that his healings – making the blind see, the deaf hear, the lame walk and the lepers clean – was a sign of his Messiahship. The consensus view of biblical commentators is that that the source for both these accounts is Isaiah 35 and 61. In contrast to Rajaram's suggestion that the Christians borrowed from the Qumranians, the scholarly verdict is that both authors drew on a common tradition and utilized it for their respective purposes.

Rajaram alleged that there was a conspiracy to prevent publication of the Dead Sea texts, but even scholars who disagreed on other issues relating to the Scrolls were united in attributing their delayed publication to factors such as professional rivalry, prevarication among the academic community and financial restrictions, and the simple fact that the enormous task of editing thousands of fragments was to be carried out by a small pool of scholars.[35]

Caustic Commentaries, Egregious Exegesis

The Hindu critics did not have an in-depth engagement with the biblical texts. The biblical narratives were addressed with a number of objectives in view. The first was to dilute their Christian distinctiveness. This approach was evident in their analysis of the Sermon on the Mount. Without substantiating his argument, Durga Prasad declared that what Jesus taught in his Sermon on the Mount did not essentially 'differ from the religions of India'.[36] Swarup, too, maintained that there was 'nothing specifically Christian about it'[37] and dismissed it as not 'organic to the Bible'.[38] Without providing any supporting evidence, he stated that the Sermon on the Mount was drawn from a variety of sources and that every sentence had a parallel in Egyptian Gnosticism, the Proverbs and the Talmud. He further diminished its status by saying that it was not a key part the New Testament since it was not referred to in two of the Gospels and was also absent from the Acts and the Epistles. Swarup maintained the offensive by repeating Renan's claim that much of the ethical teaching of Jesus was obscured by 'Paul's cloudy theology'.[39] Its spiritual element was totally out of sync with a prophetic and evangelically-minded work like the New Testament, whose main aim was proselytization. For Swarup, its utility value was limited to providing suitable quotes for theological debates.

A second method used to reduce the significance of the Sermon on the Mount was to draw attention to its impracticability. The Hindu commentators cited instances where Jesus himself was unable to practise the lofty principles he preached. For example, while the Sermon urged one not to judge, the critics pointed out that a great deal of judging and condemning was done by Jesus himself. The Gospel records of Jesus referring to a group of people as serpents and a brood of vipers and condemning some of them to hell were used to support the Hindus' case. For Goel, the Sermon was a heartless and cruel document, with sayings such as pluck out your eyes and cut off your limbs. He denounced it as a 'sanctimonious humbug' and a charter for bullies, thieves and squanderers.[40] Swarup contended that the morality of Christianity was based largely on the Ten Commandments and not on the Sermon on the Mount, as evidenced in the *Catholic Catechism*, which had seventy-five pages on the Decalogue but only three lines on the Sermon on the Mount. Although the content of the Sermon provided inspiration for Gandhi's political activism, it was derisively dismissed by the Hindu ideologues.

In general, the biblical texts were regarded as proof of the imperial intentions of the early Church, with Paul's conversion used to illustrate the point. Rajaram treated the incident on the road to Damascus not as a conversion experience but as a brainwave – 'one of the most fateful and fruitful brain-waves in history'.[41] In his reckoning, Paul did not go to Damascus on behalf of the High Priest of Jerusalem but as an agent of Rome. Rajaram dismissed scholarly suggestions that the light that had flashed around Paul was due to a seizure or sunstroke, and offered what he called a 'simpler explanation'. This was that Paul had deliberately set out to hijack and neutralize the widening power of the militant early Church, endow it with an expansionist ideology and use the name of Christ to propagate it. This would undermine the threat that Paul perceived and turn the Church into an agent of the Roman Empire.

Damascus therefore was both a political awakening and a moment of spiritual enlightenment. It was here that Paul abandoned the Law and the Prophets in favour of faith in Jesus.

Sometimes the Hindu apologists indulged in personal and idiosyncratic exegesis, as in their re-reading of Paul at Athens (Acts 17). While Christian theologians saw this episode as an endorsement of inter-faith dialogue, Swarup interpreted it as Paul opportunistically seeking to impose the monotheistic ideals of the biblical God. What happened at Athens was an example of Paul's 'passionate attachment to a fixed idea',[42] disregarding wider perspectives and the larger truths of life. Paul did not feel comfortable in an environment famous for its free inquiry and diversity. The dedication on the altar 'To the Unknown God' was for him a sign of superstition and a chance to propagate the Christian god. He could have offered his audience a 'spiritual' interpretation, but instead went on to reveal who God was and how the world was created, and spoke about the Day of Judgement and the resurrection, calling upon those assembled to repent. In the course of the speech, the multiplicity of gods which the Romans celebrated and adored were erased, to be replaced by Paul's one true God revealed by Jesus. By doing so, Paul destroyed the essential 'unknowability' of God'[43] – a cardinal element of the Indian tradition, which was remarkably in accord with the ancient pagan traditions. Paul's gravest mistake was to make the unknown known.

The Hindu commentators presented biblical and Upanishadic texts side by side to demonstrate that the Christian texts were simply echoes of Hindu spirituality. The biblical texts used for this exercise were from the Christian Apocrypha. Without considering context, quotes were plucked from Hindu and Christian material and the assertion made that they said similar things. As noted earlier, the Gnostic notion of God as invisible and incomprehensible was matched with the Upanishadic *neti, neti*, while the Genesis phrase 'Male and female created he them' was taken to mean God was androgynous, partly male and partly female, like the Hindu passage that begins with *invisible and*.[44] An excerpt from the Gospel of Philip, 'receive the resurrection while they live', referring to the resurrection as an ongoing phenomenon and not an exclusive event that happened to Jesus, was linked to a quote from Brihadaranyaka Upanishad to support the general thesis of similarity.

The juxtaposition of Sanskrit and Semitic texts was intended to bring the Mediterranean texts into the Hindu fold, but a long-term ambition of some Hindu apologists is also to integrate religions such as Buddhism and Sikhism into the Hindu family and regard them as emanations of the parental faith – Hinduism. In this context, the Hindu scholars emphasize the Vedic influence and claim that these Indic traditions exhibit affinities with and echoes of Hinduism. Their attempt to also co-opt the Semitic faith to Hinduism reflects an imperialist motivation – a reversal of the earlier 'textual colonialism' of Western missionaries and Indian Christian theologians. In the latter case, the Hindu texts were regarded as little more than rough copies of the Christian Bible – suggestive and incomplete and waiting for the final truth. But now the Hindu texts were lauded as fine depositories of the ultimate truth, which nourished and enriched other texts. Any faint textual resemblances to Hindu Scripture in any of the Buddhist, Sikh or Christian texts were seized on to support the argument that all such texts are part of a Hindu framework. The desire to link everything and anything to the Hindu way of life is relentless and obsessive. Rajaram denounced the idea of equality between religions as being 'based on superficial comparison of stray passages taken out of context' – a criticism that could easily be directed at him and his fellow Hindu warriors.

Misappropriating Western Scholars

All these Hindu thinkers draw heavily on both popular and scholarly works on the Bible and the historical Jesus. They rely on four main types of writing. One is the mass-market production, often written by authors of dubious expertise or who are simply destructive critics. Books in this category include Hugh Schonfield's *The Passover Plot*, Baigent, Leigh and Lincoln's *Holy Blood, Holy Grail*, Ian Wilson's *Jesus the Evidence*, and Morton Smith's *Jesus the Magician*. Although these books deal with different aspects of the subject and their treatment of Christ varies, each seeks to get behind the supernatural Christ to the 'real' Jesus. The Hindu commentators tend to simply repeat the content of these works, especially in relation to the unreliability of the New Testament writings; the flawed depictions of Christ's birth, life, death and resurrection; and the denial of the deity of Christ – as if biblical scholars had not already noticed these points or provided adequate answers.

The second type of Western work drawn on is that of Jewish polemicists, who have their own theological axe to grind. These include Hyam Maccoby and Géza Vermes. The third type of publication is that by Western rationalists like Tom Paine and J. M. Robertson, an advocate of Christ Myth theory who belonged to a fringe group of the same name. Chowdhuri, who made use of Robertson, was blithely unaware of Conybeare's *Historical Jesus* (1910), which exposed the serious shortcomings of Robertson's work. The fourth type of work used by the Hindu polemicists is that by Western mainstream scholars. Here the focus has been on the allegedly anti-Christian argument of these scholars, but the material has mainly been taken from secondary sources, with no evidence of having read the originals.

Within the limited space of this chapter, I will focus on a few Western mainstream scholars that these Hindus deployed to augment their anti-Christian diatribe. One such scholar is D. F. Strauss, who figures in the work of Varma, Chowdhuri, Goel and Swarup. Albert Schweitzer's comment that the many opponents of Strauss 'certainly wrote without having studied the fourteen hundred pages of his two volumes'[45] is certainly applicable to the Hindu apologists. They would not have had the chance to read the four versions of *The Life of Jesus* and the changes he made in each of them, and most importantly, his *Life of Jesus for the German People* (1864), which was 'stiff and sober' and presented a 'positive historic picture of Jesus', ultimately delivering a liberal portrayal of its subject.[46] Nonetheless, Strauss's contention that the Church inherited religious and literary traditions from the Hebrew Scriptures and fitted Jesus into this schema was a gift to the Hindu polemicists. Yet there is only a veiled reference to these points in Chowdhuri. The chance to build up their case by exploiting Strauss's negative statements, including his attack on the miracles and his questioning of the ancestry of Jesus, was squandered by the Hindu commentators.

Contrary to the interpretation offered by these Hindu thinkers to their readers, Strauss's *Life of Jesus* was not an attack on Jesus. In his preface, Strauss made it clear that his intention was not to cause 'injury' or 'threaten' the Christian faith, and he accepted that the essentials of the Christian truth – the supernatural birth of Jesus, his miracles, his resurrection and ascension – would remain 'eternal truths, whatever doubts may be cast on their reality as historical facts'.[47] What he did take issue with was the 'supernatural nimbus' with which Jesus was surrounded, as he wanted to make him truly human. The Hindu commentators also overlooked the particular context in which Strauss's life of Jesus emerged. This was the point when the Christian Church and theologians were struggling to understand the impact of the Enlightenment on the Bible, when faith was being replaced with reason and when there was a realization that humans were capable of acting rationally and morally without guidance from a higher being. Strauss wanted to release Jesus from the traditional authorities and the orthodox framework in which he was caged. His denial of the miracles and his questioning of the reliability of the Gospels was in order to establish an 'empirical-historical Jesus'. The advocates of Hinduism failed to notice Strauss's assertion that the 'God-manhood, the highest idea conceived by human thought, is actually realized in the historical personality of Jesus.'[48]

These Hindu nationalists seemed to be unaware that the controversial issues that Strauss raised in his time had all become the everyday orthodoxy of current biblical scholarship, namely the impossibility of constructing a purely historical Jesus from the Gospel sources; the inferior historical quality of John; and the miracles as divine acts. Schweitzer's criticism that Strauss had 'dissolved the life of Jesus into myth' was an 'absurdity' often repeated by people who had not read his book or who had 'read it only superficially', something that applied to these Hindu commentators. Strauss had warned that his book was not 'destined' or designed for the laity, who might want to read it but lacked the capacity understand it. Rather than regarding Strauss as a 'destroyer', as these Hindu revivalists claimed him to be, Schweitzer eulogized him as a 'prophet of a coming advance in knowledge'.[49]

Another scholar who featured in the writings of the Hindu polemicists was Elaine Pagels, whose work on the Gnostic gospels, Swarup claimed, 'shattered the imagined picture of the early Christianity'. However, Pagels did not regard the Gnostic Gospels as a rival that would supplant or threaten orthodox Christianity but rather as a 'powerful alternative' to it. For Pagels, both 'Gnostic and orthodox forms of Christianity could emerge as variant interpretations of the teaching and significance of Jesus',[50] and that the suppression of Gnostic Christianity impoverished the Christian tradition. She was not advocating Gnosticism as such, nor was she trying to destroy the credentials of Christianity, as Swarup claimed, but in fact was writing, as she explained, as someone who was 'powerfully attracted to Christianity'.[51] Pagels could in fact be critical of Gnostic teachings – something that Swarup conveniently ignored. For example, while she found some Gnostic teaching attractive, such as that on inner divinity, she was discouraged by its exclusionary stance, which she considered a serious weakness that ultimately led to the demise of the Gnostic Gospels. In contrast, Pagels commended the institutional Church for its openness and for being more welcoming to people.

Swarup was probably one of the 'casual readers' Pagels probably had in mind when she spoke of those who might deliberately mistake her as someone who 'side[d] with' Gnostic ideals. She saw herself as a historian who opened up a new perspective for understanding the history of Christianity. For Pagels, the Gnostic Gospels were the work of a 'restless, inquiring people' set on a path of self-discovery, similar to creative people such as Blake, Rembrandt, Dostoevsky and Tolstoy, who drew on Christian symbols to express their faith, yet rebelled against orthodox institutions. Pagels saw no political shenanigans between orthodox and Gnostic

Christianity, as Swarup wanted his readers to believe. As she had shown, the struggle was more about interpretation and whose authority one depends on for one's faith – the Scriptures, the apostles or the Church. In other words, it was a question of what constituted authority and what gave it legitimacy. The Gnostic texts had the confidence to ask questions that orthodoxy claimed had all been settled. Pagels believed that such questions would further the understanding of Christianity rather than undermine it. The Gnostic writings were a reminder that orthodoxy always disparaged those on the fringes – those who challenged and questioned.

Other Western scholars who featured in these writings were Martin Kähler and Rudolf Bultmann. Contrary to Goel's claim, Kähler's *The So-Called Historical Jesus and the Historic, Biblical Christ* did not sound an 'alarm-bell'.[52] Kähler differentiated between 'historical', as that which materialized in the past with no significant implications for future, and 'historic', as that which occurred long ago with ongoing ramifications. For Kähler, what mattered most was the historic, biblical Christ and not the reconstructed historical Christ. He did not 'pour scorn' on the historical Jesus, as Goel asserted. For Kähler, any historical construction was subject to change, and its position was contingent on the ideological vagaries of historians, producing scholarly debates that ordinary Christians would have no ready access to. Kähler argued that the Gospels were 'confessions and proclamation of the apostolic preaching' rather than historical documents, and thus did not provide sufficient evidence to reconstruct the life of Jesus. This was a startling position at that time, but somewhat stale by now. Kähler argued for a Christ that early Christianity found in the New Testament. It was not the historical Jesus but the Christ of the Church's proclamation that was significant. As Kähler put it in near confession-type language, 'to commune with Jesus one needs nothing more than the biblical presentation'[53] and one's view of the 'Saviour is continually clarified and deepened by the witness of the Bible'.[54] Kähler was not as dismissive of the Bible as these Hindu exponents asserted, holding the view that it was only in and through faith in Christ that the Bible could meaningfully be called the Word of God.

Another German scholar who found favour with these ardent promoters of Hinduism was Rudolf Bultmann. Goel imputes a sinister motive to Bultmann's *kerygmatic* Christ, and considered the German to be a 'crooked and crafty' theologian.[55] Writing in a clumsy style, and relying on uninterrogated secondary sources, Goel made the outrageous assertion that the Bultmannian programme of transforming the historical Jesus into the Christ of faith had a hidden purpose, namely to absolve the Church of the atrocities done in the name of the historical Jesus, which varied from wanton imperial aggression to the atrocities of the Nazis. The kerygmatic Christ was an attempt to 'legitimize' the preaching of the Church and to have a good 'conscience'. Goel provided no solid evidence for his wild claims and was unaware that Bultmann's only brother had died in a concentration camp.[56] While fellow Hindu defenders reprimanded Christian theologians for being obsessed with historicism, Goel accused Bultmann of not being historical enough. Bultmann did not doubt that something could be unearthed about the historical Jesus, but he felt that this was a tedious and uncertain historical process. What he rejected were the biographical narratives that were deployed to define Jesus' personality. What Bultmann prized was not the historicity of Jesus but rather the religiously satisfying Christ. His hermeneutics were in the service of the Church and his goal was to make the Gospel relevant to a German society that was modern, industrialized and technologically advanced. He endeavoured to draw significance from biblical stories so that they could be repurposed for preaching rather than focusing on their intricate historical details. For both Kähler and Bultmann, the historical 'lives' of Jesus were a modern phenomenon which prevented believers from experiencing the living Christ. The kerygmatic formulations were not false statements about a person who had lived, as Goel wanted his readers to believe, but religious affirmations to underpin the faith of Christian congregations. For these German theologians, the historical Jesus was a person who was confined to the past or embodied in a text. The way to interact with the living Jesus was through the Word. Bultmann even concluded a supposedly academic work with words which televangelists would come to proudly own: 'Are we ready to hear?'[57]

The Hindu thinkers were are considering seem to have been oblivious to scholarly responses to the impact of higher criticism of the biblical narratives. Today, most mainstream biblical scholars regard the Gospels as faith documents of the early Christian communities and not histories, explaining the discrepancies in the narratives as due to different Gospel writers trying to articulate who Jesus was.

Paranoid Interpreters, Passionate Polemicists

The hermeneutical strategy of the Hindu promoters was to celebrate the Hindu Scriptures as universal, open-minded and free-spirited and at the same time to condemn the biblical texts as limited, bigoted and authoritarian – in other words, show that biblical religion was exclusivist and judgemental, whereas Hinduism was pluralistic and benevolent. In practice this often meant juxtaposing the pluralistic statement of one religion with an exclusivist statement of the other. For example, a compassionate passage from the Bhagavad Gita, 'Whoever, by whatsoever path approaches me, I accept him for salvation', was contrasted with a darker, segregatory verse from the Bible: 'Thou shalt have no other gods before me.' For Rajaram, the Bible was the 'apotheosis of exclusivism', dividing the world into believers and non-believers, the latter deserving death and damnation.

The irony was that the accusations levelled by the Hindu defenders at the Gospel writers could have been equally directed against them. Their charge that the evangelists constructed Jesus from the various portrayals of the expected Messiah prevalent at that time was a crime they also committed by piecing, patching and recycling materials from both notorious and well-known authors to bolster their own hermeneutical mission. You might say that they turned borrowing into an art form. Their work amounted to the uninterrogated mindless repetition of already available material. The work of Western scholars, irrespective of the context in it had emerged, was recycled to support a weak case. The end product of this strategy was biased, based as it was on a limited range of reading and of sources.

Much of what was written by the Hindu apologists was based on assumptions rather than substantive argument, something flimsily assembled like a piece of flatpack IKEA furniture. The utmost contempt and scorn was exhibited for the Christian Church, especially the Roman Catholic Church and ecumenical bodies like the World Council of Churches. To apply current jargon, they were equal opportunity multifaith abusers.

The written work produced by this group was caustic, confrontational and plainly contemptuous of people who were not Hindus, and the tone is ranting. Their assessment of their opponents was not always fair, but even worse, it was often blatantly inaccurate, full of inventive mis-citations. They cherry-picked from dubious sources and relied on secondary materials. For example, Goel's sole source for Crossan's *Jesus: A Revolutionary Biography* was a *Time* magazine article. The result was a book full of unattributed and derogatory observations about Jesus. Goel made the remarkable claim that social scientists in the West took Jesus to be an earlier incarnation of Lenin, Stalin and Hitler and that psychologists had diagnosed him as suffering from melancholia, a mentally sick man, even stark mad. Goel did not furnish the names of the social scientists or the psychologists in question. Like most polemicists, he was at his most venomous when attacking religions other than Hinduism, but had nothing to offer in terms of solutions to problems and issues associated with faith.

The defenders of Hinduism do not provide their readers with any guidance as to what was real history or what was fictional. In a chapter entitled 'Jesus of Fiction', Goel assembled an array of serious and pseudo works on the historical Jesus, and placed them alongside an imaginary life of Jesus drawn from Western novels, thus giving the cursory reader the impression that all these genres had equal value.[58] Much worse was his acceptance of the claims of some of the novelists as historical facts. For example, he endorsed the portrayal of Jesus as a fanatic who contrived his own trial and crucifixion in order to make the Old Testament prophecies come true. Another outlandish claim that was passed off as historical truth was that an influential Brahmin took Jesus under his wing and that both went to Egypt where he taught Jesus philosophy and hypnotism. On his return to Palestine, Jesus mesmerized fashionable ladies and healed many of them. Then, when Jesus became aware of a plot to kill him, he made a pact with Joseph of Arimathea. Accordingly, while on the cross, Jesus went into cataleptic trance and feigned his death and Joseph then took him down from the cross as quickly as possible and placed him in the grave. While in the tomb, Jesus revived and made several appearances to his disciples, but he was so badly hurt that he dragged himself to Nazareth and died at the door of his Brahmin benefactor.

The Hindu apologists also utilized silence to prove the non-existence of the historical Jesus. Since the secular historians of the period hardly mentioned Jesus, the inference of Varma and Chowdhury was that he had never existed. Applying the same reasoning would suggest that the great missionary work undertaken by Emperor Asoka to propagate Buddhism was a fiction because his conversion to that faith after his battle with the state of Kalinga was not recorded in the *Mahavamsa*, the fifth-century-CE historical chronicle.

All of these Hindu scholars were quick to highlight the internal contradictions in the Gospels as a weakness of the Christian Scriptures, but turned a blind eye to the contradictions in their own Vedas. The nineteenth-century Hindu reformers were well aware of these inconsistencies, with the Vedas speaking of both the 'personal and impersonal Absolute', while in the Upanishads, God was depicted as both 'pervading the world and as eternally separate from it'.[59] Rammohun Roy, with whom these Hindu enthusiasts had a love–hate relationship, regarded the Hindu Scriptures as a declaration of the unity of God, yet he was aware of these 'apparent contradictions between different passages of the Veda' and eventually concluded that due to their errancy the Vedas were 'altogether unintelligible'.[60] Some Hindus like Debendranath Tagore questioned the authority of the Vedas and the Upanishads and produced a compilation drawn from the above mentioned texts called *Brahmdharmagrantha*.[61] Inconsistency was also to be found in the Bhagavat Gita, which is regarded as a Hindu bible. One of its salient features is action, yet Krishna, who initially extolled the virtues of action, went on to advocate that one should give up all action and become a yogi. The Hindu religionists required the Gospels to be consistent in order to prove their divine sanction. However, the Gospels were written over a long period of time by various unknown authors in different theological contexts. It was unreasonable to expect these Gospel writers to agree on every subject matter, any more than we would expect modern authors to concur on every issue.

Some of the criticisms levelled against the Bible by these Hindu apologists – concerning biblical monotheism, that the Jesus of the Gospels was a confected personality, and the continuing imperial intentions of the institutionalized Church – were not particularly original but did merit attention. To this list, one could add Christians' obsession with the literal reading of the Bible, which effectively killed off allegorical, spiritual and anagogical interpretations. Instead of simply dismissing these matters as the rants of Hindu fanatics, it would have been in their own interest for the Indian Church and Indian Christian interpreters to try to make the Christian message more relevant and accord these critics a fair hearing.

Despite the spiteful motivation behind them, a few of the Hindu group's criticisms are worth taking note of. One was their constant call on Christians to recover the often overlooked pluralistic tradition intermittently embedded in the biblical narratives. Swarup used the case of Ruth, the Moabite, and her words to her mother-in-law as indication of a biblical time when other gods had validity and when adopting other peoples' gods was not seen as a mark of disloyalty to one's own god.

The Hindu exponents always maintained that the monotheistic ideal was bound up with the 'imperial needs' of the great power of the time, whether it be the Romans or the British, and that the shameful deeds done in the name of a single God should not go unnoticed. Swarup produced a verse from the Secret Book of John (The Apocryphon of John) as proof that other gods did exist in the biblical time: 'For, if there were no other God, whom would he possibly be jealous of'?[62] He even reminded Christians that the Hebrew words for God – Elohim and El – were plural in 'origin, form and sense'.[63]

Linked to the above argument is the espousal of polytheistic ideals by the Hindu scholars. The case was put forward that monotheism induced stark choices which were no longer relevant to those whose life experiences were marked by multiple realities and identities. They routinely pointed out that polytheistic thinking continued as a norm in Israel even after the Yahweh-alone idea triumphed in the eighth century BCE, as exemplified in a verse from Micah: 'For all the peoples walk, each in the name of its god, but we will walk in the name of the Lord our God forever and ever' (Mic. 4.5). The Christian churches' survival and relevance may depend on their embracing a multicultural approach, including a variety of gods. The Hindu group's constant advocacy of the Hindu belief in the incomprehensibility of God beyond form and words also merits more consideration. At a time when Western Christians are searching for a spirituality beyond an institution, a personality-free godless mysticism could be a way forward.

What these writings did was give an academic veneer to the habitual Hindutva diatribe. Much of what they said was familiar, their arguments riddled with conspiracy theories and crude misrepresentations. They warned their faithful supporters that a secret cabal of international Christian organizations existed that was intent on wiping out Hinduism.

What is very obvious is that these Hindu agitators failed to live up to the lofty ideals they espoused. They lauded the open and pluralistic nature of Hinduism and were proud of its ideal of *sarva-dharma samabhāva* ('equal respect for all religions')[64] but at the same time showed no regard or respect for Christianity or Islam, which they vilified from a malignant impulse.

These Hindu exponents, mainly men, were largely driven and inspired by power, patriarchy, purity of faith and purity of nation. They were unconcerned about finding solutions to multicultural and multi-religious existence but stuck to the same old rhetoric about the predatory nature of Christianity, with Hindus being crushed by the overwhelming force of its institutional might. They disdained diversity and sought to convince their readers that people of different religions could not live peacefully together – that the very idea was unworkable. In this respect, they seemed to have been unaware of the existence of multicultural communities in Sasanian Persia, medieval Spain, Mughal India and the Ottoman Empire. Indeed, very few nations have ever existed in an ethnically 'pure' and sheltered state. Inevitably, each nation has its share of the 'Other'.

The writings of the Hindu propagandists contain many citations from Western sources and they always make a point of providing the rank, title and university position of the academics quoted, in order to lend intellectual credence and justification to their ethno-nationalistic positions. In spite of their anti-Western stance, they still rely on Western scholars, some of whom are of dubious reputation, to bolster their argument.

The underlying motive of these Hindu commentators was to sound the alarm – an alarm concerned with those who had become targets of the Christian Church's expansionist ideology. They believed their cause was a righteous one – to rescue Hindus from missionary propaganda and defamatory Christian literature. Varma, witnessing Hindus being taken away from their ancestral faith, posed the question,

'[S]hould I not try to save them by proclaiming the truth?'[65] He now felt a 'duty to obey the national call'[66] and refute the missionary tracts which he called 'trash'. He counselled his fellow Hindu brethren (it is always brethren) not to embrace a faith which was started by an imaginary figure – 'Never believe in the Christian religion by a mythical Christ.'[67] Chowdhuri, in his preface, wrote that if his book could turn just one person away from the Christian Church, his labour would have been adequately 'recompensed'. The Hindu scholars said that their aim was not to revile Christianity, yet their writing is full of venom. In addition to warning Asians that they had become the 'largest target in the church's struggle for survival', Rajaram said that his task involved educating the Christian public, including Christians who had been tutored at prestigious seminaries but had only received a 'sanitized version'[68] of their own history.

Just as the British used Greek classical culture to serve their colonial aims, now these Hindu nationalists employed their own classical sources – the very sources disparaged by the British – to strengthen the case for Hindu imperialism. Rajaram pointed out that both cultures – Greek and Indian – had certain characteristics in common. Both valued a plurality of personal gods who offered multiple ways to reach the divine and who made to claim to exclusivity. Both cultures were extremely rich in mythology and saw no conflict between the rational and the mystical. Both offered complete autonomy to those who sought a belief system and did not impose any intermediaries, such as priests or prophets. Neither culture had an 'enforcing agency' such as the clergy, and their doctrines were not mandatory. The spiritual freedom and pluralistic heritage of the Greek and Indian cultures had been overpowered by Christianity and its claim of exclusivity. Ironically, the same classical culture the British had used to deprecate the manners and backwardness of Indians was now employed by Indians to present Indian culture as diverse, tolerant and open.

The aim of these Hindu nationalists was to revive the ancient Vedic glories in order to reimpose them on the world. With considerable chutzpah, Swarup claimed that ancient cultures, such as those of Greece, Egypt, Rome, Persia and the Americas, and the Germanic, Celtic, Scandinavian and Baltic nations, were closer to India in their spiritual orientation and reflected the Hindu ideal. Their gods and goddesses were the same as those of India, while their beliefs were not 'polytheistic but, in deeper interpretation, advaitic'.[69] Since these world cultures manifested older and deeper advaitic impulses, Hindus should help these cultures recover the Vedic religion and see the Vedic gods in a new light as part of this renewal process. The Hindu apologists had no difficulty with gathering almost all religions under a Hindu banner and claiming that they shared a Hindu vision and ideal. This all-inclusive and imperialistic mindset was grounded in the Vedic verse, 'Truth is one, it is expressed in various ways' (Rig Veda 1.164.46).

The writings of these Hindu scholars might be described as hermeneutically self-centred, self-absorbed and introverted. They live in their own imaginary little Aryan spaces, lacking the ability to empathize with or enter into the emotional or cultural realities of non-Aryans. They show little interest in dialogue or a desire to interact with others. The general perception of these Hindus is that there is 'nothing common between Santana Dharma and the sinister cult of the Only saviour, that Hindus have nothing to learn from Christianity but a lot to teach'.[70] Their hermeneutics gives the impression that they do not care about others, especially Christians and Muslims, for whom they display only hostility.

It is worth recalling here the words of a clergyman to a schoolmaster who was distressed by reading Strauss, as the clergyman's advice chimes with the Hindu thinkers we have just considered: 'Now I hope that after the experience which you have had you will for the future refrain from reading books of this kind, which are not written for you, and of which there is no necessity for you to take any notice; and for the refutation of which, should that be needful, you have no equipment.'[71] The Hindu scholars could say the same words to Christians who read their sacred writings.

Notes

1 N. S. Rajaram, *The Dead Sea Scrolls and the Crisis of Christianity: An Eastern View of a Western Crisis* (London: Minerva Press, 1997), 85.
2 Thakur Kahan Chandra, *Christ A Myth: The Historicity of Christ Proving the Christ of the New Testament a Myth and the Gospels Spurious*, 12th edition (Lahore: K. C. Varma, 1928), 81.
3 Chandra, *Christ A Myth*, 82.
4 Sita Ram Goel, *Jesus Christ: An Artifice for Aggression* (New Delhi: Voice of India, 1994), 70.
5 Rajaram, *The Dead Sea Scrolls and the Crisis of Christianity*, 219, n. 87.
6 Ram Swarup, *Hindu View of Christianity and Islam* (New Delhi: Voice of India, 1992), 62.
7 Varma, *Christ A Myth*, 47.
8 Rajaram, *The Dead Sea Scrolls and the Crisis of Christianity*, 250.
9 Goel, *Jesus Christ*, 25.
10 Dhirendranath Chowdhuri, *In Search of Jesus Christ* (Calcutta: Brahma Mission, 1927), 237.
11 Rajaram, *The Dead Sea Scrolls and the Crisis of Christianity*, 162.
12 Rajaram, *The Dead Sea Scrolls and the Crisis of Christianity*, 163.
13 Goel, *Jesus Christ*, 75.
14 Swarup, *Hindu View of Christianity and Islam*, 80.
15 Swarup, *Hindu View of Christianity and Islam*, 41.
16 Ram Swarup, *The Word as Revelation: Names of God* (New Delhi: Voice of India, 1980), xvii.
17 Rajaram, *The Dead Sea Scrolls and the Crisis of Christianity*, 91.
18 Swarup, *Hindu View of Christianity and Islam*, 103.
19 Swarup, *Hindu View of Christianity and Islam*, 58.
20 Swarup, *The Word as Revelation*, 116–17.
21 Rajaram, *The Dead Sea Scrolls and the Crisis of Christianity*, 106.
22 Goel, *Jesus Christ*, 68.
23 Goel, *Jesus Christ*, 67.
24 Goel, *Jesus Christ*, 27.
25 Chowdhuri, *In Search of Jesus Christ*, 370.

26 Varma, *Christ A Myth*, 32.
27 Swarup, *Hindu View of Christianity and Islam*, 41.
28 Chowdhuri, *In Search of Jesus Christ*, 371.
29 Chowdhuri, *In Search of Jesus Christ*, 304.
30 Rajaram, *The Dead Sea Scrolls and the Crisis of Christianity*, 135.
31 Chowdhuri, *In Search of Jesus Christ*, 137.
32 Varma, *Christ A Myth*, 18.
33 Rajaram, *The Dead Sea Scrolls and the Crisis of Christianity*, 343.
34 Ram Swarup, *Pope John Paul II on Eastern Religions and Yoga: A Hindu–Buddhist Rejoinder* (New Delhi: Voice of India, 1995), 36; Ram Swarup, *Hinduism and Monotheistic Religions* (New Delhi: Voice of India, 2009), 341.
35 Timothy H. Lim, *The Dead Sea Scrolls: A Very Short Introduction* (Oxford: Oxford University Press, 2005), 12.
36 Duraga Prasad, *A Dissertation upon the Dogmas of Christianity* (Lahore: Empress Press, n.d.), 42.
37 Swarup, *Hindu View of Christianity and Islam*, 404.
38 Swarup, *Hindu View of Christianity and Islam*, 89.
39 Swarup, *Hindu View of Christianity and Islam*, 410.
40 Goel, *Jesus Christ*, 66.
41 Rajaram, *The Dead Sea Scrolls and the Crisis of Christianity*, 155.
42 Swarup, *The Word as Revelation*, 134.
43 Swarup, *The Word as Revelation*, 159.
44 Swarup, *Hinduism and Monotheistic Religions*, 345.
45 Albert Schweitzer, *The Quest of the Historical Jesus: A Critical Study of its Progress from Reimarus to Wrede* (London: A.C. Black, 1910), 98.
46 Schweitzer, *The Quest of the Historical Jesus*, 96.
47 David Friedrich Strauss, *The Life of Jesus Critically Examined*, vol. 1, trans. Marian Evans (New York: Calvin Blanchard, 1860), 4.
48 Schweitzer, *The Quest of the Historical Jesus*, 79.
49 Schweitzer, *The Quest of the Historical Jesus*, 95.
50 Elaine Pagels, *The Gnostic Gospels* (Harmondsworth: Penguin Books, 1982), 152.
51 Pagels, *The Gnostic Gospels*, 147.
52 Goel, *Jesus Christ*, 62.
53 Martin Kähler, *The So-called Historical Jesus and the Historic Biblical Christ*, trans. and ed. with intro. by Carl E. Braaten (Philadelphia: Fortress Press, 1964), 78.
54 Kähler, *The So-called Historical Jesus*, 86.
55 Goel, *Jesus Christ*, 74.
56 Rudolf Bultmann, *Existence and Faith: Shorter Writings of Rudolf Bultmann* (London: Colins, 1964), 338.
57 Bultmann, *Existence and Faith*, 201.
58 Goel, *Jesus Christ*, 35–59.
59 Amiya P. Sen, 'Debates within Colonial Hinduism', in Brian Hatcher (ed.), *Hinduism in the Modern World* (New York: Routledge, 2016), 70.
60 Rajah Ram Mohun Roy, *English Works of Rajah Ram Mohun Roy* (Bhowanipore: Oriental Press, 1885), 95
61 Sen, 'Debates within Colonial Hinduism', 70.
62 Swarup, *Hindu View of Christianity and Islam*, 46.
63 Swarup, *The Word as Revelation*, 115.
64 Goel, *Jesus Christ*, 99.

65 Varma, *Christ A Myth*, 161.
66 Varma, *Christ A Myth*, 154.
67 Varma, *Christ A Myth*, 163
68 Rajaram, *The Dead Sea Scrolls and the Crisis of Christianity*, 14.
69 Swarup, *The Word as Revelation*, 139.
70 Goel, *Jesus Christ*, 84.
71 Schweitzer, *The Quest of the Historical Jesus*, 100.

AFTERWORD: CHALLENGES AND CONFRONTATIONS

Sacred books are often read and interpreted within the existing framework of religious allegiances, conventions, associations and loyalties. What we saw in the preceding chapters were the appropriations of a religious text by an outside community. The reasons for these Hindus' engagements with the Bible had more to do with repairing the damage done to their own religious texts than with reading it for devotional purposes.

These articulations were not principally written for Western Christians but largely for their fellow Hindus. They reassured Hindus that they need not worry about this imported text – what was to be found there had already been revealed to the ancient rishis. Their readings also had other subsidiary benefits. They provided textual ammunition to 'talk back' to the missionaries' misrepresentation of their texts and faith. Their expositions made some of the inassimilable Semitic concepts, rituals and images easier for a Hindu readership to understand. In their interpretation, they found it hard to avoid the Hindu triumphalism associated with the hermeneutics of 'talking back'.

These Hindu reformers not only read the Bible but also rewrite it through their interpretative strategies and intentions. What is apparent is that the Bible, a Christian text, takes on different meanings in non-Christian contexts, thus becoming virtually independent of its original Jewish provenance. In their appropriation and consumption of the Bible, these Hindus produced a totally different material. It was a daring and constructive, yet at the same time destructive intrusion into other people's texts, in which salvageable parts were used to form or create something else – a Vedic text in the case of Radhakrishnan, a Saiva shastra in the case of Ramanathan, and a code for rituals in the case of Navalar. The faith of these Hindus remained unshaken, but their understanding of biblical religion risked making it look like a close variant of Hinduism.

What these writings have shown is a reawakening of the pre-critical methods of biblical interpretation, which placed a strong emphasis on the spirit of the word rather than its literal meaning. The authors did not subscribe to the view that the primitive meaning of the biblical writers was the only authentic one. They regarded literal reading as providing only one possible meaning – and not necessarily an important one. This was an important reminder that one need not be endowed with the hubris of historical criticism to unlock meaning.

Yet, these Hindus were hermeneutically handicapped. While Jewish readers had the pesher and midrash to explain the Hebrew Bible, and Catholics had extensive citations from the Church fathers, and the medieval and Reformation Protestants had theologians to augment and explicate the biblical texts, these Hindu interpreters were bereft of resources to explain an alien and intrusive text to their fellow Hindus. Their approach was to lift verses out of their context and try to place them within Hindu Scriptures, either to weaken the Christian texts or strengthen the Hindu claim. Their most common and specific hermeneutical strategy was to quote verses out of context, thus facilitating the ascendency of the verse over the whole narrative. The Bible was treated as a compendium of statements or a set of statements that provided straightforward information about Christian teaching without becoming immersed in contextual complexities. Effectively, they reduced the Bible to a series of user-friendly, engaging and empathetic verses.

Just as the Orientalists and some missionaries instructed the Hindus that they should go back to the Vedas to recover the 'original' Hinduism, these Hindus flipped this imperious instruction back onto the Christians and told them that they should go back to the *ur* message of Jesus found in the Gospels.

Among their many hermeneutical follies was mistaking self-criticism and internal interrogation of the biblical discipline, especially exposure of contradictions in the biblical narratives, as its flaw and weakness. There is an impression among these Hindus that the biblical writers should provide a uniform view in order to have credibility. The biblical books were written over a long period of time, stretching across centuries, as theological approaches and social attitudes changed. It was as unrealistic to expect uniformity and agreement among biblical writers on every issue in these circumstances as it would be to expect present-day biblical scholars or even Hindu expositors to concur on every issue.

Like all interpreters, the Hindu reformers suffered from a 'confirmation bias' – a search for evidence to support their hermeneutical agenda. The Bible was to be their proof-text, a justification for their claims. However, this hermeneutical approach was similar to any biblical interpreter: to engage the biblical narratives with a set of pre-suppositions aiming for validation of their point of view.

Ironically, the Hindu scholars enlisted for this purpose the very Hindu texts which were denigrated by the missionaries – texts that were largely confined to or understood only by a minority of brahmins or high-caste communities. In so doing, they became absorbed by two European preoccupations. First, as with Semitic traditions, was the implied belief that the Hindu faith must be contained in ancient texts and other written sources. This ignored the fact that the vast majority of Hindus had little engagement with or knowledge of these Sanskritic texts, instead experiencing their faith through art, music and dance. Second, the Hindu scholars succumbed to the Orientalist habit of taking the texts of the dominant Hindu minority to be representative of Indian realities that were in fact much more diverse.

To meet the challenge of the King James Version, which was introduced to India by the British, these Hindu apologists, especially Gandhi, successfully promoted the Bhagavad Gita not only as India's national and principal philosophical book but also as a major text for the world. Ironically, it was the Western Orientalists' discovery of the Bhagavad Gita in the late eighteenth century which prompted these Hindus to latch on to it as an eternal spiritual narrative. Another text, to use the modern parlance, that went viral was the Panchatantra, a collection of five treatises. Before 1600 CE and the advent of the modern colonialism, the Panchatantra had been translated into several languages, including old Syriac, Arabic, Latin, Greek, and Slavonic. One version represented dharma and moral duty; the other was about intelligence and wisdom in ethically uncertain times. A popular text which fired the imagination of the people was replaced by a text which until that time had remained abstruse and suited only to professional researchers and philosophers.

For many of these Hindu thinkers, Christianity as it was practised failed to measure up to the moral standard prescribed in the Bible. They were confident in their belief that the West was only notionally Christian and that it was not familiar with the true Jesus or his message. The colonial atrocities, the double standards in international dealings, their stratified social structures and the ostentatious lifestyle of the foreign clergy in India made the West less than Christian in the view of the Hindu scholars. Many of them would have concurred with the words of Vivekananda when he pointed out how miserably the Christians failed to live up to the injunction of Jesus to 'Let your light so shine before men, that they may see your good works, and glorify your Father which is in heaven' (Mt. 5.16). Max Müller, who was himself the patroniser-in-chief, dismissed such observations and allegations by these Hindus as 'patronising' remarks.[1]

Most of the Hindu interpreters studied here came from the Brahmanical community, the exceptions being Ramanathan, Navalar and Vivekananda, who belonged to high castes. That upper-caste status gave them enormous power and authority and they took upon themselves the traditional Brahmanical task of expounding and imparting ancient knowledge. They saw their interpretative task as a responsibility entrusted to them by their community so that the truth about the Bible should be known.

Most of the Hindu personalities studied here earnestly believed that the Scriptures of the world belonged to all people, and so they unashamedly raided and sought to profit from them. Ironically, at the same time they were reluctant to reveal the Hindu sacred texts to their own people. Navalar and Gandhi believed that these texts should only be accessible to a select group of Hindus and prescribed certain ground rules and conditions for having this privilege.

There was an assumption among the majority of the Hindus studied here that as a people they had lost an awareness of their own Scriptures, which made them vulnerable to invaders, be they Muslims or Christians. These thinkers believed that this decline could be corrected by reclaiming and reviving the ancient books. In similar circumstances of decay, the Buddhists, the Christians and the Muslims had ready-made texts – the Dhammapada, the Bible and the Koran. In the absence of such resources among the Hindus, they rediscovered the Vedic texts, which had little resonance for the majority of Hindu people. Nonetheless, they claimed that these texts helped to 'preserve our national character'. It could be argued that the hermeneutical engagements of this group of scholars was an early example of identity politics. They used Vedic Hinduism as a key component to define both India and Hinduism. They claimed that as Hindus, their culture, especially the high-caste Hindu culture, was distinctive and represented a different way of thinking. They extrapolated the Advaita Vedanta from these texts and interpreted the entirety of Hinduism in its light. As India's self-appointed cultural and intellectual guardians, they developed, consolidated and promoted a specific and often abstract interpretation of a Sanskrit version of Hinduism.

The writings of this group of Hindu scholars occurred in an India that was beginning to embrace diversity and multiculturalism. Today's India is marked by the mandir (Hindu temple) and the market and follows the new narrative of the populist religious belligerents, who are less likely to have the time or inclination to pursue the hermeneutical work of their predecessors.

On the surface it appears that there is an anti-Semitic element in their writings, but this can in fact be traced to a lethal strain of anti-Semitism in the polemics of the early Christian Church rather than to later racially-inspired theories. Furthermore, some of their writings predated the great atrocities committed against the Jews in the twentieth century. These Hindus were simply replicating uncritically some of the common features of Christian anti-Semitism pervasive at the time. Another distinction that should be noted is that the anti-Semitism of the Hindu writers was not directed against Jews as a racial group but against the triumphal tone of their theology. Raised on multiple gods and goddesses, these Hindus found Jewish disdain for polytheism ('Thou shalt have no gods before me', Exod. 20.2), their stubborn insistence upon a single revelation coupled with the idea of an elect people of God to be both antagonistic and narrow-minded. Radhakrishnan spoke for many when he criticized the idea of a chosen people and the Jewish consciousness of not being like other people, as depicted in both testaments, because such beliefs condemned a 'large part of Humanity to sit in darkness and death'. The Hindu commentators rejected this 'spiritual exclusiveness' which led to an 'us' and 'them' scenario, and considered the idea of a 'Chosen People' and 'a jealous God' as 'sacred egoism'.

The trouble with trying to produce a balanced evaluation of the writings of these Hindus is that their interpretations were initially assessed by Indian Christian theologians who were rooted in Christian orthodoxy. Apologists like M. M. Thomas, Stanley Samartha and Robin Boyd repeated the standard cliché that the Christian faith required the study of the 'whole Bible' and not the fragmented approach in which the Hindus engaged. These Indian Christian critics conveniently overlooked the fact that the reformers had reduced the entire Bible to the abstract notion of justification by faith. Even these Hindus' advocacy of the pre-critical fourfold meanings was chided with the advice that they should seek 'first the obvious and literal meaning of the text' rather than search for allegorical or moral meanings. The Christian critics took it for granted that the ancient answers were definitive, especially the pronouncements of the early ecumenical councils on Jesus, as if it was not possible to come to a new understanding or take a different position.

One of the sensitive areas of the Christian mission was its obsession with conversion. From Roy onwards, this met with strong resistance. Ironically, the writings of the Hindus in question resulted in some leading Hindus of the time converting to Christianity. For example, it was Roy's *Precepts* that led to the conversion of Pyari Mohun Rudra, who came from the oldest of the aristocratic families of Bengal. Pandith Ramabai's attendance at the Brahmo Samaj meetings and hearing Keshub's lectures paved the way for her to become a Christian, while Vengal Chakkarai, a leading member of the Rethinking Group in India, admitted that it was Vivekananda's interpretation of Christianity as 'essentially an oriental faith'[2] that made him change his mind on the subject.

Though these Hindus took strong objection to the idea of Christian exceptionalism, they had no qualms about making a similar claim for Hinduism. They denied the universal applicability of the Gospel message, but endorsed the Vedanta as a remedy for all the ills of the world. This was an example of how some biblical concepts associated with colonialism were repurposed by these Hindu reformers for the nationalist cause.

The missionaries placed great emphasis on the historical personality of Jesus, which they thought was important for Indians who, as a nation, lacked real personality. India's pantheistic beliefs tended to further weaken individuality, hence in response to this perceived deficiency the Christian message was presented in terms of the life and work of the historical Jesus, devoid of any mystical embellishments.[3] Furthermore, as far as the missionaries were concerned, Indian thinking was dominated by metaphysical and ethical abstractions, and much worse, the Hindu mind was simply unhistorical.

In turn, the Hindu thinkers examined here concentrated on a variety of non-historical ethical visions which emphasized responsibility and accountability. They largely rejected the historical personality of Jesus and embraced the principles he manifested. In short, they placed no value on the historical details of Jesus, but primarily focused on his self-understanding and awareness of himself and his God. The Jesus they constructed resonated with the Jesus of the liberal theology of the time. Crucially, the Hindu interpreters distanced themselves from the apocalyptic Jesus who was popular in academic circles. Their Jesus was not an end-time prophet but a sage dispensing moral precepts. None of them saw Jesus as a single man who could and would change history. Radhakrishnan summarized their position: 'If the Christian thinkers admit that men may have access to God and be saved, other than through the mediatorship of Jesus, the Hindus will heartily subscribe to the essential features of the religion of Jesus.'[4]

The Hindu commentators studied in this book were convinced that the Christian Bible could not serve as the guiding text for India, let alone for the world. Its aggressive and divisive monotheistic God, its insistence that one man was the saviour of humanity, its division of humanity into the chosen and the fallen were all seen as part of the West's effort to dominate and control other societies.

The Bible came to India at the height of the British Empire – an empire on which, it was claimed, the sun never set. Now the empire has gone, and, more importantly, the 'Bible-soaked' earlier Indian generation is hardly evident. The

Bible has been enrolled, enlisted and encroached upon for a variety of religious and secular purposes. The Bible's fate, in securing a lasting place in the hot Indian sun, depends on what kind of a text it wants to be – a single text, with a single God and a single saviour and aligned with selected people with a view to dominate the world; or a text comfortable among India's many gods and goddesses and embodying multicultural and multi-religious sensibilities and aspirations. The Bible's survival and its relevance in India depends on the choice it makes between John's 'I am the way, and the truth', or Micah's 'All peoples may walk, each in the name of their Gods' (Mic. 4.5).

Notes

1. Max. F Müller, *Biographical Essays* (London: Longman, Green, & Co., 1884), 29.
2. *Vengal Chakkarai*, vol. 2, ed. P. T. Thomas (Madras: Christian Literature Society, 1981), 41.
3. Arthur Hirtzel, *The Church, the Empire and the World* (London: Society for Promoting Christian Knowledge, 1919), 64.
4. S. Radhakrishnan, 'The Heart of Hinduism', *Hibbert Journal* 21, no. 3 (1922): 9.

GENERAL INDEX

Acts of John, the 189
Acts of Thomas, the 164, 165
Apocalypse of Peter, the 190
Apocrypha
   Christian 181, 189, 193
   Jewish 164
apocryphal Gospels 189
apocryphal writings 79, 165
Appasamy, A. J. 10, 11, 98, 145
Arumukampillai (Arumuka Navalar)
   Bible 26, 31, 34
   Bible as an abusive book 41
   Bible as book of a cult 36
   biblical texts and temple performances 33
   Bible translation 26, 27
   on conversion 42
   Hebrew Scriptures/Old Testament 29, 32, 33, 36, 37, 38
   on Hindu priests 42
   Missionaries 29, 34
   on Paul 34
   on polytheism 32, 42
   and social thinking 46
   temple rituals 29, 34, 41, 45
Arya Samaj 1, 181
Asiatic 1, 52, 53, 57, 65, 70, 74, 141
   Bible 57, 71
   characteristics 141
   Christ 54, 64, 65
   credentials 141
   effeminacy 12
   faiths 141
   Jesus 64

Baggini, Julian 11
Banerjea, K. M. 11, 91
Barker, Margaret, 37, 39, 41
Barth, Karl 74, 94, 98
Bhagavad Gita, the 63, 68, 104, 108, 130, 135, 144, 147, 156, 159, 166, 172. 174, 176, 177, 197, 206, 207

Bible, the
   King James Version 73, 113, 145, 146, 148, 206
   Navalar Version 27, 28
   as oriental book 105
   Tentative version 27, 28
Brahmo Samaj 1, 51, 59, 60, 103, 181, 209
Brahmoism 61, 121
Brihadaranyaka Upanishad 193
Bultmann, Rudolf 19, 183, 196, 197
Burkitt, C. K. 172

Caivatūṣana parikāram (Remedy for Invective on Saivism) 25, 26, 28, 31, 35, 43, 46, 47
Chowdhuri, Dhirendranath 181, 182, 183, 184, 194, 201
   On Jesus 185, 186, 187, 188
   on New Testament Greek 184
   on Paul 188
   on resurrection 187
Crossan, Dominic 198

Dhammapada, the 156, 157, 207
Dharmapala, Anagarika 45, 98
Dead Sea Scrolls 40, 41, 181, 189, 191
Deism 11
Devdas, Nalini 121
Diatessaron 10
Dibelius, Martin 172

Gandhi, M.K.
   ahimsa 132, 133, 135, 136, 138
   Beatitudes 137
   on Bhagavad Gita 135, 144, 147
   Bible classes 126, 127, 134, 1345
   Biblical narratives 133, 134
   Bible translation 145–6
   on the Buddha 138, 141, 147
   on conversion 142–3
   on cross 133

General Index

and Hebrew Scriptures/Old Testament 125, 126, 127, 132
  on Jesus 138–141
  on Paul 141–142
  Sermon on the Mount 125, 134, 135, 136, 137, 138
  Upanishads 127, 144, 147
Gnana Prakasar, S 98
Goel, Sita Ram 181, 194
  on cross 198
  on Gospels 183
  on Jesus 183, 186, 196, 198
  on the Sermon the Mount 192
Golden Rule, the 21, 60, 111, 112
Gospel of Philip 189, 190, 193
Gospel of Thomas, the 10, 190

Harrison, R.L. 82
Herzl, Theodore 98

Imitation of Christ, The 108

Jefferson, Thomas 11
Jones, William 36

Kempis, à Thomas 108
Kulandran, Sapapathy 27

Lake, Kirsopp 172
liberalism 11, 18, 172
'Literature of Refutation' 43, 44
Lord's Prayer, the 10, 33, 61, 85, 111, 191

Marshman, Joshua 7, 10, 12, 15, 17, 18, 19, 22
missionaries
  hermeneutical strategy 30
Müller, Max 69, 118, 134, 207
Murdoch, John 44
Muthukumāracuvāmi Piḷḷai, 43, 99

nationalism 41, 86, 98
  Buddhist 47
  English 141
  Hindu 46
  Indian 181
  Jewish 93

Orientalists 6, 12, 91, 168, 175, 206, 207
Otto, Rudolf 164, 166, 172

Pagels, Elaine 195, 196
Paramahamsa, Ramakrishna 103
Parekh, Manilal 67, 73
Percival, Peter 26, 27, 28, 32, 34
Pope, G. U. 119
polytheism 23, 30, 32, 42, 208
Prasad, Durga
  on Jesus 186
  on the Sermon on the Mount 191
Precepts of Jesus, The 5

Qumran
  communities 189, 191
  documents 182, 191

Radhakrishnan, S
  Advaita Vedanta 160, 161, 176
  ahimsa 160, 161
  on Bible 159
  biblical narratives 162
  book of *Enoch*, 164
  on Buddha 158, 160, 163, 164, 165, 166, 169, 176
  on cross 163, 169
  exegesis 169, 170, 172
  his hermeneutics 169, 173
  on Jesus 165-6
  karma 161, 170, 171, 176
  on Paul 167
  on resurrection 167, 169
  on Scriptures 156–8, 160, 164
  the Upanishads 156, 160, 164, 165, 176
rationalism 11, 18, 53, 103, 107
Rajaram. N. S.
  on Damascus incident 192
  on Dead Sea Scrolls 191
  Hebrew Scriptures 184
  on Jesus 186
  on Paul 188
  on resurrection 188
Ramanathan, P
  on Bible 80
  on Bible translation 87–8
  his commentaries 85, 94
  on Hebrew prophets 86-7
  and Hebrew Scriptures 85, 86, 97
  on Jesus 92–4
  on karma 90
  on logos 84

on Matthew 82, 83
his nationalism 98
on oral tradition 81
on parables 88
on Paul 92–4
on Sermon on the Mount 84
on resurrection 89, 90
Rashtriya Swayamsevak Sangh (RSS) 181
Roy, Rammohan
    on authority of the Bible 15
    Beatitudes 7
    biblical narratives 19, 20106
    on conversion 42
    Demythologization 19
    hermeneutics 19, 20, 22, 23
    on Hindu Priests 42
    on Jesus 11–14
    missionaries 6, 7, 9, 10, 12, 13, 15, 16, 17, 18, 19, 20, 21, 22, 23
    Parables of Jesus 8
    on polytheism 42
    on resurrection 9, 14
    Upanishads 16

Saiva Siddhdnta 39, 91, 95
Schweitzer, Albert 194, 195
Second Apocalypse of James, the 189
Selvanayagam, S. J. V. 47
Sen, Keshub Chunder
    on Bible 70
    on the Buddha 63, 65
    on conversion 71
    on the cross 63
    on Jesus 64–68
    on kenotic theory 74
    on Old Testament, 56, 57, 58, 59
    Sermon the Mount, the 7, 21, 111, 134, 139, 181
    Song of Solomon, the 104
    on the resurrection 63
    on the transfiguration 62, 63
Strauss, D. E. 183, 194, 195, 202
Swarup, Ram 182

on Bible 184, 185
on Gnostic Gospels 190
on Jesus 185. 187
on Paul 188
Paul at Athens 192–3
on resurrection 190

Tāmōtaram Piḷḷai, C. W 43, 99
'textual colonialism' 193
Thirukural 119
Thiruvasagam 119
Thomas, M. M. 67, 208

Upanishads 68
Upanishads, the 2, 199

Varma, K.C.
    on the Bible 182, 183
    on non-canonical gospels 189
    on Jesus 185, 198
    on New Testament Greek 184
Vivekananda, Swami
    Advaita Vedanta 104, 118, 121
    on the Bible 104, 105, 106, 107, 108, 109, 110, 113, 114, 118
    on biblical narratives 113, 106, 109, 113, 118
    Book-worship 107
    on the Buddha 108, 112, 115, 116, 117
    comparative exegesis 111
    on cross 116
    on crucifixion 116
    on the Golden Rule 112
    on historical criticism 109, 110113
    on Jesus 113, 114, 115, 117, 116, 118
    on the Sermon on the Mount 111, 112
    on Song of Solomon 104–5
    Upanishads 109, 121
Vēṅkaṭ.ācala-pati A. R. 43

Zoroaster 63, 117, 138, 147, 160
Zvelebil, Kamil 26

BIBLICAL SCRIPTURE

Old Testament

Genesis 36, 126, 129 161, 162, 193
    1.27   160
    3.19   130
    18.2   32
Exodus 161
    25   29
    27.20-1   33
    29. 37   12
    37   29
Leviticus
    17   29
    24   29
    24.1-4   33
Numbers
    6.14-17   35
    10.8   33
    16   29
    19   29
    21   29
Joshuva
    5.14   32
2 Samuel
    6   29
    6.5   33
1 Kings 126
    6.8   33
1 Chronicles
    15.14   33
Job 126
Psalms 60, 62, 86, 87, 90, 126, 163
    80   29
    98.6   33
Proverbs 90, 126, 161, 163, 185, 191
Ecclesiastes 58, 90
Song of Solomon 104
Isaiah 62, 68, 162, 187
    35   191
    53.2   89
    61   191

Jeremiah 30, 90
    31.33   160
Ezekiel 90, 158
    18.20   161
    32.33   68
Hosea 162

New Testament

Matthew
    5.33-44   7
    5.48   80, 87, 92
    8.20   114
    9.1-8   170
    10.25   81
    11.35   84
    13.35   84
    13.52   88
    15.9   166
    20.22   88
    22.1-14   88
    23.8   88
    23.23   87
    24.30   92
Mark
    2.1-5   170
Luke
    7.21-2   191
    11.21-2   162
    11.52   96
    13.1-5   171
    15.18   89
    17.20   113
    17.21   92
John
    1.18   112
    9.2   171
    14.21   92
Acts of the Apostles
    17   192

Romans		Philippians	
1.14	163	2.7	66
1 Corinthians		1 Timothy	
3.16	92, 158, 171	4.7	83
15.44	167	6.4	81
Galatians		Titus	
5.19-21	171	3.9	83
5.19-23	171	Hebrews	
6.8	171	1.1	68
Ephesians		10.28, 29	30
4.13	80, 92	Revelation	
4.18	92	3.12	163

HINDU SCRIPTURE

Bhagavad Gita		Rig Veda	
9.23	184	1.164.46	201
9.31	148		
18.63	166		

www.ingramcontent.com/pod-product-compliance
Lightning Source LLC
Chambersburg PA
CBHW051522230426
43668CB00012B/1705